A Short History of American Poetry

Donald Barlow Stauffer was born in East Orange, New Jersey, in 1930. He received a B.A. from Wesleyan University and his M.A. and Ph.D. from Indiana University. He is presently Associate Professor of English at the State University of New York at Albany. He has also taught at Indiana University, City College of New York, and Williams College. His major interests are Poe studies and American poetry, and he has published articles on Poe and Frost in scholarly journals.

A Short History
of American Poetry

BY

DONALD BARLOW STAUFFER

A Dutton dep *Paperback*

E. P. DUTTON & CO., INC., NEW YORK   1974

Published simultaneously in Canada
by Clarke, Irwin & Company Limited, Toronto and Vancouver.

ISBN 0-525-20365-6 (Cloth)   ISBN 0-525-47318-1 (DP)
Library of Congress Catalog Card Number: 69-13347

PS
303
S 67

ACKNOWLEDGMENTS

Grateful acknowledgment is made to the following for permission to quote
from copyright material:

Léonie Adams: "Pity of the Heavens," "Evening Sky," and "Light at
Equinox." Reprinted from *Poems: A Selection,* copyright 1954 by Léonie
Adams, by permission of Léonie Adams.

Conrad Aiken: "Senlin: A Biography," "And in the Hanging Gardens,"
and "South End." Reprinted from *Selected Poems* by permission of Oxford
University Press.

John Ashbery: "Landscape," copyright © 1962 by John Ashbery. Reprinted
from *The Tennis Court Oath* by permission of Wesleyan University Press.
"The Skaters," copyright © 1962, 1963, 1964, 1966 by John Ashbery. Reprinted from *Rivers and Mountains* by permission of Holt, Rinehart and
Winston, Inc.

John Berryman: "Young Woman's Song" and "The Dispossessed," from
The Dispossessed, and lines from *Homage to Mistress Bradstreet* and *77
Dream Songs* reprinted by permission of Farrar, Straus & Giroux.

Elizabeth Bishop: "Brazil, January 1, 1502," "The Fish," "The Man-Moth,"
and "Invitation to Miss Marianne Moore." Reprinted from *Complete
Poems* by permission of Farrar, Straus & Giroux.

John Peale Bishop: "Speaking of Poetry," "A Recollection," "The Return," and "The Hours." Reprinted from *Now With His Love* by permission of Charles Scribner's Sons.

Louise Bogan: "Rhyme" and "Ad Castitatem." Reprinted from *Blue
Estuaries: Poems 1923–1968* by permission of Farrar, Straus & Giroux.

Gwendolyn Brooks: "We Real Cool." Reprinted from *The World of
Gwendolyn Brooks,* copyright © 1959 by Gwendolyn Brooks Blakely, by
permission of Harper & Row, Publishers, Inc.

Hart Crane: Lines from *The Bridge,* and "The Wine Menagerie." Reprinted from *The Collected Poems and Selected Letters and Prose of*

Hart Crane. Copyright 1933, © 1958, 1966 by Liveright Publishing Corporation. Reprinted by permission of Liveright, New York.

ROBERT CREELEY: "The Way." Reprinted from *For Love: Poems 1950–1960* by permission of Charles Scribner's Sons.

E. E. CUMMINGS: "POEM, OR BEAUTY HURTS MR. VINAL," "(im)c-a-t(mo)," and "now does our world descend." Reprinted from *Complete Poems 1913–1962* by e. e. cummings by permission of Harcourt Brace Jovanovich, Inc.

H. D.: "Storm," "Oread," and "Acon." Reprinted from *Sea Garden* by permission of Norman Holmes Pearson, owner of the copyright.

EMILY DICKINSON: "Title divine—is mine!" "I taste a liquor never brewed," "What Mystery pervades a well," and "I can wade Grief." Reprinted from *The Complete Poems of Emily Dickinson*, edited by Thomas H. Johnson, by permission of Atlantic-Little, Brown and Co.

ROBERT DUNCAN: "Tribal Memories." Reprinted from *Bending the Bow*, published by New Directions Publishing Corporation, by permission of Robert Duncan.

RICHARD EBERHART: "Vision," "The Place," and "O Christ of Easter." Reprinted from *Collected Poems 1930–1960* by permission of the Oxford University Press.

JOHN GOULD FLETCHER: "Green Symphony," "The Ozarks," and "Journey Day." Reprinted from *Goblins and Pagodas* by John Gould Fletcher, by permission of Charlie May Fletcher.

ROBERT FROST: "Build Soil," "Dust of Snow," "The Witch of Coös," and "On Going Unnoticed." Reprinted from *The Poetry of Robert Frost*, edited by Edward Connery Lathem. Copyright 1923, 1928, © 1969 by Holt, Rinehart and Winston, Inc. Copyright 1936, 1951, © 1956 by Robert Frost. Copyright © 1964 by Lesley Frost Ballantine. Reprinted by permission of Holt, Rinehart and Winston.

ALLEN GINSBERG: Lines from *Howl & Other Poems*, copyright © 1956, 1959 by Allen Ginsberg. Reprinted by permission of City Lights Books.

ANTHONY HECHT: "A Letter," copyright © 1962 by Anthony E. Hecht. Appeared originally in *The New Yorker*. Reprinted from *The Hard Hours* by permission of Atheneum Publishers.

RANDALL JARRELL: "The Märchen" and "The Orient Express." Reprinted from *The Complete Poems* by permission of Farrar, Straus & Giroux. "The Lost World" and "In Galleries." Reprinted from *The Lost World*, © 1963, 1965 by Randall Jarrell, by permission of the Macmillan Publishing Company. "The Woman at the Washington Zoo." Reprinted from *The Woman at the Washington Zoo*, copyright © 1960 by Randall Jarrell, by permission of Atheneum Publishers.

ROBINSON JEFFERS: "Margrave." Reprinted from *The Selected Poetry of Robinson Jeffers*, copyright 1927, 1928, 1929, 1932, 1938, by Robinson Jeffers; copyright 1924 by Peter G. Boyle; copyright 1925 by Horace Liveright, Inc.; copyright 1935 by The Modern Library, Inc.; copyright 1931, 1933, 1937 by Random House, Inc.; copyright renewed 1951, 1953, © 1955, 1956, 1957, 1959 by Robinson Jeffers. Reprinted by permission of Random House, Inc.

STANLEY KUNITZ: "Hermetic Poem," "Father and Son," and "The Fitting of the Mask." Reprinted from *Selected Poems: 1928–1958,* published by Atlantic-Little, Brown and Company. Copyright © 1956, 1958 by Stanley Kunitz. Reprinted by permission of Atlantic-Little, Brown and Company.

DENISE LEVERTOV: "Matins, vii," and "Marvelous Truth." Reprinted from *The Jacob's Ladder,* copyright © 1961 by Denise Levertov Goodman, by permission of New Directions Publishing Corporation. "The Instant." Reprinted from *Overland to the Islands,* copyright © 1958 by Denise Levertov Goodman, by permission of Denise Levertov.

ROBERT LOWELL: "Colloquy in Black Rock" and "Mary Winslow." Reprinted from *Lord Weary's Castle* by permission of Harcourt Brace Jovanovich, Inc. "Grandparents." Reprinted from *Life Studies* by permission of Farrar, Straus & Giroux.

ARCHIBALD MACLEISH: "Mother Goose's Garland," "Le Secret Humain," "Invocation to the Social Muse," and "Background with Revolutionaries." Reprinted from *Collected Poems 1917–1952* by Archibald MacLeish, by permission of Houghton Mifflin Company.

EDGAR LEE MASTERS: Lines from the *Spoon River Anthology,* published by the Macmillan Publishing Company, reprinted by permission of Ellen C. Masters.

W. S. MERWIN: "I Live Up Here," copyright © 1966 by W. S. Merwin. "The Asians Dying" and "The Dry Stone Mason," copyright © 1966 and 1967, respectively, by W. S. Merwin; both appeared originally in *The New Yorker.* Reprinted from *The Lice* by permission of Atheneum Publishers.

MARIANNE MOORE: "He 'Digesteth Harde Yron,'" copyright 1941 and renewed © 1969 by Marianne Moore. "The Fish," copyright 1935 by Marianne Moore, renewed © 1963 by Marianne Moore and T. S. Eliot. "Nevertheless," copyright 1944 and renewed © 1972 by Marianne Moore. Reprinted from *Collected Poems* by permission of the Macmillan Publishing Company.

HOWARD NEMEROV: "Lobsters," and "Grace to Be Said at the Supermarket." Reprinted from *The Blue Swallows,* copyright © 1967 by Howard Nemerov. Reprinted by permission of the Margot Johnson Agency.

CHARLES OLSON: "Letter 3." Reprinted from *The Maximus Poems* by permission of Corinth Books.

SYLVIA PLATH: "Ariel," "Lady Lazarus," and "Morning Song." Reprinted from *Ariel* by permission of Harper & Row, Publishers, Inc.

EZRA POUND: "In a Station of the Metro," "Cino," "Salvationists," "The Seafarer," "The Jewel Stairs' Grievance," and "Hugh Selwyn Mauberly, v." Reprinted from *Personae* by Ezra Pound, copyright 1926 by Ezra Pound. Reprinted by permission of New Directions Publishing Corporation.

EDWIN ARLINGTON ROBINSON: "Walt Whitman." Reprinted from *The Children of the Night: A Book of Poems* by permission of Charles Scribner's Sons. "Pasa Thalassa Thalassa," "For a Dead Lady," "Octave XV," and "Richard Cory." Reprinted from *Collected Poems* by permission of Charles Scribner's Sons.

THEODORE ROETHKE: "Open House," copyright 1941 by Theodore Roethke. "Root Cellar," copyright 1943 by Modern Poetry Association, Inc. "The Minimal," copyright 1942 by Theodore Roethke. "Words for the Wind," copyright © 1958 by Theodore Roethke. "The Far Field" and "The Abyss," copyright © 1962 and 1963, respectively, by Beatrice Roethke as Administratrix of the Estate of Theodore Roethke. Reprinted from *The Collected Poems of Theodore Roethke* by permission of Doubleday & Company, Inc.

CARL SANDBURG: "Chicago," "To a Contemporary Bunkshooter," and "Prairie." Reprinted from *The Complete Poems of Carl Sandburg* by permission of Harcourt Brace Jovanovich, Inc.

KARL SHAPIRO: "Auto Wreck," "A Cut Flower," and "From the Top Floor of the Tulsa Hotel I Gaze at the Night Beauty of the Cracking-Plant." Reprinted from *Selected Poems*, copyright 1940, 1941, 1942, 1943, 1944, 1945, 1946, 1947, 1948, 1949, 1950, 1951, 1952, 1953, 1954, © 1956, 1957, 1958, 1961, 1962, 1963, 1964, 1967, 1968 by Karl Shapiro. Reprinted by permission of Random House, Inc.

GARY SNYDER: Lines from *Riprap*. Reprinted by permission of Gary Snyder.

WALLACE STEVENS: "Sunday Morning," "The Idea of Order at Key West," "Like Decorations in a Nigger Cemetary," "The Man With the Blue Guitar," "Credences of Summer," "The Poems of Our Climate," "Thirteen Ways of Looking at a Blackbird," "A Primitive Like an Orb." Reprinted from *The Collected Poems of Wallace Stevens*, copyright 1923, 1931, 1935, 1936, 1937, 1942, 1943, 1944, 1945, 1946, 1947, 1948, 1949, 1950, 1951, 1952, 1954 by Wallace Stevens, and *Opus Posthumous*, copyright © 1957 by Elsie Stevens and Holly Stevens. Reprinted by permission of Alfred A. Knopf, Inc.

ALLEN TATE: "The Subway," "Ode to the Confederate Dead," and "The Mediterranean." Reprinted from *The Swimmers and Other Selected Poems*, copyright © 1970 by Allen Tate. Reprinted by permission of The Swallow Press and Allen Tate.

EDWARD TAYLOR: "A Funerall Poem Upon the Death of my ever Endeared and Tender Wife Mrs. Elizabeth Taylor . . ." and 10 lines from *Gods Determinations touching his Elect*. Reprinted from *The Poems of Edward Taylor*, copyright © 1960 by Yale University Press. Reprinted by permission of Yale University Press. "The Joy of Church Fellowship Rightly Attended," Prologue to *Preparatory Meditations*, and 13 lines from *Gods Determinations touching his Elect*. Reprinted from the *New England Quarterly*, copyright 1937 by the *New England Quarterly*. Reprinted by permission of Thomas H. Johnson and the *New England Quarterly*. Lines from Meditation 26, Second Series. Reprinted from *American Literature*, copyright © 1957 by Duke University Press. Reprinted by permission of Duke University Press. Lines from Meditation 29, First Series. Reprinted from *The Poetical Works of Edward Taylor*, copyright Rockland, 1939, Princeton University Press, 1943. Reprinted by permission of Princeton University Press.

SARA TEASDALE: "Blue Squills." Reprinted from *Collected Poems* by Sara Teasdale, copyright 1920 by the Macmillan Publishing Company, renewed 1948 by Mamie T. Wheless. Reprinted by permission of the Macmillan Publishing Company.

MELVIN B. TOLSON: Lines from *Harlem Gallery*, copyright © 1965 by Twayne Publishers, Inc. Reprinted by permission of Twayne Publishers, Inc.

FREDERICK GODDARD TUCKERMAN: "Margites," "Sonnet II, First Series," "Sonnet XXIV, Second Series," "Sonnet XVI, Second Series," and "Sonnet X, Third Series," copyright 1931 by Alfred A. Knopf, Inc., renewed © 1959 by Witter Bynner. *The Cricket*, copyright 1950 by Margaret Tuckerman Clark. Reprinted from *The Complete Poems of Frederick Goddard Tuckerman*, edited by N. Scott Momaday, by permission of Oxford University Press.

ROBERT PENN WARREN: "Original Sin: A Short Story," "Nocturne: Traveling Salesman in Hotel Bedroom," and "Founding Fathers, Nineteenth-Century Style, Southeast U.S.A." Reprinted from *Selected Poems: New And Old, 1923–1966*, copyright 1936, 1940, 1941, 1942, 1943, 1944, © 1955, 1957, 1958, 1959, 1960, 1963, 1966 by Robert Penn Warren. Copyright renewed © 1964 by Robert Penn Warren. Reprinted by permission of Random House, Inc. "After Night Flight Son Reaches Bedside of Already Unconscious Father, Whose Right Hand Lifts in a Spasmodic Gesture, as Though Trying to Make Contact: 1955." Reprinted from *You, Emperors, and Others: Poems 1957–1960*, copyright © 1958, 1959, 1960 by Robert Penn Warren, by permission of Random House, Inc.

RICHARD WILBUR: "Bell Speech" and "Junk." Reprinted from *The Poems of Richard Wilbur* by permission of Harcourt Brace Jovanovich, Inc.

WILLIAM CARLOS WILLIAMS: "The Red Wheelbarrow." Reprinted from *Collected Earlier Poems*, copyright 1938 by New Directions Publishing Corporation, by permission of New Directions Publishing Corporation. Lines from *Paterson*, copyright 1946, 1948, 1949 by William Carlos Williams, reprinted by permission of New Directions Publishing Corporation.

JAMES WRIGHT: "Having Lost My Sons, I Confront the Wreckage of the Moon: Christmas, 1960." Reprinted from *The Branch Will Not Break*, copyright © 1961 by James Wright, by permission of Wesleyan University Press.

ELINOR WYLIE: "The Fairy Goldsmith," "South," and "Little Elegy." Reprinted from *Collected Poems of Elinor Wylie*, copyright 1921, 1923, 1924, 1925, 1926, 1927, 1928, 1929, 1932 by Alfred A. Knopf, Inc.; copyright 1949 by William Rose Benét; copyright © 1956, 1957, 1960 by Edwina C. Rubenstein. Reprinted by permission of Alfred A. Knopf, Inc.

For John Donald
1962–1966

Contents

xi

Contents

Preface

The Poetic area is very spacious—has room for all—has so many mansions!

—Whitman

Give me initiative, spermatic, prophesying, man-making words.

—Emerson

What is American poetry? What large generalizations can we make about it? What are its traditions? William Carlos Williams said once, half-facetiously, that "American poetry is a very easy subject to discuss, for the simple reason that it does not exist." But it does exist, in great profusion and variety, and one aim of this book is to bring it into some sort of focus. I shall make two large generalizations, which I hope will be adequately supported in the chapters to come. The first is that American poetry is heterogeneous: it is large, it contains multitudes, as Walt Whitman might say. Like the land itself, America's poets are diverse in attitude and character: they are scholars, roughnecks, scholar-roughnecks, traditionalists, innovators, bards, aesthetes, city poets and country poets, Anglophiles and Anglophobes.

The other, also demonstrable by numerous examples, is that American poets are in the main antitraditional, or at least forward-looking. The early ones praised their new-found land; in the nineteenth century they kept trying to be different from the English; in the twentieth century "new" and "revolutionary" have been bywords of poets and critics alike. It would seem that much American poetry has been written out of defiance, and sometimes even ignorance, of what went before.

This book is not an attempt to support these or other generalizations, however. In the process of writing I discovered they were there, but I began it as, and it remains first of all, a historical and critical survey of poetry written in America during the past three hundred and fifty years. I have not been able in a short history to include everybody, and there are many omissions: Phillis Wheatley, Royall Tyler, Amy Lowell, Mark Van Doren, Delmore Schwartz, John Hall Wheelock, Ogden Nash, Kenneth Rexroth, Louis Zukofsky, A. R. Ammons—the list, especially of moderns, could go on and on. I have my favorite poems and poets, and many of my selections—and omissions—reflect my own taste or my own view of their significance, though I hope I have not written an eccentric book.

I have tried to do several things: to provide biographical and historical information where necessary, to make connections between various poets and periods, and to give a sense of the range of a poet's work; but principally I have tried to give a sense of the quality of each writer—to try to see what makes him unique, what makes him stand out from his contemporaries and his ancestors. This has required a great many quotations, and these should not be skipped like indigestible small-type lumps; the reader should consider them as illustrations and read them as continuations of the text.

With some exceptions, the book is organized around two major poets for each chapter, surrounded by a group of contemporaries. Some distortion of chronology results, but I believe this is offset by a greater sense of coherence than a straight chronological treatment would have allowed. As I have said, my principles of selection have followed my own view of what is significant; however, I like to think my views are shared by many readers of poetry. In fact, to say that I am giving my own view is inaccurate, since I owe a great deal to the historians and critics whose names appear in the bibliographies.

The bibliographies serve two purposes: they list works

consulted and they document references I have made in the text. I have supplied a general bibliography for the entire book, as well as a bibliography for each chapter. The bibliographies are arranged in this way because I wished to avoid footnotes; the reader should therefore be able to find in the chapter bibliographies full citations of every source to which I have referred in the text.

A word about dates. When individual poems have appeared in a collection which is dated in the text, I have generally not repeated the dates for each poem. Dates of poems in parentheses are always the earliest known date; however, sometimes this is the date of composition, sometimes the date of periodical publication, and sometimes the date of first book publication. When dealing with so many hundreds of poems, which were written and printed under so many widely varying conditions, I found this to be unavoidable.

I wish to acknowledge the support of the Research Foundation of the State University of New York for two summer research grants, and to thank the staffs of the State University of New York at Albany Library, the New York State Library, the New York Public Library, and the Harmanus Bleeker Library in Albany for various courtesies. Guy Cardwell read the entire manuscript, and my colleagues M. E. Grenander, Perry Westbrook, Vivian Hopkins, and William Rowley read parts of it and offered suggestions and encouragement. Other debts are recorded in the text and the bibliography. Thanks should also go to Morag Stauffer, Sally Dague, Arlene Alderman, and Alice Kenny for typing the manuscript. I owe the largest debt to my wife Morag and my children, who have lived with this book over too many years.

Altamont, New York
June 1, 1973

CHAPTER ONE

The Beginnings to 1765

Early histories and narratives, the Dutch poets, "Bacon's Epitaph," Urian Oakes, John Wilson, John Fiske, The Bay Psalm Book, Anne Bradstreet, Michael Wigglesworth, Edward Taylor, Richard Steere, William Livingston, Mather Byles, Thomas Godfrey

The large quantity of Colonial poetry that survives today deals with a narrow range of subjects in a wide variety of forms. Like poetry written in other times and other places, it is an imaginative expression of the hopes, fears, and concerns of its culture, but because of the uniqueness of the culture of the settlers in the New World in general and the Puritans in particular, early American poetry has a curiously limited range.

An occasional spark of eloquence does appear, but considering the circumstances under which it was written, we cannot expect or demand the kind of literary polish and perfection from writers living in the early settlements that we would from their European contemporaries. For one thing, most of them had a quite different conception of the function of verse. They took as their purpose just one half of the twofold Horatian ideal of pleasure and instruction. Poetry, for the Puritans at least, was another mode of instruction, or "edification"; another way to equip themselves for living a spiritual life both in this world and in the next. Another of their aims was frankly propagandistic, however, and many early poems are narratives, or "histories," proclaiming the virtues and wonders of the New World in an effort to lure additional settlers to its shores. One such effort, written by William Morrell (*fl.* 1623–1625), a churchman commissioned to superintend church activities in Plymouth, reports his experiences with the benighted Indians after living with them for a year. His closing lines attempt to persuade

> our mighty and renownèd state
> This poor blind people to commiserate,
> Or painful men to this good land invite,
> Whose holy works these natives may inlight;
> If heaven grant these, to see here built, I trust,
> An English kingdom from this Indian dust.

Morrell's English rendering of his own Latin poem, *Nova Anglia,* perhaps does not strictly qualify as American poetry, since both Latin and English versions were published in London in 1625, yet in its attention to the details of climate, topography, and natural history of New England it is typical of many such reports, in verse and prose, written in the American Colonies.

The reasons for the absence of high-quality poetry are well known. The first settlers brought with them their carpenters, millers, glaziers, bootmakers, and chandlers, but they left their poets at home. Many were educated men, to be sure, but they were first of all ministers, soldiers, administrators, and farmers, and only incidentally writers of verse; therefore, the poetry they wrote reflected the everyday concerns of these men of purpose and action as they confronted a vast and novel wilderness inhabited by hostile Indians and wild animals. The number who died from sickness, overexposure, fatigue, childbirth, and Indian massacres is as much an explanation of their preoccupation with the subject of death as was any morbidity of temperament or theology they might have had. Practically every Colonial versifier wrote an elegy or "funeral poem" in memory of a wife, a child, a parent, or a friend. Poems on the transitory world and on the vanity of all things arose in part from the continual presence of death from

violent or natural causes. But these men and women were also
proud of their undertaking, and were filled with wonder and
hope at the promise of success that greeted their efforts at
taming the land. As they saw their fields prosper and gathered
the rich yields of the forests and streams, they knew they had
a good thing and were eager to spread the news in poems
about it.

Three types dominate the early history of American
poetry: the poem of providential mercy or disaster, the elegy
or epitaph, and the personal narrative or history. The first
and third of these tend to blur into each other, depending
upon whether the purpose is to demonstrate God's Providence
or to create propaganda for prospective colonists. When John
Wilson wrote *A Song of Deliverance for the Lasting Remem-
brance of Gods Wonderful Works* in 1626 he was interested
mainly in making history palatable for children. His rhymes
follow closely certain prose tracts on the Gunpowder Plot, the
Spanish Armada, and the plague of 1603, but they are arranged in such a way that they illustrate the operation of
God's Providence. The collection and assembling of "provi-
dences" took on the proportions of a major industry among
New England writers, from William Bradford's (1590–1657)
History of the Plimoth Plantation (1646–1651) to part six of
Cotton Mather's (1663–1728) *Magnalia Christi Americana*
(1697), which was specifically devoted to cataloguing events in
which God directly revealed his power in the Colonies: "all
wonderful *deliverances* of the distressed: *mercies* to the godly;
judgments on the wicked; and more glorious fulfillment of
either the promises or the threatenings in the Scriptures of
truth." This "reading" of historical events in an effort to relate
them to an overruling providential God sustaining the order of
things is, as Charles Feidelson has pointed out, a basically
symbolic process, even though the Puritans themselves were
not consciously aware of the literary or metaphorical possibility of such a fusion of discrete historical events and a unified
apocalyptic vision.

Edward Johnson's (1598–1672) *Wonder-Working Providence of Sions Saviour in New England,* first published in

London in 1654, is another of these works, an epic in prose
and verse that describes the settlement of New England with
the assistance of a benevolent God. Johnson takes the Puritan
view of history, in which New England is a New Jerusalem
where the Christian counterparts of the Children of Israel
have come to establish a Heaven on earth. This sweeping
historical view is tempered by passages of humor and satire,
including his own unorthodox views of the excommunication
and banishment of Anne Hutchinson from Massachusetts.
Although the verses are mediocre and labored, the work as a
whole is a revealing insight into the workings of a mind that
was far from commonplace. Johnson is probably also the
author of an earlier poem, *Good News from New-England*
(1648)—not to be confused with Edward Winslow's (1595–
1655) *Good Newes from New England* (1624)—which is much
more factual and realistic, with less emphasis on the high
purposes of the westward migration and more on the selfish
or mixed motives of many of the individuals involved. Taken
together, the two poems show Johnson's ability at humor and
satire as well as his sense of proportion and emphasis in placing individual events in a larger historical setting.

Benjamin Tompson's (1642–1714) *New Englands Crisis*
(1676) is another history written in a satirical vein, this one
warning its readers to give up their erring ways and return
to the simpler and purer ways of the earliest settlers. Mixing
solemn warnings and lurid descriptions of Indian warfare with
satirical portraits and other humorous sketches, Tompson,
who published the poem the same year in England with the
title *Sad and Deplorable Newes from New England,* takes the
same view of the decline of the colony that Michael Wigglesworth had earlier taken in *God's Controversy with New-
England* (1662). These are a few examples of the kind of poem
that many writers, some with talent, were writing. Of the
more obviously propagandistic poems, William Morrell's *Nova
Anglia* and the Dutch poet Steendam's panegyrics stand out,
while John Danforth, in "The Mercies of the Year, Commemorated: A Song for Little Children in New-England,
December 13th 1720," is pleased with the New Englanders

having averted the fears and dangers that preoccupied Bradford, Tompson, and Wigglesworth.

Historical narrative and the elegy seem to dominate Colonial verse, but there are many other forms. A lot of the verse was not published at the time, and much of it is fragmentary or is interspersed in prose passages, but we can be sure that verse writing was a popular pastime among the settlers of the coastal Colonies, from New England and Nova Scotia down to Virginia and the Carolinas. Harold Jantz, in his history of early New England verse, lists almost two hundred writers from that region alone and asks whether "we perchance know only a haphazard fifth of the verse of our Middle and Southern Colonies." Almost all of the poets listed by Jantz wrote elegies or epitaphs, but in addition to these almost universal forms, one finds odes, hymns, translations of psalms, almanac verse, religious lyrics, love lyrics, laudatory prefaces and epistles, historical and biblical narratives, anagrams and acrostics, satires, and "effusions" and other personal poems. These appear in almanacs, broadsides, sermon collections, hymn books, personal memoirs, diaries, wills, poetry collections, and even on tombstones. Some of the almanac verse, particularly that of Thomas Shepard (1605–1649), Samuel Danforth I (1626–1674), and John Danforth (1660–1730), is quite readable. There are the satirical verses of Samuel Sewall (1652–1730) in his diary and Nathaniel Ward in *The Simple Cobbler of Aggawam* (1647). Many Colonial writers whom we think of only as prose writers also wrote poetry; William Bradford, for example, wrote several elegies and poems of warning to straying colonists. In his will he left an admonitory poem, "Of Boston in New England," reminding Boston of her humble beginnings and warning her against putting on airs. Over fifty elegies, songs, hymns, and lyrics have been counted by Jantz as the work of Cotton Mather (1663–1728). And Roger Williams (*c.* 1603–1683) is the author of thirty-three charming lyrics, which come at the end of each of the sections of his description of the Indian language, *A Key into the Language of America* (1643). Here is a sample of these witty moralizing poems:

God gives them sleep on Ground, on Straw,
   on Sedgie Mats or Boord:
When English softest Beds of Downe,
   sometimes no sleep affoord.

I have knowne them leave their House and Mat
   to lodge a Friend or stranger
When Jewes and Christians oft have sent
   Christ Jesus to the Manger.

'Fore day they invocate their Gods,
   though Many, False and New:
O how should that God worshipt be,
   who is but One and True?

From this evidence it is safe to conclude of the American colonists in general, as Kenneth Murdock has of the New England Puritans in particular, that far from being hostile to poetry, they both needed and loved it.

Although there are differences between them, seventeenth-century American poetry is by and large like seventeenth-century English poetry, since the colonists used many of the traditions and forms current in England and on the Continent. Many wrote in the Baroque tradition, using the elaborate conceits, tricky wordplay, and gnarled reasoning characteristic of Donne, Herbert, Vaughan, and other English Metaphysical poets. The anagram and acrostic enjoyed a vogue among several practitioners, who perhaps felt secure in a tradition rooted in the Middle Ages and the Renaissance. They knew Guillaume Du Bartas, whose epic on the creation of the world, *La Première Semaine* (1578), had been translated by Joshua Sylvester and was widely read and admired in England. They knew Jonson, and, by the last quarter of the century, were familiar with Milton. Late in the seventeenth century Dryden quickly became fashionable, and the amount of verse written in imitation of Dryden and Pope continued to grow throughout the eighteenth century.

The task of bringing some sort of order to this period is complicated by a number of problems. From the beginning,

America has been a country of regions, and the story of American poetry often must be told in terms of regional poets and regional interests. Also, even if we exclude the Indians, we still have several nationalities to deal with: principally the English, the French, and the Dutch. If Spaniards and Norsemen wrote verse on North American soil we shall ignore them here, but for the record it is perhaps of interest to note at least one French poet who was writing in Nova Scotia soon after the settlement of Jamestown. This was one Marc Lescarbot (*c.* 1570–1642), a young Parisian lawyer, who lived in Port Royal, in what is now Nova Scotia, from 1606 to 1608. During this time, in order to keep up his spirits, he wrote odes, an Indian narrative in verse, and a pageant. These were collected and published in Paris in 1609 under the title *Les Muses de la Nouvelle France.*

The Dutch colonists are represented by three poets who spent some time in New Netherland in the seventeenth century: Jacob Steendam (1616–1672), Henricus Selijns (1636–1701), and Nicasius De Sille (1610–?). Steendam achieved the greatest prominence of the three as a poet, both in the Netherlands and in New Amsterdam, where he spent several years as a merchant. When Steendam arrived in New Netherland around 1651 he had already published a volume of verse in Holland called *Den Distelfink* (*The Thistle Finch*), containing conventional love lyrics, pastorals, and spiritual exercises. After several years' residence he wrote a short political allegory in which he gave voice to the Dutch colonists' complaint that their efforts at establishing New Amsterdam as a trading outpost were being frustrated by the warlike intentions of the Dutch government. This poem, *Klacht van Nieuw-Amsterdam* (*Complaint of New Amsterdam*), was published as a broadside in Amsterdam in 1659. In lines heavily burdened with rhetorical figures and Greek gods and goddesses, Steendam personified New Amsterdam as the beautiful daughter of the old mother city who had grown up rich and handsome and in danger of being despoiled by the English "swine" unless returned to her mother's protective bosom. Two years later he published another panegyric poem that more fully praised the virtues of the colony: *'T Lof van Nuw-Nederland* (*The Praise of New Netherland*). This poem, organized according to the Aristotelian scheme of the four elements—air, fire, water, and earth—is a full and elaborate description of the richness of the natural resources of New Netherland likely to appeal to prospective settlers: pure air, fresh winds, clean water, fertile earth, fish (lamprey, eel, perch, crabs, lobster), game (beaver, otter, raccoon, fox), birds (hawk, duck, goose, turkey), minerals, and herbs. This poem is characteristically Dutch in its appeal to the materialistic attractions, in contrast to the altruistic and spiritual appeal of Morrell's *Nova Anglia,* written some thirty-five years earlier, but it is clearly in the same genre of personal history as such works as Sir William Vaughan's (1577–1641) *The Golden Fleece* (London, 1626), a description of the beauties of Newfoundland written partly in verse, and John Holme's *A True Relation of the Flourishing State of Pennsylvania.* (1686). Steendam's last efforts on behalf of the Dutch colony were some "spurring verses" written in 1662 as a preface to a plan for recolonizing a settlement that had been wiped out in a massacre. The third stanza of these verses, translated by his biographer, H. C. Murphy, captures some of the flavor of his longer poem:

> The birds obscure the sky, so numerous in their flight;
> The animals roam wild, and flatten down the ground;
> The fish swarm in the waters, and exclude the light;
> The oysters there, than which none better can be found,
> And piled up, heap on heap, till islands they attain;
> And vegetation clothes the forest, mead, and plain.

Steendam was a businessman and adventurer, not a poet, and we would look in vain for any lyrical flights. These are competent and interesting works of an intelligent observer, however, and are highly typical of one kind of verse being written in both the Dutch and English colonies.

Peter Stuyvesant's First Councillor, Nicasius De Sille, a soldier and administrator, was appointed by the Dutch government to keep Stuyvesant in line. As one of the founders of the

Long Island settlement of New Utrecht he performed the functions of first citizen and, eventually, town chronicler, in his *Description of the Founding or Beginning of New Utrecht,* which he wrote from 1657 to 1660. Scattered among the documents and the chronicles are three poems inspired by his experience in the village. One is an epitaph for the first-born baby of the village; the second, "The Earth Speaks to its Cultivators," is a celebration of the fertility of the earth; and the third, "Song in the Manner of the 116th Psalm," reflects his trust in God's protecting arm and his belief that God had brought the Dutch to New Netherland to sing His praises in a land of pagans. These three poems neatly typify the three kinds of verse written by many English colonists in New England and Virginia.

Henricus Selijns, one of the founders of the Dutch Reformed Church in America, was a learned clergyman in Brooklyn whose verses show more variety in style and subject matter than the other two. If not as accomplished a poet as Steendam, Selijns was less narrow and less bound by rhetoric and tradition. Some of his verses reflect his pastoral duties, and several poems are written as advice to women, while others are indirect love poems to actual or imaginary women. Elegies, birthday poems, and epithalamia also appear in a manuscript volume of poems now in the possession of the New-York Historical Society. Some of his most interesting poems are concise "tomb-inscriptions" that outline with an almost impressionistic spareness of detail a few of the murders that occurred in the area. One such elegy, concerning an unwed mother's murder of her child, ends on a moralizing note:

Although unwed she played the wife upon her bed,
   Grew large of girth, denied what was self-evident.
  To hide her loss of maidenhood, she lost her soul,
And choked her tender child. O impious times and morals!
                (trans. from MS. by E. L. Raesly)

These Dutch writers, interesting as they may be historically, stand outside the tradition of American poetry. Their

works were published in Dutch or remained in manuscript, and
little, if any, Dutch culture was assimilated by the English after
the fall of New Amsterdam. Even though the French and
Dutch (and perhaps the Spanish) were writing verse on American soil, our concern is, of course, mainly with poetry written
by the English colonists. We may go further and assert that
even though poetry was written in the middle and southern
Colonies, the only poetry of lasting literary worth before 1700
was written by the Puritans of the Massachusetts Bay Colony.
The poetic traditions established by the Puritans in the seventeenth century are deeply embedded in much American poetry
up to the present. As Roy Harvey Pearce has written, "In form,
substance, and method, American poetry from the seventeenth
century to the present is on the whole a development of the
Puritan imagination, with its compulsion to relate, even to
make identical, man's sense of his inwardness and his sense of
his role in the world at large."

One notable exception to the preeminence of Puritan
poetry in this period is a remarkably finished and genuinely
moving epitaph written for Nathaniel Bacon (1647–1676),
leader of the rebellion against the Governor and Assembly of
Virginia in 1676. The poem, actually an elegy, is one of two
on Bacon appearing in a manuscript probably written in that
year known as "The Burwell Papers." The two poems reflect
diametrically opposite views of Bacon, but taken together
could possibly represent a kind of debate as to Bacon's character by a writer who himself is uncertain of his attitude.
"Bacon's Epitaph, Made by His Man" the better of the two, is
written by someone acquainted with the English Metaphysical
poets. It is formal and stately in tone, yet reflects sympathy
with Bacon's cause and outrage at his death. Jay B. Hubbell
has convincingly argued that the probable author of both
poems is John Cotton (1640–1699) of Queen's Creek near Wil-
liamsburg, a conservative planter and neighbor of the elder
Bacon. The poem opens with a complaint against the tyranny
of death and a plea for the justice of Bacon's cause:

Death, why so cruel? What! no other way
To manifest thy spleen but thus to slay
Our hopes of safety, liberty, our all,
Which through thy tyranny with him must fall
To its late chaos? Had thy rigid force
Been dealt by retail and not thus in gross,
Grief had been silent. Now we must complain
Since thou in him hast more than thousands slain
Whose lives and safeties did so much depend
On him, their life, with him their lives must end.

Although it is not, as some readers have claimed it to be, the best poem written in seventeenth-century America, it still stands out as a superior elegy in a form that had more practitioners than any other, and we can still agree with Moses Coit Tyler that if much of the seventeenth century was for Virginia a "literary desert, these verses form a delightful oasis in it."

"Bacon's Epitaph" is matched in quality by another fine elegy written in New England the following year, 1677, by Urian Oakes (*c.* 1631–1681), while he was acting president of Harvard College. Oakes's one published poem, *An Elegie upon The Death of the Reverend Mr. Thomas Shepard, Late Teacher of the Church at Charlestown in New-England,* is a moving and genuinely felt testimonial to the memory of the son of the influential Cambridge pastor and theologian. Shepard himself was the author of two fine elegies on John Norton and John Wilson, but he is remembered principally as the subject of Oakes's fifty-two stanzas in his memory. The length of the poem and the handling of the six-line stanza allow the poet a stateliness of tone and pace with which he enumerates the many virtues of his subject: his wit, learning, judgment, charity, wisdom, generosity, etc. In a tone that narrowly avoids bitterness and frequently expresses genuine despair, Oakes consciously and deliberately avoids elaborate conceits, rhetoric, and extensive allusion in favor of a direct testimonial to his friend's virtues:

Poetick raptures are of no esteem,
Daring *Hyperboles* have here no place,
Luxuriant wits on such a copious Theme
Would shame themselves, and blush to shew their face
    Here's worth enough to overmatch the skill
    Of the most stately Poet *Laureat's Quill.*

The poem ends with a simple statement of the loneliness and
bereavement that pervade it:

My Dearest, Inmost, Bosome-Friend, is Gone!
Gone is my sweet Companion, Soul's delight!
Now in an Huddling Croud I'm all alone,
And almost could bid all the World *Goodnight:*
    Blest be my Rock! God lives: Oh let him be,
    As He is All, so All in All to me.

Among those Puritan writers who are remembered for
their elegies are two accomplished practitioners of the anagram,
John Wilson (1588–1667), and John Fiske (1608–1677). The
device of transposing the letters of a person's name into a
phrase applicable to him hardly seems a promising one for
the production of poetry. The idea was to use the phrase thus
derived as the theme of the poem, and to apply one's ingenuity
to the development and restatement of the theme or the key
word of the phrase throughout the poem. It shares in its emphasis on intellectual dexterity and artificiality some of the
traits of the English religious poets; we are reminded of Herbert's "Easter Wings" and "The Altar." But it is not entirely
clear why Wilson, and later, Fiske, made such extensive use
of the anagram, since by this time English and Continental
poets looked upon the practice with scorn.

Thomas Shepard the Older was the subject of four such
elegies by Wilson; one in Latin and three in English. In one,
his name is anagrammatized to "o a map's thresh'd" and begins:

Loe her's a map, where we may see
Well thresh'd an heap of corn to be

By Thomas Shepard's happy hand
Which from the chaffe pure wheat hath fan'd

The two other English poems on Shepard are built upon the
anagrams, "More hath pass'd" and "Arm'd as the Shop." In
elegies on John Norton, his name is appropriately transposed
to "into honnor," while its Latin equivalent (Johannes Nor-
tonius) becomes "Jesu! Annon Thronos?" and "Annon Jesu
Honor Sit?" Wilson memorialized Elizabeth Tompson's happy
transference to Heaven by the anagram, "o i am blest on top,"
even though this requires the spellings "o i am blesst on top"
and "Elisabot Tompson." Taking liberties with spellings and
substituting letters was a commonly accepted practice, however, and allowed the anagrammatist some freedom in his
choice of appropriate phrases. Perhaps Wilson's best elegy,
judged on the basis of the verse as well as the appropriateness
of the anagram, are the lines upon the death of Mrs. Abagaill
Tompson: "i am gon to all bliss." The sixty-one lines of
rhymed couplets (with a concluding triplet) are spoken by the
triumphant Mrs. Tompson as she finds herself in Heaven at
last:

The blessed news i send to the is this:
That i am goon from the unto all bliss,
Such as the saints & angells do enjoy,

Wring not thy hand, nor sigh, nor mourn, nor weep,
All tho thine Abigaill be fain a sleep.
Tis but her body—that shall ryse again;
In Christs sweet bosomb doth her soule remain.

There is much more to be found here than mere quaintness
or eccentricity; we can share in the simplicity and direct expression of a sincere Calvinist belief in the triumph of God's
mercy, done cleverly but with no affectation. Wilson's accomplishments in the anagram were famous among his contemporaries and prompted Cotton Mather to print a poem in
Magnalia Christi Americana (1702) celebrating

His Care to guide his *Flock,* and feed his *Lambs,*
By, *Words, Works, Prayers, Psalms, Alms,* and *Anagrams.*

And Nathaniel Ward (*c.* 1578–1652), that astute and witty
observer of the New England scene, addressed these bantering
verses to his friend Wilson:

> We poor Agawams
> are so stiff in the hams
> that we cannot make Anagrams,
> But Mr John Wilson
> the great Epigrammatist
> Can let out an Anagram
> even as he list.

If Wilson popularized the anagram, John Fiske brought
it to a high state of perfection and ingenuity. He is the author
of no less than four anagrams on John Cotton, the best of
which is "O, Honie knott," which very aptly expresses two
sides of Cotton's character: his personal charm and his subtle
intelligence. The poem itself is a series of wordplays on the
"knotts" of mystery, of sweetness, of truth, etc., which Cotton's
intelligence and character opened. Every possible variation on
the word is used in what is a highly complex Baroque poem,
full of fantastic conceits and sudden and surprising shifts in
meaning:

> Knotts we doe meet with many a cue daily
> which crabbed anggry tough unpleasing bee
> But we as in a honi-comb a knott
> of Hony sweete, here had such sweetenes Gott
> the knotts and knobbs that on the Trees doe grow
> the bitterest excressences we know.

In an even more complex application of this technique, Fiske
related his anagram to his imagery and theme in an elegy to
the near-centenarian Anne Griffin. The anagram, "In Fanne:
Rig," is developed by two sets of images: the threshing fan

of a Christian life that leaves the pure wheat of the saved soul, and the "rig" of the cargo ship ready to transport the soul to its destination. The poem is difficult and obscure, and not wholly unsuccessful in its efforts to hold these two dissimilar images together thematically.

The poems of Wilson and Fiske are not the only examples of the Puritans' obvious delight in words for their own sake. Although they had the pious intention of searching for signification in the very names of their subjects, just as they sought "emblems" and "types" in nature and in Scripture, there was more than a little sheer enjoyment in the working out of an intellectual exercise for its own sake. Probably the most elaborate of such conceits is a "Threnodia," written around 1663 by E. B. (probably Edward Bulkeley), in which Samuel Stone of Hartford is described as a diamond, a loadstone, a whetstone, a stone for David's sling, and "A stone acute, fit to divide and square; / A squared stone became Christ's building rare." It is not hard to see from these few examples that Edward Taylor was using a well-established convention in such poems as Meditation 48, Second Series, with its play on "might" and "mite," or Meditation 4, First Series, "I Am the Rose of Sharon," with its conceits on the image of the rose.

Some of the earliest verses written in America were written not as self-expression, but to fulfill a practical and essential need. The authors of the much-maligned Bay Psalm Book were under no illusions that what they were producing was art or literature. The harsh judgment of Moses Coit Tyler that this book was "a poetic phenomenon, happily unique, we may hope, in all the literatures of English speech" rests partly on the assumption that the translators of the psalms were trying to produce poetry. By their own assertion they were not; their efforts were directed toward making the most literal translations possible and setting them to well-known tunes.

There had been earlier metrical versions of the psalms in English, but they were unsuitable to the Puritans, whose fundamental Calvinism demanded an absolute fidelity to the written word of God as revealed in the original Hebrew. As Thomas Cartwright wrote in his *Treatise of the Christian Re-*

ligion (1616), "the Scriptures are the rule, the line, the squyre and the light, whereby to examine and trie all judgements and sayings of men and of angels, whether they be such as God approveth, yea or no."

The Whole Booke of Psalmes Faithfully Translated into English Metre—to call it by its correct title—was the result of a collaborative effort of many clergymen and scholars in the colony under the supervision of John Cotton, John Wilson, and Richard Mather (1596–1669). John Cotton wrote a preface, and the book—the first to be printed in English America—was printed in 1640. It was not long, however, before even the relatively unlettered congregations found objections to many of the more awkwardly phrased passages, and Cotton Mather remarked that "a little more Art was to be employ'd" on it. In 1651 a revision was published, *The Psalms Hymns and Spiritual Songs of the Old and New Testament, faithfully translated into English Metre*. In this version, which came to be known as the New England Psalm Book, many psalms were considerably recast, but the larger number remained essentially the same. Even in its revised version the book was not a success, probably because of the difficulty of trying both to remain literally faithful to the Hebrew and to use English meter and rhyme. The translators were under no illusions about what they were doing, however, as Cotton clearly shows in his preface. He laboriously argues that there should be no scruple against singing the psalms in English and in meter, since they should be accessible to all and they were originally in Hebrew meter. He makes their intentions clear in his remarks on the quality of the verse:

> wee have therefore done our indeavour to make a plaine and familiar translation of the psalmes and words of David into english metre, and have not soe much as presumed to paraphrase to give the sense of his meaning in other words; we have therefore attended heerin as our chief guide the originall, shunning all additions, except such as even the best translators of them in prose supply, avoiding all materiall

detractions from words or sence. . . . If therefore
the verses are not alwayes so smooth and elegant as
some may desire or expect; let them consider that
Gods Altar needs not our pollishings.

Even if we make allowances for the intentions of the
translators, however, we cannot overlook the fact that most
of the verse delivers no more than it promises. Its meter is
lame, its diction often ludicrous, its rhymes forced, and its
syntax crabbed and inverted from attempts to fit it to the
tunes. Some translators based their versions on the King James
text, with interpolations from the earlier Sternhold-Hopkins
or Ainsworth psalters, scholarly commentaries, and their own
ingenuity. The 23rd Psalm, probably done by Cotton, follows
the King James Version fairly closely, as in the opening verses:

> The Lord to mee a shepheard is,
>   want therefore shall not I.
> Hee in the folds of tender-grasse,
>   doth cause mee down to lie:
> To waters calme me gently leads
> Restore my soule doth hee;

Although this has been frequently ridiculed, it is somewhat
better and certainly no worse than several earlier and contemporary versions by English clergymen and scholars. Norman Grabo has studied most of these and has shown that every
attempt at translation errs in the direction of either literalness
or paraphrase. Even a translation by Sir Philip Sidney, respectable poetry though it may be, is inadequate for public singing
because of its tricky metrical structure.

If we are obliged to recognize the generally poor quality
of the Bay Psalm Book itself, we may nevertheless be less apt
to pass judgment on the illiteracy or insensitivity to art of its
collaborators when we realize that they themselves had no illusions about what they were doing. For any true conception of
the nature of Colonial poetry, we shall have to look elsewhere
than this Procrustean bed.

From some of the worst poetry of the time let us turn to some of the best. It is easy to be patronizing toward Anne Bradstreet as a quaint oddity; a poetess in homespun; "the tenth muse lately sprung up in America." The singular fact remains that the first genuine poetry in English produced in America was written by a woman, and we must allow her to share with Edward Taylor the distinction of having produced most of the poetry of any merit in America's first century and a half. In her work also is the beginning of a tradition of fine poetry written by women in America, from Emily Dickinson to H. D., Marianne Moore, Elizabeth Bishop, and Denise Levertov. Today she is remembered not so much for the poetry that first made her famous as for her later poetry—the personal lyrics and meditations that not only are written from a part of herself of which she was not earlier aware, but show a ripening of her poetic powers and a maturity of vision that is not present in the verse of her apprenticeship to European models.

Daughter of one Massachusetts governor and wife of another, Anne Dudley Bradstreet (1612–1672) came to this country as the eighteen-year-old wife of Simon Bradstreet and eventually settled in North Andover. Few external facts about her life are known; we know she raised eight children and performed the official social duties of a governor's wife and that she took time away from this busy life to pursue an interest in books and in writing that had begun when she was a girl in the Earl of Lincoln's household. This interest took the form of writing verse imitations of two of her favorite books: Du Bartas' *La Première Semaine* and Sir Walter Raleigh's *History of the World* (1614). Using these works as models, Anne Bradstreet wrote five long, dull "quaternions" in a singsong iambic pentameter couplet that plod along methodically and tiresomely. These probably were little more than exercises by a woman with an active and inquiring intelligence who was searching for supports for a not very steady faith. In later years she confided to her children that she was undergoing a spiritual struggle at the time, and her dogged poetizing seems to have been less a creative act than an effort to occupy a doubtful and wavering mind. The manuscript of these poems, together with some written around 1649, was the basis of the book published without her knowledge in England in 1650, the first book of verse by a British American, as well as the first by an English woman. The book, with its well-known descriptive title, usually shortened to *The Tenth Muse Lately Sprung Up in America,* was warmly received and praised in both England and America. And although she was herself surprised at the presumption of her admiring brother-in-law for having taken the poems with him secretly to England to be published, she was dismayed at what she called the "ill-formed offspring of my feeble Brain." In her poem "The Author to her Book," written while preparing a second edition, she humorously recounts her efforts at dressing up her "rambling brats" after they had been snatched from her "by friends less wise than true." But she modestly—and rightly—admits that while she "stretched thy joints to make thee even feet, / Yet still thou runnest more hobbling than is meet."

Seeing her poetry in print must have worked as a healthy corrective, since she turned from her poems on history and morals to lyrics and meditations that were both more personal and more memorable as poetry. Some of the promise inherent in her verse written before 1650 can be seen in the shorter pieces toward the end of *The Tenth Muse.* Of these, the best are "Davids Lamentation for Saul and Jonathan" (1649), which, although still written in couplets, shows a new freedom and ease of handling, and "Of the vanity of all Worldly creatures," also written in a freer couplet. In the opinion of Josephine Piercy, whose study of Anne Bradstreet gives many fresh illuminations of her work, the latter poem is the one poem of the first edition that prophesies her independent lyric expression.

The poems written after 1650 include those intended for the 1678 edition, *Several Poems,* published in Boston, and those which remained in manuscript until John Harvard Ellis included them in his fourth edition of her work in 1867. The poems may also be classified by subject matter, and include the religious meditations, domestic poems, love poems, "The Flesh and the Spirit," elegies, and the "Contemplations."

The poems of her religious meditations are records of
what must have been an extremely personal search for the
True God. They are cast in the meter of the Bay Psalm Book
and, in fact, echo some of its lines. Her search was troubled
and guilt-ridden, and the fact that she eventually triumphed
and found a deeply felt faith does not lessen the moving pleas
for assurance in such lines as these:

> I sought him whom my Soul did Love
> With tears I sought him earnestly;
> He bow'd his ear down from Above,
> In vain I did not seek or cry.

The domestic poems are among her most personal, including the well-known verses on the burning of her house on July
10, 1666, and poems on members of her family, including two
hymns written upon the departure to England and return of
her husband. Her love lyrics vary from the simple and eloquent
to the artificial and witty. The best-known of these is "To My
dear and loving Husband" (1678), a forthright and deeply
felt expression of devotion unequaled in the scanty number
of Puritan love lyrics that have survived.

"As Loving Hind," another of Anne Bradstreet's poems
written in a consciously artificial manner, shows that she was
not unaware of the seventeenth-century fondness for puns,
epigrams, emblems, and conceits. It begins with the wordplay
typical of Elizabethan and seventeenth-century verse:

> As loving Hind that (Hartless) wants her Deer,
> Scuds through the woods and Fern with harkning ear,
> Perplext, in every bush & nook doth pry,
> Her dearest Deer, might answer ear or eye;

Two other examples of her growing versatility and maturity are "The Flesh and the Spirit" and "Contemplations,"
both of which appeared in the second edition (1678). The
former is in the manner of a medieval debate, based on the
conflict described in St. Paul's Epistle to the Romans. Her own

frankly acknowledged passion for her husband obvio
doubts in her mind on this subject, and her trouble
ing of the orthodox view of the triumph of the sp
flesh sounds like much more than a mere spiritual ex.
The verse, written in tetrameter couplets, is marked by a compression of phrasing that is quite different from her long-
winded quaternions. "Contemplations" is a single poem com-
prised of thirty-three rhyme royal stanzas, each of which may
be read separately. It takes the form of an extended religious
meditation, in manner and substance much like the meditations of Edward Taylor. But where Taylor was to concentrate
on a biblical text or a religious idea ("Wits run a wooling
over Edens parke"), Anne Bradstreet contemplates nature itself as the product of God's handiwork and draws from it
thoughts concerning the glory of God, the mortality of man,
and the joys of eternal life. She is more English than American
in her choice of birds and trees; the oak, the cricket, and the
"sweet-tongued philomel" are indiscriminately placed in her
landscape; yet if she is not an Emily Dickinson in her sharpness of natural observation, she achieves here a dignity and
sureness of tone that are unsurpassed elsewhere in her poetry.
The lesson of the poem seems to come from her own new-
found religious certainty, but not without overtones of her
earlier convictions of the vanity of all things:

> O Time the fatal wrack of mortal things,
> That draws oblivions curtains over kings,
> Their sumptuous monuments, men know them not,
> Their names without a Record are forgot,
> Their parts, their ports, their pomp's all laid in th' dust
> Nor wit nor gold, nor buildings scape times rust;
> But he whose name is grav'd in the white stone
> Shall last and shine when all of these are gone.

One of the best-known, and without a doubt the most influential, poems of the entire period is Michael Wigglesworth's
monument to Calvinist dogma, *The Day of Doom* (1662). In
224 stanzas of rollicking and incongruous fourteeners, Wiggles-

worth presents to his readers a horrifying vision of the damnation of sinners and a bland but genuinely felt description of the redemption and salvation of the elect. Although it is not his best poem, *The Day of Doom* is responsible for making Wigglesworth's name stand out above many of his contemporaries. It has been frequently noted that it was the Puritan equivalent of a best seller; eighteen hundred copies, or roughly one copy for every thirty-fifth person then living in New England, were sold in 1662, the year it was first published. It was immediately reprinted in both America and England, and was later published in broadside and hawked up and down the land. The influence of the poem is out of all proportion to its literary quality, but since it embodied so exactly the tenets of New England Puritanism, it served both as an inspiration to the faithful and a warning to backsliders. For most Americans today it stands as an accurate and full representation of the nature of Puritan belief, even though it fails to emphasize the deeply felt joy, almost akin to mysticism, that the devout Puritan experienced in his personal relation to his God. Nevertheless, the poem obviously struck a sympathetic chord in thousands of readers, and its influence can be seen in the works of later writers, including Edward Taylor, whose attitude toward the poem can best be seen in the closing lines of his funeral poem on the death of his wife, "A Funerall Poem Upon the Death of my ever Endeared, and Tender Wife Mrs. Elizabeth Taylor . . ." (1689):

The Doomsday Verses much perfum'de her Breath,
Much in her thoughts, and yet she fear'd not Death.

Michael Wigglesworth (1631–1705) was a dedicated, kindly, and sympathetic pastor to his congregation at Malden, but for a considerable period after he first went there he was too ill to preach, perhaps suffering from some kind of physical and nervous collapse. In what must have been an abnormally morbid frame of mind he turned to the composition of his poem, written partly as a substitute for preaching and instruction and partly to occupy his thoughts with his lifelong con-

cern with Calvinistic theology. It is written deliberately in
what he described as a "Plain Meeter," in order to make its
ideas more readily accessible: the "fourteener," or septenary
line, with an internal rhyme on the fourth and eighth syllables
of each line and an *aabb* rhyme scheme. All considerations of
artistry or craftsmanship are obviously put aside in favor of
making the poem's rhymes and inappropriate rhythms create
an indelible and lasting impression. Judged by these standards,
it is probably an unqualified success, since for over a hundred
years the New England faithful committed it wholly to memory, shuddering rather than snickering at such lines as

> His winged Hosts file through all Coasts, together gathering
> Both good and bad, both quick and dead, and all to
>   Judgment bring,
> Out of their holes those creeping Moles, that hid
>   themselves for fear,
> By force they take, and quickly make before the Judge
>   appear.

In spite of its more ludicrous moments, however, the poem
cannot be denied a certain effectiveness in its more vivid passages. After a lame opening describing Christ's sitting in judgment, Wigglesworth builds up to a truly horrifying description
of the torments of the damned. There is a genuine drama of
the soul's internal torment objectified in a succession of vivid
images of writhing, screaming, and agonized sinners. Six
stanzas from the end, Wigglesworth pictures the satisfaction
of his justifiably self-righteous saints at seeing "all those that
were their foes thus sent to punishment." But these stanzas
describing the triumphant ascent of the saints to Heaven do
not compare in their expression of joy to those of Edward
Taylor at the end of his *Gods Determinations touching his
Elect,* which was influenced partly by *The Day of Doom.* Wigglesworth's Stanza 220 reads:

> Thus with great joy and melody to Heav'n they all ascend,
> Him there to praise with sweetest layes, and Hymns
>   that never end,

> Where with long Rest they shall be blest, and nought
>   shall them annoy:
> Where they shall see as seen they be, and whom they
>   love enjoy.

Taylor, unhampered by an uncongenial metrical pattern and writing out of the fullness of his soul's harmony with God, begins "The Joy of Church Fellowship Rightly Attended" with this magnificent stanza:

> In Heaven soaring up, I dropt an Eare
>   On Earth: and oh! sweet Melody:
> And listening, found it was the Saints who were
>   Encoacht for Heaven that sang for Joy.
>   For in Christs Coach they sweetly sing;
>   As they to Glory ride therein.

The Day of Doom as poetry hardly merits attention but for the fact that it was the single most widely read book, aside from the Bible, in seventeenth-century America. Tyler, rightly observing that no narrative of our intellectual history during the Colonial days can justly fail to record its influence, quotes with relish Lowell's remark in the "Harvard Book" that it "was the solace of every fireside, the flicker of the pine-knots by which it was conned perhaps adding a livelier relish to its premonitions of eternal combustion." It is unjust, however, to base our opinion of Wigglesworth's abilities as a poet on this one didactic poem. A much better poem, perhaps his masterpiece, is *God's Controversy with New-England*. Written in the year of a drought in 1662, the manuscript of this 446-line poem was not published until 1873. Its argument is similar to that of other historical narratives from which lessons concerning God's Providence are drawn. Wigglesworth's vision is of a New England sadly delinquent in its piety and riddled by moral and physical decay. Its present "languishing" state is partly a result of the original state of the North American wilderness, the residence of Satan and his devils, and partly a result of the Puritans' own backsliding. God's punishment has been meted out in the form of drought, disease, and other natural catastrophes. In spite of his view that God's punishments are just, Wigglesworth in an address to the reader at the end clearly shows his love for New England in his hope that she will mend her ways: "Cheer on, sweet souls, my heart is with you all, / And shall be with you maugre Sathan's might." *God's Controversy* is more sophisticated and shows somewhat more versatility in technique than *The Day of Doom*, and it should be read in order to correct the false impression of Wigglesworth as a poet that the earlier poem is likely to create.

Other poems worth looking at are "A Song of Emptiness," a very personal and moving poem on the vanity of vanities theme, and some of the religious meditations, or songs, printed in *Meat Out of the Eater* (1670) and in *Riddles Unriddled, Or Christian Paradoxes Broke Open* (added to the 1689 edition of *Meat Out of the Eater*). The title is not meant to be grotesque, but is an allusion to the riddle propounded in Judges 14:14. These are uneven in quality, and do not compare very favorably with the meditations of Anne Bradstreet or Edward Taylor, but there are some good lines here and there. Song V: "Light in Darkness: A Dialogue between the Flesh and Spirit," is done in the tradition of the medieval debates between the body and the soul, a tradition that Anne Bradstreet used much more effectively in her "The Flesh and the Spirit."

Wigglesworth's poetry is well known, but it is not representative of the quality of Colonial verse. In the past, our limited knowledge of the period and the inaccessibility of texts too often led us to judge the poetry of New England largely on the basis of *The Day of Doom*. Fortunately, we have now been able to revise many of these opinions and in doing so place Wigglesworth several rungs down the ladder. He had, perhaps, more ability than many other Puritan rhymesters, but his single aim of enlightening and "edifying" his audience to the greater glory of God too often led him to subvert his talent in favor of his purposes.

Such was not the case with Edward Taylor (*c.* 1644–1729), who was at least as devout a Puritan as Wigglesworth, but who

found that his genuine delight in the creation of poetry overcame the teachings of restraint and plainness of style that were
part of his creed. Taylor knew to what end his poetry was
directed, as his Prologue to the *Preparatory Meditations*
clearly shows:

> I am this Crumb of Dust which is design'd
> To make my Pen unto thy Praise alone

yet he was not immune to the temptations against which Cotton Mather warned all clergymen who found themselves be-
guiled by reading or writing poetry:

> you may . . . make a little recreation of poetry, in
> the midst of your painful studies. Nevertheless, I can-
> not but advise you. Withhold thy throat from thirst.
> Be not so set upon poetry, as to be always poring on
> the passionate and measured pages. . . . let not the
> Circaean cup intoxicate you.

Mather is no doubt describing his own dangerous encounters
with a too-tempting muse, but he could just as well be describing the even more dangerous struggle of Edward Taylor with
a creative impulse that perhaps brought him close to intoxication by the Circaean cup.

Taylor's life partially explains the unique quality of his
poetry, which shares many characteristics with the Anglo-
Catholic poet George Herbert and yet is both Puritan and
American in its inwardness and its eccentricities of language
and thought. He was born sometime between 1642 and 1646
in the county of Leicestershire, England, and received some
training for the ministry—perhaps attending Cambridge for a
year or two—before emigrating to New England in 1668. En-
tering Harvard with advanced standing, Taylor graduated in
1671 and assumed the pastorate of the newly formed congregation at Westfield, Massachusetts, where he remained until his
death in 1729. In the course of almost a half century as a

country parson, Taylor established a reputation as an able minister and a good preacher, but not as a poet.

Although he was known to have written some poems, the manuscript of the *Poetical Works* remained in the possession of his family and was still unpublished when it was deposited in the Yale library in 1883. The poems were discovered in 1937 by Thomas Johnson, who printed a small selection of them in the *New England Quarterly* and in 1939 edited a volume containing *Gods Determinations* and many of the *Preparatory Meditations*. In 1960 a more nearly complete edition of his poems was prepared by Donald Stanford, giving us for the first time a look at the complete *Preparatory Meditations* and making tacit recognition of the fact that Edward Taylor is a major American poet.

In his school training in Leicestershire during the early years of the Restoration, Taylor had no doubt come into contact with contemporary literature and religious thought. It is possible that he had read Richard Baxter's *Saints' Everlasting Rest* (1650) and the poetry of George Herbert, as well as Donne, Crashaw, Vaughan, and Quarles. But as a country parson in the American wilderness he became acquainted with the practical side of medicine, law, agriculture, and domestic life. It is known that he accumulated a library of unusual size, representing a wide range of interests: practical books of medicine, Hebrew, Greek, and Latin grammars, Raleigh's *History of the World,* as well as theological and metaphysical treatises and volumes of biblical commentaries and lore.

The two influences of an early background and training in English literature and religion and his later life as a frontier minister are what give Taylor's poetry its particular qualities. There are echoes of lines and phrases from Herbert throughout the *Preparatory Meditations,* which are all written in a six-line stanza adapted from Herbert's introductory poem to *The Temple* (1633), "The Church-Porch." But whereas Herbert's poems are often didactic, Taylor's meditations are personal and private. Also, as Donald Stanford has pointed out, Herbert had the flexible mind of an Anglican priest, whereas

Taylor had the inflexibility of a Puritan minister forced to
cope with the rigors and hardships of life in a frontier settlement. The result is a poetry that has formal resemblances to
Herbert but marked differences in tone. At his best, Taylor
is a skillful and effective poet; as in the Preface to *Gods Determinations,* for example, where he uses the couplet of Sylvester's
translation of Du Bartas to make a poetic statement of Job-like
grandeur. This poem illustrates well the curious blend of eloquence and quaintness typical of Taylor's poetry. It begins
with lines reminiscent of Vaughan's "The World":

> Infinity, when all things it beheld
> In Nothing, and of Nothing all did build

Then follows a series of questions recalling God's to Job out
of the whirlwind:

> Upon what Base was fixt the Lath, wherein
> He turn'd this Globe, and riggalld it so trim?
> Who blew the Bellows of his Furnace Vast?

His conceits are extravagant and bold, rooted in such homely
things as games, crafts, and the domestic arts:

> Who made the Sea's its Selvedge, and it locks
> Like a Quilt Ball within a Silver Box?
> Who Spread its Canopy? Or Curtains Spun?
> Who in this Bowling Alley bowld the Sun?

We can see here the kind of verbal and intellectual playfulness—perhaps quirkiness is a better word—that cuts through
the expectations of the reader to a level of spontaneous response. But we are in danger of being sidetracked by the charm
of the incongruous language and allowing this playfulness to
offset the basically serious tone of the poem. Taylor goes on to
describe the awesome power of the Almighty God and ends by
describing the effects of man's apostasy in lines that grow

progressively slower and end with a suitable image of blackness and hardness:

> But Nothing man did throw down all by Sin:
> And darkened that lightsom Gem in him.
> That now his Brightest Diamond is grown
> Darker by far than any Coalpit Stone.

The poem takes several unexpected turns in language and tone that, in the absence of an overruling idea and certainty of purpose, could be disastrous. As it happens, this is one of Taylor's finest achievements.

What most distinguishes Taylor from Herbert, and, for that matter, from Anne Bradstreet, is this use of homely imagery and commonplace language to express in a personal way the abstractions of his highly formalized theology. Some of his more extravagant conceits, such as "And bring my Soule in Surges of rich flame / Of love to thee," are influenced by Crashaw, but "In this sad State, Gods Tender Bowells run / Out streams of Grace" comes nearer to being Taylor's own. Cut off from the mainstream of English culture, he came to rely more and more heavily on images and diction drawn from the life he knew. He can beg his Lord to soak his soul in "Zions Bucking-tub," see his sinful heart "at Cudgells, Kit-Cat, Cards and Dice here prance," or build a poem full of references to poisonous and medicinal herbs: "Root up my Henbain, Fawnbain, Divells bit. / My Dragons, Chokewort, Crosswort, Ragwort, vice, / and set my knot with Honysuckles." He can express his spiritual and intellectual confusion in such homey lines as "My tazzled Thoughts twirld into Snick-Snarls run." The result is a poetry marked by a charm and quaintness, which the modern reader might mistakenly take for the crudeness of an unlettered backwoodsman. Actually, Taylor is following the widespread tendency among the Puritans to look everywhere for evidence of God's truth, to correlate the facts of everyday reality with the spiritual facts of divine revelation.

This belief in the symbolic possibilities of the physical

world, which we shall see reappearing in the poetry of the Transcendentalists, this view (to quote Emerson) 'that "particular natural facts are symbols of particular spiritual facts," explains two qualities of Taylor's poetry. His use of a wide variety of terms drawn from many kinds of activities is the product of a frame of mind that habitually explains doctrine in terms of the individual life. Kenneth Murdock has commented on this tendency, which he noted in Puritan diaries: "Wherever possible theological abstractions were related to the concrete facts of personal experience, and doctrine was explained in terms of the individual life." Where the diarists sought to discover those meanings in the "emblems" of their everyday experience that would assure them of their own spiritual progress, Taylor in the bulk of his poetry also made his theology an intensely personal and individual affair. It is this personal note in his poetry that makes it come alive.

Taylor's best poetry is in the *Preparatory Meditations before my Approach to the Lords Supper. Chiefly upon the Doctrin preached upon the Day of administration,* a collection of 217 lyrics. They were written between 1682 and 1725, an outgrowth of his meditations on the sacrament of the Lord's Supper and they reflect his belief that in the administration of what he called the "royall banquet" he was experiencing an actual union with Christ, whose spirit was present in the bread and wine. The meditations are on various themes, but they differ radically in emphasis from many Puritan poems in their concentration on the elect, rather than the damned. Christ is viewed throughout as the loving Mediator and Savior who acts on God's behalf to bring regenerate man to salvation. Various aspects of this theme appear in individual poems dealing with the sinfulness and insignificance of natural man and the glorification of the elect, the Atonement, the sweetness of God's grace, the power and absolute sovereignty of God, and the experience of mystical union that takes place between the believer and Christ at the celebration of the Lord's Supper. After reading a number of these meditations, the reader perceives a pattern in which the poet moves from a state of despair and painful awareness of the sinful state of natural man, through a series of highly intellectual reflections using the metaphor or image in which this despair was first cast, and ends in a statement of mystical ecstasy or triumphant joy. This pattern is not accidental, and probably is based on an outline for meditations by Richard Baxter in *The Saints' Everlasting Rest*. Baxter's method of meditation consisted of three acts corresponding to the old division of the "powers" of the soul into Memory, Understanding, and Will. First, by *cogitation* one searched the Memory for the subject of his meditation. The subject was then presented to the *Judgment,* which "doth, as it were, open the door, between the Head and the Heart." Then, through argument and debate the soul was aroused to feel the Affections (emotions or feelings) of the Will: love, hope, desire, courage, and joy.

The general movement of the meditations, then, is from despair to triumph, as the poet searches for a subject for meditation and, finding it, brings himself methodically to a state of religious ecstasy. "Swamp, Brake, Thicket Vile of Sin. / My Head's a Bog of Filth," — "Was ever Heart like mine? / A sty of Filth, a Trough of Washing-Swill / A Dunghill Pit, a Puddle of Mere Slime," — "I'm but a Flesh and Blood bag," — "I am a dish of dumps: yea ponderous dross," —or this opening stanza from Meditation 26, Second Series:

> Unclean, Unclean: My Lord, Undone, all vile
> Yea all Defild: What shall thy Servant doe?
> Unfit for thee: not fit for holy Soile,
> Nor for Communion of Saints below.
> A bag of botches, Lump of Loathsomeness:
> Defild by Touch, by Issue: Leproust flesh.

But this same meditation, after following the kind of pattern described above, ends with a song of praise arising out of the speaker's realization of God's saving grace:

> Oh! wash mee, Lord, in this Choice Fountain, White
> That I may enter, and not sully here
> Thy Church, whose floore is pav'de with Graces bright
> And hold Church fellowship with Saints most cleare.

My Voice all sweet, with their melodious layes
Shall make sweet Musick blossom'd with thy praise.

(1.26, 1688)

The poet has not actually discovered anything, of course, since he knew from the beginning the certainty of God's infinite mercy and grace; but he has come to feel as well as know it through the exercise of his intellect upon this certainty. The logical structure of most of Taylor's meditations is based upon a single image, such as a tree, which is used for the sake of exploring as many meanings inherent in it as possible. In Meditation 29, First Series (1688), one of his best, the central image of the Tree of Life is used to develop the conceit of himself as "a Withred Twig, dride fit to bee / A Chat Cast in thy fire," until he is grafted onto God, or the Tree of Life, and partakes of His glory:

I being grafft in thee am graffted here
　　Into thy Family, and kindred Claim
　　To all in Heaven, God, Saints, and Angells there.

In the same way he will sustain and develop the image of a rose, representing Christ, or bread, representing God's mercy. God's mercy is, in fact, represented by a variety of images: the bread, cake, beer, wine, olive oil, aqua vitae, and water of His grace are conveyed to regenerate man by means of gullies, pipes, gutters, channels, pitchers, pipes, platters, and other mechanical contrivances. These images are not all equally successful, and at times Taylor strains too hard in his efforts to see God's truth everywhere. The result is a series of poems the cumulative effect of which is somewhat tiresome, yet if they are read individually, many have a power that goes far beyond the mechanical scaffolding upon which they are erected. We find in these poems an intense religious emotion released from the bonds of convention by a vigorous and original imagination. There are few things like them in either England or America for their fusion of mysticism and intellectual power, and indeed one must look to the sermons of Jonathan Edwards for a similar combination.

Taylor's other major work is an undated, long dramatic poem in the manner of a medieval debate: *Gods Determinations touching his Elect: and The Elects Combat in their Conversion, and Coming up to God in Christ together with the Comfortable Effects thereof.* It should be compared with *The Day of Doom* (1662), to which it owes some debts, as well as to Anne Bradstreet's "The Flesh and the Spirit" (1678). Unlike Wigglesworth's poem, *Gods Determinations* concentrates on the elect, rather than the damned, and describes their final triumph after a series of arguments and counterarguments between Satan and God. It contains more variety in form and meter than the meditations: some sections are lyric set pieces, some are dramatic dialogues, some are straight narrative passages. Taylor, following Du Bartas, uses couplets, six-line Herbertian stanzas, or quatrains. In facing the demands of characterization, Taylor falls into some of the same temptations Milton did by making Satan the more interesting figure, some of whose lines are the best, such as these threats to the converted Christians:

> For when I shall let fly at you, you'l fall:
> And so fall foule Upon your Generall.
> Hee'l Hang you up alive then; by and by.
> And I'le you wrack too for your treachery.
> He will become your foe, you then shall bee
> Flanckt of by him before, behinde by mee.

> * * *

> What will you do when you shall squezed bee
> Between such Monstrous Gyants Jaws as Wee?

Or in this sly appeal by Satan through his use of proverbial wisdom:

> Soon ripe, soon rot. Young Saint, Old Divell. Loe
> Why to an Empty Whistle did you goe?

But the saints win the day, and their victory is celebrated in the closing lyric, "The Joy of Church Fellowship Rightly Attended."

Also bound in the manuscript volume containing these poems were a number of shorter poems, the best of which are "Huswifery," which develops the theme of religious devotion in the language of cloth manufacture, "Upon Wedlock, and Death of Children" (c. 1682), on the deaths of four of his children, and that enigmatic and powerful poem, "Upon the Sweeping Flood Aug: 13.14.1683."

A little-known contemporary of Taylor has remained in almost total obscurity, even though several of his poems deserve to be ranked along with the best produced in the Colonial period. His name is Richard Steere (1643–1721), a London gentleman of culture and means who settled in New London as a merchant in the late 1680s after having made several previous journeys to the New World. Steere is one of several poets, including John Saffin (1626–1710), whom Jantz has brought to light in his efforts to demonstrate the variety and good quality of poetry written in New England's first century. Rare copies exist of two of Steere's works: the first is an entertaining and lively narrative poem, *A Monumental Memorial of Marine Mercy,* published in 1684 after a harrowing ocean voyage; the other is a collection of his poems issued in 1713 called *The Daniel Catcher.* In *A Monumental Memorial* Steere relates how, after five weeks of gentle winds, his ship encountered a storm near the English coast and was so battered by high seas that it threatened to founder. He recites a tragic episode of seeing another ship sink with many of its passengers aboard. Like many other such narrative and historical poems, the author sees his experience as a testimony to the power and mercy of God, but our interest in the poem lies in the vivid descriptive passages, such as one describing the ship "tost like a ball in sport, / From wave to wave in Neptunes Tennis Court." The title poem of Steere's second collection, *The Daniel Catcher,* is a narrative "Life of the Prophet Daniel," which he had first published in 1682 as a reply to Dryden's *Absalom and Achitophel* (1681). Of more interest are a philosophical poem, "Earth's Felicities, Heaven's Allowances: A Blank Poem," which celebrates the beauties and goodness of this world. However accustomed we may be to think of New England writers as hostile to the allurements of earthly beauty, the fact remains that from William Morrell to Edward Taylor poets celebrated the world they saw about them. Steere's poem is frankly dedicated to a celebration of the delights of all the senses:

> *Pleasures* are many and of Divers Kinds,
> *Riches* and *Honour* only serve to *please;*
> And ev'ry good seems to this end ordain'd;
> How many sweet felicities are found
> Contributing to pleasure ev'ry scence
> *Visus, Auditus, Gustus,* & *Olfactus.*

There are several shorter pieces in this collection, among them a charming poem on the birth of Christ that appears to have been influenced by Milton's *Paradise Lost* in its description of the angels, and a descriptive lyric, "On a Sea-Storm nigh the Coast." This poem alone demonstrates Steere's ability at handling rhythm, diction, and imagery with a fine attention to detail and skillful shifts of rhythm and emphasis:

> All round the Horizon black Clouds appear;
> A storm is near:
> Darkness Eclipseth the Sereener Sky,
> The Winds are high,
> Making the Surface of the Ocean Show
> Like mountains Lofty, and like Vallies Low.
>
> The weighty Seas are rowled from the Deeps
> In mighty heaps,
> And from the Rocks Foundations do arise
> To Kiss the Skies
> Wave after Wave in Hills each other Crowds,
> As if the Deeps resolv'd to Storm the Clouds.

How did the Surging Billows Fome and Rore
         Against the Shore
Threatning to bring the Land under their power
         And it Devour:
Those Liquid Mountains on the Clifts were hurld
As to a Chaos they would shake the World.

The Earth did Interpose the Prince of Light
         'Twas Sable night:
All Darkness was but when the Lightnings fly
         And Light the Sky,
Night, Thunder, Lightning, Rain, and *raging* Wind,
To make a Storm had all their forces joyn'd.

Steere has neither the emotional range and intensity nor the craftsmanship of Taylor, nor perhaps even of Anne Bradstreet, yet he deserves comparison with these better-known poets on the basis of the few poems we have by him. His poetry in its directness and openness is like a breath of fresh air, blowing in upon some of the crabbed, introspective verse of lesser-known, more orthodox Puritan writers. It carries with it suggestions of a wider world than the New England Colonies and, if it is not so clearly the precursor of certain traditions in American poetry, it is clearly in the tradition of English poetry.

By the time Edward Taylor died in 1729 he was already an anachronism in the rapidly changing world of the eighteenth century. Calvinism was fast giving way to deism, and with the publication of Newton's *Principia* in 1687 and Locke's *Essay Concerning Human Understanding* in 1690 men's belief in an arbitrary and capricious God was being transformed into a belief in a benevolent and reasonable God who had established a well-ordered universe run according to discoverable laws. In 1729 Benjamin Franklin—a nonpoet by deliberate choice—was writing essays on deism and publishing them in his *Pennsylvania Gazette*. Calvinism lingered on through the century, however, and received fresh vigor from Jonathan Edwards (1703–1758), who brilliantly fused the old religion with the new appeals to reason of Newton and Locke. But the poetry of New England became increasingly secular and ceased to dominate as writers in the middle colonies and the South wrote and published poems that had many of the earmarks of the Neo-classic verse of Dryden and Pope as well as the pre-Romantic verse of Gray and Collins.

Seventeenth-century writers were less imitative of their English predecessors and contemporaries than the writers of the eighteenth century because they were almost completely uninterested in matters of style or literary form for their own sake. A poet such as Wigglesworth would choose his "Plain Meeter" not for any literary reason but because it lent itself more easily to memorizing; similar principles governed the composition of the Bay Psalm Book. The influence of English writers in the seventeenth century is there: we can see that their Colonial counterparts were for the most part educated at Oxford or Cambridge and were writing in the modes they were familiar with in their youth; hence the similarities to Donne, Herbert, Sylvester's translation of Du Bartas, Sidney, and Spenser. But these echoes were more unconsciously assimilated than deliberately used, and after 1700, writers like Mather Byles, Thomas Godfrey, and Richard Steere were aware of style and of the prevailing fashions and tastes abroad. So we see a movement toward blandness and smoothness, in diction, meter, and philosophic attitude, which can be directly traced to Denham, Dryden, Pope, and Churchill.

The smooth and rather bookish verses of Governor William Livingston's (1723–1790) *Philosophic Solitude* (1747) are typical of this movement toward neoclassicism. This is a bland reworking of John Pomfret's widely read "Choice," written in England almost fifty years earlier, which describes the satisfactions of life in a pastoral setting and celebrates a God whose existence is inferred from the beauty and order of nature. Livingston's poem is also interesting because of the writers he mentions as his choices for his personal library: Milton, Dryden, Pope, and Isaac Watts among the English poets, and Bacon, Boyle, Newton, and Locke among the philosophers.

Mather Byles (1707–1788), a grandson of Increase Mather, illustrates the movement toward satire, frivolity, and the conventionalized meter and diction of the eighteenth century that most American poets were taking at the time. He describes fish as a "scaly nation," rivers flow in "cozy beds," and his long poem, *The Conflagration* (1755), is written in standard heroic couplets:

> While twinkling stars their glimmering beauties show,
> And wink perpetual o'er heavenly blue.

Byles's *Poems on Several Occasions* (1744) reflect the diversity and relative frivolity of his subjects for poetry, some of which he treats with wit and urbanity; his best poem, however, is "The Teaching of the Grave," an elegy on the death of Governor Belcher's wife in 1736.

The first half of the eighteenth century is generally a quite fallow period, however, and we must be charitable indeed to take a more than historical interest in the works of such minor poets as Joseph Green (1706–1780), Ebenezer Cook (*fl.* 1708), John Adams (1704–1740), John Seccomb (1708–1792), and many others whose names are mentioned and quickly dismissed in the literary histories. No major or even significant poets appeared until the emergence of the Connecticut Wits and Philip Freneau, all of whom will be treated in the following chapter. One or two poets of the Philadelphia circle of the teacher and publisher William Smith (1727–1803) might have fulfilled their early promise if they had not died young. Nathaniel Evans (1742–1767) and Thomas Godfrey (1736–1763) were both steeped in the classics and Milton and were addicted to the Pindaric and Horatian ode forms that the pre-Romantic English poets, Collins, Gray, and the Warton brothers were fond of using. Godfrey's posthumous collection of verse, *Juvenile Poems on Various Subjects* (1765), contains a poem written in the mood and stanza of Gray's "Elegy" (1751) and a five-hundred-line poem, "The Court of Fancy," in which he acknowledged his obligation to Pope. His most memorable piece of writing, however, is his blank-verse tragedy, *The Prince of Parthia* (1759), usually described as the first play by an American to be produced professionally. Godfrey makes skillful use of his Elizabethan and Jacobean models and shows an ability to handle a dramatic blank verse line in the manner of Shakespeare, Marlowe, and Beaumont. The poetry of these two young men from Philadelphia shows them to be far more eclectic and literary than either their New England or southern contemporaries, while at the same time it suggests the mixture and confusion of the Augustan and pre-Romantic era in America that had their counterparts in England.

CHAPTER TWO

The Late Eighteenth Century

Timothy Dwight, Joel Barlow, John Trumbull, Philip
Freneau

In 1726, three years before he visited America, George Berkeley (1685–1753), the English philosopher, circulated some
verses among his friends, "On the Prospect of Planting Arts
and Learning in America," which ended with these prophetic
lines:

> There shall be sung another golden age,
>   The rise of empire and of arts,
> The good and great inspiring epic rage,
>   The wisest heads and noblest hearts.
>
> Not such as Europe breeds in her decay;
>   Such as she bred when fresh and young,
> When heavenly flame did animate her clay,
>   By future poets shall be sung.
>
> Westward the course of empire takes its way;
>   The four first acts already past,
> A fifth shall close the drama with the day;
>   Time's noblest offspring is the last.

Bishop Berkeley was not the first to see the epic possibilities in
the American experience, nor was he the last. In the seven-

teenth century Edward Johnson had cast his *Wonder-Working Providence* in Vergilian rhetoric and Cotton Mather began his *Magnalia* in an epic strain: "I write the wonders of the Christian religion, flying from the depravations of Europe to the American strand."

In the eighteenth century, the essentially optimistic spirit of the Age of Reason found fertile ground in the minds of American colonists who could see a new country taking shape before their eyes. The nebulous and still largely unformed ideas of progress that were to dominate American thinking in the nineteenth century had their confusing and even contradictory origins in this very tangible evidence they had before them, as well as in the philosophical optimism of Shaftesbury, the perfectionism of Rousseau, and even, strangely enough, in the predestination of Calvin. Progress was everywhere, and at all levels of sophistication, from college undergraduates to Benjamin Franklin.

All four of the poets mentioned in this chapter wrote at least one poem about progress, and the major work of one of them, Joel Barlow, is an epic treatment of the theme. In 1771 at Princeton, Philip Freneau and Hugh Henry Brackenridge (1748–1816) collaborated on a commencement poem whose title, *The Rising Glory of America* (1772), could be used interchangeably with most of them, including John Trumbull's "Prospect of our Future Glory," delivered at the Yale commencement a year earlier, and poems by two other Yale men, Timothy Dwight's "America, or a Poem on the Settlement of the British Colonies" and Barlow's *The Vision of Columbus* and *The Columbiad*.

The rising glory of America seemed ripe for celebration in the epic strain, as Freneau and Brackenridge declared in an outburst of literary nationalism that was to be echoed and reechoed by every major American writer of the next fifty years:

> I see a Homer and a Milton rise
> In all the pomp and majesty of song

* * *

A second Pope, like that Arabian bird
Of which no age can boast but one, may ˙yet
Awake the muse by Schuylkill's silent stream,

* * *

And Susquehanna's rocky stream unsung

* * *

Shall yet remurmur to the magic sound
Of song heroic.

The hopes of these young men (who were still loyal British subjects) included a new Paradise in America, where tyranny would have subsided under the rule of a benevolent monarch:

Paradise anew
Shall flourish, by no second Adam lost,
No dangerous tree with deadly fruit shall groan,
No tempting serpent to allure the soul
From native innocence.—A *Canaan* here,
Another *Canaan* shall excel the old.

These lines are strangely prophetic, since in the same year in New Haven a young Yale tutor was seriously turning his mind to writing what he later claimed to be "the first epic poem to have appeared in America." Timothy Dwight (1752–1817), who became one of Yale's most distinguished presidents, early decided he was destined to literary greatness, and as a test of his talents set himself the task of composing an epic in which he would combine the best of two popular modern epics —Milton's *Paradise Lost* and Fénelon's *The Adventures of Telemachus.* He chose as his subject the conquest of Canaan by Joshua, whose exploits he felt were suitable for an epic hero. When the poem was tardily published in 1785, his readers were accustomed to making the kind of analogies that the Puritan writers had made for generations and turned Dwight's biblical Promised Land into a Revolutionary America and Joshua into General Washington. Since Dwight was more interested in the moral effects of his poem upon his readers than he was in historical or political parallels, he was actually dismayed and irritated by attempts to read *The Conquest of Canaan* (1771–1773) as allegory. What he tried to create in Joshua was a hero "favour'd by Heaven" whose actions would "raise the Admiration, and inspire the Love of Virtue" in his readers. But since he took a great deal of pains to instill in Joshua the qualities of an ideal general, it is not altogether surprising that his patriotic readers a decade later were certain he was describing George Washington.

If *The Conquest of Canaan* was mistakenly read in retrospect as an American poem, another of Dwight's poems follows the pattern of the "vision" poems being written in this period. "America: Or a Poem on the Settlement of the British Colonies" (1780) traces the history of the discovery of America and ends with a vision of an allegorical figure of freedom giving a prophecy of the future glory of America—a device that Barlow was to use in *The Vision of Columbus*.

Dwight, like his literary classmates at Yale, was not wholly at ease with the English poets, even though he had read most of them. He was especially attracted to Pope, however, and decided when he began his epic to use the couplet Pope had used in his translations of Homer. But Dwight was too cautious and unpracticed to give his couplets much of Pope's suppleness or resonance, and they fall with a thunderous deadness on the ear. *The Conquest of Canaan* consists of eleven cantos of correct but inert couplets, which Leon Howard has said are "full of eighteenth-century Americans with Hebrew names who talked like Milton's angels and fought like prehistoric Greeks."

Dwight's *Greenfield Hill* (1794) was composed in a much more relaxed mood and atmosphere, when he was a pastor in Greenfield, Connecticut. In order to occupy his mind while he took long daily walks, he composed verses that he later dictated to a secretary. Then, to give them some form, he proposed to write a topographical hill poem about the beauties and virtues of his native state. In conception it recalls Denham's *Cooper's Hill*, Dyer's *Grongar Hill*, and Pope's "Windsor Forest," but it is a conglomerate of styles—with echoes of

Pope, Milton, and Vergil's *Georgics*—in a variety of verse forms, including blank verse, couplets, octosyllabics, and Spenserian stanzas. The poem's theme is Dwight's rather smug love of his native land, which he compares to a Europe he knew only at second hand through his reading. He was an arch conservative, whose mind, V. L. Parrington observes, "was closed as tight as his study windows in January," and his poem does little to correct the notion of many of his readers that Connecticut was the garden spot of the world. Part Two, "The Flourishing Village," is an imitation of Goldsmith that draws a favorable contrast between America and Europe. Other parts celebrate the beauty of local scenery, the romance of local history, and reflect Dwight's Calvinistic notions of human nature, with an emphasis on its improvement through the cultivation of good habits. The poem ends in the spirit of the times with a section called "Vision, or Prospect of the Future Happiness of America."

Dwight's is strictly a minor talent, and it is partly a reflection on his age that his poetry stands out as it does. Although there are some worthwhile passages in *Greenfield Hill*, these are notable more as versified philosophy than as poetry, and the poem as a whole stands as witness more to the wide and varied tastes of the writer than to his gifts as a poet.

Another of the Connecticut Wits who pursued the will-o'-the-wisp of the epic was Joel Barlow (1754–1812), who founded his hopes of lasting literary fame on a poem of epic dimensions celebrating the life of Columbus. As he came to realize that the events in the life of Columbus were not of much interest, he leaned more and more toward a philosophical poem, using the machinery of a vision in which the future of America would be revealed to the hero of the poem. One of his difficulties, aside from the tediousness of his couplets and the blandness of his style, was his apparent indecision whether the poem was to be an epic or a philosophical poem. There are long passages in which the narrative is suspended for the sake of the optimistic vision of a future millennium toward which man and society are inevitably heading; these suggest that the narrative structure should have been abandoned entirely. The poem opens with the appearance of an angel to Columbus languishing in prison. The angel takes him to the top of the Mount of Vision to give him a view of the future of America, much as Michael does for Adam in *Paradise Lost*. The poem becomes loose and episodic as a result of the influence of various books Barlow picked up while he was writing, including a history of Peru and Robertson's *History of America*. The last two books of the poem outline recent scientific accomplishments and prophesy an age of scientific and technological progress, with nations united in peace.

The Vision of Columbus (1787) was original neither in its political ideas, nor in its philosophy. The mediocrity of its verse may be explained partly by the rapidity of composition, for although Barlow had the poem in hand for four years, he actually composed most of it in two spurts of strenuous activity, sometimes writing six hundred lines in a week. When he looked for money to publish it in 1783, he turned to his officer friends from the army. Their response in subscribing to over one-fourth of the first edition has been described as "the greatest exhibition of patriotism since the siege at Yorktown." It was published in 1787 and dedicated to "His Most Christian Majesty, Louis the Sixteenth, King of France and Navarre."

In the next twenty years Barlow and the world changed considerably; he was no longer living in times of turbulence and anarchy but in an era of republicanism and industrial progress. Barlow changed from a conservative and orthodox Yale graduate to a cosmopolitan and humanitarian follower of Tom Paine; from an admirer of Louis XVI to the author of a tract on human liberty called *Advice to the Privileged Orders* (1792). During those two decades Barlow never gave up his dream of producing a true epic, and in 1807 he tried to transform *The Vision of Columbus* from a philosophical poem into a kind of modern *Aeneid*. *The Columbiad* (1807), as he called the revised version, begins in epic fashion:

> I sing the Mariner who first unfurl'd
> An eastern banner o'er the western world.

His intentions, as he stated in his new preface, were frankly political: "to encourage and strengthen, in the rising generation, a sense of the importance of republican institutions; as being the great foundation of public and private happiness, the necessary ailment of future and permanent ameliorations in the condition of human nature." This kind of statement looks forward to Walt Whitman, who also wanted to replace the superstitions and feudalism of Europe with an appeal to the scientific spirit and democratic ideals.

The first five books of *The Vision of Columbus* were allowed to remain almost intact in the revised version, but the account of the American Revolution in the next two books was expanded to three. The poem's philosophical speculations are updated in the light of modern science, and he now sees progress coming about as a result of the overthrow of old superstitions. He replaced a biblical account of creation with a geological one, and even though he still saw progress as the result of a predetermined plan, the plan is now Nature's rather than God's. With all its changes, however, *The Columbiad* is not so good a poem as the old one. It is even more coldly intellectual, and the philosophical content sits, even more uneasily on its narrative framework. Perhaps one source of the difficulty is the nature of the epic itself, a form traditionally rooted in a stable society with clearly defined aims and purposes. The epic as used by Homer and Vergil celebrated and consolidates already well-established institutions through mythic heroes. Even Milton, with all his departures from orthodoxy, is celebrating essentially the great Christian myth that had provided the framework of his society for over a thousand years. One great weakness of *The Columbiad,* as Roy Harvey Pearce has pointed out, is that it has no hero: Columbus is merely someone to whom things happen. We might add that the events, and, even more, the ideas, presented in the poem are not at all recognizable aspects of the society but rather projections—possibilities of the society that was to come—a positing of one possibility among many inherent in the nation and the political system of which Barlow was a part. In short, it was too early for an epic poem. Men like Barlow and Dwight felt the epic quality of the times and the great deeds performed in them, but they were too much a part of them and were too much restricted by their conventional notions of what an epic is and what it does to make effective use of their material. Barlow passed up a unique opportunity to write a history—a true epic of the times—using private papers that Jefferson had sent him, in favor of writing a sterile, literary epic.

For all their pretensions to literary sublimity it is ironic that both Barlow and Dwight are remembered today for less ambitious productions that they made for their private amusement and that of their friends. It may seem strange to compare Barlow's "The Hasty Pudding" (1792) with Dwight's *Greenfield Hill*, yet both poems show their writers' limited talents at their best, when they loosened up and expressed their true feelings without worrying about their reputations or restricting themselves by their awareness of rules.

When Barlow was in France in 1795 his homesickness for New England was unexpectedly brought to the surface when he was served a dish of that New England variety of cornmeal mush known as hasty pudding. The experience, as one of his biographers has suggested, was Wordsworthian, or perhaps even Proustian, in the way it called up a vivid set of feelings and memories associated with his Connecticut boyhood, and prompted him to write a mock epic in three cantos that is better than either of his serious epics. With his experience in the epic form and his knowledge of *The Rape of the Lock* and other mock-heroic poems, Barlow treated his subject with a sureness and consistency of tone that he never surpassed elsewhere:

> Ye Alps audacious, thro' the heav'ns that rise,
> To cramp the day and hide me from the skies;
> Ye Gallic flags, that o'er their heights unfurl'd,
> Bear death to kings, and freedom to the world,
> I sing not you. A softer theme I chuse,
> A virgin theme, unconscious of the Muse,
> But fruitful, rich, well suited to inspire
> The purest frenzy of poetic fire.

Barlow wrote "The Hasty Pudding" for private circulation, but the friends to whom he sent it in America allowed it to be republished in book form. It has been frequently republished and anthologized since then, and ironically it remains Barlow's best-known poem, far surpassing in quality the reputation of his stillborn epics.

Barlow and Dwight were two members of that heterogeneous group known as the "Hartford Wits," or the "Connecticut Choir." What they had in common were a brief and loose association as the authors of some satirical poems inspired by Shays's Rebellion and a marked antipathy to Philip Freneau. During the years of their collaboration they produced, in one combination or another, *The Anarchiad* (1786–1787), *The Echo* (1791–1805), *The Political Greenhouse* (1799), and other satires directed against the enemies of New England conservatism. Other members of the group were John Trumbull, Richard Alsop (1761–1815), Noah Webster (1758–1843), Lemuel Hopkins (1750–1801), and Theodore Dwight (1764–1846).

Trumbull's (1750–1831) abbreviated literary career extends roughly over the eleven-year period between his graduation from Yale in 1770 and the publication of the final version of *M'Fingal* in 1782. Like Philip Freneau, Trumbull was diverted by circumstance from his early intentions to become a writer of serious verse. But whereas Freneau had already demonstrated real talent in writing lyric and philosophical poems before turning to satire, Trumbull's efforts at serious verse were stilted and dull.

The circumstance that quickened Trumbull's already formed taste for satire was specifically the mediocrity of the Yale undergraduate curriculum. When Trumbull, Timothy Dwight, and, later, Barlow, entered Yale College in the late 1760s and 1770s it was a bastion of religious orthodoxy, devoted to preserving the status quo in Connecticut, whose citizens still largely adhered to the theocratic principles of the Mather dynasty of half a century ago. The curriculum was a dry rehearsal of classical authors, the rudiments of mathematics, and outmoded but safe writings of orthodox Puritan divines. The senior year tried to make up for the shallowness of the other three by plunging the students into "metaphysical studies," which used as textbooks Locke's *Essay Concerning Human Understanding* and Jonathan Edwards' *Inquiry into the Freedom of the Will*. Most of the students were too dull-witted to benefit from these rigorous intellectual exercises, however, and the few bright ones had already lost any interest they might have had in the academic side of college life. Student riots and pranks were commonplace, the ineffective president was forced to resign, and much of the faculty had also resigned in disgust. It is surprising, considering this state of affairs, that Trumbull chose to stay on for his master's degree, but he did so and during that time he wrote the first of the two satires for which he is known today.

The Progress of Dulness (1772–1773) is a three-part poem written over a period of two years, which began as a satirical attack on two aspects of college education in Connecticut: the selection and training of candidates for the ministry and the weaknesses of college education in general. Trumbull uses the octosyllabic couplet of Butler and Swift to describe the "progress" of a character named Tom Brainless, from his youth as a witless farmboy to his career as a graduate of Yale and ordained minister. After graduation and a year as a country schoolmaster, Tom goes to a priest to "learn the art of preaching,"

> And settles down with earnest zeal
> Sermons to study, and to steal.

He is then examined by the clergy and receives a license to preach:

> What though his wits could ne'er dispense
> One page of grammar, or of sense;
> What though his learning be so slight,
> He scarcely knows to spell or write;
> What though his skull be cudgel-proof!
> He's orthodox, and that's enough.

The poem clearly demonstrates Trumbull's satiric and comic abilities. It was received with a great outcry of indignation and surprise, both because of its easily recognized portraits of some clergymen and because it was rightly read as an open attack on the Connecticut ministry as a whole.

Perhaps chastened by these rebukes, Trumbull toned down the second part considerably, but not without prefacing it with some bitter remarks toward those who had misunderstood his intentions in the first part. The Second Part, published in January 1773, is much more moderate in tone and conventional in subject matter. Trumbull's literary antecedents, particularly Addison and Pope, are plainly visible in his portrait of Dick Hairbrain, a run-of-the-mill English fop. The satire is no longer directed toward the college itself or toward Connecticut clergymen, and it loses much of its bite because of its comparative irrelevance. Part Three, "The Adventures of Miss Harriet Simper," traces with easily recognizable debts to Swift the upbringing and career of a typical and not very interesting coquette. Toward the end of the poem Trumbull tries without much success to bring the narrative threads of all three sections together, and finally ends in out-and-out burlesque that departs radically from the controlled and pointed satire of the earlier sections. The result is a poem that is uneven in quality overall, but shows some brilliance in individual lines and sections. Trumbull had found his most congenial form of expression in the octosyllabic couplet, a form he would use once again in his most successful poem, *M'Fingal*. *The Progress of Dulness* enjoyed a brief popularity, but the Revolution put it into eclipse, where it has since pretty much remained. It is not that bad a poem, however, and a reader picking it up today will be surprised at its freshness of wit and its general technical finish. Many satires by minor English poets are certainly much worse and are even more imitative of current literary fashions than this reasonably successful application of the satirical tools of Swift, Butler, and Churchill.

Between *The Progress of Dulness* and *M'Fingal* Trumbull wrote several minor poems that reflect his wavering interests. In spite of the rebellious nature of his satire, Trumbull, as a member of one of the established families of Connecticut, was conservative in temperament and background, and he was never to vent his spleen in the uncontrolled manner of Freneau. He turned again to "serious" verse in two poems, one a poor Miltonic imitation, "Ode to Sleep" (1773), the other "An Elegy on the Times" (1774), a bookish protest in flawless quatrains against the King's closing of the port of Boston following the Boston Tea Party. In its concern with the political events of the day it forecasts his much more vigorous satire, *M'Fingal,* which he began in 1775.

Like *The Progress of Dulness, M'Fingal* was composed and published in sections. The occasion that prompted Trumbull to begin this poem was the pompous proclamation by General Thomas Gage declaring martial law in Boston in 1775. Freneau about the same time produced a bitter satire called "General Gage's Soliloquy" (1775), and Trumbull, who had not seen this poem, also attacked Gage's outrageous pomposity. *M'Fingal* is not so much a poem about the war as it is an accomplished and sophisticated satire of human foibles. Compared to Freneau's enthusiastic and highly partisan satires, *M'Fingal* also is politically a conservative poem, full of ideas and sentiments that, if they are not openly Tory, are at least detached and cool in their treatment of the ideas of both sides.

For his central figure, Trumbull chose a Tory squire who embodies the comic properties of Butler's Sir Hudibras and is ironically named after the lofty hero of MacPherson's *Ossian.* M'Fingal is a militant figure, complete with rusty sword, who naïvely and disastrously takes the Tory position in a town meeting debate with Honorius, an equally pompous spokesman for the Whigs. Honorius and M'Fingal both are victims of Trumbull's wit, and he takes no sides in his treatment of the affectations of orators. It appears from this and from the generally high quality of the poem that Trumbull was more interested in the literary possibilities of the poem than he was in any effectiveness it might have had as propaganda. He worked on it slowly and carefully, and "Canto I," later divided in two, was not published until early in 1776. Later, when he saw more clearly what he wanted to do with the poem, Trumbull added a third and fourth canto and published the entire poem of three thousand lines for the first time in 1782.

The third canto contains a battle between M'Fingal and Honorius in mock-epic style, and the fourth ends with a comic "vision" of events between 1775 and 1782, in which a long series of disasters leading up to the surrender of Cornwallis in 1781 is related, followed by the hasty exit of Squire M'Fingal to Boston and oblivion. The events in the poem are so topical and the allusions so dependent upon a detailed knowledge of the events of the time that the poem has little appeal to the reader today. It is difficult now to realize how extremely popular it was after the Revolution, when Honorius' inept speeches were read straight as patriotic oratory rather than as satire. It went through more than twenty editions between 1782 and 1820, to become the most popular American poem between Wigglesworth's *The Day of Doom* (1662) and Longfellow's *Evangeline* (1847). As political satire it compares favorably in quality with James Russell Lowell's *Biglow Papers* (1848, 1867), which it resembles in its use of local expressions, and with the more hastily written and bitter satires of Freneau.

Philip Freneau (1752–1832), like the others, wrote both satires and poems of progress; he also aspired to rise above the march of events and obey what he thought was his true calling as a poet of philosophy and nature. What is particularly disappointing when we read his poems is our sense that he barely missed becoming the kind of poet he wanted to be. As we turn to the old anthology pieces: "The Wild Honey Suckle," "The Indian Burying Ground," "The Power of Fancy," we are struck by pale but unmistakable suggestions of a romantic feeling for nature and an idealism of spirit that nevertheless promise more than they deliver. We remember Freneau's traditional place in literary history as the "father of American poetry," and we look hopefully for something more than the suggestions, the tentative hints, of a major talent that was never realized. It is unsettling to read Freneau, however, because we feel we are bored more often than we ought to be and because we feel there is something hidden from us on a first reading that might reveal itself after a second. But usually a second look will only make us more sad at the spectacle of what Lewis Leary, his most sympathetic biographer, has called a literary failure.

It is not easy to explain why Freneau failed; it may have been a combination of his own character, the instability of the times, and the lack of an appreciative audience. Freneau himself was bitterly aware of the conflict between his own poetic aspirations and the reality of a provincial audience totally preoccupied with war and political turmoil. At various times in his career he composed rueful valedictories to his life as a poet as he returned to the sea or went into newspaper editing or semiretirement. One of these, "To an Author," written in 1788, describes his situation vividly:

> On these bleak climes by Fortune thrown,
> Where rigid *Reason* reigns alone,
> Where lovely *Fancy* has no sway,
> Nor magic forms about us play—
> Nor nature takes her summer hue
> Tell me, what has the muse to do?—
>
> An age employed in edging steel
> Can no poetic raptures feel;
> No solitude's attracting power,
> No leisure of the noon day hour,
> No shaded stream, no quiet grove
> Can this fantastic century move.

No doubt readers of the day were not receptive to the kind of "fanciful" poetry he wanted to write; still, Freneau was always ready to plunge headlong into battle over the issues of political liberty, Jeffersonianism, Anglophobia, and Francophilia that formed the substance of much of his polemical and satirical verse. He found he could not stay out of trouble, even though as a young man he had deliberately done so at the outbreak of hostilities in 1776. When he returned to this country from Santa Cruz two years later, however, he became a militiaman and fought for the Revolutionary cause in a variety of ways from that time on. These lines, written about the time of his return, are full of self-castigation:

> Sylvan Bards who deal in flow'ry themes,
>   Who sing the meadows and the purling streams,
> Who yet remote from blood and murder stray.

Freneau himself was certainly partly responsible for the direction his poetry took; nevertheless, his audience was not very sophisticated and therefore demanded either political lampoons, topical verse, or innocuous light verse. It is more a commentary on his audience than on his abilities as a poet that Freneau's two most popular and most widely reprinted poems during his lifetime were doggerel newspaper verses, "The Tea Drinker" (1790) and "The Jug of Rum" (1792). Here is a sample of the latter:

> Within these Prison-walls repose
> The seeds of many a bloody nose,
> The clattering tongue, the horrid oath,
>   The fist for fighting nothing loth,
> The nose with diamonds glowing red,
> The bloated eye, the broken head.

The career of Philip Freneau is less a development than a series of vacillations between two types of poetry that may be loosely categorized as "poems of freedom" and "poems of romantic fancy." The second of these labels, however, fails to suggest the variety of genres he tried. As an undergraduate at Princeton, Freneau, like Dwight, wrote a biblical epic; his was in heroic couplets celebrating the story of Jonah. He also tried what Barlow had started out to do—an "epic" on the life of Columbus, which uses a variety of metrical forms, including four-line octosyllabic stanzas, octosyllabic couplets, heroic couplets, and blank verse. Freneau was in no sense an originator, and his verse is full of echoes of Vergil, Milton, and the poets

of the eighteenth century, particularly Pope and Gray. Two
other early poems, "The American Village" and "The Deserted Farmhouse," are, as their titles suggest, clearly indebted
to Goldsmith.

One precocious poem written at seventeen, "The Pyramids
of Egypt," contains suggestions of two characteristic strains in
his poetry, a preoccupation with darkness and gloom and the
theme of transience:

> 'Tis darkness all, with hateful silence join'd—
> Here drowsy bats enjoy a dull repose,
> And marble coffins, vacant of their bones,
> Shew where the royal dead in ruin lay!
>
> * * *
>
> Where art thou ancient Thebes?—all buried low,
> All vanish'd! crumbled into mother dust,
> And nothing of antiquity remains
> But these huge pyramids, and yonder hills.

These themes were to receive their fullest treatment ten years
later in "The House of Night: A Vision" (1775), a grotesque
and fanciful dream poem full of charnel horrors relating the
death of the allegorical figure of Death. Another of Freneau's
early poems, "The Power of Fancy" (1770), suggests his kinship with the English romantics. The poem owes something in
its conception to Joseph Warton's "Ode to Fancy," and it also
bears a startling resemblance to Keats's "Fancy," written almost fifty years later. Freneau's poem begins:

> Wakeful, vagrant, restless thing,
> Ever wandering on the wing,

and Keats's begins:

> Ever let the fancy roam,
> Pleasure never is at home.

But while Keats fills his poem with rich and sensuous imagery, Freneau gets bogged down in classical allusions and echoes of Catullus and Vergil. While he was still an undergraduate, Freneau, in collaboration with Hugh Henry Brackenridge, wrote "The Rising Glory of America," already discussed above.

When Freneau went to Santa Cruz in 1776 he wrote a descriptive poem celebrating the lush tropical beauty that appealed to his own romantic nature. "The Beauties of Santa Cruz" is a rather lifeless and mechanical affair, full of attempts at vivid description and touches of local color: a good example of the difficulties American poets at this time had in reconciling the opposing tendencies of romantic material and Neo-classical forms. If Freneau had been freer and less self-conscious in his form and diction, the poem would not have suffered from the kind of artificiality that makes Santa Cruz seem more like Windsor Forest than a tropical paradise. The sea is "the billowy deep," the sun is a "Spangled traveller"; whole stanzas fall prey to the outworn eighteenth-century diction to which Freneau was too often captive:

> The happy waters boast, of various kinds,
> Unnumbered myriads of the scaly race,
> Sportive they glide above the deluged sand,
> Gay as their clime, in ocean's ample vase.

When he returned Freneau found his own country changed substantially. He had known at second hand of the injustices of the British in New England and New York, but he had not felt directly affected until in 1778 he saw evidence everywhere of tyranny and bloodshed. He joined the militia as a private soldier and later, having received some experience in navigation, sailed as captain of merchant ships that were running arms and supplies from the West Indies to New Jersey for the Continental forces. When he was taken captive by the British and placed aboard a prison ship, he had an experience that was to change his attitude toward the British for the rest of his life. "The British Prison Ship" (1781), describing his captivity, is the strongest anti-British poem ever written in America, recounting in detail the horrors that the prisoners underwent at the hands of incompetent and brutal captors. In addition to expressing his outrage at their brutality, Freneau included a passage from an earlier poem angrily denouncing the loyalists in America who were supporting what he viewed as an unjust cause:

> But that those monsters whom our soil maintain'd,
> Who first drew breath in this devoted land,
> Like famish'd wolves, should on their country prey,
> Assist its foes, and wrest our lives away,
> This shocks belief—

From this time on, to the end of his life, Freneau devoted most of his energies to the cause of freedom, first against the British and later against the Hamiltonian Federalists, whom he saw as undermining hard-won individual liberties. His popularity throughout the period of the Revolution continued to grow as he poured out lampoons and satires against George III, Benedict Arnold, Lord Cornwallis, and others.

But his best poetry is to be found not in his satires, which were for the most part ill-considered and hastily written, but in those poems that retain some of his earlier life. One of his best poems, "To the Memory of the Brave Americans, Under General Greene, in South Carolina, who fell in the action of September 8, 1781," is based on a historical event, but he turns the occasion into a reflection on the heroism of the soldiers who fell rather than a celebration of the victory itself.

The poems that mark Freneau as the father of American poetry are those in which he abandons polemic for the quieter moods and philosophical reflection that he celebrates in "The Power of Fancy," and those in which he uses a fresh diction and imagery that look forward to the poetry of Wordsworth. Without a doubt, his best poem was written hastily, almost unconsciously. "The Wild Honey Suckle" (1786) shows most clearly the promise in a poet whose talents were never fully developed. To create what Paul Elmer More calls its "rather languid beauty" he uses a natural diction, and without pretense celebrates the simple emotion aroused from the contemplation of a native American wildflower.

Although Freneau can hardly be called a philosophical poet, those poems that adopt a philosophical or meditative tone are the ones to which we return for oblique glimpses of a vision of life so often obscured by more pressing political concerns. His beautiful "The Indian Burying Ground" (1788) and his reflections on the idea of the noble savage in "The Indian Student" (1788) show him at his best. In "A Moral Thought," also printed as "The Vanity of Existence," Freneau in 1781 gave expression to one of his periodic fits of disillusion:

> In youth, gay scenes attract our eyes,
>   And not suspecting their decay
> Life's flowery fields before us rise,
>   Regardless of its winter day.
>
> But vain pursuits, and joys as vain,
>   Convince us life is but a dream.
> Death is to wake, to rise again
>   To that true life you best esteem.
>
> So nightly on some shallow tide,
>   Oft have I seen a splendid show;
> Reflected stars on either side,
>   And glittering moons were seen below.
>
> But when the tide had ebbed away,
>   The scene fantastic with it fled,
> A bank of mud around me lay,
>   And sea-weed on the river's bed.

But in spite of the lyric quality of this poem, with its vivid and appropriate image in the concluding lines, he continued to the end of his life to react with rage and bitterness to political injustices in verses that do him no credit as a poet.

Paul Elmer More has said that "The Wild Honey Suckle"

has "the slender brittleness of a costly vase, marred in the burning." Some such description could be applied to all of Freneau's verse. It is a charred landscape, burned over with the fires of rage and frustration that he could not control, yet among the ruins one can pick out some salvageable items that contain hints of a promise never fulfilled before he died, long forgotten and even despised, in 1832.

CHAPTER THREE

Early Nineteenth-Century Romanticism

Washington Allston, Richard Henry Dana, Sr., Fitz-Greene Halleck, Joseph Rodman Drake, James Kirke Paulding, N. P. Willis, William Cullen Bryant, Edgar Allan Poe

Bryant and Poe are the important early poets of American Romanticism: Bryant, the traditional poet arriving at his worship at the shrine of nature through Thomson, Cowper, and Wordsworth; Poe, the radical poet denying the material world following his reading of Tom Moore, Coleridge, and Shelley. If we were to tear the *Lyrical Ballads* in half, we would have a rough approximation of the difference between Bryant and Poe. Coleridge writes in his *Biographia Literaria,* "It was agreed that my endeavours should be directed to persons and characters supernatural or at least romantic . . . Mr. Wordsworth, on the other hand, was to propose to himself as his object, to give the charm of novelty to things of every day." Similarly, Bryant cautiously but firmly adapted the Wordsworthian idiom and attitude to his own native fondness for the New England landscape, while Poe created fantastic landscapes of his own imaginings that would reshape in much more radical ways the direction of American poetry.

The different directions they took, in fact, suggest the complexity of the Romantic movement in America. Both men spent a good part of their lives in New York, yet for neither was it a wholly congenial environment. New York's atmosphere of Addisonian London, with its cultivated amateurishness and dilettantism, was equally far removed in spirit from the rural simplicity of Bryant's beloved Berkshire Hills and Poe's ideal world of "Supernal Loveliness." Although Bryant's reputation as a poet was established before he was thirty-five, there remained throughout his life a tension between his public role as newspaper editor and champion of liberal causes and his exalted ideas of the nature of poetry. After his early poetic efforts Poe perhaps found the climate of the New York Knickerbocker group too congenial, as the increasingly satirical and topical quality of his own work suggests. But if New York itself was of doubtful direct value to the best poetry of either Poe or Bryant, it can be used as a convenient focal point for them. A number of tendencies and influences were working together in different combinations on such New York writers as Halleck, Paulding, and Willis, and the poetry of Poe and Bryant can be more clearly evaluated against the background of their contemporaries' work. The strong feelings of nationalism rampant during the twenties and thirties, the pervasive influence of Byron and Scott, the awakening awareness of nature and the beauties of the American landscape, and the emphasis on the individual are just a few of the forces working in a variety of combinations on the poets of this period. Byron, in fact, was almost universally admired, as we can see in Bryant's early verses, and in Poe's "Tamerlane" (1827), Halleck's *Fanny* (1819), Willis's "Lady Jane," Dana's *The Buccaneer,* and many more. W. E. Leonard once made the claim that Byron "stood to the lyric poetry of his age . . . as Shakespeare had stood to the dramatic poetry of Elizabethan times," yet both Poe and Bryant laid low the ghost of Byron in their movement away to their own characteristic modes.

One of the earliest American Romantics was the poet and painter Washington Allston (1779–1843), who formed a close friendship with Coleridge and whose verse was influenced by Wordsworth. Allston first demonstrated his poetic leanings at Harvard, where he delivered a poem at the college's memorial service for George Washington. But having chosen painting as a career, he went to England in 1801, where he met his countryman Benjamin West, who had succeeded Sir Joshua Reynolds as president of the Royal Academy. After studying with West, Allston moved to Paris and then to Rome. There he met Coleridge, who introduced him to the associationism of Hartley and Archibald Alison. The subject matter of several of Allston's poems shows the possible influence of Wordsworth: "The Mad Lover at the Grave of His Mistress" and "Will, the Maniac" are both ballads dealing with abnormal states of mind and men of lowly origin. Will, once "the gayest swain" whose flock "was all his humble pride," mourns his untold and hopeless love for an "heiress of the land" and lives out his life on a lonely mountain.

These poems were collected in the one volume of verse published in Allston's lifetime, *The Sylphs of the Seasons, and Other Poems* (1813). The title poem is a dream-allegory in the manner of Thomson and other followers of Milton, in which each season is represented by nature imagery appropriate to it. Two of the satirical poems deal, as does much of his work, with the subject of painting. One of them, "The Paint-King," a burlesque of Scott's "Fire-King" and Lewis's "Cloud-King," satirizes the theme of the artist's effort to embody the ideal on canvas. In thirty-eight five-line stanzas Allston describes a fiendish "Paint-King" who seizes a young girl and grinds her up into an oil jug before quite literally placing her body on his canvas. The questions raised about art are those raised by Coleridge in his pursuit of the ideal and its transformation into art. "The Two Painters, A Tale" is a long Hudibrastic poem describing a controversy between two painters who, after their death, come before Minos for his judgment of their sins. One is a "colorist"; the other a champion of "Mind"; each presents the case for his critical position. The judgment is that both should be yoked together on earth to paint for five hundred years, since " 'one leg alone shall never run, / Nor two Half-Painters make but One.' "

The sonnets are also principally related to painting. In them Allston displays considerable technical virtuosity, even experimenting with departures from the Shakespearean and Petrarchan forms. He echoes Coleridge's transcendental notions about the organic relationship of art to nature in poems describing the poet's response to the spirituality he discovers in the paintings of great masters. A sonnet on Raphael's group of three angels before the tent of Abraham begins:

> O, now I feel as though another sense,
> From heaven descending, had informed my soul;
> I feel the pleasurable, full control
> Of Grace, harmonious, boundless, and intense.

Allston also shows Coleridge's influence in his distinction between the reason and the understanding in his sonnet on Rembrandt's "Jacob's Dream." The painting's "visionary scenes" are like "the rambling of an idiot's speech" and give no "thought significant in Reason's reach." And its "random shadowings" give birth

> To thoughts and things from other worlds that come,
> And fill the soul, and strike the reason dumb.

In a later sonnet, Bienaimé's statue of an angel makes Allston's heart rise "to the world above" and he is reminded of the existence of the soul of the sculptor. The art sonnets are, in fact, a combination of poetic sensibility and art criticism, as in the sonnet to Raphael, in which the poet's eyes

> impelled as by enchantment sweet,
> From part to part with circling motion rove,
> Yet seem unconscious of the power to move;
> From line to line through endless changes run,
> O'er countless shapes, yet seem to gaze on One.

Allston's final tribute to Coleridge is the sonnet in which he asserts his friend's search for a transcendental unity in these lines:

> No, never more thy gentle voice shall blend
> With air of Earth its pure ideal tones,
> Binding in one, as with harmonious zones,
> The heart and intellect.

The only other poem published in Allston's lifetime was his tribute to the benign influence of England on America, "America to England" (1810), of which Coleridge had such a high opinion that he printed it in the first edition of his *Sibylline Leaves* in 1817. The poem, said Coleridge, should be admired "for its moral, no less than its patriotic spirit"; it ends with an affirmation of the unity between the two countries:

> While the manners, while the arts,
>   That mould a nation's soul,
> Still cling around our hearts,—
>   Between let Ocean roll,
> Our joint communion breaking with the Sun:
>   Yet still from either beach
>   The voice of blood shall reach,
>   More audible than speech,
>   "We are One."

Allston's verses are interesting early examples of the cultural dialogue between America and England that was to continue for the next half century. Admired by Wordsworth and Southey as well as Coleridge abroad, Allston had a small following among his own countrymen, including Irving and the elder Dana. His poems display considerable technical skill and the best are as good as any written in this country between Freneau's "The Wild Honey Suckle" and Bryant's "Thanatopsis."

An enthusiastic reviewer of Allston's poems was Richard Henry Dana, Sr. (1787–1879). As one of the founders of the *North American Review,* Dana was among those champions of a native literature who sought to improve the state of American letters. However, he was too eclectic in his literary tastes and he was finally forced to leave the editorial board because of his defense of the poetry of Keats. Moving to New York, he founded *The Idle Man* (1821–1822), modeled on Irving's and Paulding's *Salmagundi Papers* (1808), and printed more of the poems of William Cullen Bryant, whose "Thanatopsis" and "To a Waterfowl" had appeared in the *North American Review* in 1817 and 1818.

Dana's own poetry, printed in *Poems* (1827) and *Poems and Prose Writings* (1833), illustrates the transitional quality of much American verse of the early decades of the nineteenth century. The heroic couplet was still widely accepted as a verse form, but the strict regularity and the relation of ideas and syntax to meter and rhyme had begun to break down. Dana wrote several long, serious, philosophical poems with such titles as "Factitious Life" and "Thoughts on the Soul," in which he moved from commonplace observations to abstruse moralistic speculation. In "Thoughts on the Soul" over half the lines are run-on, and the ideas have no internal organization within the line; the effect is closer to blank verse than to the smooth, urbane instrument of Pope. Other poems show Dana's tendencies toward Romantic verse forms and subject matter. In "The Dying Raven" and "The Little Beach-Bird" he abandons the couplet for blank verse and a six-line stanza to express his feelings of identity with external nature. His tribute to the dying bird echoes the cry of Coleridge's Ancient Mariner:

> Who scoffs these sympathies,
> Makes mock of the divinity within;
> Nor feels he gently breathing through his soul
> The universal spirit. Hear it cry,—
> How does thy pride abase thee, man, vain man!
> How deaden thee to universal love,
> And joy of kindred with all humble things,—
> God's creatures all!

Dana is best known for a long Gothic horror narrative called *The Buccaneer* (1827), in which he surrounds a Byronic pirate hero who is a law unto himself with Coleridgean stage effects, including a spectral horse and a burning ghost ship. The poem does not succeed, because Dana's own Puritan temperament inclines him toward passing too many moral judgments upon a hero whose very reason for being is his defiance of morality. The poem's sea scenes are occasionally good, but the ghostly effects do not come off; to us they seem bad second-hand Coleridge or Scott or Ann Radcliffe. Among his contemporaries Dana was highly regarded as a poet, yet he is remembered today principally for his criticism and his life-long friendship with Bryant.

In New York in the 1820s the best-known poet, with the possible exceptions of James Gates Percival (1795–1856) and Mrs. Lydia Sigourney (1791–1865), was Fitz-Greene Halleck (1790–1867), who was thought by many to offer a serious challenge to England's supremacy in the world of letters. If his name is now practically forgotten, the reason is as much his own disinclination to take himself seriously as it is his lack of talent. Halleck is probably most typical of the practitioners of poetry in New York at the time. Like his friend Drake, he did not take his role as poet seriously; to him it was an avocation, to be pursued in a gentlemanly way rather than obeyed as a calling. Many young New Yorkers of wealth and family wrote verses, and the Knickerbocker attitude toward letters as an occupation to while away idle hours in harmless amusement is reflected in the title of Dana's periodical, *The Idle Man,* as well as the other numerous imitators of the *Salmagundi Papers* and Washington Irving's pseudonymous *History of New York* by Diedrich Knickerbocker (1809).

Many of them wrote under pseudonyms, and Halleck's first success was a series of poems contributed to various New York newspapers over the name Croaker, Jr. In the spring of 1819 Joseph Rodman Drake had printed a poem called "To Ennui" in the New York *Evening Post* and signed it "Croaker," after a minor character in Goldsmith's *The Good-*

Natur'd Man. This mildly satirical poem, the result of a collaboration between Drake and Halleck, was followed shortly by others, some signed by Croaker (Drake), some by Croaker, Jr. (Halleck), and some by Croaker and Co. Their verses satirized topical and political subjects and well-known local figures such as Alexander Hamilton; Samuel Woodworth, the author of "The Old Oaken Bucket" (1826); James Kirke Paulding, who had just published *The Backwoodsman* (1818); and General Jackson. Their authorship remained a secret and was never publicly acknowledged, but the "Croakers"—thirty-five in all—immediately caught on. They were widely imitated and were eventually illicitly reprinted in book form before being republished by Halleck himself. The Croaker poems have no poetic merit and must be judged as journalism rather than as poetry, in spite of the praise of Bryant and others who admired their lightness of touch. The best-known of the Croaker poems is Drake's "The American Flag," which was declaimed by generations of schoolchildren. The last stanza of that poem, however, was actually composed by Halleck, when Drake was dissatisfied with his own conclusion:

> Forever float that standard sheet!
> Where breathes the foe but falls before us,
> With freedom's soil beneath our feet,
> And freedom's banner streaming o'er us?

Halleck himself made no claims for them as poetry, and later wrote that they "have never desired or deserved any other than a short life." Poe, looking back at them thirty years later, accurately judged them "local and ephemeral."

Later in 1819 Halleck published anonymously a satirical poem in the vein of Byron's *Beppo* called *Fanny*. The poem concerns the rapid rise into society of a poor merchant and his daughter Fanny, a framework that gave Halleck the opportunity to lampoon the follies of the *nouveaux riches* and make passing comments on local politics and literature. The stylistic similarities between this poem and the "Croakers" was noticed immediately and added to its success. Although he did not acknowledge his authorship, Halleck was known to be the author of the poem, and he acquired from it a considerable local reputation. A bookseller prevailed on him to bring out an expanded version, printed in 1821 and reprinted in England, where it was less admired because of the number of purely local and topical allusions. Halleck's satirical handling of his material clearly shows his debt to Byron's *Beppo* and *Don Juan,* both of which were popular in America. *Fanny* uses a modified *ottava rima* similar to that of *Don Juan,* but Halleck was no Byron. He was too American, too provincial, too much the product of his Connecticut origins. There was enough affinity between them, however, for Halleck to bring out an edition of the English poet's works, and N. P. Willis remarked that Byron would have been like Halleck had he been born in Connecticut.

A trip abroad in 1822 deepened Halleck's perceptions and prompted him to write several of his more memorable poems. "Alnwick Castle" (1827) reflects Halleck's sense of the contrast between the ideal and the actual as he describes a visit to the castle of the Percys, which he sees in two different ways: as an ancient monument, clothed in the romance of the Middle Ages, and as a building erected centuries ago and now inhabited by modern man, including a guide who takes the narrator through for "ten-and-sixpence sterling." The poem is a strange combination of the serious and comic, a quality that prompted Bryant to remark: "What particularly distinguishes his poetry from that of our native writers . . . is that vein of playful humor, which breaks out, seemingly in spite of his efforts to repress it." Another result of his trip to Great Britain is his fine tribute to Burns, in which Lowell saw a "genial manliness."

Halleck's stirring poem, "Marco Bozzaris" (1825), celebrates the exploits of the Greek hero in the war against the Turks. It reflects Byron's involvement in the Greek cause and recalls the martial tone of Thomas Campbell's poetry. The popularity of the subject gave it a wide audience on both sides of the Atlantic. English and American publishers reprinted it and countless schoolboys recited it. The poem for which Halleck should be remembered is his very moving and terse expression of personal grief, "On the Death of Joseph Rodman Drake," said to have been written on the day of his friend's death in 1820. The "union of tender sentiment and simplicity" that Poe admired in this poem makes it still one of the finest elegies in American literature. It opens with the stanza:

> Green be the turf above thee,
> Friend of my better days!
> None knew thee but to love thee,
> Nor named thee but to praise.

It is too easy to pass over Halleck as just another poet in the Knickerbocker group. Although he cannot be said ever to have attained real distinction, a few of his poems suggest a sensibility that was never seriously cultivated. But he was largely derivative in both thought and style and, as Nelson Adkins says in his detailed study of Halleck, there was always something of the amateur about him. Adkins points out his concern with the contrast between the romance of the past and the stark reality of the present, but suggests that he was perhaps never seriously enough committed to the practice of poetry to attempt a reconciliation between them.

One of the earliest poets to make imaginative use of native scenery was Joseph Rodman Drake (1795–1820), who is remembered principally as the friend of Halleck and the author of "The Culprit Fay," which Poe subjected to abusive attack in 1836. The poem, written in two days in 1816, is an early example of the growing interest in the picturesque qualities of the Hudson River landscape. The towering palisades and craggy cliffs of the Hudson were beginning to attract the attention of a number of artists, including Washington Irving, who used them as the settings for his transplanted European folk tales; Paulding, who had alluded to "fair Hackinsack" and Weehawken in his "Lay of the Scottish Fiddle" (1813); Thomas Cole, the founder of the so-called Hudson River school of landscape painting; and Robert Weir, another Hudson River painter whose "misty mid-regions" are recalled in Poe's evocation of this same region in "Ulalume." The theme of "The Culprit Fay" is the expiation by a fairy ouphe of the crime of loving a mortal maiden, and the setting is the Hudson highlands, not far from West Point. The work, as Poe pointed out, is a work of fancy, in Coleridge's sense of the word, rather than imagination. It is quite mechanically contrived in its imitation of the manner, but not the spirit, of Shelley's "Queen Mab." Yet in 1816 this production, flawed as it is by false-sounding and strained fairy-world effects, is something new in American poetry. As a fairy tale, it departs from the didacticism, satire, and pure lyricism that were the dominant strains in American verse; and in its use of the American landscape as setting it opens up possibilities that were later fully realized by Cooper and Irving. The poem is also technically significant, since Drake employed an iambic meter based on the metrical principle of Coleridge's "Christabel," in which each line has four primary stresses irrespective of the number of syllables, achieved by the free substitution of anapests. Gay Wilson Allen, in his study of American prosody, describes this adaptation of Coleridge's principle as Drake's "most important contribution to American prosodic history."

"The Culprit Fay" circulated in manuscript for several years after Drake's death in 1820 and achieved a kind of *sub rosa* reputation, which was enhanced by the publication in London of a paraphrase by N. P. Willis, with about half the lines of the original. In the same year, 1835, George Dearborn published *The Culprit Fay and Other Poems* for Drake's daughter. The volume included his effusive patriotic outburst, "The American Flag," written for the "Croaker" series, and some other songs and fragments. The extravagant claims of his admirers that he was the American Keats, suggested partly by his early death from tuberculosis, did nothing for either Drake or Keats, and distorted the value of the youthful production of this promising but unfulfilled American Romantic poet.

Although the vogue of Scott and Byron was widespread, it was not universal, and one Knickerbocker writer took strenuous objection to it. James Kirke Paulding (1778–1860) based

his dislike for Scott and Byron principally on the strong nationalistic feelings that he retained throughout his career as
novelist, playwright, and critic. Paulding combined an extreme
nationalism with a Neo-classical point of view in his poetry
and criticism. At first his nationalism was negative: the result
of his animosity toward most things British during the War
of 1812, but, unlike his fellow Knickerbockers, he was a fervent
champion of the little man—a Jeffersonian Democrat who considered himself a true son of the people and a singer of the
untold stories of unknown men. Paulding's critical orientation
remained with the eighteenth century—with Pope, Swift, Field-
ing, and Goldsmith—but his nationalist sympathies led him to
write about the virtues of the unspoiled frontiersman and
settler as opposed to corrupt easterners and Europeans. His
satirical attitude toward Tory England and his insistence on
the hope inherent in a democratic America would not again
be given such full poetic expression until they took new form
in the transcendental outpourings of Whitman. In "The Lay
of the Scottish Fiddle" Paulding attacks the imitators of Byron
in America who,

> like the wretched prodigal of old
> Whose plaintive story is in scripture told,
> The plenty of our Father's house resign,
> To starve on offal, and to herd with swine.

This poem was published anonymously in 1813 as *The Lay of
the Scottish Fiddle: A Tale of Havre de Grace,* "Supposed to
be Written by Walter Scott, Esq." It is built around the invasion and burning of Havre de Grace by the British, but its
setting somewhat inexplicably shifts to the Hudson River, and
is full of local references to Jersey City, "fair Hackinsack," and
"Gotham."

Although Paulding continued to write and publish verse
throughout his life, he is better known as Irving's collaborator
on the *Salmagundi Papers,* as the author of *The Dutchman's
Fireside* (1831) and other novels of early settlers and frontier
life, and as a playwright. For his most popular play, *The Lion
of the West* (1830), he created the character of Nimrod Wild-

fire, the Kentucky backwoodsman who visits the East and displays his frontier wisdom. This same theme of the virtues of self-reliance and independence that reside in the unspoiled Western settler had already appeared in his long narrative poem, *The Backwoodsman* (1818), in which Paulding answers the persistent and sustained cries of the period for a national literature using native themes and subject matter. The poem was intended, he said, "to indicate to the youthful writers of his native country, the rich poetic resources with which it abounds, as well as to call their attention *home,* for the means of attaining to novelty of subject, if not to originality in style or sentiment." In six books of some eight hundred relentless heroic couplets, *The Backwoodsman* continues to develop the theme of hope in the natural virtues of frontier life that was so dear to the heart of Crèvecoeur and so questionable to the mind of Cooper. The hero of the poem is a New York tenant farmer named Basil, who hears rumors of the West and decides to join the westward movement and become, like Crèvecoeur's Andrew the Hebridean, a free farmer on fertile soil. The poem loosely follows the adventures of Basil, with frequent digressions and interludes describing the Hudson highlands and the Allegheny Mountains, celebrating the virtues of independence, recalling the heroism of Washington, and recounting episodes from an Indian war and the War of 1812. Basil reappears from time to time, and at the end is seen as an old man enjoying the fruits of his years of labor on the frontier, surrounded by green fields and prosperous neighbors. His rejection of the Old World and its decadent ways serves as an example to others in the poem's closing lines, an apostrophe to the "lone and spotless virgin" of the West:

> Do thou the nations of the earth inspire
> With the deep glow of thy celestial fire;
> Teach them a sober way to break their chains;
>
> *   *   *
>
> Then may those nations freed fresh chaplets bring,
> And to their Western sister praises sing.

The poem's theme was later to be restated by Paulding in his plea for a "National Literature" in the second *Salmagundi* series (1819–1820), where he attacked the "ascendancy of foreign taste and opinions" and deplored the use in fiction of "ghosts, fairies, goblins, and all." In *The Backwoodsman* the simplicity of Basil's home life on the frontier is contrasted to the abasement and enslavement of human beings for the sake of art. Basil and his neighbors would not "sell their heritage of rights / For long processions, pomps, and pretty sights." Paulding continues in this vein as he states:

> Among them was no driveling princely race
> Who'd beggar half a state to buy a vase,
> Or starve a province haply, to reclaim
> From mother earth a lump without a name.

This sustained effort in verse displays more of Paulding's novelistic gifts than his talents as a poet, and its pathos and flatness of diction were justly satirized by both Drake and Halleck. But his passages of exalted moral sentiment praising democratic man as the backbone of the nation are occasionally eloquent, and his descriptions of the native landscape westward to the Ohio from the Hudson are something new in American poetry, even though they are not viewed with the closeness of the naturalist's eye. For that, one would have to turn to a poem published by the Scottish-American ornithologist and poet Alexander Wilson (1766–1813), who describes some of the same territory in *The Foresters: A Poem, Descriptive of a Pedestrian Journey to the Falls of Niagara, in the Autumn of 1804* (1805).

Paulding continued throughout his life to experiment with verse. A few of his poems were printed in magazines, and several dozen more that he called his "careless verses" have been found among his papers. His most ambitious poem among these is an 810-line narrative in Spenserian stanzas that is a kind of reverse *Backwoodsman*. Apparently written to illustrate how the easterner's greed can lead to personal tragedy on the western plains, "The Pilgrim and His Guide"

(1825) concerns a native of Massachusetts who travels to the prairies in search of "accursed gain." He and his Indian guide outrun a prairie fire, only to die miserably of starvation and thirst. His other verse contains a variety of themes and types. He wrote love poems, elegies, "graveyard" poems, patriotic poems, and satires, including some unpublished lines on the death of John Jacob Astor called "On the death of J . . . J . . . A . . . who after a long life of meanness, trickery, and overreaching, died with several millions, leaving a large legacy to a Public Library, in consequence of which he was lauded to the skies for his liberality."

Another member of the group of poets and essayists known as the Knickerbocker group was Nathaniel Parker Willis (1806–1867). In his series of sketches in *Godey's Magazine* describing "The Literati of New York City," Edgar Allan Poe ranked his contemporary poets in the following order: Longfellow, Bryant, Halleck, and Willis. Poe's omission of his own name from this list is understandable on the grounds of assumed modesty, but the inclusion of Willis sadly suggests the state of American poetry in 1846. This is a distortion, of course, since James Russell Lowell (1819–1891) had published several volumes of verse, and John Greenleaf Whittier (1807–1892), though not a great poet, should have been ranked above Willis. Willis, however, was a commanding literary figure in the New York of the thirties and forties. His newspaper sketches from abroad recounting the doings of English society, his light pieces characteristically titled *Pencillings by the Way* (1835), his two romantic tragedies, and his six volumes of verse made him a formidable contender for the kind of honor Poe was claiming for him. But in Poe's case, Willis' personal kindness and generosity should also be taken into account, since he helped Poe out of several financial scrapes and republished "The Raven" in the *Evening Mirror* in 1845 with a description of it as "the most effective single example of fugitive poetry ever published in this country."

Fugitive poetry was a favorite expression of Willis, who had used it as the title of his first collection of poems in 1829.

There is something "fugitive" about Willis himself; the impression he leaves lies somewhere between the literary dandy and the Sunday-school poet. About a third of his verses are "religious poems"; some are retellings of scriptural stories, such as "Hagar in the Wilderness," "The Sacrifice of Abraham," "Lazarus and Mary," and "Scenes in Gethsemane," while others are hymns and meditations. The rest are on a variety of subjects, ranging from the death of a young girl to light descriptions of country scenes. It is too tempting to characterize his verse by listing such titles as "To Helen in a Huff," "Sunrise Thoughts at the Close of a Ball," and "The Lady in the White Dress, Whom I helped into the Omnibus," yet there remains the feeling that with one or two exceptions the tone and attitude of most of his verse are on this level. There is a kind of smooth diffuseness about his verse that in many cases leads to excesses of sentimentality and floridness of diction. When he curbs these impulses, however, Willis writes a lucid, simple, and direct verse that is unpretentious and light in tone. "To M—, from Abroad" (1834), for example, a love poem to a girl he was prevented from marrying, is sentimental verse with the stickiness left out:

> The sad, sweet bells of twilight chime,
> Of many hearts may touch but one,
> And so this seeming careless rhyme
> Will whisper to thy heart alone.

Perhaps the principal reasons for Willis' success as a poet were his wholesomeness, his piety, and his moralizing tone—qualities that were not present in his other writing. Certainly there is nothing in his poetry that would offend the Young Person. His "Dedication Hymn" (1829) exhibits his religious impulses at their best, since his piety was restricted to the simple form of the hymn stanza, where the sentimental excesses and flatness of tone of his more sustained religious efforts disappear.

A theme running through a series of four of Willis' poems is the corrupting effect of ambition and fame. In "The Wife's

Appeal" (1837) a man is stirred to the pursuit of fame by his wife and loses his self-respect and love of life. The poem opens with a description of the husband's study typical of the hollow splendor of Willis' attempts at atmosphere:

> The sunlight, streaming through the curtain's fold,
> Fell with a rose-tint on his jewell'd hand;
> And the rich woods of the quaint furniture
> Lay deepening their vein'd colors in the sun.

"Parrhasius" (1831), another poem on a similar theme, is a blank-verse narrative about an artist who tortures a slave in order to capture an expression of agony for his painting of Prometheus. The artist loses all humanity and pity for the sake of ambition and fame. The central part is spoken by the artist himself in six-line stanzas before Willis returns to blank verse to warn against the false idols of life that divert us from "truth, and fervor, and devotedness." This is probably the best of the four, the other two of which are "The Dying Alchemist" and "The Scholar of Thebet Ben Khorat" (1837).

Willis' best poem is one of his "city poems," some of which are flimsy and vulgar salutes to white-chip hats and to ladies in chemisettes with black buttons. But "Unseen Spirits" (1843) is quite different in tone from these; it is a moralistic poem in which Willis expresses his feelings about the differences between a lady who has kept her chastity ("For all God ever gave to her / She kept with chary care") and one who has not. For the latter:

> No mercy now can clear her brow
>   For this world's peace to pray;
> For, as love's wild prayer dissolved in air,
>   Her woman's heart gave way!—
> But the sin forgiven by Christ in heaven
> By man is cursed alway!

The poem impressed Poe as the one by which Willis would most likely be remembered. In his essay on Willis in "The

Literati" he wrote: "There is about this little poem (evidently written in haste and through impulse) a true imagination. Its grace, dignity, and pathos are impressive, and there is more in it of earnestness of soul than in anything I have seen from the pen of its author."

Two other contemporary judgments of Willis are worth quoting here. One is by Paulding in a four-line poem printed over his pseudonym, "Gnoman," in *Graham's Magazine:*

ON NINCOM,

Who is very devout in his poetry, and very licentious in his prose.

> Two different muses Nincom must inspire,
> As opposite as water is to fire;
> In verse, one is a saint devout and civil,
> In prose, the other is a very d - - - l.

The other is from Lowell's *A Fable for Critics* (1848):

> Over-ornament ruins both poem and prose,
> Just conceive of a Muse with a ring in her nose!
>
> *　*　*
>
> In a country where scarcely a village is found
> That has not its author sublime and profound,
> For some one to be slightly shallow's a duty,
> And Willis's shallowness makes half his beauty.
>
> *　*　*
>
> And he ought to let Scripture alone—'t is self-slaughter,
> For nobody likes inspiration-and-water.

In the 1830s, during which he published four more editions of his poems, the position of William Cullen Bryant (1794–1878) came to be widely acknowledged, while his friend Halleck's reputation began slowly to decline. As Bryant became increasingly active in politics and journalism, he wrote less and less nature poetry, even though he regretted his absence from the scenes of his inspiration. In the previous decade, his rambles in the Berkshire Hills had furnished the materials for the nature poetry for which he was well known. To Bryant, poetry was a high art and a sacred calling, a view that frequently has a distressingly dampening effect on his work. Nature was a shrine at which the poet worshiped and received his inspiration. If the impulses from the vernal wood frequently have a Wordsworthian ring, it is no accident, since Bryant early arrived at a view of nature that he was later gratified to learn was strikingly similar to that of his English contemporary. "The Burial-Place," "Green River," "Oh Fairest of the Rural Maids," "A Winter Piece," "The Rivulet," and many others are full of the closeness of observation and the use of natural objects as analogies for moral truths that are typical of Bryant's poetry. It was this attitude toward nature and poetry that led Bryant to state in his later years that "the elements of poetry lie in natural objects, in the vicissitudes of human life, in the emotions of the human heart, and the relations of man to man. He who can present them in combinations and lights which at once affect the mind with a deep sense of their truth and beauty is the poet for his own age and the ages that succeed it."

Bryant was the son of a small-town New England doctor, who was an accomplished violinist, a reader of the classics, and a political activist with strong Federalist leanings. And although his mother and grandfather shared the strongly orthodox Calvinism of Cummington, Massachusetts, and put him to reading the Bible at four, Dr. Peter Bryant was a religious liberal who subscribed to the journals of the Boston Unitarians. In his father's classical library Bryant received a grounding in versification and syntax that he soon put to use in early attempts at verse of his own. It is not surprising that his first published poem, written at the age of ten, is a versification of the 104th Psalm, or that his second is a verse satire in the manner of the Connecticut Wits entitled *The Embargo; Or Sketches of the Times, A Satire; by a Youth of Thirteen* (1809). His Federalist sympathies are those of his father, who saw Jefferson's policies as a threat to New England mercantilism. In his immoderate abuse of Jefferson, Bryant writes with the emotional maturity of a thirteen-year-old and the poetical skill of his eighteenth-century predecessors:

> Go, wretch, resign the presidential chair,
> Disclose thy secret measures, foul or fair.
> Go, search with curious eye, for hornèd frogs,
> Mid the wild wastes of Louisianian bogs.

But from the evidence of his other youthful poetry, the wonders of nature and the mystery of death were of more interest to Bryant than the Federalist politics of his father. In his early adolescence, after a bout with Byronism, he entered into a dialogue with nature in which he sought the answers to moral and philosophical questions. The yellow violet, for example, when it is overshadowed by brighter flowers, reminds him that "they, who climb to wealth, forget / The friends in darker fortunes tried." In "Thanatopsis" he combined his view of nature as analogue with an increasingly unorthodox view of death to arrive at a poem of originality and power. The poem for which Bryant is best remembered was composed in stages over a period of almost ten years, beginning with an early version written when he was sixteen or seventeen. By his own account, he had been reading the morbid lyrics of Henry Kirke White, as well as Blair's "The Grave," the poems of Southey, and the blank verse of Cowper, and had come to a liking for "poetry of a querulous caste." The history of the revisions of the poem is a history of Bryant's own exploration of the meaning of death in secular rather than religious terms. What bothered Bryant particularly was the question of the future of the human consciousness after death, and he could not accept the pat answers of the Christian promise of eternal life. Instead, he leaned toward a belief in death as the final union with an insensate universe. This, combined with a Stoic acceptance of death as a release from the miseries of human existence, resulted in a poem that answered the question raised by his reading of Blair and White: "How shall a man face death?" In the form in which "Thanatopsis" was submitted to the *North American Review* in 1817 the answer concentrated on the universality of death:

> what if thou withdraw
> In silence from the living, and no friend
> Take note of thy departure? All that breathe
> Will share thy destiny.

But when he revised the poem in 1821 for his first volume of verse, nature was no longer a mere example by means of which the understanding of death was suggested by metaphor and analogy; it had become a teacher with whose "visible forms, she speaks / A various language." The "still voice" of this personified Nature emphasizes the need for dignity in life in order to face the pleasant mystery of death that can be only partially explained in terms of human reason. The influence of Wordsworth on these additions is obvious.

The poem is remarkable for the way it handles a religious question in secular terms. The question of immortality is phrased with echoes from Calvin and the Bible, yet the answers are given by an amorphous spirit of nature rather than an anthropomorphic God. The consolations of death as a natural fulfillment of an organic process narrowly miss a shallow sentimental optimism, which Bryant avoids by his refusal to do more than suggest that nature is a mystery that reveals itself only partially to the human understanding.

"Thanatopsis" is also a good example of Bryant's favorite and most characteristic verse form. The rhythm of his blank verse is fairly regular, yet he uses several variations and makes free use of run-on lines and caesuras placed at various points within the line. The irregularities of the trisyllabic foot, to which he was giving serious thought at this time, make few appearances in this poem, however. This blank verse was even then an effective instrument, and its sonorous quality perhaps

best captures Bryant's true voice. But its dependence on alliteration, on repeated vowel sounds, and on a heavily monosyl-
labic vocabulary frequently gives its sonorities a hollow ring.
When several poems in this blank verse, such as "The Antiquity of Freedom" (1842), "A Forest Hymn" (1825), and "The
Flood of Years" (1876), are read aloud, they become, as Marius
Bewley has pointed out, a little like listening to a harmonium
with the pedal stuck.

Other early poems show more directly the influence of
Wordsworth in their use of simple diction and of natural
objects to evoke corresponding emotions in the poet. The
blank-verse "Inscription for the Entrance to a Wood" (*c.* 1815)
is imbued with the associationism of Archibald Alison and
Wordsworth in its celebration of the solace nature offers to the
spectator:

> The calm shade
> Shall bring a kindred calm, and the sweet breeze
> That makes the green leaves dance, shall waft a balm
> To thy sick heart.

Placed face to face with nature, Bryant, in the role of poet,
allowed its influence to play over his mind and suggest "analogies and correspondences which it beholds between the things
of the moral and the natural world." This attitude, expressed
in 1825, anticipates Emerson's *Nature* (1836) by a decade, but
Bryant never arrived at the rich and heady mixture of Sweden-
borgianism and German idealism that evoked the full possibilities of language as a symbolic utterance. His method can
be seen in "To a Waterfowl" (1818), another famous early
poem, in which the vividly realized image of the bird seen
against a dying sunset suggests the analogy of the "way" of
the poet guided by an unseen hand. Bryant makes no attempt
at subtlety or "organic" fusion of meaning and symbol. His
faith in a somewhat less pantheistic God than that of "Thanatopsis" moves him to state explicitly the poem's "lesson" in
the last stanza:

> He who, from zone to zone,
> Guides through the boundless sky thy certain flight,
> In the long way that I must tread alone,
>   Will lead my steps aright.

Bryant was not only a nature poet; he was also a poet of his own age who gave strong support to the nationalism and faith in progress that we associate with the Age of Jackson and the Era of Good Feeling. He was basically a liberal—from his reading of Adam Smith and David Ricardo perhaps more of an English liberal than the homegrown American variety with its strain of French social thought. Although he retained a faith in democracy, he was never a Jeffersonian or even a Jacksonian; V. L. Parrington calls him simply "anti-Whig." Bryant was an early advocate of the rights of labor and abolition, and the pages of his *Evening Post* promoted the causes of Free-Soilers, Barnburners, fugitive slaves, John Brown, and Abraham Lincoln. In supporting abolition, Bryant repudiated his youthful belief in the right to secede and became an advocate of relentless war upon the Confederacy.

His early political poems were blandly optimistic paeans to progress characteristic of the Era of Good Feeling—an optimism later tempered by a more cautious attitude. At the Harvard Commencement of 1821 he delivered the Phi Beta Kappa poem, "The Ages," which was so conventional in its outlook and in its occasional quality that he is said to have been made "sick" by composing it. In thirty-five Spenserian stanzas he traced the history of man to show how the present peak of civilization had been reached through a long series of strife and bloodshed. His Puritan distaste for Catholicism can be seen in his description of crimes perpetrated in the Middle Ages:

> And vice, beneath the mitre's kind control,
> Sinned gayly on.

His description of the Reformation made it appear to be a release from bondage from

Horrible forms of worship, that, of old,
Held, o'er the shuddering realms, unquestioned sway.

Although decidedly inferior in quality, "The Ages" stands as a poem almost perfectly expressing the spirit of a decade that was turning violently away from everything in Europe and the past.

In his later poems in which the idea of progress appears, "The Fountain" (1839) and "The Antiquity of Freedom" (1842), Bryant rejects the bland optimism of "The Ages" for a less positive hope for the future. Bryant uses the fountain in the first of these poems as a structural device; scenes from various stages of history from prehistoric times to the present appear by the fountain. But having arrived at a present of serenity and civilization, the poet wonders about the future, and the poem ends with hints of dark prophecy suggestive of geologic upheaval, which may have derived from his reading in Sir Charles Lyell's *Principles of Geology* (1830–1833). "The Antiquity of Freedom" is another corrective to the simple-minded view of progress put forth in "The Ages." The allegorical figure of Freedom grows continually stronger and better able to guard against the encroachments of its enemy, Tyranny, but is warned to maintain a vigilance against it.

In versification Bryant, like Wordsworth, leaned toward the breakdown of strict metrical regularity. He was, in fact, the first important critic of poetry in America and a student and experimenter in prosody. In an 1819 essay defending the use of the trisyllabic foot against the prevailing rules of metrical regularity, Bryant observed that they sacrificed "beauty of expression, and variety and vivacity of numbers." Elsewhere he criticized the Connecticut Wits for their "balanced and wearisome regularity." Gay Wilson Allen in his study of American prosody half seriously suggests that Bryant could be called the "father of American prosodists" and points out that by both example and precept he pointed the way for at least the American poets of his generation. His technical facility in a wide variety of verse forms and his movement away from correctness and metrical regularity toward the "organic verse" of Emerson make him an important figure in the development of typically American cadences.

But if his experiments were metrically successful, they often do not carry with them a corresponding weight of intellectual or emotional conviction. His sonnets, odes, and Spenserian stanzas satisfactorily solve their formal problems, but the results frequently are empty intellectual exercises. As for his use of the language and imagery of nature, he never fully realized the possibilities of the symbolic quality of language; his verses are never "organic" as are Emerson's in such poems as "Each and All." Even the best of Bryant's nature poems make use of natural objects as simple analogies; he learns a lesson from the waterfowl or sees a parallel between the yellow violet and life. Perhaps even with his marked affinities with Wordsworth, Bryant is in this respect closer to the eighteenth-century use of nature as a basis for moral statement, as in the ending of Freneau's "The Wild Honey Suckle," than to the nineteenth-century use of it as an expression of a way of feeling.

Still, we should accept Bryant for his strengths rather than criticize him for what he could not become. As an accurate observer of the flora and fauna of his own New England he remains unsurpassed and without precedent, as in this description of the anemone from "A Winter Piece" (1821):

> Lodged in sunny cleft,
> Where the cold breezes come not, blooms alone
> The little wind-flower, whose just opened eye
> Is blue as the spring heaven it gazes at

His sensuous involvement with nature, although tempered by his generalizing and moralizing tendencies, still points toward the much more intense immersion of the soul into nature of the radical Transcendentalists. Embracing the wind in one poem and being embraced by it in another, Bryant, as Tremaine McDowell observes, "took his place among the Romantic generation who clasped rocks to their hearts and bestowed kisses on the universe." Bryant in 1824 wrote in "Summer Wind":

> For me, I lie
> Languidly in the shade, where the thick turf,
> Yet virgin from the kisses of the sun,
> Retains some freshness, and I woo the wind.

Yet the impulse is the same—even if the mode is radically different—as that in Walt Whitman's famous lines in "Song of Myself":

> Smile O voluptuous cool-breath'd earth!
> Earth of the slumbering and liquid trees!
>
> * * *
>
> Far-swooping elbow'd earth—rich apple-blossom'd earth!
> Smile, for your lover comes.

In the year Edgar Allan Poe (1809–1849) was born, Bryant had already published his youthful diatribe against Jefferson. Twenty-six years after Poe's death, when his body was moved from an unmarked grave, Bryant was the grand old man of American letters whose bearded portrait hung in many parlors along with those of Longfellow and Lowell and Whittier. Bryant was only one of the many American poets who stayed away from the ceremony in which a marker donated by some Baltimore schoolteachers was placed over Poe's grave. The only American poet present, in fact, was Walt Whitman, who later described the event and placed Poe "among the electric lights of imaginative literature, brilliant and dazzling, but with no heat." Bryant was an octogenarian, of course, and could not be expected to journey to Baltimore to pay tribute to a man whose reputation had steadily declined since Rufus Griswold's notorious memoir was published shortly after Poe's death. Still, the irony of Poe's eclipse is compounded by the fact that two years later, when he was eighty-three, Bryant presided over an unveiling by President Hayes of the first statue erected to the memory of an American poet: his friend Fitz-Greene Halleck. Here is still another measure of the distance between Bryant and Poe; one the established and recognized man of letters, the other the eccentric and erratic poet, short-story writer, and critic whose biography, for the nineteenth century at least, was of far more interest than his writings. Henry James expressed a widely held attitude toward Poe in this country when he remarked in his essay on Baudelaire that an enthusiasm for Poe was "the mark of a decidedly primitive stage of reflection," and today the mention of Poe's name is still the cause of uneasiness and disagreement among critics and literary historians.

By the time he was twenty-two Poe had written about half of his poetry and had published three volumes of verse: *Tamerlane and Other Poems* (1827), *Al Aaraaf, Tamerlane, and Minor Poems* (1829), and *Poems* (1831). The first volume, published anonymously "By a Bostonian," went almost completely unnoticed, and so did the other two. In the second, Poe printed a revised version of "Tamerlane" and added his long, obscure exploration of the world of dream and imagination, "Al Aaraaf." The third volume, issued shortly after he left West Point, is dedicated (ironically, one suspects) to "The U.S. Corps of Cadets."

These are poems of youth—Poe claims he wrote several when he was fourteen—and they abound in Byronic posturing and vague Shelleyan vaporings about stars and dreams and spirits of the dead. "Stanzas" has an epigraph from Byron, and "Tamerlane" is about a Byronic hero who rants about a passionate love and embodies the combination of pride and morbidity that Poe admired in *Childe Harold* and "Giaour." The themes that Poe was to develop in both poetry and fiction appear in "Tamerlane": pride, love, beauty, and death; and although the heroic conqueror gradually recedes in later poems into the poet-as-hero, Tamerlane remains a seminal figure in Poe's work. The poem in its original version was over four hundred lines, but Poe thought enough of it to revise it repeatedly until it was reprinted in 1845 with only 234 lines. In spite of the fact that these three volumes were greeted by an almost complete critical silence, they are important, since, with the exception of Bryant, they are the first publications in book form of the poems of a major American poet in the nineteenth century. Longfellow, two years older than Poe, did not publish *Voices of the Night* until 1839, and Emerson did not publish a volume of verse until 1847.

The poems themselves, however, are gropings, half-successful attempts to render that vision of Supernal Loveliness that Poe conceived of as the object of poetry throughout his life. His failure to accomplish his own incompletely defined aims can be measured by the almost total absence of communication exhibited in "Al Aaraaf." Shifting from the Byronic dramatic monologue of "Tamerlane," in which the hero defines his alienation in terms of his own superior passions and gifts, in "Al Aaraaf" Poe turns even farther away from the "real" world, placing its setting on a distant star. The Al Aaraaf of the title is the star in Cassiopeia discovered by the Danish astronomer Tycho Brahe in 1572; in Poe's hands it becomes an otherworldly Paradise, or, more accurately, Purgatory, on which the world of thought and physical sensation is left behind. This is the first of the many "Aidenns" and secluded vales and islands that are scattered through Poe's work. The narrative thread with its almost completely submerged allegory concerns the fall of Angelo, an earthborn youth, from the realm of the ideal because of his passion for the maiden Ianthe. His loss of innocence is followed by a fall to destruction as the lovers fail to heed the summons sent to them by Nesace, the presiding spirit of the wandering star. The *Paradise Lost* theme is explicit in several passages, including the lines: "They fell: for Heaven no grace imparts / To those who hear not for their beating hearts," and Milton is echoed directly and indirectly throughout the poem. In spite of some fine passages and dexterous handling of open iambic pentameter couplets, the poem's obscurity makes it a failure (even Poe later stated he did not understand it fully). It may be one of the reasons he was led to claim, in "The Poetic Principle," that there is no such thing as a long poem and that Milton preferred "Comus" to *Paradise Lost*. His pursuit of the "Idea of Beauty," here dramatized through the creation of a world apart from our own, was still so nebulous and unformed in his own mind that the poem falls just short of chaos.

Looking back at this poem and others through such short stories as "Ligeia" and "The Fall of the House of Usher" we can see more clearly the theme of the war of the spirit with the external world and the quest for Supernal Beauty, which is a dominant theme of both the poetry and fiction. His exploration of the world of fantasy and dream was in effect a denial of the value placed on the material world revealed through the senses, and was also a repudiation of Descartes and Locke. In search of the truths of the realm of Supernal Beauty that lay beyond the "real" world, Poe's efforts were directed toward stripping away its falsehoods. From "Al Aaraaf" to *Eureka,* Poe viewed man as an Israfel figure, existing in a fallen state and aspiring to return to an original wholeness by transcending physical reality, even at the price of self-destruction. Thus, unlike Emerson and the Transcendentalists, who approached their vision of the ideal *through* physical nature and achieved their sense of a monistic universe through positing a dualistic one, Poe approached his ideal through a *negation* of the physical, but paradoxically retained a dualistic universe while denying its assumptions. Richard Wilbur has aptly defined this process as a "mechanism of destructive transcendence," and in his view Poe's subject thus becomes the war between the poetic soul and the earthly self to which it is bound. We can see this in his tales about reunions with dead women, such as "Morella" and "Ligeia," where the narrators' attempts to become reunited with their ethereal heroines are the efforts of "fallen" men to merge themselves with "Psyche" figures associated with the absolute. Or we can see in Poe's voyage tales, such as "MS. Found in a Bottle" and *The Narrative of Arthur Gordon Pym,* an allegory of the poet's journey toward discovery of the unknown and his destruction at the moment of discovery.

But to demonstrate how Poe effectively achieves his aims in his tales is only to show how imperfectly they are accomplished in his poems. This is not to suggest that Poe ever considered himself other than a poet. "With me poetry has been not a purpose, but a passion," he wrote in the preface to *The Raven and Other Poems* in 1845, and we have no reason to doubt him. It is in "The Poetic Principle" (1850) where he makes his aims most explicit, and it is this essay that has mis-led many critics of Poe into believing that his poems achieve what he lucidly expounds in his critical prose. "The struggle to apprehend the Supernal Loveliness," he writes, echoing Shelley, is "the desire of the moth for the star." Invoking the Bards, the Minnesingers, and Thomas Moore, Poe asserts that music comes closest to expressing Supernal Beauty and arrives at his famous definition of poetry as *"The Rhythmical Creation of Beauty."* Beauty, therefore, is the only province of the poem, not truth, or morality—Poe's comments to this effect are legion—and "the *vagueness* of exaltation," as he wrote in a letter to Lowell in 1844, "aroused by a sweet air (which should be strictly indefinite and never too strongly suggestive) is precisely what we should aim at in poetry."

Poetry, then, is itself the subject of Poe's verse. Not until Wallace Stevens would any American poet be similarly con-cerned with the relationship of imagination to reality. The difference between them lies in the fact that Poe denies reality and ultimately is defeated by his inability to make his poems convey the world of dream, whereas Stevens, starting from reality, makes his poems out of the continuing tension be-tween it and the imagination. For Poe the pursuit of Beauty becomes finally a self-defeating one. The absence of ideas and his refusal to express any emotion other than the aesthetic one lead to a repetition of private images and symbols without referents and to a distortion of language so severe that it threatens to break down completely. In "Dream-Land" (1845) the reader is plunged directly into an unknown and unknow-able world, "Out of SPACE—out of TIME," where there are

> Bottomless vales and boundless floods
> And chasms, and caves, and Titan woods,
> With forms that no man can discover
> For the tears that drip all over;

Mountains toppling evermore
Into seas without a shore;
Seas that restlessly aspire,
Surging, unto skies of fire;
Lakes that endlessly outspread
Their lone waters—lone and dead,—
Their still waters—still and chilly
With the snows of the lolling lily.

This is a hypnagogic world of fantasy and dream that leads directly into impressionism and surrealism. It has about as much relation to reality as Roderick Usher's underground vault illuminated by an unknown source of light—or the "caverns measureless to man" and "lifeless ocean" of Coleridge's "Kubla Khan," which it resembles in tone as well as language.

There is evidence that as Poe abandoned poetry for the short story he gradually learned that even the most evanescent subjects must be captured not by the hit-or-miss techniques of "Al Aaraaf" but must be subjected to discipline and form. His stories are examples of his own suspicion of inspiration and his recognition of the function of craftsmanship: "carefully, patiently, and understandingly to combine" in order to achieve the desired effect. Perhaps he learned his lesson too well, as the evidence of "The Raven" (1844), "The Bells" (1845), and "Annabel Lee" (1849) suggests. Even if we cannot accept literally "The Philosophy of Composition" (1846) as a description of the composition of "The Raven," it still clearly demonstrates Poe's attitude that a poem was the product of deliberate efforts to create a certain effect by the combination of sounds and images.

Out of his total output of fifty poems, then, only a handful have real poetic value. His anthology piece, "To Helen" (1831), certainly deserves the popularity it has had; the other "To Helen" (1848), a dream poem addressed to Sarah Helen Whitman, is also good, although it reflects Poe's poverty of imagination at this point in his life by echoes of images and phrases from earlier poems. "To One in Paradise" (1834) is one of his finest, with its beautiful last stanza:

> And all my days are trances,
>   And all my nightly dreams
> Are where thy grey eye glances,
>   And where thy footstep gleams—
> In what ethereal dances,
>   By what eternal streams.

And there are memorable lines scattered throughout his work:

> While from a proud tower in the town
> Death looks gigantically down.
>   ("The City in the Sea," 1831)

and

> Hast thou not torn the Naiad from her flood,
> The Elfin from the green grass, and from me
> The summer dream beneath the tamarind tree?
>   ("Sonnet—To Science," 1829)

"Eldorado" (1849), in addition to being a satire of the Gold Rush and a moralistic commentary on the vanity of human wishes, is a demonstration of the direction Poe's interest in sound for its own sake was taking him. This poem should be seen for what it is: a skillful and deliberate blending of sound and meaning; one of the few of Poe's poems, in fact, that has a clearly paraphrasable meaning. Finally, "The Bells" is a brilliant *tour de force* in the use of sounds, yet here once more the sound is used not solely for its own sake but, surprisingly for one so generally hostile to allegory, is constructed on a very obvious and forthright allegory of the four ages of man.

The assessment of Poe continues, but one thing is clear. He is one of the most important American poets of the nineteenth century. Untypically American in many ways, he is typically American in one: his denial of the old and his search for the new. In an age in which the immediate past and European traditions and institutions were being denied by writers and statesmen alike, no writer went further than Poe in his complete denial not only of the past but of the present as well. The romanticized picture that Baudelaire paints of Poe as the *poète maudit* cast adrift in an unsympathetic environment of philistines is exaggerated, yet Poe in his art was uncompromising in his fidelity to a vision of the unattainable knowledge of beauty. In this respect he was alone among his contemporaries.

CHAPTER FOUR

The Transcendentalists

Ralph Waldo Emerson, Henry David Thoreau, Christopher Pearse Cranch, Jones Very

The Transcendentalist poets come the closest of any in nineteenth-century America to being a "school" of poetry. They were bound together by a commonly held set of ideas and attitudes that are loosely grouped under the heading of Transcendentalism. Many thought of themselves as poets, while others, who thought of themselves as ministers, reformers, or seers, found the production of verse a satisfying outlet for the visions of spiritual unity and mystic idealism that crowded upon them singly and in groups. The Transcendentalists, as they were first described by their enemies, were radicals—New England visionaries whose shared ideas included the divinity of man, an intuitive idealism, self-improvement as the way to social improvement, individualism, and freedom and spontaneity in life and art. What they lacked in numbers and sympathizers they made up for in energy, will, perseverance, single-mindedness, and literary talent. They wrote, published, and spoke to such effect that their influence on American thought and letters has become deep and permanent. In Emerson, American poetry for the first time found a truly native voice; Freneau and Bryant had both championed the cause of a native American poetry—and so had Poe—and both had shown in their poetry a mild tendency toward a romantic identification with nature, but Emerson, working from a fully developed theory of the function of poetry, succeeded in breaking away from the influence of English nature poetry to produce something new and original.

Many of those associated with the Transcendentalists wrote poetry; it seemed to come to them naturally. Bronson Alcott (1799–1888), the author of the "Orphic Sayings" (1840) in *The Dial,* wrote verse that could just as easily have been put in prose. William Ellery Channing (1818–1901), Thoreau's walking companion, wrote volumes of verse, which Thoreau in one of his uncharitable moments described as "sublimo-slipshod." The Sturgis sisters, Caroline Sturgis Tappan (1818–1888) and Ellen Sturgis Hooper (1812?–1848), were gifted and intelligent women who wrote tributes to Emerson and graceful stanzas on art and life. Margaret Fuller (1810–1850) directed her enormous versatility and intellectual energy to the composition of some verses on the fullness of life.

Ralph Waldo Emerson's (1803–1882) poetry is an uneasy mixture of the traditional and the experimental—a mixture that reflects the conflicts in his own mind between his ideas about the nature and function of poetry and his strong sense, however much he tried to submerge it, of history and tradition. Emerson was steeped in the poetry of Donne, Herbert, Herrick, and Marvell, yet at an impressionable time in his career he discovered German Transcendentalism through the poetry and criticism of Coleridge and Wordsworth. As the chief spokesman, although not the chief theoretician, of American Transcendentalism, Emerson's thought was directed by the idealism and romanticism of the participants in that movement as well as by the intellectual rigors of the English Metaphysical poets and the Cambridge Platonists.

Like Poe, whom he contemptuously dismissed as "the jingle man," Emerson thought of himself throughout his life primarily as a poet. "I am born a poet," he wrote to his fiancée, Lydia Jackson, "of a low class without doubt, yet a poet.

That is my vocation. My singing, to be sure, is very 'husky,' and is for the most part in prose. Still I am a poet in the sense of a perceiver and dear lover of the harmonies that are in the soul and in matter, and specially of the correspondence between these and those." While both Poe and Emerson thought of themselves as intermediaries between another, purer, world and the world of men, and while both saw that the poet was the destined transmitter of his visions, each differed from the other in his conception of this privileged role. Emerson parallels Poe's flight into the world of Supernal Loveliness in his search for the world of spirit. But whereas Poe sought the destruction of the natural world in order to grasp an ephemeral reality that lay beyond it, Emerson sought a union of nature and spirit through the medium of language, which, if it was successful, would equate the word with the object and result in a truly symbolic poem. Poe, who became distracted by his own Byronic posturings in his efforts to set down his glimpses of the unknown, failed to bring off the correspondence between symbol and object that his aesthetic theories demanded. His rhythmic and resonant cadences failed to perform the symbolic functions he demanded of them. Emerson, too, had high hopes of giving poetic form to those "untaught sallies of the spirit" that revealed the fact beneath the natural symbol. But only in one or two poems was Emerson able to make the symbol and the meaning coalesce. When he did, in such poems as "Each and All" and "Days," he was on the verge of doing something quite new in American poetry, making the words themselves an organic part of the structure of the poem. But both Emerson and Poe, important as their theories are in shaping the direction American poetry was to take for the next hundred years, lacked the synthesizing power and the adventurous spirit that enabled Walt Whitman to answer Emerson's own call for a truly American poet.

Emerson as poet was a role player; he thought of himself as a kind of mage—a gifted seer and prophet—or as a Celtic bard in the tradition of Gray's *The Bard* or Macpherson's *Ossian*. He would assume the oracular role of the soothsayer, or shroud himself in the robes of "Saadi," the Persian poet. In all of these roles he saw himself as the divinely prompted spokesman transmitting knowledge that has always existed. The poet is not a creator, he tells us in the verse epigraph to his essay, "Fate," but an instrument that vibrates to impulses that have existed for all time: "the foresight that awaits / Is the same Genius that creates." He was fond of using the stock Romantic image of the Aeolian harp, played upon by the wind, to convey this idea. Both Emerson and Thoreau wrote poems about Aeolian harps because they suggest the poet's passive role in the creative process: that of merely transforming the inaudible sounds of the spiritual universe into audible poems.

His standards for his poetry were high but far from orthodox, and he expressed his own sense of inadequacy and frustration in an early draft of "Merlin," which, aside from his essay on "The Poet," reveals the most about his attitude toward poetry:

> I go discontented thro' the world
> Because I cannot strike
> The harp to please my tyrannous ear:
> Gentle touches are not wanted,
> These the yielding gods had granted.

These lines were later revised to express even more strongly his desire for a poetry that would be jarring and harsh; a poetry that would "make the wild blood start" in its freshness and novelty:

> Thy trivial harp will never please
> Or fill my craving ear;
> Its chords should ring as blows the breeze,
> Free, peremptory, clear.
> No jingling serenader's art,
> Nor tinkle of piano strings,
> Can make the wild blood start
> In its mystic springs.

The kingly bard
Must smite the chords rudely and hard,
As with hammer or with mace;
That they may render back
Artful thunder, which conveys
Secrets of the solar track,
Sparks of the supersolar blaze.

Emerson wrote this poem in 1846, when he was forty-three, the year he published his first volume of poetry. The poems collected in this first volume reflect the two contradictory tendencies in his poetry. On the one hand are the cryptic, elusive poems, such as "The Sphinx," with which he opens the volume; on the other are such conventional pieces as "Musketaquid" and "Concord Hymn." But Emerson was not trying for popular verse, and he made no compromises with his readers in a collection with titles such as "The World-Soul," "Uriel," "Hamatreya," "Astraea," and "Initial, Daemonic, and Celestial Love." Even those poems with such everyday titles as "The Humble-Bee" and "Berrying" lead the unwary reader far from the simple nature poetry of Bryant, even though there are echoes of Bryant in them.

Technically, Emerson's poems are the freest and loosest of any American's up to his time. By example as well by his criticism Emerson was working to release poetry from the restrictions of meter and language that he felt worked against uninhibited expression. He had said in "The Poet" that "it is not meters, but a meter-making argument that makes a poem," thereby placing the form of the poem in a position subservient to its thought. The irregularity of meter in many of his poems suggests that their arguments did indeed suggest meters of their own. In many this impression is reinforced by his use of a four-stress line, which Oliver Wendell Holmes maintained most nearly matched the rhythms of human breathing. This rhythm of inhalation and exhalation no doubt appealed to Emerson's theories of the principle of action and reaction, but in many of his poems it is distracting, or at least ineffective. "The Sphinx," for example, follows this pattern, although the lines are divided in two to form an eight-line stanza:

> The Sphinx is drowsy,
>   Her wings are furled:
> Her ear is heavy,
>   She broods on the world.
> "Who'll tell me my secret,
>   The ages have kept?—
> I awaited the seer
>   While they slumbered and slept:—

The hopping rhythm of such lines makes Emerson seem almost as much a jingle man as Poe. Still, in the same poem we find the lines, "Sea, earth, air, sound, silence, / Plant, quadruped, bird," to remind us that Emerson was not afraid to try for unusual effects by departing drastically from conventional metrical practice. Another striking example that illustrates his belief in the relationship of form and thought are these lines from "Merlin":

> Bird that from the nadir's floor
> To the zenith's top can soar,—
> The soaring orbit of the muse exceeds that
>   journey's length.

The last line is an obvious effort to break out of a poetic mold and may perhaps derive as much from Pope's *Essay on Criticism,* with its advice to relate sound and sense, as it does from Emerson's own theories of organic form.

Poems contains most of Emerson's best poetry, even though his second volume, *May-Day and Other Pieces* (1867), includes such well-known pieces as "Brahma," "Two Rivers," and "Waldeinsamkeit." "Days," the poem Emerson himself thought his best, is also one of his more regular. In fact, his successes, as Stephen Whicher has noted, all tend to be more

regular in form, even though his freer ones are more interesting for what they try to do.

At the heart of Emerson's creative impulse lies his belief
in the symbolic correspondence that exists between all objects
in the created universe and the reflection of this correspondence in the unseen world of spirit. The poet exists, he says, to
recognize the presence of this "divine *aura*" and employ the
symbolic qualities of language itself to transform it into poetry. Words themselves are symbols, but in his heavy reliance
on the symbolic properties of "truth-speaking things" Emerson does not always succeed in making the truth clear. When
he does attempt to make the relationship between image and
idea clear to the reader, he leans too often toward discursiveness and direct statement rather than upon the organic fusion
of the two through image and metaphor that was his aim.
"Seashore" (1856), a late poem, is an example of this tendency
merely to list the ideas suggested by the image rather than to
make the image work symbolically to reveal them:

> Behold the Sea,
> The opaline, the plentiful and strong,
>
> * * *
>
> Sea full of food, the nourisher of kinds,
> Purger of earth, and medicine of men;
> Creating a sweet climate by my breath,
> Washing out harms and griefs from memory,
> And, in my mathematic ebb and flow,
> Giving a hint of that which changes not.

But when he is able to make the image work as a vital symbol
of an idea, he can do it with considerable compression and
power. He does this in "The Snow-Storm" (1835), which
opens with a series of closely observed details. The second
stanza makes some shrewd analogies and contrasts between
the natural forms created by the winds of the storm and the
man-made forms of houses and barns. The closing lines state
the idea suggested by the images throughout the stanza, but

the effect is not a tag line or moral; rather it is the kind of "organic" outgrowth of the poem itself that Emerson tried for in many of his poems but only rarely succeeded in achieving:

> Leaves, when the sun appears, astonished Art
> To mimic in slow structures, stone by stone,
> Built in an age, the mad wind's night-work,
> The frolic architecture of the snow.

In "Days" (1851) he does achieve that rare combination of form and idea that makes the images in the poem truly symbolic. The poem is written with a compression of thought and language that Emerson always sought after but too often slipped away from into mere aphorism in one direction or diffuseness in the other. In "Days" Emerson comes closest to perfection in presenting that central paradox of his own desire to live each day to its fullest: enjoying the commonplace pleasures of the natural world while aspiring to a transcendent fulfillment of the soul. In this poem Emerson sustains the desired balance between image and idea, by means of contrasting images: diadems and fagots, bread and stars, morning wishes and herbs and apples. His tragic self-awareness and condemning introspection revealed in the closing lines have been prepared for by a vital use of figurative language that is neither empty nor affected.

In "Each and All" (1834) Emerson also succeeds in building up a series of images that contain and are related to the central idea: "I yielded myself to the perfect whole." And "Two Rivers" (1856), although not as concrete in its use of imagery, is one of his most tightly structured poems, with the closing stanza working both to unify the two levels on which the poem is working and to give it a circular structure by echoing the language of the opening stanza. "Two Rivers" is exceptional in its merging of symbol and idea through attention to structure. "Days" and "Two Rivers" show that Emerson could write good poetry in conventional verse forms. In these poems, in which his role as a "liberating god" is played down, he is writing with the full weight of the English literary tradition behind him. And even though we find some characteristic Emersonian touches, such as the dervishes of "Days" or the "goblin strong" of "Two Rivers," he avoids by and large the eccentricities of diction, rhyme, and meter of his experimental poems.

Of the latter, the most interesting are "Uriel" (1846), an adroit mingling of satire, allegory, and transcendental doctrine; the "Ode Inscribed to W. H. Channing" (1846), an attack on the Mexican War; and "Merlin" (1846), which in both technique and attitude looks forward to Whitman:

> With the pulse of manly hearts;
> With the voice of orators;
> With the din of city arts;
> With the cannonade of wars;
> With the marches of the brave;
> And prayers of might from martyrs' cave.

And these lines from an early draft of the same poem outline the same program for a new poetry that Emerson called for in his conclusion to "The Poet":

> I will not read a pretty tale
> To pretty people in a nice saloon
> Borrowed from their expectation,
> But I will sing aloud and free
> From the heart of the world.

But if Emerson's search for the ideal poet ended with the appearance of Walt Whitman, Emily Dickinson also closely followed many of Emerson's attitudes and techniques. Emerson's poems on nature subjects, such as "The Humble-Bee" (1837), occasionally reflect the same kind of close observation that gives Emily Dickinson's poetry its freshness and its individual angle of perception:

> Insect lover of the sun,
> Joy of thy dominion!

> Sailor of the atmosphere;
> Swimmer through the waves of air;
> Voyager of light and noon;
> Epicurean of June;
> Wait, I prithee, till I come
> Within earshot of thy hum,—
> All without is martyrdom.

The language here is somewhat more relaxed than in the best of Dickinson; still, the hesitant movement of the lines, the oblique rhymes, the direct address to the subject of the poem and the straining for originality in the figurative language all point to Emily Dickinson's lifelong effort to create a poetry that would contain the full impact of a momentary perception.

The poetry Emerson wrote in his freer moods is a release from the restraints of eighteenth-century verse, and an adaptation of the Romantic verse of Wordsworth and Coleridge that strains toward becoming a truly native American voice. The need for such a voice was felt by Freneau and Bryant, in whose poetry we can hear the first tentative notes. Emerson, who indulged in no self-deception, admitted he could not, like the great poet he wanted to be, "make lofty arguments in stately, continuous verse, constraining the rocks, trees, animals, and the periodic stars to say my thoughts." But this conception of the role of the poet as a "liberating god" gave his poetry whatever vitality and force it has. He was torn between the desire to be free and the tendency to be discursive and diffuse. The aphoristic quality of his essays carries over to his verse, in which there are many memorable lines but only a scattering of good poems. He is truly a transitional poet, making use of nature in ways first explored in America by Bryant, but working toward the kind of bardic freedom that Whitman was finally able to achieve.

As a writer in verse, Henry David Thoreau (1817–1862) had even less success than Emerson in putting his theories of what constitutes a good poem into practice. As a student at

Harvard and during his early years in Concord, Thoreau was intensely interested in writing poetry. Emerson, who was actively seeking the paragon he described in "The Poet," wrote to Carlyle that Thoreau's poetry was "the purest strain and the loftiest that has yet peeled from this unpoetic American forest." But over the years, as Thoreau's promise as a verse-writer waned, Emerson was forced to curb his early enthusiasm. His final judgment upon the poetry of Thoreau recognizes the fact that he "had the source of poetry in his spiritual perception," but that he "wanted a lyric facility and technical skill." Today, in spite of an increased interest in the experimental nature of Thoreau's verse, we are forced to agree pretty much in substance with this judgment of his earliest champion. It is quite possible, in fact, using Thoreau's own wide application of the term, to say that his best poem is *Walden* (1854). One might go even further and suggest, as he did in this untitled poem (1849), that his greatest poem remained unwritten:

> My life hath been the poem I would have writ,
> But I could not both live and utter it.

Although Thoreau wrote poems throughout his life, his greatest period of activity was during the years 1839 to 1842. Many were published in Margaret Fuller's *The Dial,* but she —and Emerson—rejected many more. On one occasion, Emerson, after grudgingly accepting a poem Thoreau had refused to alter into more regular form, remarked, "Our tough Yankee must have his tough verse." Altogether, Thoreau published seventy poems, most of them in his 1868 edition of *A Week on the Concord and Merrimac Rivers.* A collection of fifty poems assembled by H. S. Salt and F. B. Sanborn was published in 1895 as *Poems of Nature,* but the bulk of some one hundred and fifty additional poems remained in manuscript in various degrees of completion and were not printed until 1943.

What this full collection reveals is a craftsman and experimenter who brought to his poetry the same meticulous atten-

tion he devoted to his prose. Making use of contrast and paradox as structural and thematic devices, Thoreau as a poet was
himself paradoxical. The paradox stemmed from his theory
of poetry as the direct utterance of the inspired seer and his
practice of carefully polishing and revising his poems. Emerson's claim that it is "the meter-making argument" that makes
the poem could easily have been made by Thoreau, whose
own ideas of organic form drove him to seek new ways to
break the bonds of conventional meter and diction. But many
of his poems were actually composed by culling fragments of
verse and prose from his journals. "Inspiration" (1863), one
of his longest poems, is one of his most self-contradictory. The
origin of poetry, which comes, "unsought, unseen," is God, or
the Over-Soul:

> A clear and ancient harmony
>   Pierces my soul through all its din,
> As through its utmost melody,—
>   Farther behind than they—farther within.

But this paean to inspiration is, as the editor of his poems has
discovered from the manuscript, assembled from many bits
and pieces of verse and prose that were revised and reshaped
several times before it reached the form in which it was first
published posthumously in the *Commonwealth*. So while his
poems may look like Merlin's "artful thunder," they are highly
polished gems with some of the surfaces deliberately left
rough.

Thoreau's early poems show a strong preference for Milton and Herbert, as in "Life Is a Summer's Day" and "Friendship" (1838), one of three poems with this title, which has
obvious debts to Herbert:

> I think awhile of Love, and while I think,
>   Love is to me a world,
>   Sole meat and sweetest drink,
>   And close connecting link
>   Tween heaven and earth.

But the poems he wrote and published after leaving Harvard begin to show strong similarities to Wordsworth, perhaps due to Emerson's influence. "My Books I'd Fain Cast Off, I Cannot Read" (1842), written in regular quatrains and published in *The Dial*, parallels Wordsworth's "Expostulation and Reply" and "The Tables Turned." Wordsworth's idea of the recollection of natural beauty that refreshes the soul is developed by Thoreau in one of his best early poems, "Within the Circuit of This Plodding Life" (1842). The sights he sees and the sounds he hears, "within the verdure of my mind" look backward to Thoreau's own "The Inward Morning" (1841), in which he makes even more explicit the correspondence between the inner and outer worlds. The movement of the blank verse of "Within the Circuit" is more Miltonic than Wordsworthian, however; one sentence runs for twenty-one lines, and he is particularly daring in three lines that run with no marked pause. The diction has a toughness and suppleness that reminds us more of Emerson than Wordsworth: "Beneath a thick integument of snow"; and the best line of the poem could have been written by Robert Frost: "The upland pastures where the Johnswort grew." Two other poems, "Music" and "Manhood," both unpublished, also contain evidence that Wordsworth provided the stimulus, in imagery and diction, for blank-verse treatments of the renewing powers of the natural world.

But Thoreau's best poems are not pale imitations of Wordsworth; they are efforts to apply his theory of the harmony of the real and the ideal in a Swedenborgian vision even more intense than Emerson's. In "The Inward Morning" the natural world is described as a reflection of an inward state of mind in a direct application of Emerson's statement that "nature is a symbol of spirit." The entire physical universe becomes a metaphor for ways of seeing and feeling, and in this poem the sun is used as a symbol of the "inner light" of intuition, which, like the divine spark of the Puritans, illuminates the being of the regenerate man. Thoreau is an Adamic man—reborn with each new dawn of his own consciousness—for whom nature is not so much inspiration as confirmation of the truths he intuitively knows.

The many irregularities in rhythm are as deliberate as they are in Emerson's verse, for the same reasons, since Thoreau was also trying to break away from convention by working experimentally with a variety of verse forms. His lines range from dimeters to hexameters, with a preference for the short line, which best suited his aphoristic and gnomic utterances. He published a number of couplets as separate poems:

> Each summer sound
> Is a summer round

and many of his longer poems seem gatherings of these fleeting *aperçus*. Or they approach free verse and even prose in their irregularities of rhythm and flatness of diction:

> What's the railroad to me?
> I never go to see
> Where it ends.
> It fills a few hollows,
> And makes banks for the swallows,
> It sets the sand a-blowing,
> And the blackberries a-growing.

These lines from *Walden* (1854) (as well as the couplet above, from the *Natural History of Massachusetts*, 1842) are good examples of the difficulty of judging some of Thoreau's poetry, since they are more or less integrated with the prose surrounding them and depend for full understanding upon an awareness of the symbolic meanings of the imagery that is developed in the prose text. This is less true of the railroad poem than of two others in *Walden:* "It is No Dream of Mine" and "Light-Winged Smoke, Icarian Bird." The first of these presents in its most compressed form the water-and-sky imagery that form the substance of the key "Ponds" chapter, while "Light-Winged Smoke," his more praised poem, comes at a point where it illuminates the fire-and-hearth image of the "House-Warming" chapter.

But Thoreau's use of the smoke image, suggesting the tangible and the intangible, as well as the upward movement of the spirit from the physical to the spiritual, comes closest to achieving the unity of subject and idea that lies at the heart of the notion of organic form. F. O. Matthiessen has asked us to compare this poem to Emerson's "The Snow-Storm," adding that its use of the smoke image to make a statement of his idea produces a work truly natural in the object and truly human in the effect—as Coleridge said the artist must do—and evolves in an appropriate form.

What we see in Thoreau as a poet is a falling short of his own aims. Like Emerson, Thoreau felt that life and art were both ways of reflecting the universal; and he too felt that the function of poetry was primarily moral or ethical: if one presented the natural images in the language of poetry they would speak for themselves as symbols of the Over-Soul. "As for style of writing," he wrote, "if one has anything to say, it drops simply and directly, as a stone falls to the ground." This is at once the strength and the weakness of his poetry, which often has the power of direct statement vividly compressed but more often veers too closely to prose. Lowell's condemnation of his lines as "worsification" is merely patronizing; he hit closer to the mark when he grudgingly admitted Thoreau had "exquisite mechanical skill in the shaping of sentences and paragraphs, or (more rarely) short bits of verse for the expression of a detached thought, sentiment, or image."

As he came to discover he could demonstrate his true mastery in the art of prose, Thoreau extended his definition of the poet and poetry to include it. His best poetry is in the finely tuned cadences of *Walden;* yet the verses he wrote show he is an important nineteenth-century experimenter: his handling of various line-lengths within a single poem, his highly developed symbolic imagination with its attempts at fusion of image, language, and object, and his precision of language point in the direction of both Whitman and Emily Dickinson.

One of Emerson's most loyal and ardent supporters was Christopher Pearse Cranch (1813–1892), whose contributions of verse to *The Dial* are among the best it published. Cranch

was one of a small band of Transcendentalist Unitarian ministers, including James Freeman Clarke and William Henry
Channing, who migrated to Cincinnati in 1835. In the *Western Messenger,* which he helped to edit, Cranch printed an
early review (1837) of Emerson's "American Scholar" and
wrote several articles in defense of Emerson. In 1839 he wrote
one of his most strongly Transcendental poems, "Correspondences," which Margaret Fuller printed in *The Dial* in 1841.
The poem develops in a long, metrically free line, which seems
to be a forerunner of Whitman's free verse, the familiar Transcendentalist doctrine of the correspondence between the natural and the spiritual worlds that Emerson had propounded
in *Nature* (1836):

All things in Nature are beautiful types to the soul that will
    read them;
  Nothing exists upon earth, but for unspeakable ends.
Every object that speaks to the senses was meant for the spirit:
  Nature is but a scroll—God's hand-writing thereon.

One of Cranch's poems most clearly expressing his admiration for Emerson was written apparently soon after attending one of his lectures and meeting him personally. "The
Prophet Unveiled" (1844) contains a description of a "prophet"
whose features and lecture-hall mannerisms correspond closely
to those of the man whom he was later to call "the master-
mind of New England." It might be noted parenthetically
that Cranch was perhaps the only member of the Transcendental Club with a comic sense; his caricatures of various
members, including the one of Emerson as a "transparent eye-
ball" with long, spidery legs, puncture the inflated self-esteem
that was one of the group's more vulnerable characteristics.

"Enosis" (1880), the best-known of Cranch's poems, was
also written under the influence of Emerson's lectures, and
describes in a less vaporous and more accessible form the Transcendental idea of the unity of soul and matter. Another poem
on the same subject, written in tripping tetrameter couplets,
called forth from Poe the grudging remark in "The Literati"

that Cranch was "one of the least intolerable of the school of Boston transcendentalists." It was published in the first issue of *The Dial.*

Cranch collected these and other poems in *Poems* (1844) and dedicated them to Emerson "as an imperfect testimony of regard and grateful admiration." Emerson's response to this adulation was lukewarm, however, since apparently by this time his enthusiasm for Cranch's poetry had cooled, just as it had for both Thoreau's and Very's. Cranch continued to write verse throughout his life, and was an Emersonian to the end. His *Ariel and Caliban, With Other Poems* (1886) is full of poems influenced by Emerson, and contains an epitaph, "Ralph Waldo Emerson," which Cranch considered one of his best poems. In many ways Cranch is typical of the minor writers of verse who were drawn to the Transcendentalist group. But unlike Bronson Alcott, William Ellery Channing, and Margaret Fuller, he had some talent for poetry, however small, and his effusions on Transcendentalism have the redeeming qualities of directness and clarity that are so rarely found among the others.

Another poet for whom Emerson had high hopes and in whom he took a special interest was a young classical tutor and divinity student at Harvard, Jones Very (1813–1880). Very was first brought to Emerson's attention by Elizabeth Peabody, who had read some of his poems and was struck by their spiritual and Swedenborgian qualities. The first meeting between Emerson and Very, arranged by Peabody in 1838, seemed to the older man to be a fulfillment of his hopes for a new poetry. Very's intense spirituality, amounting to a religious fervor, seemed at first to Emerson to promise much. But Very was so intensely devout and so single-minded in his conviction that he was a special messenger from God that he seemed to his students and colleagues at Harvard to be insane. Both his personal behavior and his poems suggested he was directly in touch with Universal Reason, or the Over-Soul, and these were reasons enough for Emerson and others of the Transcendental circle not only to accept him but to find in him a stimulus and an inspiration.

Nevertheless, Very's behavior at Harvard eventually became so eccentric that he was asked to leave, and he spent a month in an insane asylum in the fall of 1838 before returning to live with his family in Salem. Frequent visits to Emerson in Concord resulted in Emerson's offer to help him publish an edition of his poems. These visits also gradually caused Emerson to revise his original opinion of Very, whom he came to find too otherworldly for his taste. Emerson sympathized with Very, who in many respects embodied the ideals he had set forth in "The American Scholar," *Nature,* and "The Poet," but Very's almost wholly passive character, his refusal to exert his will, and his ignorance of and contempt for the world around him eventually forced Emerson to reject him. "Here is Simeon the Stylite," Emerson confided to his journal, "religion divorced, detached from man, from the world, from science and art; grim, unmarried, insulated, accusing; yet true in itself, and speaking things in every word. The lie is in the detachment; and when he is in the room with other persons, speech stops as if there were a corpse in the apartment."

In spite of his rejection of Very as an influence and friend, Emerson saw his small book of writings through the press. *Essays and Poems* (1839) contained sixty-five poems and three critical essays on "Epic Poetry," "Shakespeare," and "Hamlet." Fifty-five of the poems were Shakespearean sonnets, many with an added foot in the concluding line; the others were written in a variety of stanzas, usually iambic pentameter or tetrameter quatrains.

The rest of Very's life was spent in preaching and living a quiet life in Salem. He continued to write verses, however, many of which were published in local newspapers. He sent some poems to Emerson, two of which were published in *The Dial* in 1842. In 1883, three years after Very's death, William P. Andrews edited *Poems by Jones Very.* The edition was practically exhausted in three years, and in 1886 a complete edition, *The Works of Jones Very,* was prepared by Very's sisters,

Frances and Lydia. This edition, like many "complete works," has the unfortunate effect of making Very look much worse than he is, since many of the poems should never have been printed. There is an annoying repetitive quality about his poems when they are read in bulk, an impression that is heightened by the slipshod editing that caused over twenty of them to be printed more than once, and one of them three times in the same volume.

Very's poems are concerned largely with nature and religion. His nature poetry recalls Philip Freneau and William Cullen Bryant, but he is closer in spirit to Edward Taylor in America, and Herbert, Vaughan, Traherne, and Blake in England. His mysticism, his complete submission to the divine will of an explicitly Christian God, set him apart from the strenuous pantheism of the Transcendentalists. Very, in his serene mystical acceptance of his oneness with God, lived in a state of beatitude, with an unwavering faith in the absoluteness of truth, the sinfulness of worldly speculation, and the illusory nature of a life of willed action. Here, as Yvor Winters has noted, is the essential point of difference between Very and Emerson and his friends. The Transcendentalists could think about the mystical state, but they could not, or would not, live in one.

But Very could, and his poems are reports of his experience of a profound and utterly submissive spiritual life. In them are assertions such as this in the opening lines of "The Hand and Foot" (1839):

> The hand and foot that stir not, they shall find
> Sooner than all the rightful place to go:

The submissiveness was directed toward the achievement of a perfect relationship with God, a return to Adamic innocence. The poems are filled with references to rebirth and reawakening: a new life made whole through the acknowledgement of God's omnipotence. "The New Birth" (1839) describes the mystical vision that follows such acquiescence and humility:

And from before man's vision melting fade
The heavens and earth;—their walls are falling now.

It ends with a tribute to the liberating powers of the perception of God:

And I a child of God by Christ made free
Start from death's slumbers to Eternity.

Some of Very's poems recall the meditative poetry of Taylor. One of these, "Life" (1839), develops the conceit of the tree as God, providing the source of strength in a way that recalls Taylor's Meditation 29, First Series, which, in a much more complex way, employs the imagery of grafting to make a similar statement. Very's poem also recalls both Herbert and Taylor in his allusion to the "bridegroom's supper." Here is the whole sonnet:

It is not life upon Thy gifts to live,
But, to grow fixed with deeper roots in Thee;
And when the sun and shower their bounties give,
To send out thick-leaved limbs; a fruitful tree,
Whose green head meets the eye for many a mile,
Whose moss-grown arms their rigid branches rear,
And full-faced fruits their blushing welcome smile,
As to its goodly shade our feet draw near;
Who tastes its gifts shall never hunger more,
For 'tis the Father spreads the pure repast,
Who, while we eat, renews the ready store,
Which at his bounteous board must ever last;
For none the bridegroom's supper shall attend,
Who will not hear and make his word their friend.

The spiritual transformation that Very describes in these extremely personal poems often identifies nature with purity and innocence. In "Nature" (1839) he shows man in tune with both nature and God, restored to Adamic innocence:

For he who with his Maker walks aright,
Shall be their lord as Adam was before;
His ear shall catch each sound with new delight,
Each object wear the dresses which then it wore;
And he, as when erect in soul he stood,
Hear from his Father's lips that all is good.

In this identification of nature with spirituality we can
see the attraction that Very's poems had for Emerson. To be
sure, other poets, such as Bryant, Longfellow, and Whittier,
were writing poems about the tonic effects of nature on their
spirits. But for them nature and poet remained separate enti-
ties; they had no inclination to be absorbed into trees and
brooks—except perhaps in death. Emerson, on the other hand,
had been preaching the necessity of bridging the gap between
the two elements of a dualistic universe and in Very he
thought he saw the poet who was doing just that. But Very's
mystical transcendence of the physical world was too uncompromising and too complete. His defiance of space and time
and his assertion of the reality of a universal Christian God,
coupled with his quietistic beliefs, finally set him apart as a
poet only peripherally associated with the Transcendentalists,
but also as one of the finest devotional poets in English. His
originality lies in his absolute and unwavering fidelity to his
vision of the spiritual life, couched in a spare, stark language
that derives its power less from his imaginative range than
from his spiritual intensity. Poems such as "The Created,"
"The Hand and Foot," "Man in Harmony With Nature," and
"The Garden" are among the best sonnets written in America
in the nineteenth century, and many passages in less successful
poems show the brilliance and clarity his mind was capable
of attaining.

CHAPTER FIVE

Wrestling With the Angel—Art

Frederick Goddard Tuckerman, Sidney Lanier, Herman
Melville, Walt Whitman, Emily Dickinson

The search for form and the search for self have always been
two major preoccupations of poets in America. In the second
half of the century five poets who had little else in common
were all engaged in this search. They seem also to have been
obeying Emerson's call for a new American poetry, each shaping his rhythms and language to forge an instrument adapted
to his own vision. In their various and individual efforts to
"make it new," Frederick Goddard Tuckerman, Sidney Lanier,
Herman Melville, Walt Whitman, and Emily Dickinson belong less to their own times than they do to the future.

Although his poems had no influence whatever on the
development of American poetry, one of the most interesting
nineteenth-century poets is the little-known Frederick Goddard
Tuckerman (1821–1873). As we look back on his work we see
that he was working outside the popular traditions, outside
the Keats-Shelley-Wordsworth vein, writing poetry in a highly
individualistic style. He stands with Henry Wadsworth Longfellow and Jones Very as one of the century's great sonneteers,
yet this unlikely company does not help define the peculiar
qualities of his strangely modern verse. His sonnets are un-

orthodox in structure and technique, his precision and clarity of language rival Emily Dickinson's, and his accurate and effective use of natural imagery goes far beyond anything by Bryant or Thoreau. Formally, he is not so radical as Whitman, Dickinson, or Lanier, yet he shares with all three a desire to work out formal problems for himself.

Tuckerman was the third son of a prominent Boston mercantile family. Edward, his oldest brother, was a professor of botany at Amherst College; his other brother, Samuel, was a musician and musicologist who published two collections of hymn tunes and anthems. His cousin Henry was a widely known journalist, essayist, biographer, and writer of sentimental verses. Frederick was named for an older cousin, whose accidental drowning is the subject of Wordsworth's "Lines upon a Young American, Mr. F. W. Goddard, who was drowned in the Lake of Zurich." He was brought up in a conventional Brahmin atmosphere, attended Harvard College, and was graduated from the law school in 1842. But as a young man he preferred the fields and woods of Massachusetts and Long Island to the urban life and social pressures that his family position demanded of him. Like that other Massachusetts naturalist, Henry Thoreau, Tuckerman withdrew from society and the world, but unlike Thoreau he remained a virtual recluse for most of his life. Shortly after his admission to the Suffolk County bar in 1844 he moved to Greenfield, in western Massachusetts, where he spent the remainder of his life as a gentleman of leisure and amateur botanist and astronomer. He became an authority on the flora of Franklin County, kept a journal on his astronomical observations, and published a few papers on eclipses. The two events that most affected his poetry were a four-day visit with Tennyson on the Isle of Wight in 1855, and the death of his wife when he was thirty-six. The death of Hannah Tuckerman is the subject of a remarkable series of meditative sonnets written during a long period of intense grief. The visit with Tennyson, which ended with his being presented with the manuscript of *Locksley Hall,* began a correspondence and friendship that lasted a lifetime and possibly had something to do with the publication of the English edition of his poems.

Tuckerman made only one effort to bring his poems before the public. In 1860 and 1861 he sent copies of a privately printed edition to a number of American writers, including Emerson, Hawthorne, Longfellow, Bryant, and Jones Very, and to Tennyson. Hawthorne and Emerson responded enthusiastically, but Longfellow was coolly polite. Emerson wrote that his narrative poem, "Rhotruda," was "a perfect success in its kind; and it should be bound up as a fifth in your friend Tennyson's 'Idyls,' as Chapman finished Marlowe's 'Hero and Leander.' " Hawthorne, in a kind reply, still doubted that the poems would be accepted widely, since they had "a kind of insight as when you look into a carbuncle to discover its hidden fire." In 1863 the London firm of Smith, Elder, and Company brought out an edition of *Poems,* and the following year Ticknor and Fields printed an American edition from the same plates, which were used again by Little, Brown in 1869. But by the time Tuckerman died in 1873 he was completely unknown, and it was not until 1909 that Walter Pritchard Eaton took an interest in him and published an essay about him in *The Forum.* This essay sparked the interest of Witter Bynner, who in 1931 published all the sonnets, including three later series that had remained in the possession of Tuckerman's granddaughter. In 1950 the Cummington Press printed Tuckerman's greatest poem, *The Cricket,* for the first time, and in 1965 N. Scott Momaday edited the *Complete Poems,* many of them from the original manuscripts.

Aside from a few poems such as "Rhotruda," "The Question," and "The Stranger," Tuckerman's stature as a poet depends entirely upon the 106 sonnets he wrote between 1854 and 1872 and upon his ode, *The Cricket.* The sonnets are a very personal and intimate record of his spiritual struggles with doubt, despair, melancholia, and grief, and his efforts to find meaning in a world where neither nature nor God provides the answers he seeks. In the first series of twenty-eight sonnets, which Tuckerman wrote before his wife died in 1857, he explores his relationship to nature and to God in a delib-

erate effort to escape a negative outlook as expressed in such
lines as this closing stanza from "Margites," one of his early
poems:

> I walk, unknowing where or why;
>   Or idly lie beneath the pine,
> And bite the dry-brown threads, and lie
>   And think a life well lost is mine.

Tuckerman was being pulled apart by the two sides of his
nature: as a naturalist he had a close and intimate knowledge
of the physical world and its arbitrary and contradictory ways;
as a man raised in a staunch Episcopalian family he felt the
need for a faith in God. In his moments of doubt he felt that
a knowledge of God should be as certain as his knowledge of
the flowers of Franklin County or the stars of his favorite
constellations: "God were not God, whom knowledge cannot
know." He states in Sonnet II the problem of resolving this
uncertainty into certainty:

> Wherefore, with this belief held like a blade,
> Gathering my strength and purpose still and slow,
> I wait, resolved to carry it to the heart
> Of that dark doubt in one collected blow,
> And stand at guard with spirit undismayed.

He proceeds, self-consciously at times and with much hesitation and backsliding, through a complex and closely inter-
woven sequence, to explore the difficulty and finally the impossibility of reconciling knowledge and intuition. By the end
of the first sequence he has discovered the not very new truth
that God resides in nature and that his existence can be
assured only by faith:

> No more thy meaning seek, thine anguish plead,
> But leaving straining thought and stammering word,
> Across the barren azure pass to God:
> Shooting the void in silence like a bird,
> A bird that shuts his wings for better speed.

The second series of thirty-seven sonnets is most inti-
mately concerned with the death of Hannah Tuckerman. Like
those in the first series, the sonnets are closely connected,
sometimes developing an idea or even continuing a sentence
from the preceding one. This often makes it hard to read
them singly; we have to read them in batches of three or four
to understand them. Just as the first series moves from doubt
to religious certainty, the second begins with feelings of profound grief and despair and ends with a reconciliation with
death and the hope of eventual reunion with his wife. The
joy of contemplating nature and living a life of personal fulfillment overrides his deep sense of loss:

> I would not hide my face from light, nor shun
> The full completion of this worldly day.
> What though beside my feet no other one
> May set her own to walk the forward way,
> I will not fear to take the path alone,
> Loving for thy sake things that cheer and bless
>
> (Sonnet XXXIV)

None of the forty-one sonnets of the last three series, written between 1864 and 1872, was published, and as sequences
they lack the thematic and structural unity that is so striking
in the two earlier ones. They make up for this lack, however,
with the deepened philosophical tone of a mind moving outward away from self toward questions about the world, the
reason, and religious faith. In these sonnets, no longer addressed to a reading public, Tuckerman avoids self-pity and
accepts his lot, moving away from his personal problems to
discover meanings in nature and in God. His true mission in
life, he finds, is to observe and record the workings of nature—
an activity that releases him from his earlier doubts and mis-
givings. At the end of Part V he arrives at an optimistic position, where he finds value in living a meaningful and personally satisfying life in the face of grief and doubt. This last
series of sixteen sonnets ends with the striking comparison of

himself in his youthful sadness to a tree struck by lightning in the spring, "Red-ripened to the heart: shedding its leaves / And autumn sadness on the dim spring day."

No summary can give an adequate impression of the unusual and sometimes even grotesque qualities of Tuckerman's poems, particularly his use of closely observed and accurately described natural phenomena and allusions so rare and obscure that Edmund Wilson was misled into thinking he had invented a private mythology. The sonnets follow no regular rhyme scheme, but rhyme is nevertheless used functionally throughout, giving emphasis to a thought here, an unusual image there.

Because his work is still relatively unknown, the temptation is strong to quote one's favorite poems and passages. One of my favorites, which illustrates his use of simple and direct language to create strange and quite disturbing effects, is Sonnet XVI, Second Series:

> Under the mountain, as when first I knew
> Its low dark roof and chimney creeper-twined,
> The red house stands; and yet my footsteps find,
> Vague in the walks, waste.balm and feverfew.
> But they are gone: no soft-eyed sisters trip
> Across the porch or lintels; where, behind,
> The mother sat, sat knitting with pursed lip.
> The house stands vacant in its green recess,
> Absent of beauty as a broken heart.
> The wild rain enters, and the sunset wind
> Sighs in the chambers of their loveliness
> Or shakes the pane—and in the silent noons
> The glass falls from the window, part by part,
> And ringeth faintly in the grassy stones.

The only unusual words in the poem are the two flower names in the fourth line. The economy and precision of diction are unusual for the time—perhaps the only clue that it is a nineteenth-century poem is the *ringeth* of the last line. Part of the disturbing quality and the obscurity come from the fact that this is a twin-sonnet: the sisters referred to in line 5 are the subject of the preceding poem.

One of Tuckerman's principal sources of imagery is the floral world of Franklin County, Massachusetts. One seldom finds references to roses or daisies; instead we find stramony, windflowers, mullein stalks, vervain-spike, spurge, and pearl-wort. The descriptions, although poetic, have the accuracy of a botanist's notebook:

> Thin little leaves of wood fern, ribbed and toothed,
> Long curved sail needles of the green pitch pine,
> With common sandgrass, skirt the horizon line.

And he knew not only the flowers, but the birds, rocks, insects, and animals of every area he visited. He also knew the sea and the sky, both of which figure prominently in his verse. He seems to have suffered a lifelong fear of the water, and many of the sea images suggest an atmosphere of foreboding or despair. Many of these are used with stunning effect at the ends of his poems, where he often places his best lines, such as these from Sonnet X, Third Series (1860–1872):

> And this high rock beneath whose base the sea
> Has wormed long caverns, like my tears in me:
> And hard like this I stand, and beaten and blind,
> This desolate rock with lichens rusted over,
> Hoar with salt-sleet and chalkings of the birds.

The doubts, the uncertainties, the spiritual agonies, the grief, and the meditations on death that make up the substance of the five sonnet-series all reappear in Tuckerman's masterpiece, *The Cricket,* which he wrote late in his life. Bynner found this poem among his papers but dismissed it as "attic poetry" and did not print it with his sonnet collection. Yvor Winters has certainly gone too far in the opposite direction by declaring it the greatest poem in English of the century, but it deserves a place next to Bryant's "Thanatopsis"

and Whitman's "When Lilacs Last in the Dooryard Bloom'd"
as a great nineteenth-century attempt to confront the question
of death through the study of nature. But where both Whitman and Bryant thought they had found answers, Tuckerman
finds none. For him death remains a mystery that both defines and intensifies life.

The poem is a loosely structured five-part ode of 131 lines
in which the poet addresses the cricket and develops its symbolic identity with death. The cricket is heard but not seen,
and in its invisibility it arouses in its hearer both feelings of
dread and a sense of its ubiquity in nature. The cricket's dron-
ing overwhelms the hearer's senses and brings back the memory of "dim accents from the grave / To him who walketh
when the day is dim, / Dreaming of those who dream no more
of him, / With edged remembrances of joy and pain." But
although the poet is reminded again of his grief and forced
to confront the question of death, the cricket's song remains
unintelligible, furnishing none of the answers given by Bryant's generalized nature or Whitman's caroling thrush. He
does not despair at this unintelligibility, however, but com-
forts himself with the same attitude of optimism and happiness
in the act of living with which he concluded his sonnet series.
The dark questions raised by the cricket's song finally do not
matter, and the closing lines affirm the poet's resolve to live
on in the face of death:

> Even while we stop to wrangle or repine
> > Our lives are gone—
> > Like thinnest mist,
> Like yon escaping color in the tree;
> Rejoice! rejoice! whilst yet the hours exist—
> Rejoice or mourn, and let the world swing on
> Unmoved by cricket song of thee or me.

This brief description cannot do justice to the technical
virtuosity of the poem: the skillful and effective use of alliteration and rhyme, the loose structure that gives the poem the
quality of both a meditation and a dramatic monologue, the

careful building up of the symbolic properties of the cricket. Part II is especially fine in the way it shifts from an apostrophe to the cricket in Part I to the revery on death in Part III. The sound patterns are carefully combined to re-create the drowsiness of the scene:

> Rising from nets of river vines,
>   Winrows and ricks,
>   Above, beneath,
>   At every breath,
> At hand, around, illimitably
> Rising and falling like the sea,
> Acres of cricks!

Like that other poem about crickets, Emily Dickinson's "Further in Summer than the Birds," *The Cricket* celebrates a change in the hearer that takes place as he listens to the song of invisible singers. But whereas Emily Dickinson concentrates on the fact of death typified by her "spectral Canticle," Tuckerman turns from the futility of trying to become the "true interpreter . . . Content to bring thy wisdom to the world" and instead finds happiness and satisfaction through the acceptance of the baffling and contradictory attributes of the physical world. Both poets, however, experience the "Druidic Difference" that Emily Dickinson describes, and both experience the sense of loneliness and alienation from nature that the cricket's song imparts. Biographers have been tantalized by the question of whether Tuckerman and Emily Dickinson knew each other. They lived about twenty miles apart, and Emily knew Frederick's brother Edward and his family, who lived in Amherst. They were both writing highly original, deeply personal poetry in semiretirement. The poetry of both is marked by an obscurity that, as Edmund Wilson has remarked, contributes to one's general impression of a soliloquy not quite overheard. Add to this the striking coincidence that both poets wrote one of their best poems about crickets and we have the basis for some very interesting speculation, but there is no evidence to support the idea that either knew, or knew of, the other.

Not all of Tuckerman's poems are like the sonnets or like *The Cricket*. He wrote a number of quite conventional lyrics, sonnets, love poems, and narrative poems. He was not completely otherworldly either; he was widely read in Chaucer, Shakespeare, and other English poets. His narrative poem, "Rhotruda," uses the same plot as Longfellow's student's tale in *Tales of a Wayside Inn* (1863), and he tells the story in half the number of lines. But he is most significant for his experimental and individual poems. Like Whitman and Dickinson, he had roots in American Romanticism in general and Transcendentalism in particular. Yet he was no more a Transcendentalist than Emily Dickinson was. He was too interested in the things of this world to pay much attention to its Swedenborgian counterpart. Like Thoreau, he was a naturalist, but unlike Thoreau he did not see natural facts as symbols of spiritual ones. Instead he discovered that the complexity and variety of nature confirmed man's need to accept on faith what he cannot explain by reason. The sea, the flora and fauna of New England, the planets and the stars all provided a rich store of concrete images in which his abstract ideas are firmly embodied. In Tuckerman's poetry image becomes idea in ways foreign to much nineteenth-century poetry —one reason that the direct, fresh, often obscure but never hackneyed poems of this lover of poetry and gardens appeal to us today.

Time and circumstance combined against Sidney Lanier (1842–1881) to place him in a unique position in the history of American poetry. His youthful aspirations to be a scholar, a poet, or a musician were all partially fulfilled, yet his artistic energy and creative drive were frustrated by illness, poverty, and by the generally uncongenial atmosphere for art and poetry that prevailed in the South during the Reconstruction era. And, like other Southern writers, Lanier had trouble getting published in the North, at least until he had become well known.

Like other literary young men in the South, he had read the romances of Scott and Bulwer-Lytton, the poetry of Keats and Tennyson. He had also read Froissart's *Chronicles* and the German Romantics Novalis and Jean-Paul Richter. He had written poetry and fiction steadily since his middle teens, and his love of chivalry shows up in an unsuccessful novel, *Tiger-Lilies,* which he published in 1867. The few poems of any real worth that he wrote before 1874 were several bitter lyrics written during the darkest days of Reconstruction, in 1868. The best of these is "The Raven Days," with its tone of desperation. Another is "Laughter in the Senate," which contains this cynical portrait:

> The tyrants sit in a stately hall;
> They jibe at a wretched people's fall;
> The tyrants forget how fresh is the pall
>   Over their dead and ours.

> Look how the senators ape the clown,
> And don the motley and hide the gown,
> But yonder a fast-rising frown
>   On the people's forehead lowers.

Lanier published four of these in the New York literary weekly *Round Table* during 1868, but withheld two others, "Steel in Soft Hands" and "Burn the Stubble," probably because he felt they were too strong.

One of his best early poems, "Life and Song," was Lanier's first popular success. Written at the same time as the Reconstruction poems, it reflects his mood of frustration at seeing his career as author and poet fail to materialize. In one five-quatrain sentence he sings of his commitment to a life of art that he despaired of attaining. There is an irony in the closing lines, written when he had already made the decision to retire from teaching and return to his father's law office in Macon:

> *His song was only living aloud,*
> *His work a singing with his hand!*

The turning point in Lanier's life was 1874, his thirty-second year, when he decided to devote the remainder of what he knew would be a short life to poetry. While serving in the Confederate Army he had been captured and sent to prison at Point Lookout, Maryland, and when he was released he was a sick man. The rest of his life was devoted to bouts with tuberculosis, as well as poverty and indecision about his career. He supported himself and his family with a succession of jobs, periodically returning to his father's law office in Macon, before he finally went to Baltimore to become first flutist with the Peabody Symphony Orchestra. There he was able to turn his love of music to practical use and at the same time devote himself to the life of the artist of which he had dreamed. In 1879 he realized still another ambition, when he was appointed to the faculty of the newly founded Johns Hopkins University to lecture on poetry and the English novel.

Between 1868 and 1874 Lanier turned from Keats and Tennyson to Chaucer and Shakespeare as models. The influence of these two poets, whom he described as his masters, is seen in "Corn," his first long poem, a Cowleyan ode in which he makes an impassioned plea for agricultural reform in the deep South, where cotton was the single money-crop. As the Fugitive group of the 1920s was later to believe, Lanier thought that the hope of the South lay in an agrarian economy with diversified crops and a built-in resistance to the morally degrading and economically disrupting influence of "trade." Although Henry Timrod had eulogized the beauties of cotton in "The Cotton Boll" (1861), Lanier believed the cotton crops were too much at the mercy of market fluctuations, placing the cotton farmer in subjection to the banks and moneylenders; whereas corn, a food crop for man and beast, offered an alternative to the "games of Buy-and-Sell" that "turned each field into a gambler's hell." "Corn" was rejected by William Dean Howells of the *Atlantic Monthly* and by *Scribner's;* however, when it was published in *Lippincott's* magazine in 1875 it was an immediate nationwide success. One enthusiastic Philadelphia critic described it as "Keats at his best . . . with an American fibre in it." "Corn" was recognized as more than a versified agricultural tract. Its impassioned lyric passages, its rhythmic freedom, and its sturdy language caused Lanier to be regarded as a new and important poetic voice in America. With this public encouragement, Lanier in 1875 wrote "The Symphony," which develops at greater length his antipathy to "trade," his term for modern capitalism in the Gilded Age. It is technically a much more ambitious poem, full of references to Spenser, Sidney, the Bible, and Madame de Staël, but it is a step down from the impassioned lyricism of "Corn." More than half of the 358 lines are in tetrameter couplets; the rest have more metrical variety than any other poem he wrote. In the latter half he ranges from two-syllable couplets to heroic couplets, with refrains and lines of varying length, giving each instrument of the orchestra a different meter. The result is uneven: there are some striking natural images and some musical passages that look forward to his later musical style, mingled with an overuse of compound words and a perhaps unavoidable discursiveness. His response to the southern landscape, combined with his immersion in Shakespeare and Keats, work to produce the kind of natural imagery for which "The Marshes of Glynn" (1878) is justly celebrated. This passage from "The Symphony" shows how his close observation of nature is combined with an awareness of the tradition of English nature poetry:

> All modesties of mountain-fawns
> That leap to covert from wild lawns,
> And tremble if the day but dawns;
> All sparklings of small beady eyes
> Of birds, and sidelong glances wise
> Wherewith the jay hints tragedies;
> All piquancies of prickly burs,
> And smoothnesses of downs and furs
> Of eiders and of minevers;
> All limpid honeys that do lie
> At stamen-bases, nor deny
> The humming-birds' fine roguery,
> Bee-thighs, nor any butterfly;

The poem, as Lanier's biographer has noted, is less important as poetry than as protest, yet it can be safely said that it is one of the few poems about economic reform that has some literary merit. "The Symphony," following the success of "Corn," assured Lanier of the audience he had so long desired. When Lippincott published *Poems* in 1876, he was recognized as a promising poet, although the volume—the only one published during his lifetime—did not have a wide sale.

During the remaining five years of his life Lanier developed and matured the style for which he is now chiefly known —the lyrical, rhythmically complex, and melodically rich verse, with its echoes of Poe and Thomas Holley Chivers (1809–1858), its spiritual affinities with Emerson, and its sweeping lines often reminiscent of Whitman. But Lanier was not an imitator. He was searching for, and partially succeeded in finding, an original voice, which grew partly out of his ideas on the affinities between music and poetry and partly out of his interest in science, which led him to make the close qualitative study of metrics that he published as *The Science of English Verse* (1880).

In 1876 he wrote the beautiful love lyric to his wife, "Evening Song," and in 1878 he wrote an ambitious narrative piece, "The Revenge of Hamish." This poem is an exercise in the use of his "logoaedic dactyls," telling a story with a plot lifted wholesale from an episode in William Black's novel, *Macleod of Dare*. Lanier distilled all his reading of medieval balladry into this poem, which moves swiftly and irrevocably to a horrifying climax.

In Florida in 1877, where he had gone in an effort to recover from a severe tuberculosis attack, Lanier discovered that the close spiritual affinity he felt between himself and nature was confirmed by Emerson, whom he had first begun to read seriously. Emerson's religious interpretation of nature lay close to Lanier's own, and he was led to explore these attitudes further in "The Bee" and "A Florida Sunday," before giving them their most eloquent expression in "The Marshes of Glynn" (1878). The coastal regions of Georgia had impressed Lanier for many years, and this most important of his poems is an outgrowth of his lifelong habit of closely observing all natural scenery. It is also an indirect response to his belated reading of Whitman. Both influences may be seen in his earlier poem, "Song of the Chattahoochee" (1877), which uses a complex combination of rhythm and sound to produce incantatory effects like those of Poe's "Annabel Lee" and "Ulalume." But "The Marshes of Glynn," although it did not receive the widespread popularity of "Chattahoochee," is a greater artistic success. Lanier was experimenting again with the free-flowing "logoaedic dactyls" he had used in "The Revenge of Hamish," and he now achieved a greater degree of metrical freedom than he had yet done in any poem. But metrical freedom alone is not what makes "The Marshes of Glynn" his finest poem. The lights and shadows, the combinations of colorful words, the variety and heavy insistence on rhyme and alliteration all work to produce a skillfully wrought, original, and yet characteristic Lanier poem. Here is a sample passage from the poem, a poem from which it is difficult to extract a quotation:

As a silver-wrought garment that clings to and follows the
    firm sweet limbs of a girl.
Vanishing, swerving, evermore curving again into sight,
Softly the sand-beach wavers away to a dim gray looping of
    light.
And what if behind me to westward the wall of the woods
    stands high?
The world lies east: how ample, the marsh and the sea and
    the sky!
A league and a league of marsh-grass, waist-high, broad in
    the blade,
Green, and all of a height, and unflecked with a light or a
    shade,
    Stretch leisurely off, in a pleasant plain,
    To the terminal blue of the main.

One danger in this kind of "musical" poetry is that the meaning and the images themselves become lost in the response of the reader to the sensuous quality of the sound. For Poe, this was enough; in fact, that was his aim. But Lanier was not trying to lose the reader in a welter of sound. He believed in the prophetic function of the poet and in poetry as a medium of ideas, not as an escape from the tyranny of reason. Nevertheless, the lushness of his verse threatens to have a narcotic effect upon the reader, and in the long run, as Edmund Wilson has remarked, one is tempted to lose patience with him. Still, as Wilson also admits, there is something noble about him—both the man and the poetry—which is felt in the passionate, even feverish, strains of his later verse.

"The Marshes of Glynn" is the most successful of a series of projected "Hymns of the Marshes" that Lanier contemplated gathering into a new book. The other great poem of his last years is "Sunrise," which he planned to make the initial poem of the new volume. It was his last completed poem, written in Baltimore during the last months of his illness, at a time when he is said to have had a fever of 104 degrees. Although it does not achieve the technical excellence of "The Marshes of Glynn," it has many of the same effects. Its theme is more closely related to the social gospel of "The Symphony," although it has a curious, and understandable, feverishness about it. "Sunrise" is not a finished or polished composition, but in it the reader feels strongly his lifelong, fervent devotion to poetry. In one of the poem's best passages Lanier addresses the sun as a symbol of a Swedenborgian God and reaches a plateau of serenity and calm that none of his other poems achieves:

> Not slower than Majesty moves, for a mean and a
>   measure
> Of motion,—nor faster than dateless Olympian
>   leisure
> Might pace with unblown ample garments from
>   pleasure to pleasure,—
> The wave-serrate sea-rim sinks unjarring,
>   unreeling,
>   Forever revealing, revealing, revealing,

> Edgewise, bladewise, halfwise, wholewise,—'tis
>   done!
>   Good-morrow, lord Sun!
>   With several voice, with ascription one,
>   The woods and the marsh and the sea and
>   my soul
>   Unto thee, whence the glittering stream of all
>   morrows doth roll,
>   Cry good and past-good and most heavenly
>   morrow, lord Sun.

This is the Lanier we remember today: a poet with a deep sense of the musical values of poetry whose experiments in rhythm and sound promised still another direction, other than those of Whitman and Dickinson, in which to escape the restrictions of traditional English verse and to find a native American voice. That all three of these poets were influenced by Emerson is perhaps no coincidence, although he influenced each of them in different ways. Lanier found in Emerson a confirmation of his own belief in a natural religion, and although the freedom of his verses seems to have come from his own metrical studies and from a belated reading of *Leaves of Grass* (1855), Lanier's connections with Whitman are significant. He did not read Whitman with any real attention until 1878, when he wrote him an effusive letter of praise, with a request for a copy of *Leaves of Grass*. Whitman was amused at what he thought was "a florid, gushing letter," inconsistent in its statement that Lanier disagreed with all his ideas on artistic form at the same time that it praised him as the master of "strong and beautiful rhythms." But even though Whitman had little direct influence on Lanier, they are linked in their mutual interest in evolving new poetic forms and their daring and courageous refusal to give in to the tastes and demands of a genteel popular audience. This is more true of Whitman than of Lanier, who on at least one occasion admitted he had trimmed some of the irregularities and excesses from a poem to satisfy an editor; nevertheless, Lanier retained a hope throughout his last years that he could inaugurate a new school of bolder, freer poetry with rhythms and language liberated from the restraints of the past. That hope was at least partially realized, and Lanier is remembered today not only as the South's greatest poet but, with Dickinson and Whitman, as one of the great experimenters of nineteenth-century poetry in America.

During the last thirty years of his life most of the writing Herman Melville (1819–1891) did was in verse. Aside from a few sketches and the long manuscript of *Billy Budd* that he left at his death, the mature Melville was not a writer of fiction but a poet. But there is a connection between his career as a romancer and his career as a poet. As Robert Penn Warren has observed, Melville's poetry is part of a search for peace in the second half of his life; turning away from an audience that had largely deserted him, he uneasily resigned himself to failure as a writer of fiction. His poetry is not a poetry of failure, however; it reveals the same toughness and integrity that characterize his best prose.

Some of the first poetry Melville wrote are the lyrics, sea songs, and elegies that are interspersed throughout his novel *Mardi,* published in 1849. It would be possible for a student of Melville's poems to see in these early ones some suggestions of the themes and language of his more mature verse. One of these, a song about a sea burial, for example (Chapter 99), is on a theme he later treated in a much more complex way in "Billy in the Darbies" (1885?). But, on the whole, there is little of intrinsic interest in these pieces.

The first poems Melville tried to publish in a separate volume are those he wrote between 1857 and 1860, after a trip to the Near East. These are travel impressions of Italy, Greece, and Egypt, which, like the *Mardi* poems, are not as interesting for themselves as for the hints of poetic ability they contain. Of course, no reader of *Moby-Dick* (1851) needs to be told that Melville is a poet, but before he could apply his talents to verse he needed to do some apprentice work. He himself apparently regarded these poems as little more than juvenilia, since he collected them under the heading, "Fruit of Travel of Long Ago" in the volume he called *Timoleon &c.,* privately published the year he died.

The events that triggered his imagination and inspired his first mature verse were, curiously enough, not central to his own life. Unlike the life aboard whaling vessels that supplied the foundations for his prose flights of imagination and metaphysics, the Civil War was something that Melville knew little about at firsthand. Still, he followed the war carefully and was affected by such events as the New York draft riots of 1863, the Battle of Bull Run, and the Battle of Shiloh. In 1864 he visited the Virginia front as a civilian observer and called on General Grant. The outgrowth of these meager experiences of a passionately concerned outsider is one of the two best books of poetry to come out of the war. *Battle-Pieces and Aspects of the War* (1866) is quite different in tone and attitude from Whitman's *Drum-Taps* (1865), however. Whitman used the war to confirm his sympathy with his fellow human beings by providing glimpses of individuals poignantly caught in the toils of war. Melville is more distant from the war, more ironic and ambiguous; finally, as Robert Penn Warren has observed, more tragic. "Whitman," he writes, "moves toward ritual," in the sense of discovering the universals of human experience contained in the events of the war, while "Melville moves toward tragedy" in his awareness of the ambiguities of life and death, meaning and meaninglessness, that war reveals.

Thus he sees the wounded young man in "The College Colonel" as having "lived a thousand years / Compressed in battle's pains and prayers," because the events of war have affected him spiritually as well as physically. In "The House-Top: A Night Piece," Melville, reflecting on the New York draft riots, laments that the situation has led to an act of suppression, since such an act violates the principle of man's natural goodness upon which the Republic is founded. His double-edged vision is most effective in "A Utilitarian View of the Monitor's Fight," in which he observes that the historic battle between the two first ironclad warships marked the end of the concept of glory in war. Now that floating machines are pitted against each other, war is placed "among the trades and artisans," warriors "are now but operatives," and, as the ironic last line says, "a singe runs through lace and feather." Melville is no less ironic in other poems about the glory of war. In "The March Into Virginia: Ending in the First Manassas" he takes a point of view similar to that of Stephen Crane in *The Red Badge of Courage*. "All wars are boyish, and are fought by boys," he writes, and ends with this stanza:

> But some who this blithe mood present,
>   As on in lightsome files they fare,
> Shall die experienced ere three days are spent—
>   Perish, enlightened by the vollied glare;
> Or shame survive, and, like to adamant,
>   The throe of Second Manassas share.

The futility of war against the backdrop of an indifferent and perpetually self-renewing nature is dramatized in "Malvern Hill" and "Shiloh," both of which have a cyclical structure. In "Shiloh: A Requiem" the swallows in the first stanza return at the end to fly over the hushed battlefield; "Malvern Hill" ends with these sardonic lines spoken by the elms of Malvern Hill: *"Wag the world how it will, / Leaves must be green in Spring." Battle-Pieces,* then, are more than war poems; they are philosophical reflections on the nature of man as he is seen in a wartime setting.

It is not easy to describe the unique qualities of Melville's verse. It is not smooth, it is not lyrical; it is irregular and even prosaic. In its roughness and irregularity it is strikingly similar to Emerson's verse, perhaps for the same reasons. The disregard for form that Emerson made explicit in "Merlin" is seconded by Melville in such passages as this opening stanza from "A Utilitarian View . . .":

> Plain be the phrase, yet apt the verse,
>   More ponderous than nimble;
> For since grimed War here laid aside
> His Orient pomp, 'twould ill befit
>   Overmuch to ply
> The rhyme's barbaric cymbal.

What one notices again and again in Melville's poems is the unusual word, the striking phrase, the apt image, or the line fraught with ambiguity or irony. But instead of calling attention to themselves as devices of style, they demand the reader's attention to the ideas they express. The closing lines of "The Portent," for example, give the figure of the hanged John Brown a significance heightened by the etymologically sound use of the word *weird:*

> But the streaming beard is shown
> (Weird John Brown),
> The meteor of the war.

The uneven, somewhat stammering quality of Melville's verse can become a hindrance to the reader. This is especially true in his long historical-philosophical poem, *Clarel,* in which he uses an octosyllabic line rhyming at irregular intervals. Obviously, however, the greatest barrier to the reader of *Clarel* is its extreme length: one hundred and fifty cantos adding up to over twenty thousand lines. Since its publication, *Clarel: A Poem and Pilgrimage in the Holy Land* (1876) has acquired, largely because of its length, a reputation as a dull, sententious philosophical treatise in verse. Recently, however, there has been a growing interest in the poem, as many readers have argued that it is not the random outpouring of an aging and weakening writer but a forceful, uncompromising work written by Melville in his maturity. *Clarel* had its origins in his tour of the Holy Land in the late 1850s, but he probably did not begin work on it until after the publication of *Battle-Pieces.* As he recalled his own travels and read widely in the literature about Palestine, Melville tied them to biblical events and put together a tortured and difficult narrative about the loss of faith and the vain search for a replacement. Starting with a numerous and shifting cast of characters representing every shade of religious belief, agnosticism, and atheism, Melville built a complex structure of historical, theological, and psychological thought that is the real substance of the poem. The central character, Clarel, is a young American divinity student who has fallen into religious doubt and made a pilgrimage to Jerusalem. His encounters with the various morality-play characters provide episodes of high drama or intense religious and psychological speculation, but, like Melville himself, Clarel ends his quest for faith with no more certainty than when he began. It is impossible to summarize this complex poem adequately; one can only describe it and compare it to other works. Robert Penn Warren agrees with Walter Bezanson, the editor of an excellent edition of *Clarel*, that it is a complex document in literary history and in the history of ideas, adding that it can be read in the same spirit we read Carlyle, Whitman in *Democratic Vistas*, William James, Henry Adams, and Thorstein Veblen. Melville himself ironically described it as "a metrical affair, a pilgrimage or what not . . . eminently adapted for unpopularity." No one will quarrel with this statement; still, *Clarel* should not be dismissed without at least giving it a fair try. It is that rare thing in any age—a body of ideas treated imaginatively and made into a work of art.

Clarel, which fully lived up to Melville's expectations of failure, was the last publishing venture of his life, but he did have two volumes privately printed in editions of twenty-five each, and these contain some of his finest poems. One was *John Marr and Other Sailors with Some Sea-Pieces* (1888); the other was *Timoleon &c.* (1891). In the first of these are four poems about sailors. Melville prefaced two of them, "John Marr" and "Tom Deadlight," by short explanatory notes giving some background to the events alluded to in the poems. It is now generally agreed that the poem "Billy in the Darbies," found after Melville's death at the end of the manuscript of *Billy Budd,* was also intended for inclusion with these sea poems. But Melville's headnote grew longer and longer as he became involved in the complexities underlying the poem itself, until it became a one-hundred-fifty-page manuscript, ending with the poem. "Billy in the Darbies" is capable of standing by itself as a poem, however; it is not a mere appendage to the story but rather gains in depth and resonance from the events of the story.

Two other poems in the *John Marr* volume demonstrate Melville's ability to find the especially vivid image and the appropriate phrase. "The Berg" is a frightening description of the collision of a sailing ship with an iceberg. At first the ship is made to appear foolish and the iceberg beautiful: it is an "infatuate ship" and an "impetuous ship," while the iceberg is trimmed with "lace of traceries fine" and "jack-straw needle ice." But as the mindless but somehow sinister indifference of the berg becomes apparent it takes on the menacing qualities that nature assumed for Ishmael in his more despondent moments:

> A lumbering lubbard loitering slow,
> Impingers rue thee and go down,
> Sounding thy precipice below,
> Nor stir the slimy slug that sprawls
> Along thy dead indifference of walls.

"The Maldive Shark" also explores the ambiguities of nature in the image of the pilot fish that direct the shark to its prey while they remain unharmed between its jaws.

Some of the poems in the *Timoleon* volume are also among Melville's best. "After the Pleasure Party" is a disturbing dramatic monologue by a middle-aged woman who has discovered the irritating persistence of sexual desire after a lifetime of repression. "Monody" mourns the death of Nathaniel Hawthorne and the end of that very special relationship between the two men. "Art" describes the torments the writer must undergo, who, like Jacob, must "wrestle with the angel—Art." This poem and another, lesser one best describe Melville's strong feelings of martyrdom to the life of art. Both re-create the sense of desperation and contempt for the opinion of a world that had returned this contempt with indifference. One of his heroes was Don Quixote, whom he once described as "that sagest sage that ever lived," and it is he who became the subject of this very personally revealing poem, "The Rusty Man," subtitled "(By a timid one)":

In La Mancha he mopeth
  With beard thin and dusty;
He doteth and mopeth
  In library fusty—
'Mong his old folios gropeth:
  Cites obsolete saws
  Of chivalry's laws—
  Be the wronged one's knight:
  Die, but do right.
So he rusts and musts,
While each grocer green
Thriveth apace with the fulsome face
Of a fool serene.

This, then, is Melville the poet. Unconventional in technique, yet powerful and vividly imaginative, he wrote some of the most interesting poetry of the nineteenth century.

The half-educated printer and newspaper editor named Walter Whitman (1819–1892), who was seen making an occasional political speech in Brooklyn and Manhattan in the 1840s, gave few outward signs of his desire to be a poet. Whitman was a political activist, well known in Brooklyn as a journalist with strong views on the Barnburners and the Free Soil issue that eventually led to his resignation as editor of the Brooklyn *Daily Eagle* in 1847. Underneath this exterior was a lonely man, a dreamer and brooder, who began about this time to record in notebooks the more and more insistent promptings that came to him from within. These took the form of apocalyptic, hesitant, and obscure symbolic fragments, many of which found their way unchanged into the first edition of *Leaves of Grass* in 1855. Although Whitman had literary aspirations and tried his hand at sentimental verse and melodramatic stories, these notebook entries show no inclination to conform to prevailing tastes. They are personal gropings and explorations of feelings reaching back to his childhood. They also reflect his wide and undisciplined reading in Carlyle, Hegel, George Sand, Emerson, and many others.

Of all the influences on him Emerson was the most immediate. He had followed Emerson's career as a lecturer, and at one time toyed with the idea of putting his own thoughts in the form of lectures. "I was simmering, simmering, simmering," he told his biographer, Horace Traubel (1858–1919), years later; "Emerson brought me to a boil."

But the precise origins and reasons for Whitman's emergence as a prophetic poet of the ego will probably always remain obscure. Possibly he underwent some kind of mystical experience that acted as a catalyst upon him and inspired him to arrange and expand his experimental writings into a group of poems. Whatever the circumstances, the book he published and placed on sale on July 4, 1855, was one of the most unusual ever published. It was a large, thin folio volume, bound in green, with the title *Leaves of Grass* stamped in gold letters sprouting roots and leaves. The wide pages were especially suited to the long lines of verse, which were broken up by an eccentric system of punctuation consisting mainly of dots. The title page contained no author's or publisher's name; instead, the frontispiece pictured a studied, self-consciously casual portrait of an idealized workingman, hands on hips, shirt open at the collar, hat on the back of his head. This rugged figure presumably was the speaker of the poems. Whitman's name appeared in only two places: once as "Walter Whitman" on the copyright page, and once about halfway through the long first poem as "Walt Whitman, an American, one of the roughs, a kosmos."

The long and declamatory preface of the first edition announced the arrival of a new age of American poetry; this was followed by twelve untitled poems, beginning with the long poem that would eventually be called "Song of Myself." All were in free verse, a loosely rhythmical, irregular line that goes much farther than Emerson in the direction of metrical freedom and has its closest analogy in the rhythmical prose of the King James Bible.

Although the book went largely unnoticed by readers and critics, Whitman had enough public-relations sense to distribute copies widely, and of course he sent one to Emerson.

Emerson's response was as much as any unknown poet could hope for. "I greet you at the beginning of a great career," he wrote. "I find it the most extraordinary piece of wit and wisdom that America has yet contributed . . . I find incomparable things said incomparably well, as they must be." Encouraged by Emerson's favorable response, Whitman published a second edition of *Leaves of Grass* in 1856. He added twenty new poems and gave titles to all the poems in the volume, which was now a conventional quarto. The most striking change, however, was Whitman's unauthorized use of a quotation from Emerson's letter, which he stamped in gold letters on the spine. At the end of the volume he also printed a long and embarrassing reply to Emerson, whom he addressed as "dear Friend and Master."

The story of the remaining seven editions of *Leaves of Grass,* which appeared at intervals during the next thirty-five years until his death, is the story of Whitman's growth and development as an artist, and, finally, of the decline of his poetic and creative powers. For although he published some of his poems separately, such as *Drum-Taps* (1865), his last, "deathbed" edition of 383 poems bears the same title as the first volume of twelve poems. This evolution and growth of *Leaves of Grass* reflects perhaps the single most important aspect of Whitman's poetry—the poem seen as process. Like Melville, who thought of *Moby-Dick* as a cathedral, Whitman conceived of his growing body of poems as a cathedral to which he was continually adding. Underlying this attitude toward his poetry is the organic principle of form derived in part from Schlegel and in part from Coleridge, who, in his discussion of Shakespeare, remarked that organic form "shapes, as it develops, itself from within. . . . Such as the life is, such is the form. Nature, the prime genial artist, inexhaustible in diverse powers, is equally inexhaustible in forms." Whitman adopted this attitude as his own, shaping and reshaping his songs as they emerged but keeping always the freedom and novelty of form he described in the preface to the 1855 *Leaves of Grass*. "The rhyme and uniformity of perfect poems," he wrote, "show the free growth of metrical laws and bud from them as unerringly and loosely as lilacs or roses on a bush, and take shapes as compact as the shapes of chestnuts and oranges and melons and pears, and shed the perfume impalpable to form."

Standing at the center of Whitman's poems is the person, or the poet himself—Walt Whitman, or the "I" of his poems —the most complex as well as the most pervasive symbol to be found in his poetry. Whitman's poetry moves from the center outward: from the "simple separate person" in an ever-widening spiral that culminates in an inclusiveness so vast that the word *cosmic* seems hardly adequate to describe it. As he approaches this rim of consciousness, the poet turns back inward and encompasses his vision in himself—in the "Personality," to use his own term, which is simultaneously the poet's individual consciousness and all with which it comes in contact: "One's self I sing, a simple separate person, / Yet utter the word Democratic, the word En-Masse." These two lines, placed at the very beginning of *Leaves of Grass*, define the basic paradox of Whitman's poetry and emphasize the central importance of the individual. "One main contrast of the ideas behind every page of my verses," he wrote in "A Backward Glance O'er Travel'd Roads" (1888), "is . . . the quite changed attitude of the ego, the one chanting or talking, toward himself and toward his fellow-humanity." "The time had come," he said, "to reflect all themes and things, old and new, in the lights thrown on them by the advent of America and democracy—to chant those themes through the utterance of one, not only the grateful and reverent legatees of the past, but the born child of the New World." This was his aim, as he saw it in retrospect; perhaps at first (as he himself suggests) it had been largely unconscious. He wanted to embrace all of objective reality in order to know simultaneously the seemingly contradictory elements of his world: himself and nature, matter and spirit, love and hate, life and death, good and evil. This turning inward and outward in an effort to reach toward the unknown is brilliantly captured in the image of the "noiseless patient spider," launching forth "fila-

ment, filament, filament, out of itself." The poet's soul is like
the spider:

> Surrounded, detached, in measureless oceans of space,
> Ceaselessly musing, venturing, throwing, seeking the
>   spheres to connect them,
> Till the bridge you will need be form'd, till the
>   ductile anchor hold,
> Till the gossamer thread you fling catch somewhere,
>   O my soul.

Although it is possible to open *Leaves of Grass* almost
anywhere and find an adumbration of Whitman's underlying
theme of the poet as cosmic consciousness, the point of departure for any reader of Whitman is "Song of Myself" (1855).
This poem is a unique combination of lyric and epic: personal revelation tied to national experience in a way that
defies all generic categories. In intention its closest parallel is
perhaps Wordsworth's *Prelude* (1805), which describes the
growth of consciousness through personal experience. But
"Song of Myself" tries also to be a national epic—a fusion of
the idealism of a democratic faith and the robust materialism
of a young and vigorous nation. It may seem at first to be a
hopelessly chaotic collection of rhetorical flights, purple passages, descriptions, word lists, and awkward prose; upon
closer study it reveals a shape to the reader that can be
roughly described as introduction, dramatic development,
mystical release and expansion, return, and conclusion. There
seems to be little doubt that something corresponding to the
mystical experience as described by such students of mysticism
as William James and Evelyn Underhill is the basis for the
poem's structure; it is dangerous, nevertheless, to try to im-
pose too rigidly any system that denies the essentially fluid
and shifting quality of the poem.

The opening stanzas contain the basic imagery of the
grass, which works as an organizing symbol, suggestive of the
many and the one. "I celebrate myself," the speaker an-

nounces in the opening line, and proceeds to describe himself as he leans and loafs at his ease "observing a spear of summer grass." His acute awareness of the physical aspects of his surroundings is combined with his sense of the equality of spirit and matter: "Clear and sweet is my soul, and clear and sweet is all that is not my soul." This apparent duality becomes resolved for him in the fifth chant of the song, where he uses a daring sexual image to suggest the union of these apparent opposites. Whitman's own sexuality and his intense, even pathological, responsiveness to physical contact is nowhere more delicately employed to express his belief in the unity of spirit and matter than in this description of the quasi-sexual union of body and soul:

I mind how once we lay such a transparent summer morning,
How you settled your head athwart my hips and gently
    turn'd over upon me,
And parted the shirt from my bosom-bone, and plunged your
    tongue to my bare-stript heart,
And reach'd till you felt my beard, and reach'd till
    you held my feet.

This is the moment of entry into the mystical state that the rest of the poem develops and describes. At this moment Whitman turns to biblical language to describe "the peace and knowledge that pass all the argument of the earth" which result from this union.

"Song of Myself" continues to develop the themes of expansiveness, unity, fellowship, and hope by moving in somewhat random fashion through a series of loosely related chants. The tone of the poem is a perilous balance between prophetic urgency, oratorical pomposity, and ironic self-mockery. The sheer intensity of Whitman's creative urge makes the receptive reader excuse the many lapses in taste, awkward expressions, and tiresome repetitions with which the poem abounds. We can find plenty of examples of his "prophetical screams" and his "barbaric yawp"; we can easily see the justice of Emerson's smiling remark, quoted by Bliss Perry, that in its mixture of diction and variety of syntax *Leaves of Grass* was a combination of the *Bhagavad-Gita* and the New York *Herald*. The impulse behind this conglomerate mixture of styles is the same as that of the poem itself, to make the words themselves contain, or be, the immense range of his experience: "My voice goes after what my eyes cannot reach, / With the twirl of my tongue I encompass worlds and volumes of worlds." But Whitman is aware of the arrogance implicit in his vision of the prophet, and is even more acutely aware of his own shortcomings and lack of confidence. He can therefore taunt himself in such a passage as this:

> Speech is the twin of my vision, it is unequal to measure itself,
> It provokes me forever, it says sarcastically,
> *Walt you contain enough, why don't you let it out then?*

Still, it is too easy to see in "Song of Myself" only diffuseness and excessive size. In spite of the sweeping, cosmic effect the poem as a whole produces, it is composed of many carefully worked lyric passages and concrete descriptions of closely observed people and places. One such lyrical passage is in Chant 21, in which he achieves a fusion of imagery of night, earth, sea, and sex in that well-known passage beginning "Press close bare-bosom'd night—press close magnetic nourishing night!" Whitman is often at his best in the accurate observation of small details. Here are a few such vignettes, which could easily be rearranged on the page to become Imagist poems.

> The young sister holds out the skein while the elder sister winds it off in a ball, and stops now and then for the knots . . .

> The lunatic is carried at last to the asylum a confirm'd case, (He will never sleep any more as he did in the cot in his mother's bed-room;). . . .

> The western turkey-shooting draws old and young, some lean on their rifles, some sit on logs,

Out from the crowd steps the marksman, takes his position,
   levels his piece. . . .

The bride unrumples her white dress, the minute-hand of the
   clock moves slowly.

The first of these has the quality of a Dutch genre painting,
while others, such as the last, look forward to the Imagists'
adaptation of the Japanese haiku, and to the poems of William Carlos Williams.

Between 1856 and 1860 Whitman's personality underwent some changes. Self-doubt and loneliness, already suggested in some sections of "Song of Myself," appear in a number of lyrics printed for the first time in the 1860 edition.
Also during that four-year interval Whitman seems to have
had a homosexual experience that troubled him with a sense
of guilt and drove him to write his most personal poems on
love and human friendship. This is not the place to explore
Whitman's ambiguous, or ambivalent sexuality—a subject that
has occupied the attention of numerous biographers. It is possible to say, however, that Whitman was probably neither
exclusively heterosexual nor homosexual, but that he was
sexually sensitive to an extraordinary degree. His strong
physical vitality and his equally strong mystical impulse to
merge with the physical universe produced in him feelings
that he could not always either understand or direct. In the
first edition of his poems he had published a poem later
called "I Sing the Body Electric," which, in its insistence on
the inseparability of body and soul, seemed to have intimate
connotations for him. This celebration of male and female
bodies reappeared in the series of poems, which he called
"Enfans d'Adam" in 1860. They are an outgrowth of the
attitude expressed in these lines of "Song of Myself":

On women fit for conception I start bigger and nimbler babes,
(This day I am jetting the stuff of far more arrogant republics.)

They are, that is, programmatic rather than personal, for the
most part, celebrating the theme of procreation and the
sacredness of the human body:

This is the female form,
A divine nimbus exhales from it from head to foot,
It attracts with fierce undeniable attraction.

Richard Chase exaggerates only slightly when he remarks that the "Children of Adam" poems, as they came to be called, "came from the pen of one for whom the love of man for woman was remote and theoretical, however much he may have been in favor of it."

The "Calamus" poems (1860), also basically sexual, are quite different in tone. This extraordinary series exposes Whitman's most intimate feelings to public view in what seems to be an effort to take stock of himself. Many poems frankly express the theme of "manly attachment," while others are veiled in ambiguous references to loneliness, self-doubt, and frustration. The opening poem asserts that he will "proceed for all who are or have been young men, / To tell the secret of my nights and days, / To celebrate the need of comrades." This need for companionship recurs in such lines as "Passing stranger! you do not know how longingly I look upon you," and in such poems as the love sonnet in free verse, "I Saw in Louisiana a Live-Oak Growing." The autobiographical relevance of the "Calamus" poems seems particularly strong in several poems that he excluded from all editions after 1860. In one of these Whitman's mood is directly opposite to the overwhelming optimism of his earlier days, consumed as he is by the emotions of his love affair:

> For I can be your singer of songs no longer—One who
>   loves me is jealous of me, and withdraws me from
>   all but love. . . .
> I am indifferent to my own songs—I will go with
>   him I love,
> It is to be enough for us that we are together—We
>   never separate again.

Whitman's feelings of uncertainty and drift are not confined to the "Calamus" series, however; they are found in their most moving and most artistically satisfying form in "As

I Ebb'd With the Ocean of Life" (1860). Here he questions all his confident posturing, all his assertions of optimism, all his notions of form and plan. He turns inward to discover that because he cannot understand himself he can understand nothing:

> before all my arrogant poems the real Me stands
> yet untouch'd, untold, altogether unreach'd,
>
> * * *
>
> I perceive I have not really understood any thing, not a
> single object, and that no man ever can

The poem ends with an image of himself as one of many bits of flotsam cast up on the shore by an unseen God, lying "in drifts at your feet." This poem is an important key to the fluctuation of feelings and attitudes contained in the poems of the 1860 edition, a book that Roy Harvey Pearce has suggested can be read as a spiritual autobiography. But in spite of its mood of despair, Whitman avoids self-pity and pathos by his remarkable ability to assume the same ironic and self-mocking tone that redeemed the exuberance of "Song of Myself" from fatuousness.

But the central poem of this volume, and in the opinion of many, the central poem of Whitman's work, echoes and at the same time transcends his deepening mood. In "Out of the Cradle Endlessly Rocking" (1859) Whitman succeeds in making artistic use of his new-found preoccupation with spiritual malaise and physical death. Displaying the technical virtuosity of a matured artist in absolute command of his craft, Whitman describes the coming-of-age of a young boy, an "outsetting bard," who discovers the sources of creative energy in "the cries of unsatisfied love" and in the "low and delicious word death." Spoken by the mature poet looking back at his own boyhood, it is a portrait of the artist as a young man told with an almost Jamesian dexterity in its handling of point of view. It is a song of experience to be placed against the innocence of "Song of Myself." Combining lyric, or aria, passages with narrative, or recitative, passages, Whitman achieves a fusion of the three central figures in the poem, the boy, the bird, and the sea. The rhythm is subtly altered to correspond to the shifting emotions of the boy and the bird, but is sustained by an underlying rocking motion that reinforces the central message of death that is whispered by the breaking waves of the sea. Whitman's diction is free of the mannerisms and affectations that mar some of his verse, and the entire poem is sustained by a unity of tone unsurpassed elsewhere in his work.

Another example of Whitman's artistic control is his great elegy on the death of Abraham Lincoln. "When Lilacs Last in the Dooryard Bloom'd" deals even more specifically with death than "Out of the Cradle," which is really about the growth of the artist. By the time Whitman wrote it, he had been exposed to the pain and suffering of the wounded soldiers he visited in Civil War hospitals, and had come to have a firsthand and intimate knowledge of death. His war experiences had stimulated him to write a new series of poems, which he published as *Drum-Taps* in 1865, a series which stands beside Melville's *Battle-Pieces* (1866) as the most significant poetry to emerge from the Civil War. Many of the *Drum-Taps* poems, such as "The Wound-Dresser," describe the suffering of the wounded and dying, while others, such as "Come Up from the Fields Father" and "Vigil Strange I Kept on the Field One Night," describe the feelings of loss and bereavement. The death of Lincoln, for whose mournful and solitary figure Whitman felt a profound attraction, focused for him all the brooding on death and loss that had occupied him during the war years. "When Lilacs Last in the Dooryard Bloom'd," written in 1865 and printed in a small supplement to *Drum-Taps*, brings together all these feelings and becomes a superb expression of his reconciliation with the fact of death. Like all great elegies, it moves away from its subject and away from the sense of individual loss to a generalized and universal statement about death. The poem is not an anguished outcry of personal grief but a carefully constructed and controlled artistic performance concerning the nature of grief that does not abandon the sense of loss that is the basis of the poem.

What we see in Whitman as a poet today is the innovator, partly in his radical use of free verse and his release of language from the shackles of convention. These are important; he "broke the new wood," as Ezra Pound said of him in "A Pact," and the exploration of new subjects and new ways of writing about old subjects that twentieth-century poets have undertaken owes much to Whitman's view of poetry as a "language experiment." But more important is the close and necessary identification Whitman made between himself and his poetry; for him they were one and the same. "No one will get at my verses who insists upon viewing them as a literary performance," he wrote in "A Backward Glance O'er Travel'd Roads" (1888), "or attempt at such performance, or as aiming mainly toward art or aestheticism." Whitman was a humanistic poet, if we mean by that that he was a poet of the human experience. He was a Romantic poet—pushing the egocentrism of the Romantic attitude to its extreme limits, finding in himself the sum of all human experience. *Leaves of Grass,* he added, "has mainly been the out-cropping of my own emotional and other personal nature—an attempt, from first to last, to put a *Person,* a human being (myself in the latter half of the Nineteenth Century, in America), freely, fully, and truly on record."

Whitman was also a maker of myth, whose myths were grounded in the science and materialism of his country and his age. By "tallying" his land and his people he translated them into an autochthonic poetry that sprung from both his material and himself. His themes—the divinity of man, comradeship and love, the democratic faith, the beauty and purpose of the natural world—are all related to his conception of the poem and the words of which it is composed as symbolic. "The substantial words are in the ground and sea, / They are in the air, they are in you," he wrote. In his poems the material of the world is translated, but not transformed. It remains what it was, with the same suggestiveness it had. The poem and the process of making poetry are the same, and in this respect, perhaps, Whitman is most American in his pragmatic fascination with process. Just as the Civil War, in which he took part, marks a turning point in American history, Whitman is a watershed in the history of American poetry. He took those elements of American romanticism that suited his own egocentric personality and wrote poems that in their originality and emotional power have had an ever-increasing influence on the direction of American poetry.

Emily Dickinson (1830–1886) the poet and Emily Dickinson the person are so closely intertwined that it is difficult to separate the two. Close readings of her poems and letters reveal a variety of psychological aberrations, from a deep fear of her father and an obvious dislike of men to an inability to cope in a "normal" way with the outside world, which taken together add up to a severe psychological disturbance bordering on psychosis. The fact that her periods of most intense creativity coincide with those times in her life when she was most troubled by events taking place in her own narrowly circumscribed life adds support to theories of correlation between art and madness. Dressing entirely in white toward the end of her life, lowering gifts of baskets of peaches to friends from her bedroom windows, speaking to visitors from behind a screen placed in the living room, presenting some of them with day lilies as she entered the room—these and dozens of other eccentricities have made the "White Nun of Amherst" almost as much a literary legend as Edgar Allan Poe. But the fact remains that her eccentricities and her neuroses were the materials of her art—not always consciously and seldom directly, as in the poetry of Robert Lowell and Anne Sexton, but surreptitiously and indirectly, through a private vocabulary and oblique references that veiled her suffering and repressed her desires. And the art she produced from her private agonies of soul stands with Whitman's as the best poetry written in America in the nineteenth century.

There was nothing exceptional about Emily Dickinson's early years. She grew up in the small college town of Amherst, Massachusetts, where her father was a lawyer and influential citizen. She spent several years of intermittent schooling at the Amherst Academy and one year when she was seventeen at what was then called the Mount Holyoke Female Seminary. The strict Calvinist atmosphere of the school was difficult for Emily Dickinson to accept, however, since her faith in God was far from being either conventional or certain. In 1862 she confided to her literary correspondent, Thomas Wentworth Higginson (1823–1911), that her family were "religious, except me, and address an eclipse, every morning, whom they call their 'Father.'" This attitude accounts for her refusal to join in daily prayers at Mount Holyoke, for which defiance she was placed among a special group of problem students. This one unsuccessful year was the last she spent away from home, except for a trip to Washington and Philadelphia and two trips to Boston.

Three episodes in Emily Dickinson's life, each involving a man, bear directly on her writing of poetry. The first of these men was a young graduate of Amherst, Benjamin Franklin Newton, who first introduced her to a number of writers, including the Brontë sisters, and communicated to her his own love of literature. In 1849 he gave her a copy of Emerson's poems, and these were to be an influence on her throughout her life. Newton died in 1853, and there is no evidence to suggest she was in love with him, but he was important to her in opening her perceptions of the world and suggesting the possibilities of giving them literary expression. Much more has been made of the relationship between Emily Dickinson and another man, much older than she, whom she met when he visited her father in 1859. The Reverend Charles Wadsworth was pastor of the Arch Street Presbyterian Church of Philadelphia, an upstanding and righteous man of God, and a family man. In him were combined the qualities of spiritual leader, father-figure, and lover that she seemed to need. She almost certainly had no desire for him to change, but he filled her need for someone to look up to and admire. A major crisis in her life came late in 1861 when Wadsworth accepted a call to the Calvary Church in San Francisco, and without his guidance she seemed to fear she would not be able to control her emotions or her reason. The poems she wrote from 1858 on show she was in a highly emotional state, and Wadsworth seemed to provide an outlet and direction for her emotions that eventually took form in the poems. It was about the time that Wadsworth went to San Francisco that Emily Dickinson began to dress entirely in white, adopting her "white election," as she called it. The name "Calvary" also first appeared in her poems, in many of which she pictured herself as a bride or "queen" who has adopted a renunciation of all she values most, as in this poem:

> Title divine—is mine!
> The Wife—without the Sign!
> Acute Degree—conferred on me—
> Empress of Calvary!
> Royal—all but the Crown!
> Betrothed—without the swoon
> God sends us Women—
> When you—hold—Garnet to Garnet—
> Gold—to Gold—
> Born—Bridalled—Shrouded—
> In a day—
> Tri Victory
> "My Husband"—women say—
> Stroking the Melody—
> Is *this*—the way?

> (1072, *c.* 1862)

Wadsworth returned to Philadelphia in 1870, and Emily Dickinson saw him once again at Amherst in 1880, but she had long ago turned to someone else for the support she seemed desperately to need.

About the time Wadsworth went west, Emily Dickinson sent her first letter and a selection of her poems to Thomas Wentworth Higginson, the Unitarian minister turned writer and editor. Her desire for an audience for her poems and for professional critical advice, as well as for a kind of literary mentor and spiritual savior, led her to turn, almost desperately, to Higginson for help. Indeed, she later wrote to him: "You are not aware that you saved my life. To thank you in

person has been since then one of my few requests." Although
Higginson was aware from the beginning that she was unusually gifted, his own tastes were too conventional to allow
him to do more than politely encourage her. He did his best
to give her the kind of criticism she wanted, but she soon
recognized his inadequacies as a critic even though she continued to value him as a friend.

Although she allowed a few of her poems to be published
by her friend Samuel Bowles of the Springfield *Republican,*
this was the last effort Emily Dickinson made in her life to
receive public recognition. A total of seven of her poems were
published in her lifetime. Higginson's "surgery," as she described his criticism, was not able to give her the direction she
needed, and after a period in which her poems betray an
intense desire for literary fame, she timidly gave up all literary
ambitions. It was a great surprise to everyone, including her
sister Lavinia, who discovered them after her death, that
Emily Dickinson had been writing poems steadily over a period
of thirty-six years and carefully revising and preserving them
in a locked box in her desk. Forty-four packets containing 879
poems on small pieces of paper were sewn together, usually
with a final version, but often with several possible variants
from which she could presumably choose. The publishing history of these scraps is a long and not wholly pleasant one,
marked by bickering among members of the family and distortion of the texts by well-meaning editors, including Higginson, who edited the volume of *Poems* in 1890. He regularized
the 115 poems he chose in rhyme, rhythm, and language so
that they would be received favorably by the public. Thomas
H. Johnson's edition of the poems in 1955 has made available
all the poems transcribed from the original manuscripts, with
all the variants. This edition retains the eccentricities of capi-
talization, punctuation, and language as they were in the original. Emily Dickinson's unique system of punctuation consisted largely of dashes, which served as periods, commas,
colons, and semicolons, but she also used them for emphasis—
to set off a word or phrase or to suggest either a sudden break
or a gradual slowing down, as at the end of her poem about

pain, "After great pain, a formal feeling comes" (*c.* 1862), which ends, "First—Chill—then Stupor—then the letting go—." And there are cases where the dash seems to have no grammatical function. At the time he printed his edition of the poems Johnson said he thought future editions of the poems should omit such punctuation, but after seeing them in this form most readers have become convinced that the ambiguity of so much of her punctuation makes almost impossible the job of deciding exactly how a poem should be punctuated. Reading them in their original state becomes both an experience of the creative process and a critical act in which the reader is forced to become as closely engaged with the poem and its ambiguities as the poet herself.

The poems of Emily Dickinson must be read in bulk— the good with the bad—in order to begin to understand what she is doing in individual poems. Although the great poems are perfectly capable of standing alone, they gain in clarity and meaning when they are read against a background of several dozen, or several hundred, of her short lyrics. Out of a total of 1,775 poems at least half are the merest effusions: letters in the form of poems, birthday poems and valentines, elegies, and funeral poems. And many of the rest are failures, or only partial successes, in which her aims were not fully realized; or they were written at times in her life in which her creative energies were not at their peak. The experience of reading a large number of Emily Dickinson's poems is the experience of coming in contact with a unique personality whose voice speaks to us in a confiding, conversational tone. It is this tone, and the set of attitudes it conveys, that stays with us long after we have forgotten the substance of the individual poems. Her voice is spontaneous but not unreflective, a voice that speaks out of a solitary meditation to report on its results. Her declaration in one of her poems that "This is My Letter to the World," is the tone of them all: they are letters of a private self who finds release in the act of communication. But there is more, of course, than the presence of a generalized "voice" to be discovered in Emily Dickinson's poems. Each poem finally becomes a unique experience, a momentary perception that she has wrought into poetry with great care. Since the form of her lyrics has little variety, and since the tone is uniform and they are all quite short, they tend to blur into one another. On the other hand, if we read each of them with the close attention that the best of them demand and deserve, the intensity with which they force us to respond soon becomes tiring. The answer lies in reading and rereading. Like the poems of Wallace Stevens, in which there is a similar concentration of language and perception, Emily Dickinson's poems gradually yield their secrets to the persistent reader. Many of her good poems, of course, such as "Bring Me the Sunset in a Cup," "What Soft—Cherubic Creatures," and "Presentiment is that long shadow on the lawn" are immediately accessible; but others—"Further in Summer than the Birds," "My Life Had Stood—a Loaded Gun," "A Route of Evanescence," and "An Ignorance a sunset"—are so economical and concise in diction, so frugal in syntax, that they must be read again and again.

Her basic stanza was the ballad stanza or the hymn stanza: four lines, with three-and-four stresses alternating, rhymed at the end of the second and fourth lines. Her experience with other verse forms, such as the sonnets of Elizabeth Barrett Browning and the blank verse of Shakespeare, never stimulated her to be very adventurous in trying out much variety in her choice of basic stanzas. Some of her stanzas are longer—she uses a six-line one in many poems—but the line seldom has more than four accents. What she did within this very restricted form was to experiment radically with rhythm, rhyme, word choice, and syntax in her efforts to pack the greatest intensity of feeling and perception into a small space, and she does this by omitting parts of speech, varying the meter, using approximate, or "slant" rhyme, and making up words of her own when she cannot find one. She told Higginson, "for several years my lexicon was my only companion," and her versatility and precision in her choice of words attest to that. Because she thinks by means of images, perceptions, sudden insights, and ironic twists, the carefully chosen word bears the weight of her thoughts.

A great number of her poems are about nature, but her attitude toward it—as toward most things, including immortality and God—is not consistent. At times she seems to be a Transcendentalist, inspired and even intoxicated by her contact with the natural world. In "I taste a liquor never brewed," for example, she states that draughts of air and water are the strongest she can take:

> Inebriate of Air—am I—
> And Debauchee of Dew—
> Reeling—thro endless summer days—
> From inns of Molten Blue—
>
> (214)

In this she echoes Emerson's view of the poet: "The air should suffice for his inspiration, and he should be tipsy with water." But at other times Emily Dickinson seems to be denying that any affinity between man and nature can exist:

> But nature is a stranger yet;
> The ones that cite her most
> Have never passed her haunted house,
> Nor simplified her ghost.
>
> To pity those that know her not
> Is helped by the regret
> That those who know her, know her less
> The nearer her they get.
>
> (1400)

Her reaction to nature, as to other experiences, is often one of dread, as in "I dreaded that first Robin so." In this and other, similar poems the intensity of her response to one small aspect of nature is so great that she experiences what amounts to an almost overwhelming physical pain. The fear of such pain inflicted by her contact with nature lies at the center of her tragic vision of life. Her acute awareness of the pain of living affects her entire existence and results in a poetry of dread that has many elements of the existential *angst*. Whether she is writing about God, or pain, or immortality, her role is often either to endure or transcend suffering, and her poems of renunciation most explicitly confront the problem of pain by asserting her hard-won belief that "Success is counted sweetest by those who ne'er succeed." Although that poem expresses a kind of triumphant resignation, others, such as "A wounded deer leaps highest," contain her familiar doctrine, harking back to her Calvinist origins, that pain is a source of strength. The best of these poems is "I can wade Grief" (*c.* 1861):

> I can wade Grief—
> Whole Pools of it—
> I'm used to that—
> But the least push of Joy
> Breaks up my feet—
> And I tip—drunken—
> Let no Pebble—smile—
> 'Twas the New Liquor—
> That was all!
> Power is only Pain—
> Stranded, thro' Discipline,
> Till Weights—will hang—
> Give Balm—to Giants—
> And they'll wilt, like Men—
> Give Himmaleh—
> They'll Carry—Him!
>
> (252)

Pain reveals to Emily Dickinson the tragic quality of a life permeated by dread and despair. The fact that one is alive is itself painful, yet paradoxically the thought of dying can be equally painful. Her obsession with immortality drives her to write countless poems about it, yet she does not conceive of the afterlife in any of the easy terms of conventional Christianity. "I don't like Paradise," she writes in one poem, "Because it's Sunday—all the time—." Yet her glimpses of immortality and eternity give promise of a release from the worldly and mortal pain to which her physical being so cruelly subjects her. In one poem eternity resembles a glimpse of Italy as the clouds momentarily clear away from the Swiss Alps. In another, consciousness itself is "captivity," and elsewhere she asks, "How have I peace / Except by subjugating / Consciousness?"

Implicit in practically every poem Emily Dickinson ever wrote is her sense of her role as a poet—the poet whose perceptions continually engage and redefine the world she sees. Her poems are all efforts at definition, and many of her poems begin with definitions of abstract nouns: presentiment, experiment, prayer, fame, crisis, grief, remorse, publication, faith. But the definitions are extremely personal and even idiosyncratic; finally it is not the definitions that are important to either the writer or the reader but the very individual mind and feelings of Emily Dickinson herself. As Roy Harvey Pearce has remarked, her grand theme is Life as it is involved in her life. The poet, Emily Dickinson writes, "Distills amazing sense / From ordinary Meanings—" The key word here is distills; in another poem about the poet's role she makes the analogy between the poet and the press that crushes the essential oils from the rose petals. In both poems she sees her gift as transforming nature into its essence. Her admonition, presumably to herself, to "Tell all the Truth but tell it slant" lies at the heart of her effort to arrive by indirection, or "circuit," at what is at once too impalpable and too overpowering to be perceived head on. These attitudes toward her world and her place in it are what make her poems what they are.

Emily Dickinson shares with Walt Whitman the impulse to merge poetry with experience until both are one. An Emily Dickinson poem, like a Whitman poem, is not *about* an experience; it *is* the experience. The poetry of both fuses the poetry with the world: Whitman's through his continuing, forward-rushing efforts to encompass everything, Emily Dickinson's by her fleeting and fragmentary acts of perception. Both distort, wrench, and make language into a highly personal instrument that has little to do with prevailing notions of poetic form or diction, and in so doing they make a new reality that is both

the poem and the world it has engaged and transformed. In
their faith in the powers of the human imagination Emily
Dickinson and Walt Whitman both resemble the singer in
Wallace Stevens' poem, "The Idea of Order at Key West":

> when she sang, the sea,
> Whatever self it had, became the self
> That was her song, for she was the maker.

CHAPTER SIX

The Old South and New England

Henry Wadsworth Longfellow, John Greenleaf Whittier, Oliver Wendell Holmes, James Russell Lowell, Paul Hamilton Hayne, William Gilmore Simms, Henry Timrod

Longfellow, Whittier, Holmes, and Lowell: the names are far more familiar than their poetry. There is a kind of similarity in our attitude toward the Founding Fathers—those periwigged and knee-breeched authors of the Declaration of Independence and of the Constitution—and toward the Fireside poets, or Household poets, whose bearded countenances seem to contain all the blandness and lack of vitality that many Americans associate not only with nineteenth-century poetry but with all poetry. Poetry for many of us still means long passages of *The Song of Hiawatha* or *Snow-Bound,* painfully memorized or perhaps even acted out, or rhyming stanzas of vague moral uplift. Although this view of poetry and of poets is less widespread now than it was twenty years ago, there are still few Americans, young or old, who read the schoolroom poets, as George Arms has named them, for pleasure. It is hard for us to imagine the widespread veneration in which Longfellow and Whittier were held during their last years, to see why their birthdays were celebrated annually by thousands of schoolchildren, and why Longfellow is the only foreign poet to be commemorated in the Poet's Corner of Westminster Abbey. What we must have in order to understand their popularity is a historical imagination which will let us see that they lived and wrote at a time when a large mass audience had come to have pretensions to education and gentility. The novel, still dominated in this country by what Hawthorne called "damned female scribblers," was not quite a respectable or serious form, so readers who wanted to find serious thoughts in literature still read poetry. They found a lot of serious thoughts, but whether or not what they were reading was poetry was, and still is, a matter of debate. Neither Poe nor Margaret Fuller, among Longfellow's early readers, was inclined to think so, though Poe's objections were fewer and more special than Miss Fuller's.

Ludwig Lewisohn once asked: "Who, except wretched schoolchildren, now reads Longfellow?" For Longfellow, one might substitute the names of Whittier, Lowell, or Holmes and characterize one extreme attitude toward them all. But the revulsion and contempt in which all attitudes, all ideas, and all art of the Victorian period were held early in the twentieth century have more recently given way to a reevaluation of these poets that, if it has not restored them to their former overblown and exaggerated eminence, has found them to be very good minor poets. All of them, and Longfellow in particular, were victimized by what Howard Nemerov has called "the encouragement of popularity"; their easily read verses, many expressing popular sentiments, invited a large and appreciative audience that read not to discover new ideas but to have old ones repeated and confirmed. The huge output of these four poets says far more about the prevailing sentiments and attitudes of nineteenth-century America than all the works of Emerson, Whitman, and Melville.

By the second half of the century New England, and Boston in particular, had become the center of the national culture, even though New York and Philadelphia were aggressive rivals in book and magazine publishing. Since the founding of the *North American Review* in 1815, New England culture dominated the country, to the disgust of many, including Poe, who referred to Boston as "Frogpondia." But a term for the privileged inhabitants of Boston that gained wider currency was "Brahmin," which implied an aristocratic background and a culture of learning and tradition. The Brahmins were not a withdrawn, effete class, however; Longfellow and Lowell were Harvard professors, Holmes taught and practiced medicine, and Whittier, on the fringe of this group, was a newspaperman and tireless worker in the Abolitionist cause. Lowell's founding of the *Atlantic Monthly* in 1857, Holmes's long association with that magazine through his Breakfast Table essays, and the formation of the Saturday Club, whose members included Emerson, Lowell, Longfellow, the younger Dana, Holmes, Prescott, Whittier, Howells, Henry James, and many others, gave the participants the character of an interlocking directorate whose literary pursuits and interests were shared and discussed among them. Younger poets and those outside the charmed circle found it difficult to be published in the *Atlantic* unless they shared the Brahmins' outlook. This was especially true when William Dean Howells took over as editor in 1871. Although he drew from a wider field than Lowell and James T. Fields had done, he was generally unreceptive to poetry that was not genteel in attitude and conventional in form.

The literary situation in the South was quite different. Before the Civil War, the centers of culture were widely scattered—in Charleston, Richmond, and Baltimore. After the war the members of the Confederacy who wanted an audience outside the South could not easily find a sympathetic ear among northern editors. Southern writers generally shared the ideals of the plantation culture upon which their economy and society were built. They tended to be lawyers, journalists, or editors of small newspapers, or itinerant schoolmasters, journeying from one country estate to another to teach rhetoric to the owners' sons and French to their daughters. The impulse for writing poetry was often strong, but the conditions for writing it and the audience for reading it were much less promising than those in the North. There was a strong tendency among southern poets to write lyrics in a faded Romantic tradition: pale imitations of Wordsworth, Keats, Shelley, and Tennyson. Aside from Sidney Lanier, the South produced few poets who are of more than local interest, but at the end of this chapter we shall look briefly at the work of a few of them.

In New England, Henry Wadsworth Longfellow (1807–1882) led all the rest. His life, like his poetry, was dominated by sunshine, with flickerings of shadow. "Life is real! Life is earnest!" he exclaims in "A Psalm of Life." He was certainly aware he had made no new discovery, yet for him the very fact that this was a truism made it an appropriate theme for poetry. Longfellow was not humorless, but he and his audience lacked the ironic sense, so closely associated with our own age, that would have prevented him from many such sententious excesses. It may be hard to believe now that when "A Psalm of Life" was published in 1838 it was read as a poem of startling freshness and newness. "Young men read it with delight," writes his brother, Samuel Longfellow; "their hearts were stirred by it as by a bugle summons . . . They did not stop to ask critically whether or not it passed the line which separates poetry from preaching, or whether its didactic merit was a poetic defect. It was enough that it inspired them and enlarged their lives." The poem was translated into eight languages, including a version in Chinese painted on a fan, and in 1855 Lady Byron wrote to a friend that it had been heard on the lips of a dying soldier on the field before Sevastopol. This is not to say that its popularity in any way makes it a great poem, but the attitudes in it, and the clarity and directness of statement in which they are expressed are the qualities that made Longfellow second only to Tennyson in worldwide popularity in the nineteenth century, and the most famous American poet who has ever lived.

Although Longfellow suffered from almost as much personal tragedy as Emerson, his bland and earnest optimism is generally untouched by the determination of spirit with which Emerson's most positive remarks are made. Longfellow's first wife died during their European trip when he was twenty-eight; his second wife, Frances Appleton, was horribly burned to death in a freak accident, yet his writing seldom reveals a deep sense of either tragedy or evil. He suffered from dyspepsia, neuralgia, and near-blindness, but he allowed neither his sense of loss nor his physical discomfort to color his poetry deeply. His fine sonnet, "The Cross of Snow" (1879), makes one of the few explicit references to the long years of suffering and sorrow following the death of his second wife—but he withheld this poem from publication.

If we try to see why so little of Longfellow's poetry contains what Melville called "the blackness of darkness," we must take a number of things into account. One is his temperament; another is his early life—a comfortable upbringing in a well-to-do family of Portland, Maine; an excellent but uneventful education at Bowdoin College; and, most important, a three-year sojourn in Europe during his most impressionable years. Appointed as the first professor of modern languages at Bowdoin at the age of eighteen, Longfellow was given three *Wanderjähren* in Europe to learn French, Spanish, Italian, and German before taking up his duties. He learned these languages not by attending the universities or by taking formal instruction, but by living, reading, and traveling in the language of each country he visited. He met Italian monks, visited medieval castles in France, and danced with Spanish peasants; he met Thomas Carlyle in England, Washington Irving in Spain, and August Wilhelm Schlegel in Germany. But he was in Europe at a time when German Romanticism had reached a point of diffuseness and mistiness that placed heavy emphasis on the emotions and little on the mind. He read Goethe and Heine, but was more captivated by Ludwig Tieck, E. T. A. Hoffmann, Novalis, and Jean-Paul Richter. Although he traveled widely and talked with many kinds of people, he remained out of touch with contemporary Europe, preferring to linger in Heidelberg and Nuremberg, where he stored up enough memories and associations to last him a lifetime. Poetry and life for Longfellow were two different things—as they were for Poe, with quite different results—and Longfellow was never completely able to accustom himself to the idea that writing poetry was not an occupation for the idle or for women. One of many revealing statements Longfellow makes about his attitude toward poetry is a journal entry of 1845, after his second visit to Germany:

> Felt more than ever to-day the difference between my ideal home-world of Poetry, and the outer, actual, tangible Prose world. When I go out of the precincts of my study, down the village street to college, how the scaffoldings about the Palace of Song come rattling and scattering down!

Although from his undergraduate days he had ambitions to make a career of poetry, Longfellow was prevented from writing any by his studies and early teaching years at Bowdoin and Harvard. He wrote "Hymn to the Night" and "A Psalm of Life" when he was thirty-two, and he was led by their popular success to collect his early poems in his first volume of verse, *Voices of the Night,* in 1839. "The aspiration of my youth," he wrote in "Mezzo Cammin" in 1842, is "to build / Some tower of song with lofty parapet." The same lofty and romantic ambition we see in his journal entry is repeated in this sonnet, but perhaps more interesting is the theme of the poem—the missed opportunities, the awareness of the passage of time—a theme upon which so many of Longfellow's poems are built. The tone in such poems is gentle regret for the past, coupled with a firm resolve for the future. The image of "footprints on the sands of time" in "A Psalm of Life" (1838) recurs in the much finer poem of his old age, "The Tide Rises, The Tide Falls" (1879), in which "The little waves, with their soft, white hands, / Efface the footprints in the sands." In "Mezzo Cammin" he sees the past as a twilit city, and hears "above me on the autumnal blast / The cataract of Death far thundering from the heights," as he becomes a kind of Lambert Strether awakening to the horrifying possibilities of the unlived life. But it is never too late, as he reminds the members of his college class at their fiftieth reunion, in "Morituri Salutamus" (1875):

> For age is opportunity no less
> Than youth itself, though in another dress,
> And as the evening twilight fades away
> The sky is filled with stars, invisible by day.

Even titles of many of his shorter lyrics and poems are on the same theme: "My Lost Youth," "Something Left Undone," and "Sand of the Desert in an Hour-Glass." In one of his best poems, "The Fire of Drift-Wood," he skillfully mingles fire imagery with the memories of lost hopes of those sitting by the hearth:

> The gusty blast, the bickering flames,
>   All mingled vaguely in our speech;
>
> Until they made themselves a part
>   Of fancies floating through the brain,
> The long-lost ventures of the heart,
>   That send no answers back again.
>
> O flames that glowed! O hearts that yearned!
>   They were indeed too much akin,
> The drift-wood fire without that burned,
>   The thoughts that burned and glowed within.

This gentle and somewhat bookish melancholy, coupled with images of the sea, of sunlight and moonlight, of wind and rain, all lucidly and directly expressed, is the hallmark of Longfellow's lyric poetry.

There are two sides to Longfellow's work: on the one hand, he is a popular poet, author of "The Wreck of the Hesperus," "The Village Blacksmith," and "Excelsior"; on the other, he is the sensitive, emotional, but never very deeply thoughtful, writer of "The Building of the Ship" (1849), "In the Churchyard at Cambridge" (1858), "The Jewish Cemetery at Newport" (1858), and "The Arsenal at Springfield" (1845). These poems are carefully built, with a simplicity of design and clarity of statement that we associate with Longfellow's best poems. Frequently we discover scattered passages in his work that have a particular brilliance or beauty, such as this one in "Kéramos" (1878), a long philosophical poem:

> What land is this that seems to be
> A mingling of the land and sea?
> This land of sluices, dikes, and dunes?
> This water-net, that tessellates
> The landscape? this unending maze
> Of gardens, through whose latticed gates
> The imprisoned pinks and tulips gaze;
> Where in long summer afternoons
> The sunshine, softened by the haze,
> Comes streaming down as through a screen;
> Where over fields and pastures green
> The painted ships float high in air,
> And over all and everywhere
> The sails of windmills sink and soar
> Like wings of sea-gulls on the shore?

Another poem, one of his best lyrics, has been underrated, perhaps because it does not build to a satisfactory conclusion. George Arms, writing about "Snow-Flakes" (1858), has shown how this poem becomes more effective when the middle stanza is dropped and the first and third stanzas are put in reverse order:

> This is the poem of the air,
>   Slowly in silent syllables recorded;
> This is the secret of despair,
>   Long in its cloudy bosom hoarded,
>   Now whispered and revealed
>   To wood and field.
>
> Out of the bosom of the Air,
>   Out of the cloud-folds of her garments shaken,
> Over the woodlands brown and bare,
>   Over the harvest-fields forsaken,
>   Silent, and soft, and slow
>   Descends the snow.

Obviously, we cannot judge a poet by rearranging and rewriting his poems according to the way we think they should have been written, but this startling and very perceptive observation does bring home to us the fact that there are some beautiful passages to be found scattered through Longfellow's work.

Longfellow's long poems, *Evangeline, The Song of Hiawatha, The Courtship of Miles Standish,* and *Tales of a Wayside Inn,* all display his gift for narration, description, and characterization. The story of *Evangeline* (1847), the first of his long poems, was offered to him by Hawthorne, who had heard it from a clergyman friend. When Longfellow began to work out the details of the poem he was influenced by several examples to write *Evangeline* in hexameters. He had recently read a translation of the *Iliad* that attempted to reproduce the classical hexameters in English; he had also translated part of the Swedish poet Esaias Tegnér's poem of the Viking age, *Frithiof's Saga,* into the English equivalent of Swedish hexameters. In addition, he had been reading Goethe's *Hermann und Dorothea,* which used a hexameter line. If we do not try to read *Evangeline* as a classical imitation, but allow the long line to move us at a rather slow and dreamy pace, we may avoid becoming annoyed or distracted by a meter that has seldom been successfully used in English verse. Longfellow's hexameters were attacked vigorously by critics of his own day, including Poe, who found fault with them because they were not classical at all but simply English dactyls. Toward the end of "The Rationale of Verse" (1848), he printed some of them as prose, and commented: "There!— That is respectable prose; and it will incur no danger of ever getting its character ruined by anybody's mistaking it for verse." There are indeed whole passages of *Evangeline,* particularly the set speeches, that do read like prose; but where he is setting a mood or describing a scene bathed in moonlight (as so many of them are), he has written some passages of great beauty.

The story of *Evangeline* is sentimental and melodramatic, but its wandering motif and its colorful French and Indian characters gave Longfellow the opportunity to let himself go in descriptions of natural scenery and in the use of folk material he had encountered in the course of his background reading. Evangeline, after her exile from Acadia, wanders all over the eastern part of North America, eventually going down the Mississippi to Louisiana. Longfellow had not visited any of the places he describes except Philadelphia, where at the end of the poem Evangeline is reunited with her former lover, and he reinforced his memories of the city with books and maps. The other descriptions of the North American wilderness are about as authentic as Chateaubriand's notoriously inaccurate ones in *Atala* and *René*. The bare and flat landscape of Nova Scotia is transformed by Longfellow's imagination into the heavily wooded countryside of Sweden, and the details are taken from an essay on Tegnér he had written ten years before. In spite of its inaccuracies, *Evangeline* remains a moving narrative poem, chiefly because of the sustained mood of melancholy and moonlight and the pathetic but not oversentimental characterization of its heroine.

When he resigned from teaching at Harvard in 1854, Longfellow began work on another long poem based on native material, much of which he found in Henry Rowe Schoolcraft's (1793–1864) monumental collections of Indian history and folklore. The hero of *The Song of Hiawatha* (1855) is a different kind of Indian from the conventional noble savage of sentimental fiction and drama; he is different, too, from Cooper's larger-than-life Chingachgook and Uncas. Hiawatha is, as Newton Arvin has said, the Gentle Savage, a kind of mild primitive who neither deceives nor tortures nor fights cruel wars. Instead, he teaches his people to hunt, raise corn, cure diseases, and love each other. He undergoes a series of trials and adventures in a sagalike poem resembling in spirit, as well as in its peculiar meter, the Finnish epic *Kalevala*. As a youth Hiawatha, like Beowulf and other primitive heroes, is sluggish and backward; later he emerges as a great culture hero, aided by friendly and helpful animals, which often have a kind of cloying, Disney-like cuteness about them. The meter of *Hiawatha* is even more eccentric than that of *Evan-*

geline—an unrhymed trochaic tetrameter with a heavy use of parallelism and repetition that attempts to reproduce the effects of primitive verse. This adaption of Finnish meter to English does not work very well, because of the monotonous regularity of the beat. Practically any passage taken at random shows the difficult limitations Longfellow imposed upon himself:

> Thus the Birch Canoe was builded
> In the valley, by the river,
> In the bosom of the forest;
> And the forest's life was in it,
> All its mystery and its magic,
> All the lightness of the birch-tree,
> All the toughness of the cedar,
> All the larch's supple sinews;
> And it floated on the river
> Like a yellow leaf in Autumn,
> Like a yellow water-lily.

If we discount a certain amount of diffuseness in these two poems and allow ourselves to be absorbed by their atmosphere of gentle melancholy, we may still enjoy them—especially if we have not previously been subjected to long and undigestible passages of them in grade school. *The Courtship of Miles Standish* (1858), also perhaps too familiar to us today, will bear up well under a fresh and unprejudiced reading. And his most ambitious effort, the *Tales of a Wayside Inn* (1863), modeled loosely on *The Canterbury Tales*, holds many surprises for those who think Longfellow is never humorous or clever or sardonic.

Whatever reservations we may have about his narrative poems, most readers today agree that Longfellow's best poetry is found in his sonnets. He wrote most of them late in his life; fourteen were published in a section of *The Masque of Pandora and Other Poems* in 1875. Among these are his tributes to Chaucer, Shakespeare, Milton, and Keats, each of which distills into fourteen lines a lifetime of immersion in their poetry. The long, rolling lines of Milton, for example, are echoed in this rhythmically magnificent single sentence of the octet:

I pace the sounding sea-beach and behold
　　How the voluminous billows roll and run,
　　Upheaving and subsiding, while the sun
　　Shines through their sheeted emerald far unrolled,
And the ninth wave, slow gathering fold by fold
　　All its loose-flowing garments into one,
　　Plunges upon the shore, and floods the dun
　　Pale reach of sands, and changes them to gold.

Even better than these are the six famous sonnets he wrote as epigraphs to his accurate but uninspiring translation of the *Divina Commedia* (1865–1867), especially the first of the Paradiso sonnets, with its skillful blending of cathedral imagery with allusions to the poem itself. Along with "Mezzo Cammin," "The Cross of Snow" (1879), and "The Broken Oar" (1886), these sonnets by Longfellow are among the best written in America in the nineteenth century.

But in spite of his experiments with a variety of stanzas and meters, Longfellow was less versatile than Holmes, less experimental than Lowell. He contributed little to the development of American verse forms; instead, he stimulated an interest in the possibilities of using a wide variety of forms, including those imported from Europe. He was more learned than Holmes, more devoted to the poetic life than Whittier, yet few of his poems have the strength of passion or depth of feeling of "The Chambered Nautilus" or "Ichabod." In the history of American poetry Longfellow's name has eclipsed all three of his Brahmin contemporaries, yet his gifts were no greater than Lowell's nor were they more fully realized than Whittier's. His very blandness and geniality—a word often applied to him—made his reputation, even while they called forth some reservations from early critics of his work.

The popularity of Longfellow was most closely rivaled by his exact contemporary John Greenleaf Whittier (1807–1892),

who never went to college, spent most of his life as a newspaperman and politician, and publicly disclaimed his pretensions as a poet. Whittier was not the simple folk bard he
seemed, however; he was a complicated man whose quiet but
fervent lines barely conceal a desire for fame, which he felt
was beyond his reach. Whittier invites labels; he is "the
American Burns," the "Quaker poet," or the "Abolitionist
poet." These labels have their origin in fact, but even taken
together they do not fairly describe the quality of his verse.
Whittier is not a great poet; like Longfellow and Holmes he
wrote too much, but a severe winnowing will turn up a dozen
or so very good poems. He has a good narrative and dramatic
sense, an ability to create vivid genre pictures of the local
New England countryside, and a talent for satire and invective.

Whittier's early life as a farmboy in Haverhill, Massachusetts, is reflected in his countless poems about simple people
set in a native New England landscape. Many of his early
poems are imitations of Burns, such as the temperance lyric,
"The Drunkard to His Bottle," written when he was twenty-
two:

> Hoot!—daur ye shaw ye're face again,
> Ye auld black thief o' purse an' brain?
> For foul disgrace, for dool an' pain
>   An' shame I ban ye:
> Wae's me, that e'er my lips have ta'en
>   Your kiss uncanny!

Whittier is probably one of the few poets whose early verses
opened the way to a formal education and the beginning of a
career. When he was eighteen he submitted "The Exile's Departure," a mawkish imitation of Byron, to the then unknown
editor of the *Newburyport Free Press,* William Lloyd Garrison, who printed it and asked for more. Whittier sent him a
second poem, "The Deity," and on the strength of this, Garrison persuaded Whittier's father to let him attend Haverhill
Academy. After two terms there Whittier was launched on a

career of newspaper editing and politics that was to absorb him for most of his life.

Meanwhile, he continued to write poetry, and for a while remained under the influence of Byron and Scott. Two early verse narratives, written in the 1830s, *Mogg Megone* and *Moll Pitcher,* both attest to Whittier's one-time aspiration to be a Scott in New England. Years later, in a note to *Mogg Megone,* he observed that his efforts to give New England an atmosphere of legend and tradition were too literary and unnatural. The poem, he said, "suggests the idea of a big Indian in his war-paint strutting about in Sir Walter Scott's plaid." He had earlier hunted out every copy he could find of his prose *Legends of New England* (1831) and destroyed them, because he realized that these, too, were the products of misguided intentions. But the spirit of Byron was also much in evidence. He had remarked in an early review that Byron was "the master spirit of his time," and a projected series of verses, "The Poem of Adrian," seems to be a parallel to Byron's *Childe Harold. Mogg Megone* (1834) and "The Song of the Vermonters," which he published anonymously in 1833, are full of violence, Byronic melancholy, self-pity, and demonism. Whittier's love for superstitions and for the exotic never left him; his readings in anthropology, Indian history, Norse legend, and primitive religions prompted him to write such poems as "The Dead Feast of the Kol-Folk" (1829), "The Khan's Devil" (1879), "Funeral Tree of the Sokokis" (1841), and "King Volmer and Elsie" (1872). Some of his best poems make use of this legendary material, often in ballad form, while others are genre pieces, such as the somewhat sentimental but realistic "Maud Muller" (1854), which evoke the people and natural settings of his native New England in a well-defined American literary tradition looking backward to Bryant's poems, set in the Berkshires, and forward to Frost's, set in the mountains of New Hampshire and Vermont.

Whittier's ballads are better than Longfellow's because they are less literary; he has the true ballad-maker's gift of narration, combined with an economy of language and a spareness of description. "Skipper Ireson's Ride" (1857) is a good poem not because the story itself is striking or unusual, but because it moves quickly and suggests, rather than states, much of the background that gives it that darkly sinister quality we associate with such folk ballads as "Sir Patrick Spens" in a way that Longfellow's "The Wreck of the Hesperus" does not:

> Fathoms deep in dark Chaleur
> That wreck shall lie forevermore.
> Mother and sister, wife and maid,
> Looked from the rocks of Marblehead
> Over the moaning and rainy sea, —
> Looked for the coming that might not be!

For simplicity of diction and uniformity of tone this ballad is Whittier's best, but he demonstrated his ability in a number of other excellent ballads, including "Kathleen" (1849), a story of the selling of a beautiful Irish girl by a wicked stepmother; "The Henchman" (1877), a ballad of hopeless love; "The Wreck of Rivermouth" (1867) and "The Garrison of Cape Ann" (1857), ballads of history and superstition; and his most famous ballad, "Barbara Frietchie" (1863). There is nothing subtle or sophisticated in either language or tone in this last poem, which has been assimilated into the national folk memory to the point where many can quote from it without having read it. This is not necessarily a sign of greatness, but Whittier's gray-headed Barbara Frietchie demonstrates better than anything in his other poems his ability to distill popular feelings into rhythmically strong and emotionally moving stanzas.

Whittier is at his best when he is describing a landscape or setting a scene. He is able to set a scene with precise and economical descriptive touches, as he does in the opening of "Barbara Frietchie":

> Up from the meadows rich with corn,
> Clear in the cool September morn,
>
> The clustered spires of Frederick stand
> Green-walled by the hills of Maryland.

Or in the opening of "Telling the Bees" (1858):

> Here is the place; right over the hill
>> Runs the path I took;
> You can see the gap in the old wall still,
>> And the stepping-stones in the shallow brook.
>
> There is the house, with the gate red-barred,
>> And the poplars tall;
> And the barn's brown length, and the cattle-yard,
>> And the white horns tossing above the wall.

"Telling the Bees" is memorable for more than its descriptive qualities, however. It demonstates Whittier's dramatic and narrative sense more fully than any of his other poems. The poem's narrator changes in mood from innocent anticipation of a reunion with his Mary to vague feelings of foreboding, as he discovers the servant girl following the New England custom of "telling the bees" of a death in the family. The final stanza is a cry of revelation and despair:

> And the song she was singing ever since
>> In my ear sounds on:—
> "Stay at home, pretty bees, fly not hence!
>> Mistress Mary is dead and gone!"

Whittier's best genre poem is *Snow-Bound* (1866), his sentimental evocation of a New England boyhood. This narrative compresses all his memories and nostalgia into a single week, during which all the members of the family are gathered around the fireside. The poem is given more unity and meaning by the fortunate choice of the hearth as the central image. Whittier draws attention to the fire in the first of the two epigraphs, from Cornelius Agrippa, which ends, "as the Celestial Fire drives away dark spirits, so also this our Fire of Wood doth the same." The second epigraph is from Emerson's "The Snow-Storm." George Arms and John B. Pickard have both called attention to the fact that the poem is not just a loosely organized series of sketches, but is built around the imagery of snow and fire and light. As it is in Hawthorne's tales, Whittier's hearth is a symbol of family love and warmth —of the inwardness of human emotion and experience in relation to the outer world. The poem opens with the image of a "cheerless" December sun rising with a "sadder light than waning moon," a portent of darkness and strangeness that is soon replaced by the strong inward light of family love. As the warmth of the family is juxtaposed against the hostile and strange forces of a nature suddenly made unfamiliar by the transformations of the snow, the reader is made to feel the sustaining power of the family through imagery that is commonplace and readily accessible yet completely appropriate.

In addition to his genre pieces and ballads, Whittier wrote innumerable Abolitionist verses. All but a few of these poems have been mercifully forgotten. One memorable exception is "Ichabod" (1850), which expresses Whittier's intense feelings of anger and dismay upon reading Daniel Webster's "Seventh of March" speech in support of the Fugitive Slave Act. "No partisan or personal enmity dictated [the poem]," Whittier later wrote. "On the contrary my admiration of the splendid personality and intellectual power of the great Senator was never stronger than when I . . . penned my protest." Whittier both denounces Webster, whom he characterizes by the biblical name meaning "inglorious one," and expresses compassion and sorrow for him as a misguided man who is explicitly described as a fallen angel. The poem ends on an elegiac note that softens the tone of angry surprise of the opening:

> Then, pay the reverence of old days
>   To his dead fame;
> Walk backward, with averted gaze,
>   And hide the shame!

A poem like this illustrates the burning intensity and fervor of Whittier's personality, which often erupted into violence or invective but was usually mitigated by the "still small voice" of the Quaker conscience.

Whittier's love for the New England countryside did not blind him to the shortcomings of its people, and he was able to describe the narrowness and meanness of many of their lives in passages such as this from the Prelude to "Among the Hills" (1869):

> Shrill, querulous women, sour and sullen men,
> Untidy, loveless, old before their time,
> With scarce a human interest save their own
> Monotonous round of small economies,
> Or the poor scandal of the neighborhood;
>
> *   *   *
>
> Church-goers, fearful of the unseen Powers,
> But grumbling over pulpit-tax and pew-rent,
> Saving, as shrewd economists, their souls
> And winter pork with the least possible outlay
> Of salt and sanctity;

These words recall Emerson's remark in the "Ode Inscribed to William Ellery Channing" that "The God who made New Hampshire / Taunted the lofty land / With little men." Other satirical poems include his "Letter from a Missionary, of the Methodist Episcopal Church South, in Kansas, to a Distinguished Politician" (1854), in which the writer laments his difficulties in keeping order among the Negro slaves (one ran away, but "my Indian converts / Found him, and treed and shot him") and in coping with the Yankee Abolitionist settlers ("grim, stalwart men, / Each face set like a flint of Plymouth Rock / Against our institutions"). Another is his humorous poem, "The Double-Headed Snake of Newbury" (1859), in which Cotton Mather's credulous account of the "wonder workings of God's providence" in the form of a two-headed snake is burlesqued in hudibrastic couplets.

Whittier worked entirely within a limited number of conventional forms: the ballad stanza and the quatrain, usually using his favorite four-stress lines, especially octosyllabic couplets. Occasionally, in his verse narratives, such as *The Pennsylvania Pilgrim* (1872), he used a three-line rhymed stanza in iambic pentameter, but he never attempted irregular odes or complicated stanzaic forms such as the sonnet. Simple, strong measures suited his direct and straightforward manner best, but they also emphasized his weaknesses when they became too prosaic in diction and tone. His diction was limited partly by his lack of formal education and partly by his lack of interest in developing versatility and polish in the use of language. He had an ear for New England dialect and pronunciation, however, and liked to use them in his rhymes: "meadows" and "ladders," "hence" and "since," "lion" and "iron," "Susquehanna" and "banner." He made his own disclaimers and modest apologies for his weaknesses in "Proem," written in 1847 and affixed to the collected edition of his poems. Here he attributes his shortcomings to "The rigor of a frozen clime, / The harshness of an untaught ear," and goes on to say:

> Of mystic beauty, dreamy grace,
>> No rounded art the lack supplies;
> Unskilled the subtle lines to trace,
>> Or softer shades of Natures face,
> I view her common forms with unanointed eyes.

His desire for lasting fame is implicit here, however, in spite of his attitude of resignation to his humbler gifts. There seems to have been a point early in his life when, as Perry Miller has observed, he rejected whatever desire for poetic fame he may have had in favor of his commitment to the Abolitionist cause. This commitment produced a lot of mediocre verse, but it also enabled Whittier to overcome a romantic passion for poetry that was foreign to his Quaker beliefs and at the same time to channel much of his intense energy into journalism and politics in such a way that poetry became not his entire life but an important adjunct to it.

The earnest and rural simplicity of Whittier's poetry is far removed in tone from the sophisticated light verse of Oliver Wendell Holmes (1809–1894). Holmes was a physician and scientist whose observations of nature were made as often in the dissecting room as they were in the fields of Cambridge, and his poetry reflects the habits of precision and close observation he developed in his professional life. He was a highly sociable man, a diner-out and joiner, who enjoyed an evening of good talk with intelligent men and charming women. His social ease and charm, his tact, and his sense of correctness and decorum are other personal qualities that found their way into his verse. And for most of his long life Holmes was a New England poet laureate. He wrote poems commemorating birthdays, centennials, Harvard commencements, openings of agricultural fairs, and other occasions requiring his ability to put the collective sentiments of his assembled listeners into gracious and agreeable language.

If this description defines his limitations it also underscores his strengths, for no one could be relied upon so well to put his best efforts into writing occasional poetry. It was an activity he enjoyed, and the reader of such poems as "For the Meeting of the National Sanitary Association" or "A Poem for the Meeting of the American Medical Association" never feels that Holmes was lowering himself from some exalted conception of himself in order to perform a perfunctory duty. Very much aware of his own limitations, Holmes once remarked that he wrote "not verses so much as the stuff that verses are made of." And in a mood of self-deprecation, which his best poems deny, he added, "I have some of the qualities . . . that make a man a poet; and yet I am not one." Throughout his life, Holmes played a variety of roles, all of which affected his verse. He was, to a large segment of his readers here and abroad, the Autocrat of the Breakfast Table, the opinionated, somewhat irascible but always lively Boston Brahmin, whose views were aggressively provincial in outlook and philistine in attitude.

Holmes made his reputation early in both medicine and poetry. At twenty-one he had published the poem with which he has ever since been most closely identified. "Old Ironsides," like so much of what he was to write, was an occasional poem, written on the spur of the moment in reaction to a newspaper account of the Navy's announced plan to scrap the frigate *Constitution*. It was published two days later on September 16, 1830, and is said to have led directly to the preservation of the ship. The three eight-line stanzas, beginning, "Ay, tear her tattered ensign down," were known to generations of schoolchildren and have become, as have so many of the poems of the Fireside poets, a part of our folk tradition. As the Class Poet of 1829 at Harvard—a duty he performed for over fifty years—Holmes had already shown his leanings toward literature, and while he was a medical student in Boston he turned out over five dozen poems, mostly in a light vein. One of these early poems was "The Last Leaf" (1831), written in an experimental six-line stanza designed, in Holmes's words, to "betray any copyist." It was much admired by Poe and was memorized by Lincoln, two facts to which Holmes pointed with pride in a note to his collected works.

Holmes's poetry has been classified by S. I. Hayakawa and Howard Mumford Jones into three categories: familiar verse, occasional verse, and "serious" verse. A good bit of his early poems were familiar verse, including *vers de société:* "The Spectre Pig" (1830), a mock-ballad ridiculing Dana's *The Buccaneer;* "The Last Leaf" (1836); and "To an Insect" (1836), which plays on the word "katydid" in a way that avoids the sentimentality of Freneau's poem on the same subject:

> Oh, tell me where did Katy live,
>   And what did Katy do?
> And was she very fair and young,
>   And yet so wicked, too?
> Did Katy love a naughty man,
>   Or kiss more cheeks than one?
> I warrant Katy did no more
>   Than many a Kate has done.

In the opinion of Hayakawa and Jones, Holmes is the best familiar-verse writer in classic American letters, and the first American in a long line including Bret Harte, Eugene Field,

F. P. Adams, Ogden Nash, E. B. White, Morris Bishop, and Phyllis McGinley to distinguish himself in this genre. The form demands a scrupulous attention to the humorous possibilities of meter and rhyme and the ability to adapt the conversational tone to the formal structure of verse. "Contentment," a poem that takes off from Oliver Goldsmith's remark in *The Vicar of Wakefield* that "Man wants but little here below," is a good example of the kind of irony that Holmes could direct toward stock sentimental attitudes in his role as Autocrat of the Breakfast Table:

> I care not much for gold or land;—
>   Give me a mortgage here and there,—
> Some good bank-stock, some note of hand,
>   Or trifling railroad share,—
> I only ask that Fortune send
> A *little* more than I shall spend.

Holmes's best-known piece of familiar verse was read by his contemporaries with no suspicion of its allegorical overtones. "The Deacon's Masterpiece; or, The Wonderful 'One-Hoss Shay' " (1858) is ostensibly a poem about the sudden and total collapse of the shay, but its subtitle as "A Logical Story" supports the idea first proposed by Barrett Wendell in 1900 that it is an attack upon Calvinism. Holmes had voiced his antipathy toward Calvinist orthodoxy in enough places—in his essay on Jonathan Edwards, in his long philosophical poem "Wind Clouds and Star Drifts" (1872), in his novel *Elsie Venner* (1861), and in many passages in the Breakfast-Table series—to make the connection between the breakdown of the logically constructed shay and the logic of Edwards a plausible one. Although the deacon's shay was built in 1755, the year after Edwards' *Freedom of the Will,* this was the year of Edwards' death, and was also the year of the Lisbon earthquake, which figures prominently in the poem and recalls Voltaire's discussions in *Candide* of the problems it raised concerning original sin and free will. Whatever its allegorical overtones (and other readers have suggested it might be a comment on

homeopathy or even manufacturing), "The Deacon's Masterpiece" remains one of Holmes's best pieces of light verse, with
its dexterous handling of Yankee idiom and its descriptions of
the details of the shay's construction:

> Step and prop-iron, bolt and screw,
> Spring, tire, axle, and linchpin too,
> Steel of the finest, bright and blue . . .
> That was the way he "put her through."
> "There!" said the Deacon, "naow she'll dew!"

Holmes's most serious poetry suffers from the qualities
that made him a successful occasional poet. Like Longfellow
and Lowell, Holmes was a public poet, and one hears in his
lines the tones of the orator addressing an audience. This is
true even in "The Chambered Nautilus" (1858), a philosophical poem using the image of the sea creature that builds itself
a paper-thin shell and then leaves it for a new one. Throughout the poem, Holmes maintains a precarious balance between the Romanticism that he avowedly despised yet had a
taste for, and eighteenth-century diction, which establishes a
connection between the universal and particular. In the first
stanza, he indulges in a lushness of diction and imagery in
these lines:

> The venturous bark that flings
> On the sweet summer wind its purpled wings
> In gulfs enchanted, where the Siren sings,
> And coral reefs lie bare,
> Where the cold sea-maids rise to sun their streaming hair.

But elsewhere in the poem, as Alexander Kern has pointed
out, he uses words in their literal sense to suggest an abstract
quality of the object as well: the ship of pearl is really pearl,
the irised ceiling is iridescent, the lustrous crypt has luster.
The last two stanzas follow the method of Bryant, in their explicit didacticism: "Thanks for the heavenly message brought
by thee, / Child of the wandering sea," and the declamatory

tone of the famous last stanza beginning, "Build thee more
stately mansions, O my soul," puts the Emersonian attitude
toward the correspondence of nature and spirit on public display. This is a line Whitman would have been proud to write,
and Holmes, like Whitman, moves outward in the last stanza
into an expansive celebration of the soul's release in death.
But instead of diffuseness and verbal freedom, Holmes maintains a Neo-classical balance and restraint:

> Let each new temple, nobler than the last,
> Shut thee from heaven with a dome more vast,
>   Till thou at length are free,
> Leaving thine outgrown shell by life's unresting sea!

Although he was a conservative and a philistine, he was
no prude, and his medical career made him see the falseness
in avoiding direct references to the physical aspects of life. In
"The Living Temple" (1858), he uses his professional medical
knowledge to create a fresh conception of the biblical text,
"your body is the temple of the Holy Ghost," again staying
within the bounds of an abstract Neo-classical diction:

> Then mark the cloven sphere that holds
> All thought in its mysterious folds;
> That feels sensation's faintest thrill,
> And flashes forth the sovereign will

"Dorothy Q." (1871), in addition to being a charming
genre piece about one of his ancestors, is a quite frank tribute
to the power of sex:

> What if a hundred years ago
> Those close-shut lips had answered No,
> When forth the tremulous question came
> That cost the maiden her Norman name,
> And under the folds that look so still
> The bodice swelled with the bosom's thrill?
> Should I be I, or would it be
> One tenth another, to nine tenths me?

In spite of the fact that Holmes's diction is firmly rooted in eighteenth-century Neo-classicism, he was given to flights of verbal fancy, as in "Musa" (1858), written in the "Chambered Nautilus" stanza:

Thou shalt be decked with jewels, like a queen,
    Sought in those bowers of green
    Where loop the clustered vines
And the close-clinging dulcamara twines,—
Pure pearls of Maydew where the moonlight shines,
    And Summer's fruited gems,
And coral pendants shorn from Autumn's berried stems.

His love of language also led him into burlesque, as in "Aestivation: An Unpublished Poem, by my Late Latin Tutor" (1858):

In candent ire the solar splendor flames;
The foles, languescent, pend from arid rames;
His humid front the cive, anheling, wipes,
And dreams of erring on ventiferous ripes.

Holmes, who took the job of writing poetry seriously, once remarked that poetry is "a cold-blooded, haggard, anxious, worrying hunt after rhymes which will be effective, after phrases which are sonorous." Still, he was not so serious that he could not describe his verses as "idle strains" or see that his future reputation was by no means certain. As a poet, he should be remembered today for a dozen or so poems that display his wit, his verbal energy, and his willingness to confront life with a combination of frankness and optimism.

Like the other Fireside poets, James Russell Lowell (1819–1891) was a spokesman for New England sentiments and attitudes. He thought and wrote from a provincial point of view, celebrating the virtues derived from close contact with the soil. He was not a farmer, although at one period in his life he raised chickens, but his sympathies, when they were not directed toward Abolition, were with the people and with nature. In several early poems celebrating the kinship of feeling and nature he sounds like Wordsworth, Bryant, and particularly Emerson. In "The Shepherd of King Admetus" (1842) he discovers the source of inspiration in nature:

> It seemed the loveliness of things
>   Did teach him all their use,
> For, in mere weeds, and stones, and springs,
>   He found a healing power profuse.

Implicit in the stanza above is an Emersonian disregard for history and tradition, which is made explicit in his dramatic monologue, "Columbus," in which Columbus rejects the Old World: "The old world is effete; there man with man / Jostles, and, in the brawl for means to live, / Life is trod underfoot." Lowell had absorbed most of the prevailing Romantic attitudes toward the primacy of feeling over intellect and primitivism over civilization that were current in mid-nineteenth-century America, even though he retained a Neo-classical cultivation and restraint. He gives these Romantic attitudes expression, for example, in his lines about a man reading Burns aloud in a railroad car:

> All thought begins in feeling,—wide
>   In the great mass its base is hid,
> And, narrowing up to thought, stands glorified,
>   A moveless pyramid.
>   ("An Incident in a Railroad Car," 1842)

As he does elsewhere in his early verse, Lowell is here indulging in a sentimental egalitarianism; later in his career this attitude was to give way to a distrust of popular opinion and a stronger reliance upon the eighteenth-century virtue of wisdom. This is his position in "The Washers of the Shroud," which he wrote during the early days of the Civil War:

> Hath he the Many's plaudits found more sweet
> Than Wisdom? held Opinion's wind for Law?
> Then let him hearken for the doomster's feet!

We find ourselves looking specifically for ideas in Lowell's poems, because in spite of their diffuseness and shifting attitudes many of them, from *The Biglow Papers* to the "Ode Recited at the Harvard Commemoration," have some philosophical or political content. Because this emphasis on ideas is so pervasive, Harry Hayden Clark's analysis of the stages of Lowell's development as a writer and thinker is a valuable aid to reading his poems in a context of widening human and philosophical concerns. As a young man, up to about 1850, Lowell was a humanitarian, influenced by the ardent Abolitionism of his first wife, Maria White; for the next seventeen years, until after the Civil War, he was a nationalist, interested primarily in the preservation of the Union. After 1867 he moved toward a broader humanism and in his political beliefs became a Jeffersonian natural aristocrat. During the first period he wrote the poems that made him famous: *The Biglow Papers, First Series* (1848), and *A Fable for Critics* (1847–1848). In the second period, while he taught at Harvard and edited the *Atlantic Monthly* (1857–1861) and *North American Review* (1864), he wrote *The Biglow Papers, Second Series* (1867), and the Harvard Commemoration Ode. The two best poems of his later years, and those which best represent his humanistic outlook, are "Agassiz" (1874) and *The Cathedral* (1869).

Throughout Lowell's career, however, there was a tension between his innate playfulness and high spirits and his attitude toward the writing of poetry as a highly serious vocation. He is a curious combination of the rough-and-ready, down-to-earth Yankee, which he projects into his persona of Hosea Biglow, and the Victorian poet of high seriousness, like the later Wordsworth, Tennyson, or Matthew Arnold. His versatility and his facility of composition in many ways worked against him, since he could compose an ode, a satire, or a lyric practically at will. He began *A Fable for Critics* (1847–1848) as a series of hurriedly improvised letters to his friend C. F. Briggs about his literary contemporaries. Although they show an acute critical perception in many cases, they were not intended to be serious criticism. The diffuseness of structure and vagueness of tone in many of his longer "verse essays" is perhaps no more than an unwillingness to conceive of poetry as a highly ordered art. "The Vision of Sir Launfal" (1848)—perhaps the most disorganized poem ever written—is the extreme example of Lowell's disregard for form. At the same time, however, "Sir Launfal" demonstrates his great technical skill in the handling of meter: its basic four-stress iambic pattern is brilliantly modulated through a variety of line lengths and meters in a movement analogous to music, as "Over his keys the musing organist, / Beginning doubtfully and far away, / First lets his fingers wander as they list, / And builds a bridge from Dreamland for his lay."

We see in Lowell, then, a poet of many and various gifts, none of which was ever fully exploited. His sensitivity to language is revealed most vividly in *The Biglow Papers,* which in his own opinion was inferior stuff compared to "The Washers of the Shroud." Lowell used the vernacular as a stylistic device; he was a connoisseur of the Yankee dialect, and the trueness of his ear in reproducing it is surpassed only by his good taste in putting it to the service of his most deeply held beliefs. In "The Washers of the Shroud," for example, Lowell had made a strong plea, in conventional language, for making war in the just cause of national unity:

> "God, give us peace! not such as lulls to sleep,
> But sword on thigh, and brow with purpose knit!
> And let our Ship of State to harbor sweep,
> Her ports all up, her battle-lanterns lit,
> And her leashed thunders gathering for their leap!"

He makes a similar plea more effectively at the end of Number VII of *The Biglow Papers, Second Series:*

> An' come wut will, I think it's grand
>   Abe's gut his will et last bloom-furnaced
> In trial-flames till it'll stand
>   The strain o' bein' in deadly earnest:
> Thet's wut we want,—we want to know

The folks on our side hez the bravery
To b'lieve ez hard, come weal, come woe,
In Freedom ez Jeff doos in Slavery.

Although Lowell's use of dialect is probably most effective
when put to the service of satire, this passage shows how his
real feelings could be given more forceful expression when
they were released from the bondage of genteel diction. "Sunthin' in the Pastoral Line" (1862), another in the Second Series, also is impressive for the way Lowell deals in a complex
and sophisticated way with the basic morality of the Northern
cause in a deceptively simple comic mode. In these poems,
Lowell was a pioneer in the humorous use of native languages,
continuing the tradition of Yankee humor found in Sam Slick
and Jack Downing and carried on in the South and West by
George Washington Harris and Artemus Ward.

Lowell was also an originator in his skillful use of meter.
Following the lead of Bryant, he worked toward greater freedom and looseness in his lines, particularly in the odes, where
he tried for a rhythm and rhyme suitable for recitation. He
was aware that a long series of uniform stanzas with regularly
recurring lines "produces somnolence among the men and a
desperate resort to their fans on the part of the women," and
for the "Ode Recited at the Harvard Commemoration" he invented a stanza of uneven lines and irregular rhyme scheme
that still had affinities with that staple of nineteenth-century
poets, the pseudo-Pindaric ode. But even though he was an
innovator in his free use of standard metrical forms, his experiments cannot be said to have had any significant or lasting
effect on the development of American verse. The "Ode Recited at the Harvard Commemoration" (1865) is an attempt to
restore the country to unity after the Civil War; to celebrate
the triumph of truth and high ideals and to urge a return
to national purpose. The best section of the poem is the sixth
strophe in praise of Lincoln, in which we find these lines:

Here was a type of the true elder race,
And one of Plutarch's men talked with us face to face.

I praise him not; it were too late;
And some innative weakness there must be
In him who condescends to victory
Such as the Present gives, and cannot wait,
    Safe in himself as in a fate.
        So always firmly he:
        He knew to bide his time,
        And can his fame abide,
Still patient in his simple faith sublime,
        Till the wise years decide.

Although Lowell wrote a number of excellent sonnets and short lyrics, including "Auspex" (1888) and "To the Dandelion" (1844), he was more at home in sustained and discursive poems, writing, as George Arms has pointed out, in the mode of the familiar verse essay. Among these longer poems are "Agassiz" (1874), a warm and deeply felt portrait of the famous scientist written after his death, *The Cathedral* (1869), and the "Ode Recited at the Harvard Commemoration." Both *The Cathedral* and "Agassiz" wrestle with the problems of faith and doubt that tormented the Victorian era. In "Agassiz" Lowell tries to resolve the conflict by emphasizing his friend's humanity. *The Cathedral*, which invites comparison with Tennyson's *In Memoriam A. H. H.*, Arnold's "Stanzas from the Grande Chartreuse," and Longfellow's *The Golden Legend* (1851), is a long philosophical plea for a return to a monolithic faith to replace the confusion of conflicting Protestant creeds. Using as his organizing image the Cathedral of Chartres, "Imagination's very self in stone," Lowell meditates loosely and discursively on the difference between the Middle Ages and his own, "an age that lectures, not creates." There are many excellent passages, one in particular that echoes Keats's "Ode to a Grecian Urn," and another that echoes Arnold's "Dover Beach," written two years before:

        . . . onward yearnings of unstilled desire;
    Fruitless, except we now and then divined

A mystery of Purpose, gleaming through
The secular confusions of the world,
Whose will we darkly accomplish, doing ours.

As a philosophical verse essay, *The Cathedral* is an impressive poem. It is flawed by the use of too many unusual words: *undisprivacied, repaganized, decuman, invirile* and the like, but its masterful blank verse conveys a philosophical depth seldom seen in American poetry.

Of all the Fireside poets Lowell had the most promise, yet he is the most disappointing in his accomplishments. With as much intelligence and more brilliance, Lowell rivals Longfellow in his range of learning, his deep love for literature, and his technical skill—but Lowell's poems were never really popular. His best-known poems were *The Biglow Papers,* and although they earned him a reputation, they reflect only one side of a many-sided individual whom Leon Howard once described as "the chameleon of nineteenth-century literature."

In the South one of the most commanding literary figures was Paul Hamilton Hayne (1830–1886), who in many ways typifies the predicament of the southern poet. Born to wealth and high social position in Charleston, Hayne became a lawyer and part-time poet. He published two volumes of verse at his own expense, one with the Boston house of Ticknor and Fields. This was a rather common practice among southern poets, since they felt this was one way they could get a hearing outside of the South. During his stay in New England to see his poems through the press, he met Whittier, Longfellow, Lowell, Dana, Whipple, and many other ornaments of northern literary life. He remained friends with many of them, and kept up a correspondence with them that lasted through the Civil War. Perhaps it was his contact with these writers that made him resent the fact he was born in the South. Like other southern writers, he felt at a disadvantage by not having access to a wide and cultivated audience and by the lack of stimulation he felt he needed in order to produce work of high quality. This was a traditional

and overworked complaint of many nineteenth-century southern poets, however, and there is little evidence in Hayne's
poetry to suggest that he would have been a better poet had
he lived elsewhere. His poems have little life in them and virtually ignore the real world in favor of polite parlor lyrics
based on medieval and Oriental subjects done up with a Ten-
nysonian sentimentality. They are ahead of their time in perhaps one respect, in that they are virtually indistinguishable
from the slightly later poems of Thomas Bailey Aldrich, Richard Henry Stoddard, Edmund Clarence Stedman, and Hamilton Wright Mabie.

The really central figure in the literature of the Old
South was William Gilmore Simms (1806–1870), who is remembered today for *The Yemassee* (1835) and other romances in the tradition of Scott and Cooper. Simms was a versatile and prolific writer who had published five small volumes
of verse before he was thirty. A long poem, *Atalantis,* was admired by Bryant in 1832, when he was arranging to have it
published in New York. But Simms, like John Pendleton Ken-
nedy (1795–1870) and the Cooke brothers, Philip (1816–1850)
and John (1830–1886), was obsessed with history, and turned
to celebrating the southerner's sense of community by writing
historical romances. He also wrote criticism, essays, plays,
short stories, biography, and history in a truly amazing outburst of energy. But his poems were even more diffuse and
otherworldly than those of Paul Hamilton Hayne; he had the
southerner's bent for verbal melody, and his short lyrics
are too much under the spell of Edward Coote Pinckney
(1802–1828) and Thomas Holley Chivers (1809–1858). Simms's
only really popular poem was "The Lost Pleiad," written before he was twenty, but Poe was particularly struck by "Indian Serenade," published in his novel *The Damsel of Darien*
in 1839.

Aside from Sidney Lanier, Henry Timrod (1828–1867) is
the only significant southern poet of this period. The son of
a minor Charleston poet, Timrod taught school for over ten

years in various South Carolina towns and began in 1849 to
contribute verse to the *Southern Literary Messenger* over the
signature "Aglaus." In 1859 he collected his early poems,
many of them technically excellent but without much substance, in a volume published by Ticknor and Fields at his
own expense. But after the bombardment of Fort Sumter,
Timrod discovered a passion and devotion to the South that
gave him his true subject. His technical ability was now combined with a genuine feeling of hatred for the North and
strong nationalistic feelings that overcame his original opposition to secession. "Ethnogenesis," first printed as a broadside
in 1861, celebrates the birth of a new nation in a way that
suggests that the Confederacy is not only a new nation but a
new race. It begins:

> Hath not the morning dawned with added light?
> And shall not evening call another star
> Out of the infinite regions of the night,
> To mark this day in Heaven? At last, we are
> A nation among nations; and the world
> Shall soon behold in many a distant port
>   Another flag unfurled!

He wrote and published in Charleston newspapers a
number of other stirring war poems before he served briefly in
the Confederate Army. In the winter of 1862, when South
Carolina was threatened with invasion, Timrod wrote two
stirring war poems, "A Cry to Arms" and "Carolina," both of
which are appeals to the men of the South to defend their
homeland. "Carolina," the better-known of the two, is a
battle cry in the manner of Burns's "Bannockburn"; it became immediately popular and in 1911 was adopted by the
legislature as the state hymn. It has little poetic merit, but was
effective as a rallying cry for southern patriots, with its
strongly accented tetrameter lines and the single word "Carolina" that concludes each stanza. When his health failed, Timrod was forced to leave the Army and return home, where he
wrote "Charleston" (1862), one of his best poems of this pe-

riod, evoking the mood of tension and uncertainty in the city that was under threat of attack from the sea.

Timrod's attitude toward war was changing, however, as he became more aware of its tragic consequences. In "Spring" (1863) he contrasts the promise of renewal in a world about to break into bloom with the destructiveness of war:

> Ah! who would couple thoughts of war and crime
> With such a blessed time!
> Who in the west-wind's aromatic breath
> Could hear the call of Death!
>
> Yet not more surely shall the Spring awake
> The voice of wood and brake
> Than she shall rouse, for all her tranquil charms,
> A million men to arms.

The controlled emotion and classical simplicity of phrase in this poem is matched and even surpassed in Timrod's finest poem, in which he has clearly abandoned the warlike tone of his earlier poems. This Horatian ode was first sung by a choir at Confederate memorial exercises in June 1866, and in July was reprinted in an amended version in the Charleston *Courier*. In form and spirit the "Ode" is comparable to Emerson's "Concord Hymn" and Collins' "How Sleep the Brave." It begins:

> Sleep sweetly in your humble graves,
> Sleep, martyrs of a fallen cause!—
> Though yet no marble column craves
> The pilgrim here to pause.

and ends with the lines:

> Stoop, angels, hither from the skies!
> There is no holier spot of ground,
> Than where defeated valor lies
> By mourning beauty crowned.

Today Timrod is remembered chiefly for his later work, even though many of his earlier lyrics and love poems stand up well in comparison to Longfellow, Whittier, and Lowell. He is not a great or original poet, but aside from Lanier, he is the South's best nineteenth-century poet. After reading his poem "Christmas" (1862) Tennyson is said to have remarked that "the man who wrote those lines deserves to be called the poet laureate of the South." This label is perhaps more fitting than the narrower and less accurate one usually attached to him, "Laureate of the Confederacy."

CHAPTER SEVEN

Moody, Crane, and the Poets of the Twilight Years

Bayard Taylor, Thomas Bailey Aldrich, E. C. Sted-
man, George Henry Boker, Trumbull Stickney, George
Cabot Lodge, William Vaughn Moody, George San-
tayana, Louise Imogen Guiney, Lizette Woodworth
Reese, Emma Lazarus, Paul Laurence Dunbar, Stephen
Crane

With a prescience not shared by many of his contemporaries
in 1900 Barrett Wendell, in his *A Literary History of America*,
wrote: "It is hard to resist the conclusion that whoever shall
make a new library of American literature, thirty or forty
years hence, will . . . find no place for many of our contemporaries momentarily preserved by our latest anthologists.
As you turn their pages, you can hardly avoid feeling that,
however valuable these may be as history, they contain little
which merits permanence." It is a sad fact that such a conclusion stands up better than most of the poetry written in
the late nineteenth century. Mark Twain's sobriquet for the
period, the Gilded Age, emphasizes the materialism and ac-
quisitiveness that underlay the widely prevalent smugness and
genteel attitudes of writers and readers. An extreme, but not
uncommon, genteel attitude may be seen in the history of
American literature that the influential teacher and critic
George Edward Woodberry published in 1903. In it he failed
to consider either Walt Whitman or Mark Twain worthy of
notice, and he later wrote that "our magnificent America has
never yet produced a poet of the rank of Gray." This kind of
cultural snobbery accounts for some of the weakness and

vapidity of the poetry written in the period that has been called "the interregnum," and makes clear the sense of outrage that led Edwin Arlington Robinson to write this "Sonnet" in 1894:

> Oh for a poet—for a beacon bright
> To rift this changeless glimmer of dead gray;
> To spirit back the Muses, long astray,
> And flush Parnassus with a new light;
> To put these little sonnet-men to flight
> Who fashion, in a shrewd mechanic way,
> Songs without souls, that flicker for a day,
> To vanish in irrevocable night.
>
> What does it mean, this barren age of ours?
> Here are the men, the women, and the flowers,
> The seasons, and the sunset, as before.
> What does it mean? Shall there not one arise
> To wrench one banner from the western skies,
> And mark it with his name forevermore?

The "little sonnet-men" to whom Robinson was referring were to be found in the pages of Richard Watson Gilder's (1844–1909) *Century*. Their strongest influence was a congenial circle of New York literary friends who gathered in the Tenth Street home of Richard Henry Stoddard (1825–1903) and formed a genteel, late-Victorian American Bohemia. The principal members were Thomas Bailey Aldrich, E. C. Stedman, Bayard Taylor, and George Henry Boker.

Another group, younger and more adventurous in tastes and attitudes, was composed of seven Harvard undergraduates led by George Santayana, then a new instructor. They formed the Laodicean Club in the nineties, devoted to the notion that the Laodiceans' lukewarm attitudes toward religion represented a commendable balance of thought and feeling. The principal members were William Vaughn Moody, Trumbull Stickney, and George Cabot Lodge, all of whom tended to be skeptical in religion but catholic in taste. The outstanding member was Moody, who transcended his academic origins to write some distinguished poems.

But poetry was no less diverse in the latter half of the nineteenth century than it was at any other time. Much of it was popular poetry, from the sentimental dialect rhymes of James Whitcomb Riley (1849–1916) to the swaggering Far-West Pre-Raphaelitism of Joaquin Miller (1841?–1913). The local-color vogue also manifested itself in the ballads of John Hay (1838–1905) and Bret Harte (1836–1902), and the seaside idyls of the Maine poet Celia Thaxter (1835–1894).

The poet of this period who stands out above all the rest is still perhaps only a minor poet, but Stephen Crane's poetry is interesting for the qualities it shares with that of the Imagists. Other poets who deserve at least a brief glance are the black poet Paul Laurence Dunbar and three women: Louise Imogen Guiney, Lizette Woodworth Reese, and Emma Lazarus.

Let us look first at the New York group, among whom Bayard Taylor (1825–1878) was the best known. Taylor was one of the most ambitious and industrious writers of the nineteenth century, determined throughout his life to make a name for himself that would rival Longfellow's and Whittier's. One of the original members of the circle of writers who gathered at the home of Richard Henry Stoddard and his wife, Elizabeth, Taylor shared their idealistic and highly romanticized views of the role of the artist in society. He published his first volume of verse, *Ximena* (1844), when he was nineteen and then embarked on a career of journalism that led to writing books based on his travels in Egypt, China, Abyssinia, Turkey, and India. His name became widely known, even though it was associated in the minds of many with the unkind epigram that he had traveled more and seen less than anybody else on earth.

Taylor, like E. C. Stedman and Thomas Bailey Aldrich, was a kind of high priest of the Ideal, who was defended in a preface to his *Poetical Works* (1879) by the poet and dramatist George Henry Boker as a man whose "sensitive poetical nature" was brought into daily contact with "the vulgarity of conceited dolts." But even Boker had to agree with the damning judgment of the sharp-tongued "Lizzie" Stoddard that all of this group—Boker, Taylor, Stoddard, Stedman, and Aldrich—were "dreary failures" as poets, none of them having attained even to such a position as "that weakling Longfellow, for whom no one can challenge more than a third class place, as compared with the mass of English poets."

Taylor issued about a dozen volumes of poetry in all, a lot of it based upon his travels: *Poems of the Orient* (1854), a collection of gushing lyrics including the popular "Bedouin Song," *Poems of Home and Travel* (1855), and *Lars: A Pastoral of Norway* (1873). Few of these have any intrinsic worth, and the pleasant experience of reading his facilely written lines was accompanied even in his own time by the realization that one could remember little of what he had read after he had put down the book. Some of his *Home Pastorals* (1875) are worthwhile, but an ode written for the Philadelphia centennial celebration the following year is a resounding failure. He worked hard on *The Picture of St. John* (1866), a long narrative poem by which he hoped to establish his reputation, but his gift for imitation and parody unfortunately led him into such pseudo-Wordsworthian passages as this description of the growth of the artist:

> And, wandering forth, a child that could not know
> The thing for which he pined, in sombre woods
> And echo-haunted mountain-solitudes
> I learned a rapture from the blended show
> Of form and color, felt the soul that broods
> In lonely scenes, the moods that come and go
> O'er Wayward Nature, making her the haunt
> Of Art's forerunner, Love's eternal want.

The flavor of the minor literary Bohemia of these New York poets is preserved for us in *The Echo Club and Other Literary Diversions,* a series of lively parodies that Taylor did for the *Atlantic* in the seventies. He continued the game of parody-writing that all of them played for a while, and the poems are interesting reflections of contemporary attitudes toward a number of literary figures. Taylor placed his "diversions" in the mouths of a cast of characters who carry on a running dialogue with each other. Among the authors he parodied are Poe, Browning, Mrs. Sigourney, Keats, Swinburne, Emerson, Whittier, Aldrich, Stoddard, Mrs. Stoddard, Willis, Stedman, and himself. Here is a parody of Thomas Holley Chivers, the southern poet whose verse had such a marked effect on Poe's later poetry:

> Many mellow Cydonian suckets,
>   Sweet apples, anthosmial, divine,
> From the ruby-rimmed beryline buckets,
>   Star-gemmed, lily-shaped, hyaline;
> Like the sweet golden goblet found growing
>   On the wild emerald cucumber-tree,
> Rich, brilliant, like chrysoprase glowing,
>   Was my beautiful Rosalie Lee!

In spite of his ability to laugh at himself and his friends, Taylor was driven in his serious verse by his devotion to a dimly conceived Ideal. Holding toward the end of the century a position of popularity similar to that held by Fitz-Greene Halleck near its beginning, this latter-day friend of Bryant has also faded to almost complete obscurity. The judgment of Lizzie Stoddard upon her husband and his friends, including Taylor, was all too accurate: "The world is not unappreciative of real genius, as you flatter yourselves is the case, only you are not up to the required standard."

If Taylor was the most ambitious among the New York group, Thomas Bailey Aldrich (1836–1907) was the most conscientious. Unlike his friends, he devoted himself to polishing and perfecting his technique, even to the point of refusing to allow his early poems to be reprinted in later editions. Aldrich was a protégé of N. P. Willis, on whose magazines he held several editorial posts. His early verses are much like

Willis's: sentimental trifles about romantic love, usually in exotic settings, with echoes of Keats, Shelley, and Longfellow; later he moved away from his early lushness toward a Neo-classical purity of line and diction. Aldrich's poetry, like that of Taylor and Stedman, suffers from a diffuseness of imagery and idea that all of them deliberately cultivated. They shied away from "materialism" and the vitality of Whitman's subject matter in their pursuit of an Ideal that kept them within narrow bounds. Eschewing free verse and other experimental forms because they were too unconventional, and avoiding elaborate French forms such as the virelay, the roundel, and the ballade because they were too effete, they wrote and re-wrote the neo-Pindaric odes, the sonnets, and the quatrains that Bryant, Lowell, and Longfellow had already made respectable. Practically the only direction a man with any poetic talent could go was toward perfecting and refining his verses in these forms, and this is what Aldrich, certainly a minor talent, did. Both his attitude toward the role of the poet and his fears about the direction contemporary poetry was taking are expressed in these lines from "At the Funeral of a Minor Poet" (1897), which are full of a faded irony directed at the state of poetry in the Gilded Age:

> we can poorly spare
> Even his slight perfection in an age
> Of limping triolets and tame rondeaux.
> He had at least ideals, though unreached,
> And heard, far off, immortal harmonies,
> Such as fall coldly on our ear to-day.
> The mighty Zolaistic Movement now
> Engrosses us—a miasmatic breath
> Blown from the slums.

Since Aldrich's typical subjects for poetry were such things as "Madonnas leaning from their starry thrones / Ineffable," it is not surprising that they seldom led to anything but watered-down Longfellow or sexless Swinburne.

Aldrich is best known as the author of the semiautobio-

graphical novel *The Story of a Bad Boy* (1870) and as the
editor of the *Atlantic* from 1881 to 1890. In this exalted position he shared with Richard Watson Gilder, editor of *The
Century,* an influence over the taste of the American reading
public that was responsible for Robinson's exasperated outcry
against the "little sonnet-men" published in their pages. Aldrich himself published over fifteen volumes of verse, including *The Bells* (1855) and *Pampinea and Other Poems* (1861),
both collections of lush sentimental poems. Later collections
included *Flower and Thorn* (1877), *Friar Jerome's Beautiful
Book* (1881), and *Judith and Holofernes* (1896), a long narrative poem that was produced as a play, *Judith of Bethulia,*
in 1904. In spite of the fact that his popular reputation as a
poet rested on such tear-jerkers as the "Ballad of Babie Bell"
(1856), Aldrich late in life produced some more restrained
verses, including the ode "Spring in New England" (1897) and
some quite passable sonnets, "By the Potomac" (1874), "An-
dromeda" (1897), and "Eidolons" (1897), for example. But
even these remain well within the narrow bounds that he and
his Tenth Street friends had imposed upon themselves

Edmund Clarence Stedman (1833–1908), a later addition
to the Stoddard-Aldrich-Taylor group, is better remembered
as a critic than as a poet. As another arbiter of American
taste, he was far more eclectic than his colleagues. Together
with Professor G. E. Woodberry he edited Poe's works, but
their views on Whitman as a poet show the extent to which
they differed. Whereas Woodberry failed to include Whitman
in his history of American literature, Stedman's praise of
Whitman shows a critical acuteness not shared by Aldrich or
Taylor. "Unrhymed verse, the easiest to write, is the hardest
to excel in," he wrote, but added, "it may be that his mode is
suited to himself alone, and not to the future poets of These
States." Certainly it was not suited to Stedman himself, who
chose to write imitations of Landor and Swinburne and repli-
cas of exotic cultures. He brought together a second collected
edition of his poems in the eighties, but there is no percep-
tible sign of development from those he wrote in the sixties;

the shadows of Poe and Tennyson hang over them all. Stedman was first a journalist and later a stockbroker in Wall Street with a seat on the New York Stock Exchange. "The Diamond Wedding" (1859), a whimsical satire on a fashionable society wedding, brought him the threat of a duel and a lawsuit after it was published in the *Tribune,* but it also brought him into the Stoddard-Taylor-Aldrich circle. Most of his poetry is sentimental rather than satirical, voicing such ideas as "true love conquers all" and bewailing the death of the "high bards." The poems of his own that he chose for inclusion in his *An American Anthology* (1900) are mainly on historical or literary themes: Lincoln, General Kearney, Falstaff, and witchcraft in Salem. One poem, written in 1888, speculates on the closed-off world of the eight-year-old Helen Keller. In his poetry as well as his criticism Stedman reiterated the poet's sovereignty in the pursuit of beauty and truth, but the criticism did it with a far greater tolerance and catholicity of taste than the poetry.

Both Taylor and Stoddard owed part of their success in getting published to their older friend and supporter, George Henry Boker (1823–1890). Best known for his verse tragedy *Francesca da Rimini* (1855), Boker was primarily a playwright, whose plays met with moderate success in his native Philadelphia, but he had ambitions to be a serious poet. His *Plays and Poems* (1856) collected many of his pieces, but there is nothing particularly remarkable about this assortment of sonnets, satires, and dedicatory poems.

Boker's most impressive work is a group of 313 "profane sonnets" discovered after his death, most of them addressed to his mistress of fifteen years. The sonnets, written between 1851 and 1887, fall into three groups. The largest number celebrate his love affair with a well-known Philadelphia lady who could not afford to have her name connected with his. Thirteen sonnets record a very casual two-week affair in Europe, and the remaining seventeen are addressed to a third lady whom he met in his later years.

That he intended to publish them is argued by E. Sculley

Bradley, who discovered them in a cupboard in the house of Boker's daughter-in-law and published them in 1929. Although he treats other subjects such as his failure to gain recognition as an artist, his hatred of ugliness and philistinism, and his joy in the beauty of nature, his overriding concern is the love affair itself. The sonnets cover a wide range of moods: extreme melancholy, tenderness, physical passion, dejection, and remorse. They are very uneven in quality, and many suffer from a Victorian flaccidity of diction and sentiment. But Boker, for whom poetic fame was a lifelong ambition, achieved his greatest success with these lyrics, which show considerable versatility and skill in satisfying the demands of the Italian form. Although they do not approach the sonnets of Frederick Goddard Tuckerman for their intricacy or subtlety in the handling of language and imagery, Boker's sequence makes it clear that he was, along with Longfellow, Jones Very, and Washington Allston, one of the outstanding sonnet writers of the nineteenth century. Here is one of them:

> Ah! could I grow in some remote degree
> Nearer the whiteness of my darling's love;
> By likening her, my darker self reprove
> Beneath the eyes of her calm purity;
> Drop from my soul the earth that sullies me,
> And struggling upward, if but slowly, move
> A little nearer to those lights above,
> Whose guiding rays I cannot choose but see!
> Even as I muse, the vision of those eyes
> Awakes the fiery current in my veins
> With longings wild, mixed thrills of joys and pains;
> Remembered kisses, burning with the dyes
> That flushed her cheeks, the struggles, sobs and sighs,
> Ere her chaste will lay vanquished in my chains.
>
> (LXXII)

At Harvard, one of the group who called themselves the Laodiceans was Trumbull Stickney (1874–1904), a promising

Greek scholar for whom the Prometheus legend became a paradigm of his own bleak view of human history. This view, which had much in common with that of his friend Henry Adams (1838–1918), was filtered through a curious combination of Greek classics and the social Darwinism of Herbert Spencer. His early lyrics have the weaknesses of abstraction and vague moralizing that were the malady of the age, but his later lyrics, published posthumously by Moody, suggest that he might have developed into a poet of originality and force. His conviction that man's destiny offers only the bleakest hopes led him to cultivate a kind of pagan Stoicism with which to supplant a weakened and failing Christianity. All one could do was to gird oneself against despair, he wrote in one of his best-known sonnets: to "live blindly and upon the hour." In another sonnet, "Be still. The Hanging Gardens were a dream," life is illusion: "Thou art a frighted owl / Blind with the light of life thou'ldst not forsake, / And Error loves and nourishes thy soul."

These attitudes took their fullest form in a seven-hundred-line verse play, *Prometheus Pyrphoros* (1900), which Stickney wrote in Paris while working on a doctorate in classics. The play explores the possibility of hope in a benighted time by seeing the fire of Prometheus as scientific knowledge, which would raise man to new levels of achievement and material welfare. But the character of Prometheus as the bringer of light and hope is not wholly convincing, and the reader finishes the play feeling that the forces of darkness and misery that Prometheus is supposed to dispel are too much for him, and that his efforts to remove them, like the ideas of progress themselves, are impotent in the face of such negative currents. Stickney's later poems are tinged with some of the Eliotian malaise and despair that were certainly being felt around Harvard Yard by the turn of the century; one poem, "Six O'Clock" (1903), uses a contemporary grimness of detail to tentatively suggest that God is dead. But as Larzer Ziff has pointed out, his "almost automatic dependence upon a traditional arsenal" of images vitiates the poem's novel effects. Still, if he had not died of a brain tumor at thirty, Stickney might have continued to work away from the dead forms of the past to come to firm grips with the present.

The death of God and the struggle for the assertion of will were also preoccupations of George Cabot Lodge (1873–1909), whose first collection of poems, *The Song of the Wave and Other Poems* (1898), adopts the mood of pessimism and despair characteristic of the Laodiceans. The poems are experiments in a variety of forms; some are in Swinburnian meters, others in Whitman's free verse or in French verse forms. They treat lost youth, lost faith, and lost love in a youthful mood that looks forward to the F. Scott Fitzgerald heroes of a quarter of a century later. The title poem is typical of many of them in its use of sea imagery and in its assertion of the problem of the individual will making itself felt against the stark background of death:

So tried it the impossible height, till the end was found:
Where ends the soul that yearns for the fillet of morning stars,
The soul in the toils of the journeying worlds,
Whose eye is filled with the Image of God,
                    And the end is Death!

This longing for freedom, coupled with the loneliness and isolation of the poet-rebel, is the theme of two verse dramas on the Promethean theme, both of them probably inspired by Stickney's *Prometheus Pyrphoros* rather than Shelley's *Prometheus Unbound*. In *Cain, a Drama* (1904) and *Herakles* (1908) Lodge depicted characters struggling to attain Promethean stature who are left in chilly isolation in a world of loneliness and fear. Lodge's poems are finally quite lifeless and sterile attempts to confront the philosophical confusion of an age pathetically trying to place its faith in a science that refused to yield answers. His use of Greek myth for this purpose was misguided, perhaps, but he and his scholarly colleagues knew of no effective substitute. Stripped of such antiquarian trappings, the poems of Edwin Arlington Robinson were asking some of the same hard questions. James Dickey quotes

Robinson's ironic remark that the world is a "kind of vast spiritual kindergarten where millions of people are trying to spell God with the wrong blocks." It could well have been made by Stickney, Lodge, or Robinson's good friend, William Vaughn Moody.

When he published *The Fire-Bringer* in 1904, a verse play also based on the Prometheus theme, William Vaughn Moody (1869–1910) was considered by many critics to be the foremost American poet. Since that time, however, his reputation has been in steady decline; in 1961 Roy Harvey Pearce dismissed him in a paragraph devoted to a list of "depressing" poets of the 1890s that includes such decidedly minor talents as Richard Hovey (1864–1900), Madison Cawein (1865–1914), and Richard Watson Gilder (1844–1909).

Although Moody is an uneven poet, typical of his time in his inclination to be discursive and rhetorical, his best poetry demonstrates a skill and sensitivity shared by few of his contemporaries. As a professor of English literature at the University of Chicago—one of the first of the breed of poet-professors who have proliferated throughout the land—Moody steeped himself in the literature of the past. His poems are consciously wrought in the great tradition of English poetry, full of echoes of Marlowe, Shelley, and Keats, and many allusions to his favorite poet, Milton.

The eclecticism of the dying Victorian period, its self-consciousness and moral striving, all found their way into Moody's work. He was not a forward-looking or innovative poet, but his moral fervor and emotional intensity were at their highest when they were touched by contemporary issues, such as America's imperialistic tendencies and the horrors of the machine age. Stickney and Lodge remained in the east, but Moody moved west, and his eastern sensibilities received a severe jolt when he moved to the brash and vulgar city of Chicago. Repelled at first by its coarseness, he came to appreciate the strengths that these comparatively ugly surroundings could give to his own poetry by their "alchemical power to change and transmute." Moody certainly cannot be classed

with the Chicago poets—Masters, Lindsay, and Sandburg—
who found in Chicago the substance for Whitmanesque celebrations of the common man, but his contact with its raw
vigor gave his poetry a strength that he would never have
found in Harvard Yard.

Still, he was at odds with the industrial order and wrote
poems ambiguously critical of it, such as "Jetsam" (1897), a
long poem denouncing the factory system, "The Brute" (1900),
and "Gloucester Moors" (1900). "The Brute" is an ode to the
machine, which alternates in tone between mockery and fear
and in attitude between admiration and contempt. Moody
sees in the machine the potential for both material freedom
and spiritual death, and his attitude toward it is neither facile
progressivism nor sentimental antimaterialism, but an uneasy
mixture of both. Comparing "The Brute" to Emily Dickinson's "I Like to See it Lap the Miles," a poem that mocks the
anthropomorphic sentimentalizing of the "iron horse," we see
extreme contrasts in both sensibility and technique. Emily
Dickinson's poem is understated, concise, ironic, and witty;
Moody's is discursive, overexplicit, and largely humorless. But
it reflects quite accurately his Arnoldian fears about the dehumanizing tendencies of the industrial age. These same fears
are voiced, again ambiguously, in "Gloucester Moors," the
Moody poem exceeded in popularity only by "An Ode in
Time of Hesitation" (1900). "Gloucester Moors" is more successful as nature description than as political allegory, however, since Moody must strain to establish an elaborate metaphor of the world as a ship with a cargo of souls. Its passages
of nature description lie in a direct line from Bryant to Frost:

> Jill-o'er-the-ground is purple blue,
> Blue is the quaker-maid,
> The wild geranium holds its dew
> Long in the boulder's shade.
> Wax-red hangs the cup
> From the huckleberry boughs,
> In barberry bells the grey moths sup,
> Or where the choke-cherry lifts high up
> Sweet bowls for their carouse.

But when he gets to social criticism the language and tone are not convincing:

> Or shall a haggard ruthless few
> Warp her over and bring her to,
> While the many broken souls of men
> Fester down in the slaver's pen,
> And nothing to say or do?

We cannot accuse Moody of being insincere—his moral outrage is genuine—but he is trapped by a gentility of language and attitude that weakens even his best poems. "An Ode in Time of Hesitation" is a case in point. This is a courageous poem of protest against America's corruption of its ideals by its imperialistic actions. It expresses Moody's disappointment in the American government's refusal to give up the Philippines after their seizure in the Spanish-American War. First published in the *Atlantic Monthly* in May 1900, it became immediately well known and made Moody a popular poet. The poem opens strongly, but its moral fervor dwindles into vague and abstract language that vitiates its effect on modern readers. The ode begins by addressing the ideals of the past, typified by the spirit in which Colonel Robert Gould Shaw died while leading the first Union Army black regiment in an attack. Moody addresses his poem to Saint-Gaudens' statue of Shaw in Boston Common, and, in his evocation of the ideals of union and national purpose that the end of the Civil War was supposed to realize, Moody makes Shaw the figure against which the deterioration of these ideals is contrasted. In spite of its occasional lapses into rhetorical din, the ode is still a good poem, written in an unmistakable tone of moral passion. Shaw, his statue, and this poem about them have captured the imagination of several other American poets. James Russell Lowell addressed his ode "Memoriae Positum" (1863) to Shaw, and Robert Lowell's "For the Union Dead" (1964) is addressed to the statue and alludes indirectly to Moody's poem. Paul Laurence Dunbar and John Berryman have also written poems about him.

Moody's interest in dramatic writing led him to devote

over two years to the writing of his verse drama *The Masque of Judgment,* published in 1900. The *Masque* eventually came to be the second in a projected trilogy, all concerned with the theme of the inseparableness of God and man. Moody's most direct inspiration seems to have been a triptych of the Last Judgment that aroused in him a sense of revulsion against traditional apocalyptic myths, and he set out to write a masque that would deny what he considered the historical role of Christian doctrine—the denial of life.

Moody wrote his second verse play in 1904 after a tour of Greece and a stay with Trumbull Stickney in Paris, with whom he read through the entire body of Greek tragedy in the original. Still concerned with the problem of man's separation from God, Moody chose the Prometheus legend as the subject of the play that he was to call *The Fire-Bringer.* Although he told Stickney that he owed a debt to his play *Prometheus Pyrphoros,* they are different enough in theme and attitude to suggest that the debt stops with the similarity of subject. Rather than concentrating, as Stickney did, on the disaster of a crumbling faith, Moody attempted to restore optimism by placing his hope in man rather than God. Prometheus' act of bringing fire to man is treated in the play as the basis for a renewed hope in man's progress. As in *The Masque of Judgment,* Moody is working against the idea of God as the denier and destroyer of human happiness; his purpose is the opposite of Milton's: to justify man's ways to God in a way that asserts Moody's belief in the need to redefine our conception of God in the light of human intellectual development. *The Fire-Bringer* has some good poetry in it: Pandora's songs, including "Of wounds and sore defeat," are among the best lyrics Moody wrote. It was during the writing of this second play that Moody conceived the idea of writing a dramatic trilogy on the Prometheus theme, treating man's separateness from God during three different periods in man's historical development: Greek, Hebraic, and Christian. But he did not plan to substantially alter the *Masque* in order to bring it into line as the second play in the trilogy. Instead, all three were to be loosely bound together by the Prometheus legend. The last play, left unfinished at his death, was *The Death of Eve* (1912); it was to be an attempt to bring about the reunion of God and man, concluding, according to his widow, with a "lyric murmur of pure human joy, based upon . . . consciousness of mutual life."

Moody's poetry today seems strangely ornate, lush, and overripe in its richness of allusion to Keats, Shelley, and Milton. His fascination with language and his love of English poetry led him to the sometimes pedantic references to the great works of English poetry and to use unusual and archaic words such as *bataillous, vesperine, margent, blooth,* and *windelstrae.* This same rich gift of expression, F. O. Mathiessen has reminded us, is the very element that Moody's contemporary critics praised most highly. He was aware of this tendency, however, and remarked that he wanted to be "pedantic in the demand for simplicity." Like his exact contemporary Edwin Arlington Robinson, he was trying to keep poetry from becoming totally ossified, and it is ironic that today we consider his efforts misguided. Although he is little read today, Moody still remains one of the few signs of vigor in the early years of the twentieth century.

George Santayana (1863–1952) shared with Moody, Lodge, and Stickney an interest in the cultivation and pursuit of beauty, which is reflected in his first published book, *Sonnets and Other Verses* (1894). His own apology for his verse, written in his Preface to *Poems* (1922), is perhaps the best criticism of it: "Of impassioned tenderness or Dionysiac frenzy I have nothing, nor even of that magic and pregnancy of phrase—really the creation of a fresh idiom—which marks the high lights of poetry." But if he wrote neither with impassioned tenderness nor in a fresh idiom, Santayana created a few carefully polished poetic statements of what he himself described as his philosophy in the making. His best poems are the series of Petrarchan sonnets (1883–1893) dealing with the pursuit of beauty. The first of these, "I sought on earth a garden of delight," is one of his most interesting poems, but, like most of them, lacks concreteness of imagery. Through them all runs a sense of detachment that allows him to view with irony rather than passion his own concern with the ethical concept of beauty. This attitude is most explicit—perhaps too much so—in "On the Death of a Metaphysician," which mocks an "unhappy dreamer" who went beyond the pleasures of earth to seek "the empty horror of abysmal night":

> You cried you were a god, or were to be;
> I heard with feeble moan your boastful breath
> Bubble from depths of the Icarian sea.

Santayana's best sonnet is "Dreamt I today the dream of yesternight" (1883), with its arresting closing line: "Truth is a dream, unless my dream is true." Some of his other poems, such as "Easter Hymn" (1896) and "King's College Chapel" (1901), explore the implications of his materialistic philosophy and question the validity of faith in a doubting age. The second of these juxtaposes his philosophic materialism against the traditional Christian myth in a mood of denial that uncannily foreshadows Wallace Stevens' "Sunday Morning" (1915) and suggests reasons for the affinity between them. At the end of a church service the poet feels the "shades depart / Into the sacred night":

> Then I go forth into the open wold
>   And breathe the vigour of the freshening wind,
> And with the piling drift of cloud I hold
>   A worship sweeter to the homeless mind

Within limits Santayana is a skillful workman, but the man who described Whitman's poems as the "poetry of barbarism" tends to be too bookish and too concerned with form. Nevertheless, he wrote a number of memorable sonnets and other poems, such as "Avila" and "Cape Cod," which may still be read with pleasure.

Among the three women who were writing good poems during these years were two who returned to the English poetry of the seventeenth century for their models and one who found her voice in the celebration of her Jewish heritage.

One of these women with strong affinities for seventeenth-century England was the Boston-born Catholic poet Louise Imogen Guiney (1861–1920), whose romantic yearning for the past led her late in life to migrate to England, where she relived the lives of the Cavaliers, rescued the grave of Henry Vaughan from oblivion, and edited an anthology of the Recusant poets. Her best volume of poems, *A Roadside Harp,* was published in 1893, with a title page bearing a motto taken from one of Sidney's *Astrophel and Stella* sonnets. The poems in this volume have a freshness and variety of interest that distinguish them from the drawing-room pieties of many of her contemporaries, male and female. The poems range in subject matter from the English countryside and the classical world to American history and legend. One of her most successful poems is a narrative based on the legend of Peter Rugg, the missing man—a legend in which Hawthorne had once had an interest. None of her later volumes, however, including *England and Yesterday* (1898), *The Martyr's Idyl* (1899), and *Happy Ending* (1909), improves on the quality of this one, and many of the poems are bookish and derivative. But among the poems worth looking at are an early anapestic pentameter narrative, "Tarpeia" (1887), and two later poems, "When on the Marge of Evening" (1909) and "A Talisman" (1909). The virtues of Louise Guiney's often refreshing poetry stem from her concern for accuracy of diction and her efforts to write lyrics that avoid the artificial restraints of form so dear to the likes of Aldrich and Richard Watson Gilder, whose tastes did so much to define the character of poetry in the 1890s.

Another daughter of the seventeenth century was Lizette Woodworth Reese (1856–1935), the Baltimore schoolteacher whose simple, crisp lyrics in *A Branch of May* (1887) were a healthy antidote to the stickiness of so much of the verse of this period. Lizette Reese admired the seventeenth century, but her verse had none of its complexity or obliqueness. Her poems are almost all short, uncomplicated lyrics, sharply observant of the natural world or solemnly aware of the fact of death. The similarity of theme and attitudes invites a comparison with Emily Dickinson, whom she resembled in several ways. She spent her girlhood in a rural village in Maryland, and her poems contain closely observed recollections of the local scenery, the houses, gardens, fields, and trees, with a sharpness of imagery and compression of language that sound like Emily Dickinson without the eccentricities of diction and syntax:

> The weather has gone mad with white;
>> The cloud, the highway touch.
> White lilac is enough;
>> White thorn too much.

Lizette Reese's verse forms are conventional, yet her mind was not, and her preoccupation with death, while not morbid, still informed her vision and gave depth and meaning to her world and to her poetry. One of her best poems, "In Time of Grief" (1916), effortlessly assimilates an appropriate natural image with the theme of personal grief in three organically unified quatrains:

> Dark, thinned, beside the wall of stone,
> The box dripped in the air;
> Its odor through my house was blown
> Into the chamber there.

> Remote and yet distinct the scent,
> The sole thing of the kind,
> As though one spoke a word half meant
> That left a sting behind.

> I knew not Grief would go from me,
> And naught of it be plain,
> Except how keen the box can be
> After a fall of rain.

She maintained her high standards through ten collections, including *A Handful of Lavender* (1891), *A Wayside*

Lute (1909), which contained her best-known poem, "Tears," *Spicewood* (1920), and *Pastures* (1933). Although there is a surface gentility and conventionality to her work, the poems of Lizette Reese reproduce a sense of place and express a vivid response to the natural world that is personal and deeply felt. The freshness of her verses, with their cameolike quality, is comparable to the finest work of such younger poets as Sara Teasdale and Edna St. Vincent Millay, and, as we have seen, will even bear comparison with the more eccentric and original poetry of Emily Dickinson.

The poetic career of Emma Lazarus (1849–1887) received an unusual impetus at an early age when she mailed a copy of her *Poems and Translations* (1867) to Emerson, whom she had briefly met. Emerson's enthusiastic response to these mournful poems written between her fourteenth and seventeenth years was encouraging, and his reply to her began a correspondence and friendship that were to last until his death. Emerson was even more enthusiastic upon receiving a copy of "Admetus," of which he wrote: "You have written a noble poem, which I cannot enough praise." His guidance and encouragement were responsible for the publication of a second volume, *Admetus and Other Poems* (1871), which Emma Lazarus dedicated (against his wishes) to "my friend, Ralph Waldo Emerson." This volume contained some imitative and rather tame verse narratives, and the strongest poetry in it was a translation of the first act of Goethe's *Faust*. Nevertheless, Emerson's favorite poem was "Heroes," an unassuming tribute to the Civil War dead.

Emma Lazarus found her real voice, however, when she became converted to the cause of Judaism. Aroused by the reports of pogroms in Russia after the assassination of the Czar, she began writing stirring emotional and propagandistic poems asserting her indignation at injustice and her pride in being a Jew. At nineteen she had already written a fine poem on the same subject as one of Longfellow's poems called "In the Jewish Synagogue at Newport," which shows a greater sympathy and understanding for her people's past. In her thirties, in poems such as "The Banner of the Jew," she let her emotions and the spirit of the hour get the better of her, and most of *Songs of a Semite* (1882) suffer from the topicality of the subject and her emotional involvement with it. Today, however, they are the poems for which she is best known, with the exception of "The New Colossus" (1883). This sonnet was written as part of a fund-raising effort for the pedestal for the Statue of Liberty. Her long experience with immigrant Jews and her own ideas about America as a refuge and the home of liberty found expression in the sonnet with its famous lines:

> Give me your tired, your poor,
> Your huddled masses yearning to breathe free,
> The wretched refuse of your teeming shore.
> Send these, the homeless, tempest-tost to me.

The poem was later engraved on the statue's pedestal where it still remains the most enduring memory of Emma Lazarus.

The first American black poet to become widely known and read was Paul Laurence Dunbar (1872–1906), the son of former Kentucky slaves who had settled in Dayton, Ohio. There are a number of ironies connected with the career of Dunbar, not the least of which is that his name has survived as a poet of black life. Although a large number of his poems are written in literary English on conventional themes, he was first admired as a dialect poet writing about plantation life. The vogue for local-color writing begun by such writers as Joel Chandler Harris (1848–1908) made poets and storytellers treating the life of the southern plantation, the backwoods, and the midwestern frontier widely popular. Almost in spite of himself, Dunbar became the spokesman for the more pleasant aspects of ante-bellum plantation life, writing sentimental dialect poems about old-time southern "darkies" fishing, loafing, telling stories, making love, grinning at the Massah and Missus, and drinking " 'lasses an' watah'." In the nineties the black was still an object of both curiosity and fear, and the inability of white Americans to see him simply as a man is demonstrated in William Dean Howells' enthusiastic essay on Dunbar that is nevertheless unconsciously patronizing and condescending. Although Howells saw his poems as "evidence of the essential unity of the human race," he went on to remark that "there is a precious difference of temperament between the races which it would be a great pity ever to lose," adding that Dunbar's verses reveal "a finely ironical perception of the negro's limitations, with a tenderness for them which I think so very rare as to be almost quite new." Certainly Howells' essay, published as the introduction to Dunbar's first collection, *Lyrics of Lowly Life* (1896), was well-intentioned, but it had the effect of stereotyping Dunbar in the mind of the public as a black poet. Although he wrote some good religious and nature verse, and a number of fine elegiac lyrics in literary English, he is best known for poems with such titles as "At Candle-Lightin' Time," "An Easy-Goin' Feller," and "Dat Ol' Mare O' Mine." His debts to the sentimental rural poems of James Whitcomb Riley are obvious and frankly acknowledged. In spite of his tendency to look on the brighter side of a life that was far from idyllic, he did notice the effects of poverty on the newly freed slave:

But it's easy 'nough to titter w'en de stew is smokin' hot,
  But hit's mighty ha'd to giggle w'en dey's nuffin' in de pot.

And in "We Wear the Mask" (1896) he calls attention to the suffering human being who lies beneath the exterior of the buffoon:

> We wear the mask that grins and lies,
> It hides our cheeks and shades our eyes,—
> This debt we pay to human guile;
> With torn and bleeding hearts we smile,
> And mouth with myriad subtleties.

Dunbar's more lighthearted celebrations of black folk customs include "A Negro Love Song" (1896), simply describing a country courtship, "How Lucy Backslid" (1899), a comic nar-

rative of religious hypocrisy, and "Possum" (1899), a frank
celebration of a food unknown to most whites:

> Possum skin is jes' lak shoat skin;
> Jes' you swinge an' scrope it down,
> Tek a good sha'p knife an' sco' it,
> Den you bake it good an' brown.
> Huh-uh! honey, you's so happy
> Dat yo' thoughts is 'mos' a sin
> When you's settin' dah a-chawin'
> On dat possum's cracklin' skin.

Dialect poems and conventional poems alternate through
such representative volumes as *Lyrics of the Hearthside* (1899),
Lyrics of Love and Laughter (1903), and *Lyrics of Sunshine
and Shadow* (1905), but in the later volumes many of the lyrics
tend toward death and despair, some, such as "Distinction"
(1899), written in the disillusioned manner of Stephen Crane:

> "I am but clay," the sinner plead,
> Who fed each vain desire.
> "Not only clay," another said,
> "But worse, for thou art mire."

Dunbar's verse is an interesting manifestation of the local-
color movement of the late nineteenth century. And, ironically, in view of his own wishes to be read first as a poet and
second as a black, his poems about blacks and black attitudes
are forerunners of the poetry of Countee Cullen, Langston
Hughes, and Imamu Amiri Baraka.

Aside from Edwin Arlington Robinson, the only poet
writing in the 1890s who is read at all widely today is Stephen
Crane (1871–1900), who disliked thinking of himself as a poet,
who called his poems "lines," who had little acquaintance
with traditional poetry, and who could write five or six of his
poems in a single evening, "drawing them off" from memory
after having composed them in his head. Tradition has it

that Crane began writing poetry after William Dean Howells read him some of the newly published poems of Emily Dickinson, yet aside from the freedom of form and the epigrammatic quality that are found in both their styles, his verses have little resemblance to hers. Crane's thumping ironies and extravagant gestures of adolescent defiance in such poems as:

> If there is a witness to my little life,
> To my tiny throes and struggles,
> He sees a fool;
> And it is not fine for gods to menace fools
> (*Black Riders* XIII, 1895)

are far from the subtle and witty poems of Emily Dickinson.

It would be more to the point to say that Crane was influenced by the French Symbolists—except for the fact that he had never heard of them. Indeed, he had heard of few poets when he wrote the untitled verses he collected in *The Black Riders and Other Lines* in 1895. Hamlin Garland has described, perhaps too credulously, how Crane came to him one night with a handful of "lines," and after remarking that he had "three more waiting in line; I could do one now," sat down and wrote a flawless poem while Garland watched. Crane's responses to the world were immediate and intense, and his posture of rebelliousness is the same that characterizes his questioning attitudes toward the glory of war in *The Red Badge of Courage* (1895). But where the style of his fiction is impressionistic and loaded with images of color and texture, his poetry is sparse and telegraphic; its short lines and flat statements seem to convey a sense of urgency that has no patience with the niceties of poetic form. Unlike Stickney, Lodge, and Moody—or even Taylor and the New York group —Crane was working outside the cultural influences of his time that led the former to write verse on classical themes and the latter to hold on to the faded flowers of late Victorian Romanticism. If the influence of Emily Dickinson on Crane is negligible and that of the Symbolists impossible, there are still some others. One is the Bible—probably the most important because its Old Testament descriptions of a wrathful and vengeful God gave Crane a model for his willful and cantankerous one. The *Fantastic Fables* (1899) of Ambrose Bierce (1842–1914?), with their use of ironic surprise, and Olive Schreiner's collection of tales called *Dreams* (1890) have also been proposed as influences by the closest student of Crane's poetry. The crude and sentimental use of allegorical abstractions in *Dreams*, says Daniel Hoffman, is the source of Crane's own tendency to use them, but with a characteristic ironic inversion of her sentimental optimism:

> There was set before me a mighty hill,
> And long days I climbed
> Through regions of snow.
> When I had before me the summit-view,
> It seemed that my labour
> Had been to see gardens
> Lying at impossible distances.
>   (*Black Riders* XXVI, 1895)

Crane was possessed with a gift for perceiving the relationships of things and ideas in a manner that Hoffman has described as a "metaphoric imagination," yet this gift is much more evident in his use of unusual images and phrases in his fiction than in his poetry, where directness of treatment and economy of phrase are his means for approaching the themes of defiance and God-baiting that are the mainstay of *The Black Riders*. Hoffman has documented the extent to which Crane's boyhood as a minister's son and member of a prominent Methodist family haunted him when he matched his experiences during his Bowery years against his memories of the fire-and-brimstone theology of his family. His uncle Jesse Peck, in particular, provides a bleak and terrifying background for Crane's allegorical characters in their strangely unlocalized landscapes. Bishop Peck's tract *What Must I Do To Be Saved?* is a relentless effort to frighten the sinner and convince him of his natural depravity, while many of Crane's consciously iconoclastic poems are assertions of his acceptance of the loathsomeness of man, along with a contrary celebration of it because it is human. In his view, man, having been placed on earth without being consulted by God, can rely finally only upon himself and not upon the capricious will of his inscrutable creator. This is the attitude that informs a well-known poem from his second volume, *War Is Kind* (1899):

> A man said to the universe:
> "Sir, I exist!"
> "However," replied the universe,
> "The fact has not created in me
> A sense of obligation."

It is easy to recognize in this poem the similarity in theme to "The Open Boat," published in 1898. The theme of that story is another longer, poem, possibly Crane's best, which he never published but probably wrote in 1897 or 1898. This is the first stanza:

> A man adrift on a slim spar
> A horizon smaller than the rim of a bottle.
> Tented waves rearing lashy dark points
> The near whine of froth in circles.
> God is cold.

The typical Crane poem is narrative rather than lyric and is usually an allegorical treatment of large moral questions. It makes statements full of heavy irony and occasionally, as in his posthumously published "A Naked Woman and a dead dwarf," relies on a kind of sentimental decadence strangely like the poems of Charles Baudelaire or Ernest Dowson. George Peck called him the Aubrey Beardsley of poetry, and the book designer for *The Black Riders* must have sensed this quality, for he adorned the gray board covers with a limp black orchid trailing over them. But Crane's concern with morality distinguishes him from the Decadents just as his interest in narrative and allegory distinguishes him from the Imagists and other followers of the

Symbolist aesthetic. He remains a strange and unassimilated product of the nineties, committed to the life of art yet refusing to become an aesthete. His later poetry reverts to more traditional forms as he wrote longer poems with a stanza-and-refrain structure. But these poems are weakened by the introduction of conventional poetic diction: "thee's" and "thou's" and "woe is me's." The style of the earlier, strangely condensed poems, with their anguished but somewhat adolescent bitterness, is their most arresting quality. The reader senses in them something strangely alien to the 1890s and akin to the poetry of despair fashionable in the second and third decades of the twentieth century. In an introduction to his poems Amy Lowell remarks that in the decade that began with 1912 Crane would have been in his element, "perfectly understood, wisely praised, forced to take the position of leader." Her final judgment is still worth reflection: "A marvelous boy, potentially a genius, historically an important link in the chain of American poetry."

It is clear that with the possible exception of Crane these poets were working with the outworn conventions of form and language of the nineteenth century. They were generally deaf to the experiments of Whitman, Emily Dickinson, and Lanier, working either from choice or ignorance in derivative modes, using a poetic diction that was exhausted or bankrupt. A mood of complacency hung like a shroud over most of them, and they recoiled from rather than welcomed the fresh breath of realism and naturalism that was then revitalizing the novel. The local-color movement in fiction found a few counterparts in John Hay, Bret Harte, and Celia Thaxter, but a regional awareness was not strong. The late nineteenth century was largely a time of waiting for a new resurgence of energy, first from the regionalism of New England and the Midwest and then from the great modern movement that revolutionized American poetry in the twentieth century.

CHAPTER EIGHT

The New Poets: Regionalism and the Renewal of Language

Edwin Arlington Robinson, Robert Frost, Edna St. Vincent Millay, Sara Teasdale, Carl Sandburg, Vachel Lindsay, Edgar Lee Masters, James Weldon Johnson, Claude McKay, Langston Hughes, Countee Cullen, Jean Toomer, Melvin B. Tolson, Gwendolyn Brooks

The "new poetry" of the twentieth century actually began in the last decade of the nineteenth with the writing of two poets whose work in many respects serves as a link between the old and the new. Both Edwin Arlington Robinson and Robert Frost worked all their lives in traditional forms, but a directness and simplicity of language distinguishes their early poems dramatically from the diffuse poeticizing that prevailed in the nineties. T. S. Eliot once remarked that the poetry of the twentieth century is best characterized by its "search for a proper modern colloquial idiom," yet even before the century had begun, and before that *annus mirabilis*, 1912, from which we traditionally date the beginning of modern American poetry, Frost and Robinson were writing in the language of ordinary men with the same objectives Wordsworth had had a century earlier: to give poetry a new vitality. The forging of a new poetic idiom did indeed become a major preoccupation of twentieth-century poets. This effort to give a purer language to the tribe had its tame beginning in Moody, was stressed by Robinson and Frost, took fresh inspiration from Whitman in Sandburg, Lindsay, and Masters, and, for reasons having more to do with black identity than with aesthetics, took still another direction in the poetry written in Harlem in the 1920s.

To make generalizations about the complex interplay of forces working to bring about what many viewed as a poetic renaissance is dangerous. Both Robinson and Frost were solitary, independent writers, refusing to identify themselves with a school or movement, yet even they were aware of the need for doing new things in new ways. The midwestern poets responded more immediately to the encouragement of Harriet Monroe (1860–1936), whose magazine *Poetry,* which she founded in 1912, bore a motto from Whitman and opened its pages to the brash voices of Sandburg, Lindsay, and Masters. In the same year, Mitchell Kennerly published an anthology called *The Lyric Year* with contributions from Vachel Lindsay, Sara Teasdale, and a twenty-year-old girl named Edna St. Vincent Millay. These are some of the "new poets," identified rather closely with their regions, particularly New England and the Midwest, who were breathing new life into American poetry. Their novelty and freshness now seem somewhat faded when seen in retrospect against the much more dramatic and radical innovations of the Imagists, yet this "new poetry," of which Robinson was considered an elder statesman, was every bit as exciting to their contemporaries. Some of it, of course, is among the best poetry ever written in America.

Both Robinson and Frost are poets of New England: Frost placing his people, lonely, joyful, frustrated, or content, against a vivid backdrop of New England scenery—the birches, apple trees, snow-filled woods, and isolated farms that every reader of his poems knows; Robinson turning inward to the psychological quirks, the inconsistencies between appearance and reality, and the visions of moral horror that fascinated the New England writer whom he most resembles, Nathaniel Hawthorne. They are also poets of tradition, using the materials and forms of Bryant, Whittier, and Longfellow; but the romantic optimism of Emerson and Whitman that had seemed so satisfactory to readers of the seventies and eighties was no longer possible in a post-Darwinian and increasingly mechanistic world. Robinson sought to break out of the bonds of materialism by searching for something new—but at best his proposals were tentative and obscure, as he groped to penetrate the universal mysteries. He was not a philosopher but a poet, reacting with a baffled intensity to the disappearance of the old certainties. The uncertain, fragmentary quality of his world is reflected in his legendary Tilbury Town, whose inhabitants seek oblivion through alcohol, fantasy, or suicide.

Edwin Arlington Robinson (1869–1935) grew up as the third son of a shipbuilder and merchant in the seaside town of Gardiner, Maine, the Tilbury Town of his poems. His older brothers, more handsome, outgoing, and enterprising than he, cast a shadow over his boyhood, although they both died early, one of morphine addiction leading to suicide and the other of alcoholism. He received some encouragement to write poetry from Alanson T. Schumann, a literary doctor of the town, but otherwise his life in this New England provincial seaport was not encouraging to a young man who had early made up his mind to be nothing but a poet. His two years at Harvard turned out to be a vitally liberating experience before he returned to a rapidly deteriorating family situation, including the bankruptcy and death of his father.

Robinson published a pamphlet of poems, *The Torrent and the Night Before,* in 1896 and another collection, *The Children of the Night,* the following year, shortly after moving to New York. Neither attracted any attention, and he had already resigned himself to a life of obscurity when in 1905 his poems came to the attention of President Theodore Roosevelt and his fortunes changed slightly for the better. Unusual as it may seem to have a president write literary criticism, Roosevelt's essay in *The Outlook* brought Robinson's poetry to a larger potential audience and made publishers and editors less reluctant to print his poems. Roosevelt also persuaded him to take a sinecure in the New York Customs House, a position that gave him some financial security, at least until the change of administrations.

As a young man Robinson had complained rather bitterly about the "little sonnet-men" of the previous generation who had emasculated poetry. He was aware also of the power of Whitman's poetry, and of the loss to America marked by his death. His poem, "Walt Whitman" (1896), which he wrote soon afterward, began: "The master-songs are ended," and continued:

> We do not hear him very much today:
> His piercing and eternal cadence rings
> Too pure for us—too powerfully pure,
> Too lovingly triumphant and too large

Certainly, in spite of Robinson's sense of the need for Whitman's powerful poetry, we hear very little of it in his own work. There are passages with a Whitmanlike ring, such as this one from a poem called "Pasa Thalassa Thalassa" (1910):

> Smoke that floated and rolled in the twilight away
>   from the chimney
> Floats and rolls no more. Wheeling and falling,
>   instead,
> Down with a twittering flash go the smooth and in-
>   scrutable swallows,
> Down to the place made theirs by the cold work of
>   the sea.

However, this passage, with its abundance of imagery and sweeping rhythms, is not typical of Robinson.

The note that Robinson sounded is quite different from Whitman's clarion call, yet we cannot say that it is less a part of the American tradition for that. Whereas Whitman was a poet of the soul, Robinson was a poet of the mind, yet of that mind that Emerson ambiguously called reason. That is, a mind that knows itself and, knowing itself, can turn outward in the act of knowing to search for truth beyond itself. Although Robinson could seldom achieve the transcendence of the material world that Emerson began and Whitman continued, he has often—and rightly—been called a Transcendentalist. Certainly he admired Emerson, once remarking to Joyce

Kilmer in an interview that he was the greatest poet who ever wrote in America. "In fact," he said, "I think that there are lines and sentences in Emerson's poetry that are as great as anything anywhere."

But if Emerson can be said to have written the poetry of success, Robinson was the great American poet of failure. The failure basically seems to be a failure of nerve—a recognition in himself of his inability to find life's satisfactions in the world of physical sensation and his unwillingness to take the transcendent leap toward Romantic release and ecstasy. This is not to say his poems are failures; but many of his best-known poems are *about* individual failures: "Bewick Finzer," "Mr. Flood's Party," "Richard Cory"; or failures to realize life's possibilities: "Eros Turannos," "Captain Craig." The characters in his poems—and no American poet has created a greater variety of characters or concentrated more intently on human nature—are often captured in attitudes of bewilderment; their search for truth and their subsequent frustration is a recurrent Robinson theme. We find in his beautiful, short elegiac poem "For a Dead Lady" (1910) both this sense of failure and the bafflement that accompanies it that underlie many of Robinson's poems:

> The beauty, shattered by the laws
> That have creation in their keeping,
> No longer trembles at applause,
> Or over children that are sleeping;
> And we who delve in beauty's lore
> Know all that we have known before
> Of what inexorable cause
> Makes Time so vicious in his reaping.

Here in this one stanza, too, are many of the qualities typical of his style: the discursiveness, the fondness for feminine endings, the tortuous sentence structure, the use of nonfunctional words ("Or over children that are sleeping"), the irregular rhythms (as in the next-to-last line). We find, even in reading this short passage, how difficult it is to read a Robinson poem quickly; how he demands our close attention, word for word and line for line, even though in other poems such close attention is not always rewarding.

Robinson was primarily a poet, not a philosopher, and his philosophical poems, even the overrated "The Man Against the Sky" (1916), never have the same force as those built around a single character. The early series of "Octaves," published in *The Children of the Night,* contain some revealing statements about his beliefs, but, with one or two exceptions, he presents the same attitudes more effectively in his character sketches. Here is "Octave XV," containing an idea realized later in "Miniver Cheevy" (1910):

> We lack the courage to be where we are:—
> We love too much to travel on old roads,
> To triumph on old fields; we love too much
> To consecrate the magic of dead things,
> And yieldingly to linger by long walls
> Of ruin, where the ruinous moonlight
> That sheds a lying glory on old stones
> Befriends us with a wizard's enmity.

How much more effective is Robinson's satirical portrait of Miniver—with the irony of the name itself—who "missed the medieval grace / Of iron clothing." That Cheevy's sentimental and romantic yearning for the past is a side of Robinson that he wanted to purge from himself is quite obvious, and this attitude reflects his contempt for romantic escapism and his sense of the need to live a life without illusions. The last lines of the poem:

> Miniver coughed, and called it fate,
>   And kept on drinking

remind us of those down-and-outers in O'Neill's *The Iceman Cometh* who retreat into their alcoholic reverie in order to avoid living a life without illusion. But whereas O'Neill came to accept and even celebrate pain as a necessary ingredient of human existence, Robinson could not; he could dwell on it, and even comment wryly on it, but he could not accept it. He even suggests in "How Annandale Went Out" (1910) that the answer to physical pain is not endurance but euthanasia. There is, then, some of Miniver Cheevy in Robinson as he balks at pain, suffering, and ugliness, viewing them as hindrances to both earthly happiness and the realization of a fully transcendent life. That he recognized this conflict between man's desire for life and the desire to transcend it is suggested in these cryptic lines:

> We shriek to live, but no man ever lives
> Till he has rid the ghost of human breath

What Robinson could not do was accept and celebrate this flawed world with the recognition that it is the only one we have. This is what Wallace Stevens, ten years his junior, could do. We can see the startling contrast in attitudes in "The Emperor of Ice-Cream," where Stevens accepts life in all its tawdriness, and in "Richard Cory," whose narrator, although implicitly suggesting he does not want to be in Richard Cory's place, still assumes an attitude of resigned hopelessness in the closing stanza:

> So on we worked, and waited for the light,
> And went without the meat, and cursed the bread

It is by the short poems—the character sketches such as "Richard Cory" (1897), "Miniver Cheevy" (1910), "Bewick Finzer" (1916), and "Aunt Imogen" (1902) and by such lyrics as "Luke Havergal" (1896) and "For a Dead Lady" (1910) that Robinson is remembered today. Although he devoted great energy to making the long Arthurian poems, *Merlin* (1917), *Lancelot* (1920), and *Tristram* (1927), come alive, they are largely unreadable today, even though he achieved his greatest popular success with *Tristram*. The philosophy in these poems is vague and ambiguous, the characters have little flesh and blood; the scenes of *Sturm und Drang* are passionless and unreal. Even less readable are the other, late long poems, which share with the Arthurian poems a weakness of structure, a sparseness of imagery, and a monotony of tone and style that make them formidable to approach and largely unrewarding to read.

But his short poems and many of his poems of middle length, such as "Rembrandt to Rembrandt" (1921), "Ben Jonson Entertains a Man from Stratford" (1916), "Tasker Norcross" (1920), "Mortmain" (1925), "The Book of Annandale" (1902), and "Sainte-Nitouche" (1902), continue, when given the attentive and sympathetic reading they demand and deserve, to assure Robinson a place among the major American poets of the twentieth century.

Robert Frost (1874–1963) was not so much in rebellion against the nineties as Robinson was, but rather worked through a period of sympathy and even identification with the Georgian poets in England. Two of his early friends in England were Lascelles Abercrombie and Wilfred Wilson Gibson, and his first volume of poems shares with them some of the yearning for the past that became their hallmark. But if the Georgians persisted in longing for a past that could not return, Frost's pastoralism eventually became his way of looking at a present he never forgot.

Frost seems to work from a more secure base than Robinson. His poems are, in his phrase, a "momentary stay against confusion," poems that begin in delight and end in "a clarification of life." Unsystematic in philosophical outlook, Frost moves backward and inward toward the source of a strength that will equip him with a sense of the self. His clarifications of life are the fragments he has chosen to shore against the ruins: a personal brand of humanism that sustains him in the face of his awareness of an impersonal and indifferent natural universe.

It was Ezra Pound who found Frost's use of language refreshing and new, who congratulated him for breaking away from "stilted pseudo-literary language." Even though Frost's subjects in the poems he showed to Pound in England in 1912 were far different from any of his, Pound, with his highly sensitive antennae, was aware of the great gifts that Frost displayed in such poems as "Mowing" (1913) and "The Tuft of Flowers" (1913). Frost, then thirty-eight years old, had not arrived at this point by accident. When he was nineteen he had told his grandfather he wanted to be a poet, and when he was told he would be given one year, his answer—prophetic, as it turned out—was, "Give me twenty." Almost exactly twenty years later he published *A Boy's Will*. His early years were crowded with odd jobs—working in a textile mill and a shoeshop, later as a newspaper columnist, schoolteacher, and manager for a Shakespearean actor. Between eighteen and twenty-nine he attended Dartmouth for a few months and Harvard for a few years, married, had five children, wrote articles for a poultry journal, taught school, and finally turned to a life of bitter and desultory farming on a worn-out farm near Derry, New Hampshire. At thirty-eight he took his wife, his children, and his poems to England, more driven than ever by his ambition to be a poet.

The critical reception in England of his first two volumes, *A Boy's Will* (1913) and *North of Boston* (1914), made him a kind of celebrity when he returned to New England, again settling on a farm, this time to produce poems rather than crops. Frost continued to celebrate his rural world and its inhabitants in the volumes that followed: *Mountain Interval* (1916), *New Hampshire* (1924), *Collected Poems* (1930), *A Further Range* (1936), and *A Witness Tree* (1942), the last four of which each won a Pulitzer Prize. He was to speak for the rest of his career as a farmer writing poetry, a voice that he consciously cultivated over the years until it became a familiar and—late in his life—even a rather tiresome one. In retrospect he could see his early years as preparation and discipline for his craft, and in one of his revealing personal poems, "Build Soil" (1932), he used his own experience as the basis for this Horatian advice:

                              we both know poets
        Who fall all over each other to bring soil
        And even subsoil and hardpan to market.
        To sell the hay off, let alone the soil,
        Is an unpardonable sin in farming.
        The moral is, make a late start to market.

    If his lyrics in *A Boy's Will* were simple and refreshing
evocations of what Emily Dickinson would call "thinking
New Englandly," the poems in *North of Boston* show that
Frost had truly discovered New England as his subject. This
"book of people," as he called it, contains narratives and dramatic monologues spoken by a gallery of up-country types,
many of them oppressed by loneliness or deranged by grief;
others content with, or resigned to, a life on reduced terms.
One of the speakers in "The Death of the Hired Man" says
that a home is "Something you somehow haven't to deserve"
and so asserts a basic human value; an old farmer in "The
Mountain" simply has never had enough ambition to climb
the mountain he has lived at the foot of all his life; the disturbed housekeeper in "A Servant to Servants" is worn out
emotionally and physically by a life of routine and hardship.
These people are both created and defined by the landscape,
an economically depressed region passed over by industrial
and technological progress. Frost's stance in these poems is a
strategic retreat from the modern industrial world, in order
not to hide from it but to look at it from the single perspective of one who lives outside it and looks at it with a wary eye.
    Frost's technique is deceptively simple. His easily scanned
blank verse and his unpretentious quatrains and sonnets mask
an art that stems from a commitment to metrical regularity
basic to his conception of the nature of poetry. "The possibilities for tune from the dramatic tones of meaning struck across
rigidity of a limited meter are endless," he wrote in his classic
critical essay, "The Figure a Poem Makes" (1930). These possibilities may be seen in the relaxed, colloquial blank verse
of such pieces as "The Death of the Hired Man" (1914) or
such carefully structured quatrains as those in "In a Disused

Graveyard" (1923). In "Dust of Snow" (1923) he achieves a *tour de force* by writing one sentence in two iambic dimeter quatrains:

> The way a crow
> Shook down on me
> The dust of snow
> From a hemlock tree
>
> Has given my heart
> A change of mood
> And saved some part
> Of a day I had rued.

This poem is typically Frostian, too, because of the way it moves from "delight"—the sharply observed natural fact of the first stanza—to "wisdom"—the gradually achieved discovery not fully realized until the last line, where its vital final word colors the entire poem. Frost saw the logic of the poem as a revelation, or series of revelations, "as much for the poet as for the reader"—and "Dust of Snow" works in its structure toward that kind of surprise. Some of his best poems, in fact, are discoveries: "The Most of It" (1942), "After Apple-Picking" (1914), "Come In" (1942), "Stopping by Woods on a Snowy Evening" (1923), and "Birches" (1916) all work this way. Other poems aim toward a balanced and purposely ambivalent view by opposing contraries; perhaps it was this technique that led Yvor Winters to accuse Frost of being a spiritual drifter. "All truth is dialogue," Frost once said. "We were not given eyes or intellect . . . for wisdom that can have no counter-wisdom." And the wisdom and counter-wisdom of such poems as "Range-Finding" (1916), "West-Running Brook" (1928), and "On the Heart's Beginning to Cloud the Mind" (1936) are illustrations of that point.

Equally important to Frost was the language of his poems, the conversational rhythms and diction of native speech rendered in meter. No poet of the twentieth century, with the exception of William Carlos Williams, has placed so much emphasis on the spoken language as the source of poetry. The blank-verse dramatic monologues, such as this passage from "The Witch of Coös" (1923), must be read aloud, or heard on a recording by Frost himself, to appreciate the way in which he shapes language while at the same time allowing it to retain something of its original quality:

> The night the bones came up the cellar stairs
> Toffile had gone to bed alone and left me,
> But left an open door to cool the room off
> So as to sort of turn me out of it.
> I was just coming to myself enough
> To wonder where the cold was coming from,
> When I heard Toffile upstairs in the bedroom
> And thought I heard him downstairs in the cellar.

Frost's nature imagery is in a direct, practically unbroken line from Bryant, Whittier, and Thoreau, yet he does not use it the way they did. Nature for Frost is neither the hallowed shrine of Bryant, nor the source of nostalgia that it was for Whittier. And Frost, for all his sympathy with Thoreau's toughmindedness and desire for simplicity, does not try to spiritualize nature or suggest that it exists in any state of kinship with man. For Frost, nature is ambivalent. It contains many lessons, such as the "backward motion toward the source" of "West-Running Brook" that suggests the same direction for man. It also contains the origins of irrational fear, or is simply a hostile or indifferent force that barely tolerates man's presence or intrusion into its domain. In "Storm Fear" (1901), the speaker is in awe of a snowstorm that threatens to overcome him, "Till even the comforting barn grows far away." The speaker in "The Census-Taker" (1923) is disturbed by the houses of the back country falling into decay; a mountain in "The Birthplace" (1928) "pushed us off her knees. / And now her lap is full of trees." In "Our Hold on the Planet" (1942) Frost suggests that nature "must be a little more in favor of man, / Say a fraction of one per cent at the very least," but in "On Going Unnoticed" (1928) he writes:

> You linger your little hour and are gone,
> And still the woods sweep leafily on,
> Not even missing the coral root flower
> You took as a trophy of the hour.

In spite of his love of the physical manifestations of beauty in nature, Frost gives us finally a sense of man's aloneness in a universe unable to respond to him, as it cannot in "The Most of It" (1942). If there are desert places in men's minds, they exist also in the world. Looking down a well, the speaker of one poem, after having seen only his reflection, thought he discerned "a something white, uncertain, / Something more of the depths—and then I lost it." He is encouraged by having seen something, no matter how vague or ephemeral, that has momentarily suggested to him the presence of meaning in nature. But this tentative gesture in a positive direction is offset by such cruelly disillusioning experiences as that in "Design" (1936), with its mocking questioning of the idea of a purposeful God. The attitude in all of these poems is what Lionel Trilling had in mind when, in comparing Frost to Sophocles, he said that he made plain the terrible things of human life. Frost himself once wrote in the Amherst College newspaper that "the background is hugeness and confusion shading away from where we stand into black and utter chaos." But he added, "unless we are novelists or economists we don't worry about this confusion; we look out on it with an instrument or tackle it to reduce it." The poems reveal a poet who refuses to shrink from truth, but steadily regards it with an unwavering gaze. Frost is neither a cynic nor a moralizer, but renders life as he has seen and lived it. As Randall Jarrell said, "the grimness and awfulness and untouchable sadness of things, both in the world and in the self, have justice done to them in the poems, but no more justice than is done to the tenderness and love and delight; and everything in between is represented too."

Two young women who began writing in the first decade of the century continued to write in traditional ways. Edna St. Vincent Millay, although identified with her Bohemian life-style, responded in her poems to little of the technical experimentation that was going on around her in the twenties, while Sara Teasdale remained a traditional lyricist from first to last. Both poets, like many others of their generation, such as John Hall Wheelock (b. 1886), Robert Hillyer (1895–1961), and Mark Van Doren (1894–1972), found the traditional forms the best for their own purposes.

Although Edna St. Vincent Millay (1892–1950) lived until the middle of the century, her poetry is inevitably linked with the 1920s. The spirit of feminist revolt and emancipation that leaps from the pages of *A Few Figs from Thistles* (1920) leaves the most lasting impression on her readers and in fact affected the response of her readers to her later work. Millay is the poet of the striking phrase, the socially daring idea, the delicate suggestiveness and handling of sex, and if she is identified now in the minds of many as a literary flapper or a female Scott Fitzgerald, there is evidence in her poems as well as in her life to support this view. As a girl in Rockland, Maine, she wrote poetry that reflected her love of the sea and the Maine landscape. Her response to her environment was much like that of other Maine writers such as Mary Wilkins Freeman (1852–1930) or Sarah Orne Jewett (1849–1909). She is perhaps even more closely linked with that other Maine poet, Celia Thaxter (1835–1894), whose delicate lyrics about the Maine coast seem to be echoed in Millay's earliest success, "Renascence" (1912). This poem, written when she was seventeen, is an unusually mature performance, with some sophisticated metaphysical speculation in the chaste language and simple imagery that are the hallmarks of all her work. Her mystical vision of a spiritual burial and rebirth through nature owes something to Wordsworth, perhaps, and something to Whitman, but it is still her own. When she submitted the poem to *The Lyric Year,* it was published but did not receive a prize. The controversy that arose out of the judges' decision made her well known on the basis of the first poem she ever published. While she was at Vassar she continued to write and publish poems, which were collected in her first volume, *Renascence* (1917).

Her life in Greenwich Village during the twenties, her association with a number of artists and writers, including Edmund Wilson, William Rose and Stephen Vincent Benét, Archibald MacLeish, and others, and her acting career with the Provincetown Players all made her a well-known figure and a symbol of Bohemian life. Her poetry, especially in *A Few Figs from Thistles,* reflects an attitude of free-and-easy living and loving. The impermanence of love and the theme of woman's fickleness—an attitude borrowed from the Cavalier poets and given a modern twist—were the dominant themes in this volume, which was widely read and imitated.

Many of her poems in this and later volumes express her defiance and unwillingness to accept the fact of death. "The Poet and His Book," in *Second April* (1921), begins in the hortatory mode typical of many of her poems: *"Down, you mongrel, Death!"* But in "Dirge Without Music," and "Moriturus," both published in *The Buck in the Snow* (1928), she comes to accept death even though she still is not resigned to it.

The best of Millay's work combines the virtues of clarity and simplicity of diction with a sure sense of the musical line. Although she was not the meticulous craftsman that Elinor Wylie is, Millay managed to infuse feelings of passion into lyrics that have a deceptively simple surface. Some of the sonnets in *Fatal Interview* (1931) reflect a deepening and maturing of the attitudes that characterized her earlier work. One of these, "Oh, sleep forever in the Latmian Cave," deals with sexual themes in a way that purifies them of all grossness. Millay's sonnets are on the whole not her most successful poems, but among her better ones are "Love is not all; it is not meat nor drink" (1931), and "Euclid alone has looked on Beauty bare" (1923). Other good poems are "Memorial to D. C." (1921), "The Cameo" (1928), and "Passer Mortuus Est" (1921), a meditation on the value of transitory love. Millay continued to write poems in the face of many personal difficulties, and turned increasingly to questions of social concern. In the late twenties she wrote "Justice Denied in Massachusetts," in protest against the trial of Sacco and Vanzetti. In the forties she wrote a number of poems about the war, including the long, dramatic verse narrative *The Murder of Lidice* (1942) and "There Are No Islands Any More," written just before the fall of France. But these pieces do not approach in quality the pure lyric vein of her verse of the twenties.

The lyrics of Sara Teasdale (1884–1933) are studiedly simple in diction and conventional in theme. There is a balladlike quality to them, with a minimum of figurative language or ornamental imagery. The poems published in *Sonnets to Duse and Other Poems* (1907) and *Love Songs* (1917), the most widely praised of her seven volumes of verse, are in the manner and spirit of Christina Rossetti, although the impulse behind them is a dedication to spiritual beauty rather than to religion. In poems such as "Barter" (1917) her devotion to life's pleasures is expressed in simple terms, and in her love songs one encounters the simple and abiding fact of the loneliness of the beloved woman tinged with melancholy thoughts of impending death. Her own physical frailty led her to write increasingly about the imminence of death, as in "Wisdom" (1917) and "Blue Squills" (1920):

> Oh burn me with your beauty, then,
>   Oh hurt me, tree and flower,
> Lest in the end death try to take
>   Even this glistening hour.

The purity of feeling and expression of Sara Teasdale's poems has seldom been matched, but they lack the intensity and, partly because of their concentration on the subject of a woman's abiding love, the interest of poets with either a wider scope or the saving grace of wit, such as Elinor Wylie and Edna St. Vincent Millay.

The poet most closely identified with the "new poetry" of Chicago was the author of the poem most shocking to its own citizens, soon notorious in the minds of countless readers as the precursor to poetic chaos and the end of genteel literature. Carl Sandburg (1878–1967) was a genuine product of the Midwest and of the people whom he wrote about throughout his life. Sandburg, the son of a blacksmith's helper, grew up in the railroad town of Galesburg, Illinois, where the memories of President Lincoln were still strong enough to make a lasting impression on him. Quitting school in the eighth grade, he entered upon a twenty-five-year apprenticeship before he became a balladeer, people's poet, folklorist, and biographer of Abraham Lincoln. His many odd jobs, his service as a foot soldier in Puerto Rico during the Spanish-American War, his abortive education at Lombard College in Galesburg, his life as a hobo, his careers as newspaper reporter and, at one period, secretary to the Socialist mayor of Milwaukee all helped form him as a poet of the nation he loved with a vague, misty idealism and strong populist sympathies.

Although he tended to cultivate his popular image as a literary roughneck, Sandburg had read widely in college as a member of a group calling themselves the Poor Writers Club, who read aloud from Kipling, Turgenev, and Twain. He also read Marx, whose ideas coincided with his own Populist dissatisfaction with capitalism. When he returned to Galesburg after a two-year period of wandering, Sandburg wrote and published several small pamphlets on the private press of his favorite professor. One of these, published in 1904, was titled *In Reckless Ecstasy,* a phrase borrowed from the mystic novelist Marie Corelli. A passage from this pamphlet bears quoting since it reflects attitudes that Sandburg continued to hold throughout his life:

> I glory in this world of men and women, torn with troubles and lost in sorrow, yet living on to love and laugh and play through it all. My eyes range with pleasure over flowers, prairies, woods, grass, and running water, and the sea, and the sky and the clouds.

The vagueness, the sentimental quality, and the simple idealism of this passage are all found many times over in Carl Sandburg's poetry.

Some of these attitudes, in spite of the surface crudities of the title poem, are evident in his first volume, *Chicago Poems* (1916). Harriet Monroe had published nine of these in *Poetry* in 1914, and had seen to it that Sandburg received the Levinson Prize for that year. Sandburg was her biggest catch so far, and the greatest support to her belief that a poetry renaissance was taking place in the Midwest. It is hard to imagine the furor that was caused by Sandburg's free-verse paean to Chicago in 1915 unless we remember that since the death of Whitman most American poetry had sunk into a morass of gentility and propriety. The vigorous accents of Whitman, when they were remembered at all, were regarded largely as historical curiosities, and the tradition of American poetry seemed in the popular mind to descend directly from Longfellow to James Whitcomb Riley. What now seem rather tame verses—perhaps not even very interesting ones—were then shocking, both for their form and for what they said about Chicago:

> Hog Butcher for the World,
> Tool Maker, Stacker of Wheat,
> Player with Railroads and the
>   Nation's Freight Handler;
> Stormy, husky, brawling,
> City of the Big Shoulders

This apostrophe is followed by a series of Whitmanesque portraits of "painted women," gunmen, hungry women and children who make up the city: "under his ribs the heart of the people, / Laughing!"

With a few exceptions, *Chicago Poems* contains the best of Sandburg's work—and all that is typical of it. By the time he wrote these poems he had already found his voice, and from that point on he never substantially developed or changed. It is often a sure and strong voice, with a deep underlying love of people; people in the abstract, but seen in individuals, in particulars. His poems about lonely or forlorn people do not probe with any of the psychological depth with which Robinson examines his inhabitants of Tilbury Town; instead they become the basis for outcries against social injustice. Sandburg is the poet of social consciousness in ways that John Dos Passos and John Steinbeck were to adopt in their social protest novels of the twenties and thirties. He is the champion of the little guy and the underdog, the fellow who never had a chance. In "Child of the Romans" (1916) a "dago shovelman sits by the railroad track" eating bread and bologna while a train goes by on which men and women sit eating steaks "running with brown gravy." One is reminded here of the end of Dos Passos' *U.S.A.,* where "Vag" stands watching an airplane wherein a transcontinental passenger is throwing up the steak and mushrooms he ate in New York. In Sandburg's "Mag" (1916) the speaker wishes he had never met Mag and had kids by her, "And rent and coal and clothes to pay for." In "Mamie" (1916) he captures the dreariness of midwestern farm life with his portrait of a girl who yearns, like Dreiser's Sister Carrie, for "romance among the streets of Chicago." The most angry and outspoken poem in this volume is "To a Contemporary Bunkshooter" (1916), which attacks the preaching of Billy Sunday by matching the revivalist's own vulgarities:

> You slimy bunkshooter, you put a smut on every
>   human blossom in reach of your rotten breath
>   belching about hell-fire and hiccupping about
>   this Man who lived a clean life in Galilee.

In *Cornhuskers* (1918) and *Smoke and Steel* (1920) Sandburg continued to explore the "unpoetic" areas of life, with a mixture of harshness and gentleness that goes no further, however, in defining his central vision. The best of *Cornhuskers* is in the long poem "Prairie"—a nostalgic evocation of what it was like to live in the open spaces and see the cities of Omaha, Kansas City, and St. Paul rising from the plains.

The Whitman manner is particularly strong here, as Sandburg tries to duplicate his expansiveness of spirit:

> To a man across a thousand years I offer a handshake.
> I say to him: Brother, make the story short, for the
> stretch of a thousand years is short.

But one senses that what was for Whitman a genuine vision of cosmic nationalism has become in Sandburg only a stylized tribute to the physical energies of a growing nation. His skyscrapers, grain elevators, and sheet steel mills are depressing reminders of Russia's poetry of social realism that cry for Whitman's all-embracing ego.

By the time he published *Slabs of the Sunburnt West* in 1922 Sandburg was a fixture on the American poetic landscape and no longer the object of shocked and outraged criticism. Whatever position he held as an innovator in 1914 had given way in the intervening years of rapidly changing attitudes to Ezra Pound and to T. S. Eliot, who published *The Waste Land* the same year. Sandburg all too often allowed his sentimentality to override his judgment. An example is "Wilderness," in which successive stanzas begin with phrases that descend to bathos or worse: "There is a wolf in me . . . There is a fox in me . . . There is a hog in me . . . There is a fish in me . . . There is a baboon in me . . . There is an eagle in me and a mocking-bird . . . O, I got a zoo, I got a menagerie, inside my ribs, under my bony head, under my red-valve heart," etc. But another poem in *Cornhuskers* gives us an idea of the range of his interests, as well as a suggestion of the influence of Pound and the Imagists. "Bilbea" is ostensibly a translation of ancient Babylonian tablet writing, and in its style and tone resembles such translations of Pound as "Exile's Letter" and "The River Merchant's Wife." In *Chicago Poems* Sandburg had written such poems as "Joy" and "Monotone" in a vaguely Imagist manner, and in "Letters to Dead Imagists" he paid tribute to Emily Dickinson and Stephen Crane, who were then widely considered to be forerunners of the Imagist movement. And his famous, over-quoted "Fog" also owes something to both the Imagists and the Japanese haiku, with which he was experimenting. He continued to write poems that could be loosely associated with the Imagist movement, although they are blurred by the romantic melancholy that his repeated use of mist, smoke, haze, and fog suggests.

Sandburg's interest in folk wisdom and popular sayings led him to use them in his poems, and even to try to make poems out of the raw material itself. *Good Morning, America* (1928) contains this kind of poetry, and shows the direction he was heading when he published *The People, Yes* in 1936. It was clear by this time that Sandburg had found his voice in the voice of the people, and some readers, including the English writer Rebecca West in her introduction to an English edition of his poems, were led to compare him with Burns as a user of authentic native language. *The People, Yes* took him about as far as it is possible to go in this direction. This is a combination of popular sayings, proverbs, poolroom slang, barbershop wisdom, and typical Sandburgiana. Some of it is poetry; most of it is not, and yet it is impossible and even undesirable to dismiss the Sandburg of this volume or the earlier ones, because he seldom exerts really effective control or sustains a unified point of view in relation to his material. In spite of the shortcomings in all of his work, many of his individual poems are excellent: "Broken-Face Gargoyles" (1920), "Four Preludes on Playthings of the Wind" (1920), "The Lawyers Know Too Much" (1920), and his tribute to President Roosevelt in "When Death Came April Twelve 1945" (1945). Perhaps a remark of Archibald MacLeish at the 1955 Boston Arts Festival most clearly defines Sandburg's role: a "poet of the American affirmation," a "singer of the city where no one before him thought song could be found, and the voice of a prairie country which had been silent until he came."

The most spectacular of the midwestern poets was Vachel Lindsay (1879–1931), who chanted, whispered, and yelled his best-known poems to large audiences all over the country. Performing in what he called the "Higher Vaudeville," Lindsay became in the twenties a well-known figure, part entertainer, part curiosity, part crusader for the "Gospel of Beauty," which he had begun preaching in 1906. For three years after leaving Hiram College in 1900 he studied art in New York, but gave it up for journalism and a variety of odd jobs. In 1906 he went on the first of his walking tours around the country, trading his poems for food and shelter, eventually ending up back in his home town of Springfield, Illinois, lecturing for the Anti-Saloon League. In one walking tour through the Southwest in 1912 he distributed his *Rhymes to Be Traded for Bread* and followed a set of rules for traveling and begging based upon what was essentially a vow of poverty.

The course of Lindsay's life was changed dramatically in 1912 by the enterprising Harriet Monroe, on the lookout for talent for her new magazine *Poetry*. Having read a magazine article about his adventures, she invited him to contribute, and he sent her "General William Booth Enters into Heaven" (1913). Lindsay had read about the blindness and subsequent death of the founder of the Salvation Army at a time when, tramping around the country and sleeping in Salvation Army quarters, he felt that he was among those unfortunates to whom General Booth had devoted his life. The poem, he said, "merely turned into rhyme as well as I could, word for word, General Booth's own account of his life and the telegraph dispatches of his death after going blind." The poem was accompanied by directions for reading: "(To be sung to the tune of 'The Blood of the Lamb' with indicated instruments)," which included a bass drum, banjos, flutes, and tambourines. The poem's immediate and sensational success led to Lindsay's extensive tours of the high-school and college lecture circuit, where he delivered his poems in an exaggerated stage whisper. The stimulus provided by these recitals led to some of his best poems: "The Congo" (1914), "The Santa Fe Trail" (1914), "Bryan, Bryan, Bryan, Bryan" (1919), and "John L. Sullivan" (1919). The first two of these, in addition to "General William Booth," were the most popular, and by 1920 he had become sick of audiences who demanded the same poems over and over; he once wrote to Louis Unter-meyer that if he had to read them once more he would go mad.

These poems, and many others like them, have their roots in popular literature and tradition. Lindsay was among the first to seize upon the minstrel show, revival meetings, vaude-ville, and college yells as a source of rhythm and language. The writing of college yells, he once said in a mood of defi-ance, is as steady an occupation among bright youths here as the writing of sonnets was in England in the Elizabethan age. This all-but-forgotten form is preserved by Lindsay in "Kallyope Yell" (1913), which he said should be whispered in unison. All poetry, he said, should be whispered, since it is first and last for the inner ear, and his own unique method of chanting may be heard on recordings he made of his work. Although jazz was often cited as an influence on his rhythms, he repeatedly denied it, stating that he had always hated jazz as "our most Babylonian disease." Babylon was Lindsay's name for cities, and as a boy growing up under the spell-binding rhetoric of William Jennings Bryan he acquired a lifelong Populist antipathy to cities, capitalism, money, and monopoly.

The stagey qualities of Lindsay's best-known verse are its most distinguishing characteristic. The response of his public to the use of stage directions in "General William Booth" led him to use a greater range and variety of such effects in "The Congo," which he subtitled, "A Study of the Negro Race." It is actually a collection of all the racial stereotypes of Ne-groes (the heading of two sections are "Their Basic Savagery" and "Their Irrepressible High Spirits"), but Lindsay himself believed it represented a true insight into their character. The poem, which has been recited by several generations of high-school students, depends heavily on rhythm and sound effects, and is accompanied by such stage directions as "Like the wind in the chimney" and "All the 'o' sounds very golden." This poem and "The Santa Fe Trail" exemplify his conception of the "Higher Vaudeville"—an effort to reach the public through poetry that is both beautiful and entertaining. They may be vulgar, they may lack taste, but they are skillfully and even sensitively written. Although the impulse lying behind them and the free-verse form may seem reminiscent of the attitudes and practices of Whitman, they lie closer to the spirit of Poe, with their heavy dependence upon musical effects. Poe and Swinburne were indeed early favorites of Lindsay, and although he shared with Masters and Sandburg their emulation of Whitman as a popular poet, he came finally to reject him.

One of his best pieces is "The Chinese Nightingale" (1917). Also good are poems in a different vein, such as his poem about World War I, "Abraham Lincoln Walks at Midnight" (1914), his many tributes to Johnny Appleseed, his three poems written in tribute to Mark Twain, the bitter social criticism of "Factory Windows Are Always Broken" (1923), and "The Eagle That Is Forgotten" (1913), which he wrote in praise of the radical governor of Illinois, John Peter Altgeld. Lindsay's *Collected Poems* (1925), however, is in many ways a disaster, since its bad poems threaten to overwhelm the few good ones. Since he had little critical judgment and less taste, the collection is heavily loaded with poems of the social gospel, tributes to movie actresses, and sentimental rhymes with titles like "Queen Mab in the Village" and "What Grandpa Mouse Said." Lindsay's voice was a strong one, heard, he claimed, by millions of people. He was eccentric and in many ways unique in his ability to stir an audience with the music of his poems. The appearance of Lindsay on the scene during the second decade is what might be described as a "cultural episode," but certainly not with any suggestion of high seriousness.

A third voice out of the Midwest was Edgar Lee Masters (1869–1950), a lawyer approaching middle age who first succeeded in publishing his poems when he abandoned the classical lyrics of his youth for the free verse of Whitman. To the chagrin of Harriet Monroe, Masters, unlike Sandburg and Lindsay, was not from Chicago; he published the poems that made him famous in William Reedy's *Mirror* in St. Louis.

The poems in the *Spoon River Anthology* had their origins in the southern Illinois towns of Petersburg and Lewistown, however; not far from Vachel Lindsay's Springfield. While Carl Sandburg was chanting of the rawness and power of Chicago as Hog Butcher for the World and Lindsay was seeing visions of Governor Altgeld over the Springfield State House, Masters was exploding the myth of small-town innocence through his collection of free-verse epitaphs spoken by the former inhabitants of his mythical Spoon River. When *Spoon River Anthology* appeared in book form in 1915 it had the effect of a revelation for the American public, many of whom still treasured the belief that small-town inhabitants were untainted and incorruptible, in spite of Mark Twain's "The Man That Corrupted Hadleyburg" and Hamlin Garland's bleak tales of the middle border. The muckraking journalism that flourished when Masters began writing was later followed by the more widespread debunking of all kinds of pretense that is found in H. L. Mencken's satiric portraits of the "booboisie" and Sinclair Lewis' descriptions of life on Main Street in Gopher Prairie. Both Lewis' caricatures and Sherwood Anderson's brooding characters in *Winesburg, Ohio* are the inheritors of the chronicles of frustrated, petty, or tragic lives that form the substance of *Spoon River Anthology*.

Masters had considered for years the idea of writing a novel about the tradespeople, bankers, lawyers, and schoolteachers in a small town, but in 1909, when Reedy gave him a copy of *The Greek Anthology*, he was led to try writing verses modeled on this compilation of epigrams and epithets. The results were quickly accepted by Reedy and his public, who eagerly demanded more. Each is a small poem, between ten and twenty lines, in free verse, spoken by one of the characters buried in the cemetery "on the hill." Their names range from the flat and commonplace to the whimsical and bizarre: Henry Phipps, Hortense Robbins, Ollie McGee, Sexsmith the Dentist, Roscoe Purkapile, Isaiah Beethoven. Masters' wide reading in English poetry and classical authors shows up in his choice of names such as Voltaire Johnson and Jonathan Swift Somers, and in references in the poems to such writers as Ovid, Wordsworth, and George Eliot. His ironies are sometimes too dependent upon such allusions: the high-minded idealist, Robert Southey Burke, and the village wastrel named Percy Bysshe Shelley, who accidentally shoots himself on a hunting trip:

> They say the ashes of my namesake
> Were scattered near the pyramid of Caius Cestius
> Somewhere near Rome.

Masters is at his best when he stays close to the soil and treats his characters with the detached sympathy and understanding contained in the opening lines of his prologue. "The Hill":

> Where are Elmer, Herman, Bert, Tom and Charley,
> The weak of will, the strong of arm, the clown, the
>   boozer, the fighter?
> All, all, are sleeping on the hill.

His characterizations of some people, such as the devoted schoolteacher Emily Sparks, Sarah Brown the devoted wife, and the happy musician Fiddler Jones, represent the happy and beautiful side of life, while others reflect life's ironies, bitterness, frustrations, and despair. Masters also knew how to titillate his audience with the raciness of village scandal and gossip: Doctor Meyers performs an abortion in an unthinking moment and dies a broken man; Lois Spears is born blind from inherited syphilis; another girl is deserted by her husband when he learns she was not a virgin when they married. Masters' sense of the substance and quality of village life is keen here, and he is especially skillful at relating the lives of the characters to each other, often in complex ways that are novelistic in their effect yet sufficiently developed in the individual poems. The *Spoon River Anthology* should perhaps be read as a realistic novel, since Masters is a kind of Theodore Dreiser in verse. Certainly Masters' attitude toward his characters, which Babette Deutsch has called "compassionate objectivity," is similar to Dreiser's toward his own characters. The best poems are "The Hill," "The Village Atheist," the portrait of Anne Rutledge, and the well-known "Petit the Poet," who spent his life writing "Triolets, villanelles, rondels, rondeaus" and fussing with "little iambics, / While Homer and Whitman roared in the pines."

Although Masters actively entered the literary life of Chicago after the publication of this collection and became associated in the public mind, along with Sandburg and Lindsay, as one of the continuators of "the Whitman tradition," the fact remains that he is essentially a one-book man. He published over a dozen more volumes of poetry, including *The New Spoon River* (1924), *Domesday Book* (1920), and its sequel, *The Fate of the Jury* (1929); several novels; and several biographies, including a bitterly hostile attack on Vachel Lindsay, but in none of this work did he ever again reach the level of *Spoon River Anthology*.

Masters did not write great poetry; much of it is not even good poetry, but he struck a responsive chord and captured a large audience. He is not the accomplished poet Sandburg was; his free verse is not very rhythmical and his diction too often falls flat. Nevertheless, the stories he told are good ones, and he remains an important figure in the efforts of the "new" poets to work toward a freedom of subject matter and technique by which they were seeking to express their vision of a modern America.

Another significant development was the new vitality in the writing of blacks, and a growing interest in their work on the part of white readers. Paul Laurence Dunbar's *Lyrics of Lowly Life* (1896) had been instrumental in creating a public for black verse, but the ironies of his own ambiguous situation, wherein he wanted to transcend his racial background yet was read because of it, were not lost on other black writers. The direction of black poetry in the twentieth century has been toward greater self-awareness, confidence, and pride in blackness, attitudes that can be summed up in the word *négritude*. As a part of this trend James Weldon Johnson (1871–

1938) can perhaps be viewed as a transitional figure. Best known for his novel *The Autobiography of an Ex-Colored Man* (1912), Johnson wrote many dialect pieces in the manner of Dunbar, as well as poems expressing racial pride and racial protest. These are collected in *Fifty Years and Other Poems* (1922). More powerful and original are the dignified and restrained *God's Trombones: Seven Negro Sermons in Verse* (1927).

Claude McKay (1891–1948) is also better known for his fiction. Born in Jamaica, he lived and worked in New York in the twenties and published one volume of verse, *Harlem Shadows* (1922). *Selected Poems* was published posthumously in 1953. He wrote some nostalgic lyrics on West Indian life and some poems expressing his bitterness as a black man, of which "If We Must Die" is his best known.

Both Johnson and McKay are associated with what is now called the Negro Renaissance, or, because so much of the activity took place in New York, the Harlem Renaissance. This many-sided phenomenon was a result of a new black awareness, out of which black writers, painters, and musicians developed into significant artists and offered their own contributions to the mainstream of American cultural life. For the blacks, there was a new pride in blackness coupled with the irony and bitterness of racial oppression, a renewed interest in their African cultural heritage, and pleasure in the folkways and indigenous art of both rural and urban blacks. For the whites, who made up a substantial part of their audience, both blacks and black literature were attractive because of their exotic and bizarre aspects, and reading black writing or listening to their music was equivalent to many to visiting a nightclub in Harlem. But Harlem was the home not only of musicians like Fats Waller and Duke Ellington. Writers like McKay, Countee Cullen, Jean Toomer, and Langston Hughes were living there; and two new publications, *The Crisis,* begun by W. E. B. Dubois in 1910, and Charles S. Johnson's *Opportunity,* provided outlets for their work.

Langston Hughes (1902–1967) began his own publishing career in *The Crisis* in 1921 when it printed one of his best poems, "The Negro Speaks of Rivers." This short poem, with its obvious debts to Sandburg, is a deeply emotional but restrained expression of the black's sense of his ancient past in which the river image is used to fuse the present and the past:

> I've known rivers ancient as the world and older than the
>   flow of human blood in human veins.
> My soul has grown deep like the rivers

Through all of Hughes's work runs a strong vein of racial consciousness, which he used to affirm his pride in blackness. Whether he was writing about race prejudice, black separatism, Harlem, the South, or black pride, Hughes was working to break down generalizations and stereotypes about the black man fostered by both blacks and whites. "I explain and illuminate the Negro condition in America," he once said. "This applies to 90 percent of my work."

One important way in which Hughes illuminated the Negro condition was in his adaptations of the rhythms of Afro-American music to poetry. He wrote poems in which he attempted to re-create the rhythms of the blues, jazz, bebop, and boogie-woogie. From the time he first heard the blues as a nine-year-old boy in Kansas City, Hughes was interested in the relationship between music and poetry. His blues poems, such as "The Weary Blues" (1926), "Song for a Banjo Dance" (1926), "Homesick Blues" (1926), and "Po' Boy Blues" (1926), are efforts to re-create black soul music—that complex of feelings associated with the blues: an incongruous combination of rhythm, warmth, ironic laughter, and tears. The blues poems attempted to re-create in words alone what blues singers did with music, gestures, and facial expressions. Some of these poems adhere more closely than others to the blues rhyme pattern and the use of refrains, but even when departing from them in form, Hughes remained faithful to them in spirit. "The Weary Blues," written about a Harlem piano player, won a prize when it appeared and is the title poem of his first collection, published in 1926. One of his best blues poems is "Evenin' Air Blues" (1941), an ironic account of the fortunes of a southern black who has made the traditional flight to the North:

> This mornin' for breakfast
> I chawed de mornin' air.
> This mornin' for breakfast
> Chawed de mornin' air.
> But this evenin' for supper,
> I got evenin' air to spare.

Jazz, even more than the blues, appealed to Hughes because of its rhythmic possibilities. In the twenties he was already reading poetry to the jazz accompaniment of Fats Waller for their Harlem friends, an early forerunner of the practice of Kenneth Rexroth and others in the fifties. Vachel Lindsay's "The Congo" in 1914 had already explored some of the possibilities of using jazz rhythms in poetry, and when Hughes met Lindsay, two of the three poems he showed him were jazz poems: "Negro Dancers" (1926) and "Jazzonia" (1926). These poems combine sexual themes, jagged rhythms, and sharp images to give the effects of jazz. One of Hughes's most interesting applications of jazz to poetry is a series of poems called *Ask Your Mama* (1961), written to be read to jazz accompaniment. The leitmotif for the entire series, he says in a note, is the traditional folk melody of the "Hesitation Blues." The marginal notes to the poems are strongly reminiscent of "The Congo," although there is a closer connection between the music and the poetry. Here is a note to one of them, called "Cultural Exchange" (1961): "The rhythmically rough scraping of a guira continues monotonously until a lonely flute call, high and far away, merges into piano variations on German lieder gradually changing into old-time traditional 12-bar blues up between verses until African drums throb against blues fading as the music ends."

Hughes wrote hundreds of poems, most of his best in the early twenties, before he turned to fiction and plays. In his work over the years he has dealt with virtually every aspect of black life in a variety of moods and attitudes from bitter and vehement racial pride to romantic lyricism and earthy folk humor. In his powerful poem "Mulatto" (1927), which opens with the line, *"I am your son, white man!,"* he raised complex and difficult questions of identity and responsibility. In "Minstrel Man" (1925) he echoes Dunbar's "We Wear the Mask" when he sympathizes with the familiar black problem of keeping up a false front in his dealings with whites:

> Because my mouth
> Is wide with laughter,
> You do not hear
> My inner cry

He attacked white generalizations about blacks in "Theme for English B" (1949), in which a black college student, told to write something about himself, muses over the difference between his white instructor's ideas of what black life is and what it really is. In his long poem *Montage of a Dream Deferred* (1951) Hughes combines a variety of techniques, using street songs, boogie-woogie rhythms, snatches of conversation, etc., to create an impression in words of black urban life. For his lifelong concern with the life of his people Langston Hughes has been aptly called the poet laureate of the Negro people.

Another poet associated with the Harlem Renaissance is Countee Cullen (1903–1946), whose first volume of poems, *Color* (1925), was published while he was an undergraduate at New York University. After taking a Master of Arts degree at Harvard he became an editor of *Opportunity*. He published several other volumes, including *Copper Sun* (1927), *The Ballad of the Brown Girl* (1927), and *The Medea and Other Poems* (1935). Cullen was not spiritually or emotionally so closely tied to racial questions as was Hughes, and his poetry is more highly literary, with a special kinship with Keats, Housman, and Edna St. Vincent Millay. His sonnet

"Yet Do I Marvel" (1925) catalogues the inscrutable ways of God and ends with the couplet, "Yet do I marvel at this curious thing: / To make a poet black, and bid him sing!" In "Incident" (1925) he recalls a boyhood incident in which a Baltimorean "poked out / His tongue, and called me, 'Nigger'." "Heritage" (1925) is historically an early expression of *négritude,* the black's sense of his cultural identity with Africa, but the poem is somewhat artificial and full of clichés of exoticism.

Other poems, such as "Wisdom Cometh With the Years" (1925), are concerned with more universal themes. Cullen wrote "To Endymion" (1927) after a visit to the grave of Keats and "Cor Cordium" (1927) in memory of Shelley. His lyrical talents are best put to the service of his racial feelings in the sonnet "From the Dark Tower" (1927). He demonstrates his considerable lyrical talents in other sonnets: "What I am saying now was said before" (1935), "These are no wind-blown rumors" (1935), and in "She of the Dancing Feet Sings" (1925) and "Nothing Endures" (1929).

Another important figure associated with Hughes and Cullen was Jean Toomer (1894–1967), who established his reputation on one book, *Cane* (1923), a miscellany of stories, sketches, and poems, ending in a one-act play. In the 1920s Toomer had known Hart Crane, Kenneth Burke, and Waldo Frank and was a contributor to such "little" magazines as *Broom, The Dial,* and the *Little Review.* However, he had ambivalent attitudes toward blackness and the question of black identity. The cane becomes a symbol of Toomer's southern black heritage, representing the sweetness of life, sexuality, and roots in the soil. In the short stories and sketches he portrays various aspects of black life in the South and North and uses such poems as "Reapers," "Georgia Dusk," and "Karintha" to set a mood or serve as lyrical commentary on the quality of that life. Although he published practically nothing afterward, he willed some thirty thousand pieces of manuscript material to the Fisk University library, some of which

could quite possibly be poetry equal in quality to what we
have.

In the intricate, colorful, highly intellectual verse of Melvin B. Tolson (1900–1966) we can see the efforts of a black
poet to blend his own Afro-American heritage with the mainstream of modern twentieth-century poetry. Born in Missouri
and educated at Fisk, Lincoln, and Columbia Universities,
Tolson spent most of his life teaching creative literature at
Langston University in Oklahoma. His poems are full of the
rhythms of black speech and song but draw their material
from wide reading in classical and contemporary literature.
He received early recognition for a group of lyrics, "Dark
Symphony," collected in *Rendezvous with America* (1944).
In 1953 he was commissioned to write a poem for the Liberian
centennial celebration. *Libretto for the Republic of Liberia*
is a long Pindaric ode written in a unique Afro-American
idiom full of Poundian allusions. It was enthusiastically received by many poets and critics, including William Carlos
Williams, who referred to it in the fourth book of *Paterson,*
and Allen Tate, who, in an introduction, called attention
to his great gift for language, his profound historical sense,
and his first-rate intelligence.

Tolson published the first book of an unfinished major
work, *Harlem Gallery,* in 1965. Using the ode form of the
Libretto, he returned to the major themes of that work, such
as the question of black identity. In his introduction to the
poem, Karl Shapiro describes it as follows: "The milieu is
Harlem, from the twenties on. The *dramatis personae* com-
prise every symbolic character, from the black bourgeois
Babbitt and the Lenox Avenue poet to the alienated Negro
professor and sage who sits in the bar and elaborates, along
with the Curator and others, a Platonic dialogue. The give-
and-take ostensibly moves on a level of talk about the arts—a
'floor' which is constantly caving in and plunging the reader
into the depth of metaphysical horror which journalists nowa-
days refer to as the Race Question."

It is not a somber poem, however. It is full of wit, cruel humor, and slapstick. Here is a sample passage:

> "The golden mean
> of the dark wayfarer's way between
> black Scylla and white Charybdis, I
> have traveled; subdued ifs in the way;
> from *vile-canaille* balconies and nigger heavens, seen
> day beasts and night beasts of prey
> in the disemboweling pits of
> Europe and America,
> in the death-worming bowels of
> Asia and Africa;
> and, although a Dumb Ox (like young Aquinas), I
> have not forgot
> the rainbows and the olive leaves against the orient sky.

> "The basso profundo
> Gibbon of Putney
> —not the lyric tenor, Thomas of Celano—
> hymns the *Dies Irae!*"

American blacks in the forties and fifties continued to write primarily as blacks, responding to their experience and their environment sometimes with bitterness, sometimes with joy, but seldom with sentimentality or false humility. Gwendolyn Brooks (b. 1917) is one of the best of the post-Harlem generation. Many of her poems are set in her native Chicago and contain insights into black life, such as the frugal life of an aging couple in "The Bean Eaters" (1960), the title poem of her third volume. "We Real Cool" in this volume makes a brilliant sociological comment without sentimentality or bitterness in four sharply etched stanzas:

> We real cool. We
> Left school. We
>
> Lurk late. We
> Strike straight. We

Sing sin. We
Thin gin. We

Jazz June. We
Die soon.

Not all of Gwendolyn Brooks's early poems are about black life, and the poem above is not a good sample of the rich textures, subtle rhymes, and sharp, incisive diction of which she is capable. *Annie Allen* (1949) won the Pulitzer Prize and *Selected Poems* was published in 1963. The title poem of *In the Mecca* (1969), a long, grim narrative about the murder of a child in Chicago's black ghetto, demonstrates her continuing concern with the life of her people and her awareness of continuing in the tradition of Langston Hughes. From the late sixties she has been one of the principal spokeswomen of the new black consciousness, and she has adapted her poetic style, as in *Family Pictures* (1970), to reflect her own growing commitment to it.

CHAPTER NINE

Pound, Eliot, and the Imagists

Ezra Pound, T. S. Eliot, Hilda Doolittle (H. D.), John
Gould Fletcher, John Peale Bishop, Elinor Wylie,
Louise Bogan, Léonie Adams

It is not a serious distortion to date the beginnings of the
modern movement in American poetry from the arrival of
Ezra Pound (1885–1972) in London in 1908, since no other
poet, not even T. S. Eliot, is so closely identified with it. The
story of Pound's early Kensington years, his friendships with
William Butler Yeats, Wyndham Lewis, D. H. Lawrence,
Ford Madox Ford, and other British and American writers,
and his central role in the Imagist movement is the story of a
revolution in poetry that challenged the attitudes of the past
and permanently changed the direction of British and American literature. For this was an international, or Anglo-Ameri-
can, phenomenon, which the ferment of those pre–World
War I years in London stimulated. Let us take a brief look
at those historic years in London just preceding World War
I, when the domestic culture absorbed the French Symbolists,
the philosophy of Henri Bergson, and the paintings of the
French Impressionists and Italian Futurists, in the process
evolving a new and cosmopolitan style in the arts that we now
call modernism. Then let us go on to look at the poets most
closely associated with the Imagists and with Eliot.

After doing graduate work in the Romance languages at

the University of Pennsylvania, Pound went first to Italy, then to London, where he remained until 1920. At about the time he collected his early poems in *Personae* (1909) Pound was introduced to the circle of T. E. Hulme, which included F. S. Flint, Francis Tancred, and Joseph Campbell. Up to this meeting, Pound had felt little or no dissatisfaction with the state of English verse at the time, and his own early verses were Victorian in style and tone, but he quickly adopted the rebellious attitudes of this group against the diffuse, sentimental poetry of the Georgians. Writing back home to William Carlos Williams, Pound remarked, "I have sinned in nearly every possible way, even the ways I most condemn. I have printed too much. . . . There is no town like London to make one feel the vanity of all art except the highest. To make one disbelieve in all but the most careful and conservative presentation of one's stuff. I have sinned deeply against the doctrine I preach."

This doctrine was Imagism, which began with Hulme's studies of poetic theory and came to be a theory in which form and meaning coexist in a poetry characterized by hardness, clarity, and restraint, and by an absence of didacticism. Hulme found his ideas in Bergson, but the French Symbolists had also gone a long way toward developing and putting into practice a modern theory of the image, and this theory had found its way across the Channel by way of Arthur Symons and the Goncourt brothers. Hulme also discovered in the Japanese haiku a formal poetic structure that lent itself to directly expressing feeling through the juxtaposition of images. As Pound later defined it, the image was "that which presents an intellectual and emotional complex in an instant of time"; it was able to free language from the limits of space and time by compression and precision. Hulme, in the few poems he wrote, worked to apply these techniques, and Pound eventually took over the program as his own. When he met the British poet Richard Aldington and the American poet H. D. in 1912 and read some of their brief and delicate lyrics, Pound informed them that they were writing Imagist poems, and at this point he became the chief apologist and propagandist for the Imagist movement. His own description of Imagism, in "A Retrospect," includes these three principles: (1) direct treatment of the "thing," whether subjective or objective; (2) to use absolutely no word that does not contribute to the presentation; and (3) as regarding rhythm: to compose in the sequence of the musical phrase, not in the sequence of a metronome. "Naturally," he added, in *Make It New* (1934), "the second clause in the Imagist triad was the first to be avoided."

The poems that Pound wrote according to these principles he deliberately stripped of all but the telling image; the poem was to be neither narrative nor didactic but was to strive toward the ideal of the intellectual and emotional complex in an instant of time. The most celebrated example of Imagist poetry is Pound's own two-line poem, "In a Station of the Metro" (1916):

> The apparition of these faces in the crowd;
> Petals on a wet, black bough.

In this poem he felt he had recorded the "precise instant when a thing outward and objective transforms itself, or darts into a thing inward and subjective," and he called attention to what he felt was a similarity between his poetry and the techniques and objectives of the Impressionist painters. In 1914 Pound and others published a number of Imagist poems in the *Egoist,* and in the same year he edited an anthology, *Des Imagistes,* which included poems by H. D., William Carlos Williams, James Joyce, Ford Madox Ford, D. H. Lawrence, Amy Lowell, and himself. By this time, the Imagist program had become sufficiently diffuse to allow for a wide variety of styles to appear in the anthology, including haiku, free verse, prose poems, and other forms of experimentation. What the contributors had in common was a rebellious spirit against the poetry of the past and a desire to "make it new."

As Amy Lowell (1874–1925) became more and more assertive and influential in the Imagist movement, Pound tended to disassociate himself from it, and finally to positively reject it in favor of another, even more short-lived movement, which he and Wyndham Lewis called Vorticism. Vorticism was officially launched in Lewis' and Pound's periodical, *BLAST*, in July 1914, in which both wrote polemical essays defining the movement. But Vorticism was perhaps more a frame of mind than a clearly definable program. Both Lewis and Pound at one time or another claimed credit for the invention of the terms *vortex* and *vorticism,* but they were both in agreement about the need in the arts for a vigorous aesthetic: "The vortex is the point of maximum energy," Pound wrote in *BLAST* in 1914, and went on to deny that Futurism or Impressionism had anything to do with his new movement. We can pass over this phase in Pound's career rather quickly, since his energies were devoted more toward gaining converts and toward drawing people away from Amy Lowell's influence than they were toward writing poetry.

Taken as a whole, Pound's early poetry—published in five separate volumes between 1909 and 1915—is an astonishing display of variety and versatility. Retaining his devotion to purity and freshness in diction and to vividness and intensity of imagery, he wrote poems in a wide range of styles and modes: Catullan satire, Imagist poems, Browningesque dramatic monologues, impressions, manifestoes, and translations from the Anglo-Saxon and Chinese. One of Pound's most influential models was the medieval poetry of the Provençal troubadours, whom he admired as the embodiment of a concept of poetry that combined innovation with tradition. In the troubadours' inventions of such complex verse forms as the sestina and villanelle Pound found examples for infusing a new spirit into his own poetry. He wrote many such poems while still under the influence of his postgraduate studies in Romance literature and published them in his first volume, *A Lume Spento* (1908). The early poem "Cino" is a mixture of the slangy tone of the Browning monologue and the purity of language and image that has characterized Pound's poetry throughout his life. The poem begins:

> Bah! I have sung women in three cities,
> But it is all the same;
> And I will sing of the sun.

After a series of irreverent reflections on women as a subject for poetry, he ends:

> I will sing of the white birds
> In the blue waters of heaven,
> The clouds that are spray to its sea.

Other poems in this volume, such as "Na Audiart" and "Villonaud for This Yule," are also successful efforts to imitate the spirit and forms of Provençal poetry.

In such poems as "The Coming of War: Actaeon" (1916) and "The Return" (1912) he demonstrated a subtlety and delicacy in the handling of language that prompted Yeats to remark of the latter poem, "it gives me better words than my own." In "Les Millwin" (1916), and the savagely satiric series, "Moeurs Contemporaines" (1919), Pound showed his contempt for philistinism and sham. He indulged himself in outright invective in "Salutation the Third" (1926) and in "Salvationists" (1916), which ends:

> Come, my songs,
> Let us take arms against this sea of stupidities—
> Beginning with Mumpodorus;
> And against this sea of vulgarities—
> Beginning with Nimmim;
> And against this sea of imbeciles—
> All the Bulmenian literati.

Some of his most outstanding work was in translations. "The Seafarer" (1912), for example, a fairly free rendering of the well-known Anglo-Saxon poem, reproduces the spirit of the original through the use of a rough-hewn free-verse line that approximates the alliterative four-beat line of the original.

> Bitter breast-cares have I abided,
> Known on my keel many a care's hold,
> And dire sea-surge, and there I oft spent
> Narrow nightwatch nigh the ship's head
> While she tossed close to cliffs.

This is not a literal translation, and was not supposed to be, but it was attacked by some because it did not follow the original closely enough. But Pound's talents as a translator lay in his ability to reproduce the spirit of the original, even if he had to distort the text to do it. He was a "creative translator," using his text as the basis for what became in his hands a new poem. In the case of one series of translations, he did not even know the original language but worked instead from prose translations of Chinese poetry made by an American Oriental scholar, Ernest Fenellosa. Pound turned these into the series of poems published as *Cathay* in 1915. Here he was able to use the Imagist techniques to advantage: the ideals of restraint, understatement, and concreteness of the Imagist program were qualities already contained in the Chinese poems, both in the dramatic monologues, such as "Exile's Letter" and "The River Merchant's Wife: A Letter," and in the shorter, haiku-like pieces, such as "The Jewel Stairs' Grievance":

> The jewelled steps are already quite white with dew,
> It is so late that the dew soaks my gauze stockings,
> And I let down the crystal curtain
> And watch the moon through the clear autumn.

Pound's role as a translator, and the importance of translation to his work, may be seen most clearly in the *Homage to Sextus Propertius,* a series of twelve poems, completed in 1917 and published in *Poetry* and *The New Age* in 1919. The poems are not, strictly speaking, translations at all: to an even greater extent than the Anglo-Saxon or the Chinese translations they are attempts to re-create the mind and attitudes of the original poet through a twentieth-century sensibility. It was Propertius' concern for art that perhaps led Pound to adopt him as still another persona, not to hide himself, but to widen his range of expression by projecting himself into the personality of another poet. Although Propertius' major subject was love, Pound's interest in him focused largely on the parallel between what he called the "infinite and ineffable imbecility of the British Empire" and the "infinite and ineffable imbecility of the Roman Empire." In effect, the *Homage* became an attack on the warlike society and culture of twentieth-century Europe that militated against artistic expression.

In many ways, *Homage to Sextus Propertius* is a preparation for Pound's sequence, *Hugh Selwyn Mauberley* (1920), a work that marks a turning point in his career (Pound himself once called it a popularization of *Propertius*). Pound's bitter and satirical exploration of the artist's relation to society, and of the opposition of private poetic morality to public compulsions are the main themes of the *Mauberley* sequence, which is told through personae whom it is often too tempting to recognize as versions of Pound himself. Noting that it was "distinctly a farewell to London," Pound mounted a vituperative attack on philistinism and the socially and morally corrupting influences of the war.

In the *Mauberley* sequence Pound uses a disjunctive, stream-of-consciousness method in which the poet's voice is heard through various personae. The principal figure in the poem, subtitled "Life and Contacts," is Hugh Selwyn Mauberley, a poet who begins as a hero and ends as a victim of the vulgarity and indifference of England in the years 1912 to 1920. The epigraph and opening stanzas establish the speaker as a heroic figure in the tradition of Villon and Ronsard, both of whom marked points of departure in the history of poetry:

> For three years, out of key with his time,
> He strove to resuscitate the dead art
> Of poetry; to maintain "the sublime"
> In the old sense

The speaker describes himself ironically, using critical cant phrases current at the time, but maintaining an Odyssean heroic stance in his remark that his "true Penelope was Flaubert." He then moves to a discussion of the forces in England working against the poet, in particular the World War, which he attacks in some of the most savage language Pound ever wrote:

> There died a myriad,
> And of the best, among them,
> For an old bitch gone in the teeth,
> For a botched civilization,
> Charm, smiling at the good mouth,
> Quick eyes gone under earth's lid,
>
> For two gross of broken statues,
> For a few thousand battered books.

A series of highly allusive sections describes the forces and counterforces of the late Victorian period that led up to the debased and degenerate atmosphere preceding the war: the philistine ignorance and scorn for Edward Fitzgerald and the Pre-Raphaelites, the mercenary attitude of the successful novelist, such as Arnold Bennett, as opposed to the self-sacrifice of the "stylist," such as Ford Madox Ford. In "Envoi" (1919), the closing poem of the first part of the sequence, Pound abandons his satire and irony for a poem that embodies the ideals he feels are threatened by the tendencies he has described. Echoing the English poet Edmund Waller, he writes a three-stanza free-verse lyric equal to his model on the enduring quality of beauty.

In the second part of the *Mauberley* sequence the Mauberley-Pound persona turns inward to examine himself in the light of his own failure to adapt himself to the cultural milieu of his time. His irony goes in two directions: toward himself, now viewed as an ineffective and emasculated aesthete, and toward his environment, which because of its cultural bankruptcy has forced upon him a dwindling of perceptions and intensity. The virile anger of the first section gives way to a faded resignation and constipated style, as Pound the poet ironically projects what the Pound-Mauberley persona would become if he were to remain in London. Turning inward becomes not a means for self-renewal in the face of his tawdry surroundings, but a state of confused and ineffective muttering:

Nothing, in brief, but maudlin confession,
Irresponse to human aggression,
Amid the precipitation, down-float
Of insubstantial manna,
Lifting the faint susurrus
Of his subjective hosannah.

Although *Mauberley* does not reach to the roots of the spiritual and moral problems of the age as Eliot's *The Waste Land* does, it still bores in more sharply on the dilemma of the artist whose commitment to his ideals forces him to turn his back on his age. Less structurally unified than *The Waste Land,* and more heavily dependent upon irony, *Hugh Selwyn Mauberley* offers many obstacles to the reader, but once they are overcome this poem can be seen as one of Pound's most impressive achievements.

Mauberley marks the end of an era, both for Pound and for modern poetry—an era of dynamic change and experimentalism that led to the great flowering of literary creativity in the twenties. Pound had been laying the groundwork for the next stage in his career when, around 1905, he wrote the earliest drafts of what were to become part of the *Cantos.* There is probably no comparable effort in all literary history to that of Pound to project himself, his reading, his attitudes— finally, his life—into the one, long work-in-progress that the *Cantos* became. For over sixty years Pound built piece by piece an open-ended sequence of poems that has become the object of extravagant praise and abusive attack.

The *Cantos* took up where *Mauberley* left off. Pound again mounted his attack on the moneyed interests, the militarists, the philistines, but these attacks are juxtaposed with lyrical visions of various periods of the past, which Pound held up as offering hopeful signs for a "new Paideuma," or cluster of ideas upon which to base a society of the future. These periods include the Italian Renaissance of the Medici, Homeric Greece, China of the time of Confucius, Provence of the Middle Ages, and the America of John Adams. Pound starts as he did in *Mauberley,* with Odysseus as his persona, but in the course of the sequence this poet-hero-voyager undergoes a complex series of metamorphoses. As the subject and theme of the *Cantos* require, the personae become Sigismondo Malatesta, Guillaume d'Aquitaine, Thomas Jefferson, John Adams, Confucius, Pound himself, and many others.

The method Pound used in the *Cantos* is an outgrowth of the Imagist-Vorticist technique of juxtaposition of ideas, images, and feelings, working to produce an unparaphrasable concept in the reader's mind. This technique becomes the "ideogrammic method," following the ideas in Fenellosa's writings on the Chinese written character as a medium for poetry, in which language is supposed to work "presentationally" to form clusters of meanings. In Pound's words, the ideogrammic method "consists in presenting one facet and then another until at some point one gets off the dead and desensitized surface of the reader's mind onto a part that will register." The idea is not new with the *Cantos;* it was already a staple of Imagist poetry. But the extent to which Pound applied it as a structural principle in the *Cantos* goes far beyond anything he or anyone else had tried. Stream-of-consciousness, free association, and a considerable amount of willful non sequitur are used to erect a poem in which there are layers upon layers of meaning. The *Cantos* become increasingly clogged with scraps and orts of Greek, Latin, Italian, and French phrases; with passages from the diaries of Malatesta, the life of Martin Van Buren, the journals of John Adams; with obscenities; and even with Chinese characters themselves; as well as musical notation from medieval psalteries. To describe the *Cantos* this way is, of course, to put them in the worst possible light and to place oneself in the camp of the philistines, yet they finally demand this description. There are beautiful lyrical passages, and passages of brilliant wit and satire, but the ideogrammic method, as well as Pound's belief that the inclusion of substance means the comprehension of substance, led him to include the flotsam and jetsam of a lifetime of reading in patterns that none but the most dedicated exegete can follow.

Yeats once compared the *Cantos* to a fugue, and also remarked that when the 100th Canto was written, the structure would become apparent. It is clear to readers today that the *Cantos* have no formal structure, that it is the first poem to use the "open" form, since emulated by Charles Olson in the *Maximus* poems (1960) and Robert Duncan in *Passages,* not to mention William Carlos Williams' *Paterson* (1958). In 1969 Pound published *Drafts and Fragments: Cantos CX to CXVII,* yet the structure is no more apparent now than it was at the time Yeats made his statement. Perhaps the most accurate description of *Cantos* is Allen Tate's: "The secret of his form is this: conversation. The *Cantos* are talk, talk, talk; not by anyone in particular to anyone else in particular . . . Each Canto has the broken flow and the somewhat elusive climax of a good monologue." Still, this is only partially true. One of Pound's two great strengths is verse as speech; the other is verse as song, and in *Cantos* there is as much song as there is speech. Pound's steadfast commitment to these ideals was the source of vitality not only in his own work but in virtually every American poet since.

Looming forbiddingly over the landscape of twentieth-century American poetry—in fact, over poetry in the Western world—in a way that threatens to strike the historian dumb is the great, good figure of Thomas Stearns Eliot (1888–1965). T. S. Eliot was known variously as a drunken helot whose poetry bordered on the totally incoherent, a towering eminence of critical dogmatism and infallibility, a radical and daring experimentalist in techniques of imagery and diction, and a poet-priest expounding the doctrines of Anglo-Catholic orthodoxy. These, stripped of their pejorative coloring, are all more or less accurate descriptions of a poet whose literary career paralleled and did much to shape and define the modernist movement.

Eliot seems never to have been a young man. His earliest poetry is marked by both an extraordinary technical mastery and a world-weariness and malaise more characteristic of middle age. This impression is sustained by the minor poems, such as "Preludes" (1917), "Dans le Restaurant" (1920), and

"Portrait of a Lady" (1917), all written in a tone of jaded cynicism and mild regret that he seemed from the beginning deliberately to cultivate. This early verse stems from a variety of diverse influences on his own sensibility. Among these is the *fin-de-siècle* atmosphere of Harvard Yard, with its mixture of gentility, Emersonianism, religious doubt, aestheticism, and antimaterialism. The mood of intellectual paralysis and spiritual despair that we see in the poems of those earlier inhabitants of the Yard, Trumbull Stickney and George Cabot Lodge, also affected Eliot, and it was reinforced by his reading the ironic, self-mocking poetry of the French Symbolist Jules Laforgue. Several of Eliot's early poems are translations or adaptations from Laforgue, and his bravura verses in French are done in the Laforgue manner. He seems, in fact, and was taken to be, on the basis of *Prufrock and Other Observations* (1917), a writer of clever *vers de société*, with some debts to Browning.

But the brooding quality and heightened sensibility in these early poems suggest the inadequacy of this description. The tentativeness, the hesitancy, and the indirectness of "The Love Song of J. Alfred Prufrock," for example, are both the manner and the substance of this crucial poem. Composed in 1911, it is the basic Eliot poem, characteristically projecting his own steady refusal to pin things down once and for all or to allow his ambiguous emotions to submit to the order of logic. J. Alfred Prufrock is a man who cannot make up his mind, who is at the mercy of subtle emotions and fleeting impressions, and who moves in irregular ways: crabwise or winding through "streets of insidious intent." The interior monologue itself begins abruptly in the middle of a reverie and moves by free association through a variety of memories and desires. This total response to experience involves both sense impressions and thought, emerging in a mingling of the two in a heightened perception of the actual. "Prufrock" illustrates this comment Eliot made in his essay on the Metaphysical poets concerning the experience of the poet: "The ordinary man's experience is chaotic, irregular, fragmentary. [He] falls in love, or reads Spinoza, and these two experiences have nothing to do with each other, or with the noise of the type-writer or the smell of cooking; in the mind of the poet these experiences are always forming new wholes." The connection between these remarks and the ideas of the English philosopher Francis Herbert Bradley is striking and relevant. In 1916 Eliot was writing his Harvard doctoral dissertation on Bradley, and was obviously struck by his doctrine of "immediate experience." In 1922, in notes he appended to *The Waste Land,* Eliot quoted this paragraph from Bradley's *Appearance and Reality* (1893):

> My external sensations are no less private to myself than are my thoughts or my feelings. In either case my experience falls within my own circle, a circle closed on the outside; and, with all its elements alike, every sphere is opaque to the others which surround it . . . In brief, regarded as an existence which appears in a soul, the whole world for each is peculiar and private to that soul.

The construction of many of Eliot's poems, after "Prufrock" and through "Gerontion" and *The Waste Land,* is based on the attitude toward the relation between interior and exterior reality that these remarks imply.

But Bradley's "immediate experience" is not necessarily to be understood as the experience of the poet, and we are reminded of this distinction by Eliot's insistence on what he called the impersonal theory of poetry. For him, poetry was not an expression of the poet's own emotions or personality, but emotions concentrated into a set of new feelings, from which the poet himself has disappeared. The "I" of "The Love Song of J. Alfred Prufrock" becomes diffused in subsequent poems—in "Gerontion," for example, where the attitudes are objectified in the persona of an old man, and in *The Waste Land,* where the "I" becomes an almost totally diffuse sensibility that broods over the sensations and events in the poem, responding to them in a way that implies the non-existence of the poet. In his essay "Tradition and the Individual Talent" (1919), Eliot said, "the progress of an artist is a continual self-sacrifice, a continual extinction of personality"; and it is this conception of the role of the artist, and Eliot's application of it in his major poems, that makes Hugh Kenner's descriptive phrase, "the invisible poet," a particularly apt one.

In "Gerontion" (1920), Eliot objectifies states of feeling just as he did in "Prufrock": the sense of frustration, boredom, lack of vitality, and the absence of spiritual qualities in modern life. Unlike Prufrock, Gerontion is removed from a specific social setting, yet, like Prufrock, he makes a particular statement about life in a series of brilliantly realized images. The dominant image is the mind of Gerontion, the old man: "Thoughts of a dry brain in a dry season." The reader is witness to the tortured and futile thoughts of a man intellectually convinced of the need for faith but too spiritually and physically desiccated to arrive at belief. His awareness of an age in which religion has been debased and even lost is objectified in Eliot's sharply drawn vignettes of characters representing various types of decadence: Fräulein von Kulp, Hakagawa, and Mr. Silvero—all vaguely cosmopolitan, sinister, and threatening in the way that such characters in *The Waste Land* as Mr. Eugenides and Madame Sosostris are. Gerontion's horrified response to his age is matched by an even more horrifying self-awareness, in which the drying up of his own emotions and a life without faith force him to face death as a dwindling and disintegration of his intellect and perceptions.

This death-in-life reappeared as the major theme of the loosely structured manuscript he first showed to Ezra Pound early in 1922. Eliot's frenzied activity between the years 1915 and 1921—completing his Harvard dissertation, marrying, working in a bank, teaching school, reviewing books, working as assistant editor of the *Egoist,* and publishing three volumes of poetry—left him in a state of exhaustion that forced him to take a rest in Lausanne, Switzerland. There, in the fall of 1921, he composed the nineteen-page manuscript, the title of which was to become a byword of twentieth-century literary and cultural history. Eliot's own state of emotional and physical lassitude may have had something to do with the unusual receptiveness and sensitivity to intellectual, physical, and emotional impressions that the poem exhibits. He seems to have concentrated all his experience and all his wide reading into this collection of loosely related fragments. In the form in which *The Waste Land* (1922) eventually appeared, a good bit of this fragmentary quality remains, but underlying it is a cohesiveness of vision and sensibility that takes the place of structure in the more conventional sense. Since the publication in 1971 of Valerie Eliot's edition of the facsimile of the original drafts, Ezra Pound's role in shaping the poem is now common knowledge, although it was publicly acknowledged by Eliot himself in his dedication to him as *"il miglior fabbro,"* printed in the 1925 edition of his poems. Pound's role approaches that of collaborator, since it was he who suggested omitting some sections from the poem entirely, as well as omitting certain discursive connecting links and changing the wording of many passages in an effort to increase the immediacy of the poem. *The Waste Land* was first published in October 1922 in the *Criterion,* which Eliot was editing; in November it was published in *The Dial* in America, for which it received *The Dial* award; in December an edition of one thousand copies was published by Boni and Liveright, to which Eliot first added the "Notes"; and in the following September it was published by the Woolfs' Hogarth Press.

This rundown of the early printing history of *The Waste Land* is interesting chiefly in connection with the "Notes," which, it now seems clear, were at least partly a hoax. Eliot created them, as Kenner has noted, out of the exigencies of modern publishing techniques, which require a certain number of pages for each gathering. The poem was too short as it stood, and Eliot added the notes to fill up the space. Many of them, such as those to Dante, Baudelaire, Elizabethan tragedies, etc., are helpful, but in others he seems deliberately pompous and pedantic. Pound's nickname for him as Ol' Possum suggests the same playful solemnity in his character that is apparent in references to bawdy ballads from Sydney, Australia, and the song of the North American her-

mit thrush, *Turdus aonalaschkae pallasii,* whose " 'water-drip-
ping song' is justly celebrated." The notes, however, have become an integral part of the poem itself, and few readers
would wish to be without them.

The Waste Land is a sequence constructed on the principles of *Hugh Selwyn Mauberley* and the *Cantos,* with the
added inspiration of using myth as a unifying device, as
Joyce had done in *Ulysses.* Through the use of primitive vege-
tation myths of burial and resurrection—found mainly in Sir
James George Frazer's *The Golden Bough* and Jessie L. Wes-
ton's study of the relation between these myths and Arthurian
legend, *From Ritual to Romance* (1920)—Eliot tied together
the strands of ancient religion, with its basis in fertility
rituals, and Christianity, with its emphasis on resurrection
and spiritual regeneration. This vital connection between
sex and religion on the one hand and sterility and lack of
faith on the other explains the heavy underlying sexuality
of the poem, and provides the way for the various uses of
these themes that are united in the complex metaphor of the
waste land. One can say that the poem as a whole is a single
metaphor, orchestrated in a variety of ways through the interaction of the themes of life and death. On the one hand, life
devoid of meaning is death; on the other, death viewed as a
sacrificial act becomes life-giving.

The critical reactions to the poem were violent and in
wide disagreement, some, like Amy Lowell, condemning it as
"a piece of tripe," others hailing Eliot as the spokesman of the
age. Undergraduates memorized large chunks of it, and other
writers almost immediately began making allusions to it, as
did Ernest Hemingway in *The Sun Also Rises* (1926) and F.
Scott Fitzgerald in *The Great Gatsby* (1925). But Hart Crane,
who had been a passionate admirer of Eliot, condemned its
negativeness and began work on *The Bridge* (1930) partly as
a reaction against it; while William Carlos Williams later recalled in his autobiography how this "great catastrophe to our
letters" had set him back twenty years: "Critically Eliot returned us to the classroom just at the moment when I felt
that we were on the point of an escape to matters much

closer to the essence of a new art form itself." It is interesting to notice, however, how much of Williams' own long poem, *Paterson,* takes on the coloration of Eliot's "unreal city" full of the walking dead.

The tone of the poem is not unremitting despair, however, as many of its admirers and detractors thought; in the last section, called "What the Thunder Said," Eliot makes a tentative affirmation of his hope for a return to belief. The cryptic Sanskrit message of the thunder, promising the return of rain to the arid land, is translated by Eliot as "the peace which passeth understanding," suggesting a means of preservation in the face of spiritual decay. Several years after having joined the Anglican Church, Eliot wrote this passage in "Thoughts After Lambeth" (1931), which points in retrospect toward the direction he was heading at the time he wrote *The Waste Land:*

> The World is trying the experiment of attempting to form a civilized but non-Christian mentality. The experiment will fail; but we must be very patient in awaiting its collapse; meanwhile redeeming the time; so that the Faith may be preserved alive through the dark ages before us; to renew and rebuild civilization, and save the World from suicide.

Eliot's major works, however, form a startlingly consistent whole, a series of poetic statements affirming his straight-line progression from spiritual doubt through spiritual certitude, culminating in the mysticism of *Four Quartets.* Following "The Hollow Men" (1925), an extension of the themes of *The Waste Land,* is the series of four religious poems, appearing at the rate of one a year, that are clearly positive in their attitude: "Journey of the Magi" (1927), "A Song for Simeon" (1928), "Animula" (1929), and "Marina" (1930). These, along with "The Cultivation of Christmas Trees" (1954), were later grouped by Eliot under the heading, "Ariel Poems." Then, in the same mood, is *Ash-Wednesday* (1930), published three years after Eliot became a British subject and joined the Anglican Church. When we look back at it, the poem seems to be part of a program, deliberately planned as a public revelation of Eliot's growing orthodoxy and conservatism, even though it is not.

Although *Ash-Wednesday* is quite explicitly a religious poem, F. O. Matthiessen is right in reminding us of its heavy use of musical effects. Eliot, the virtuoso technician, has left behind his irony and wit and has returned to some of the sense of mystery through the use of repetition and incantation that is found in that important early poem, "La Figlia Che Piange" (1917). *Ash-Wednesday,* like that poem, and like all the best of Eliot's poetry, finally cannot be understood on the intellectual level without allowing oneself to succumb to the power of its musical effects. Matthiessen hardly goes too far when he remarks that the poem is for someone who cannot read or write. The subject of the poem is the power of the religious emotion that brings about humility in one's relationship to God, but rather than describing this emotion Eliot succeeds in reproducing it or objectifying it through the directness, simplicity, and clarity of his imagery and language.

This same "music of meaning" informs the style of Eliot's *Four Quartets* (1943), his four-part meditative poem that attempts to do the impossible—re-create the feelings of an individual who has had a mystical experience. Such a description of his masterpiece is itself inadequate, of course, but it focuses our attention on the two essential aspects of the poem: the poet and his experience. We are made very much aware throughout the poem of the poet's own difficulties in making himself understood, of his "intolerable wrestle / With words and meanings" in the process of conveying the sensations of spiritual serenity.

His basic structural and thematic device is musical form. Each of the four poems, "Burnt Norton" (1935), "East Coker" (1940), "The Dry Salvages" (1941), and "Little Gidding" (1942), has the same five-part structure. They begin with a meditation on a philosophical problem, followed by a lyric section, a personal, introspective meditation, another lyric, and a final meditation that resolves the problems of the particular poem. The musical analogy goes beyond mere structure, however, since Eliot introduces images, themes, and phrases that recur throughout the poems, culminating in a dense and highly charged grouping of them in the closing section of "Little Gidding." The symbolic quality of these images and phrases—the rose garden, the tongue of fire, the dove, the dance, the sea, air, and earth—derives from their occurrence and reoccurrence throughout *Four Quartets;* Eliot's earlier use of literary and historical allusions has been partly replaced by images and phrases that, even though they may have their origin in Dante, Heraclitus, or the Upanishads, still generate their own meaning primarily within the poem itself, rather than from their original context.

Eliot's main objective in this poem was clarity—not so much clarity of meaning as clarity of feeling: the words tend to wrap themselves around the reader by means of incantation and repetition and draw him into the mood of the poem. The diction itself is therefore stripped and simple, even though the syntax is deliberately sinuous and tortuous.

The movement of the poem is away from and out of time into timelessness and eternity—a thrust toward the mystical, still point of eternity that lies, to recall a relevant phrase from *The Waste Land,* in "the heart of light, the silence." To achieve this stasis Eliot develops the idea quoted in the epigraph from Heraclitus: "The way upward and downward are one and the same." These are the two directions by which one can move away from time past and time future, away from the distractions of everyday life, toward a still point of inaction and contemplation. One can go downward through Hell and the fires of Purgatory, or upward toward the light. The search for humility on the moral plane, or grace on the mystical plane, is equated with the "right action" of Oriental philosophy—action without desire—the way to that union with the Absolute called Liberation. At the conclusion of "Little Gidding" the Heraclitean fire imagery, suggesting a translation from Becoming to Being, and the fire imagery from Dante's *Paradiso,* which embodies a universal form of love, are merged in a transcendent, Pentecostal vision of the "crowned knot of fire" in which "the fire and the rose are one." This ultimate evocation of the mystery of religious emotion is the plane on which the poem ends. The emotion itself is completely foreign to most readers, and the attempt to convey it is—as Eliot makes clear he is himself aware—almost impossible. *Four Quartets,* therefore, depends heavily on the willingness of the reader to respond not only intellectually but with his whole being if he is to apprehend the quality of an experience that is both personal and universal. This, in varying degrees, is what all of Eliot's poems demand: a response to the dramatized projection of a complex experience playing upon a highly refined sensibility.

Because so many of the poems of Hilda Doolittle (1886–1961) conform closely to the doctrines of the Imagists, her name has always been associated with them. She began writing her short free-verse poems before 1911, the year she arrived in London, met Richard Aldington, her future husband, and renewed her friendship with Ezra Pound. When Pound saw these small, carefully wrought, single-image poems, they seemed to him to be illustrations of T. E. Hulme's theories. He therefore informed her she was an Imagist poet and insisted that the poems he submitted for her to Harriet Monroe's *Poetry* should be signed "H. D., Imagist." She signed her name as H. D. from then on. The daughter of an astronomer at the University of Pennsylvania, H. D. attended Friends' Central School and Bryn Mawr, and during the years 1902 to 1906 came to know Pound, William Carlos Williams, and Marianne Moore. In addition to becoming engaged to be married to her, Pound took it upon himself to continue the classical education that had begun in her childhood with Poe's "To Helen," Bulwer-Lytton's *The Last Days of Pompeii,* and Hawthorne's *Tanglewood Tales.*

H. D.'s poetry may seem to epitomize the aims of the Imagists, yet few of her poems have the haiku-like balance and internal tension of Pound's Imagist poems. Hers have motion and passion, coupled with a clarity of speech and freshness of perception that make them simultaneously earthy and spiritually pure. "Storm," published in her first volume, *Sea Garden* (1916), gives us a series of sharp observations in language that suspends them all like the swirl of colors in agate:

> You crash over the trees,
> you crack the live branch—
> the branch is white,
> the green crushed,
> each leaf is rent like split wood.
>
> You burden the trees
> with black drops,
> you swirl and crash—
> you have broken off a weighted leaf
> in the wind,
> it is hurled out,
> whirls up and sinks,
> a green stone.

And in "Oread" (1913), the poem made famous by Pound as an example of Vorticist poetry, is the same sense of violence in stasis:

> Whirl up, sea—
> whirl your pointed pines,
> splash your great pines
> on our rocks,
> hurl your green over us,
> cover us with your pools of fir.

H. D.'s loose rhythms are controlled both by the short irregular lines and by an ear so sensitive to the cadences of natural speech that Pound in 1912 exclaimed to Harriet Monroe, "It's straight talk, straight as the Greek!" Her language, especially in her descriptions of flowers, is precise, as in this stanza from "Acon" (1913):

I choose spray of dittany
cyperum, frail of flower,
buds of myrrh,
all-healing herbs,
close pressed in calathes.

Her images, however, do most to define the texture of her
verse: rain, snow, marble, granite, silver, the sea, and rocks
mingle with myrtle, laurel, cornel buds, violets, lilies, and
roses to create a world of remote yet attainable beauty, a
world of classical calm toward which she strains with romantic yearning.

The world of H. D.'s poetry is a world of sea-battered
rocks, Grecian temples, Aegean islands, cliffs and mountains,
and the gods and heroes who once roamed over them. Yet
she is neither a romantic escapist nor a heroic poet, but a
classicist in the purest sense who seeks spiritual stability
through the perception and celebration of timeless beauty.
This is not the sterile beauty of ruined palaces, but the
vibrant, sun-filled beauty of lush fields, grape-laden hillsides,
and snow-covered peaks, as well as the fierce beauty of storm-
lashed waves and their aftermath. Nor is H. D. an antiquarian, although most of her poems are inhabited by figures from
classical legend. Her highly disciplined, taut lines speak
directly from a modern sensibility in recoil from the failures
of her own civilization to recognize the humanity of man and
to maintain the links between man and nature.

The poems in her *Collected Poems* (1925) and *Red Roses
for Bronze* (1931) are concerned entirely with themes from
classical legend, with titles such as "Adonis," "Pygmalion,"
"Heliodora," and "Phaedra." In the *Collected Poems*, also,
are translations of choruses from Euripides. After writing two
novels and a classical drama, H. D. published from 1944 to
1946 a trilogy of poems based on her experiences in London
during World War II: *The Walls Do Not Fall, Tribute to the
Angels,* and *The Flowering of the Rod,* the last two each composed within a space of two weeks. These are written in
spare, unrhymed free-verse couplets and deal with both the

present and the past. Her vivid and moving descriptions of war-torn London are matched by other poems returning once again to the gods of the ancient cities of Greece, Egypt, and Israel, whose pure spirits retain the eternal qualities of truth and love that in the present city are threatened with destruction. There are in these poems the same qualities found in the verse written more than a decade earlier: precision of image and word, directness of statement, but with a sureness and evenness of tone that show how firmly she was in control of the world she had chosen to re-create.

This war trilogy and the book-length philosophical poem, *Helen in Egypt* (1961), are explorations, in which she is seeking answers to ultimate questions about religion and philosophy and their relation to history. In them she was applying her Imagist techniques in new ways, working toward an openness of form analogous to the *Cantos* and *Paterson*. These poems, not widely known to American readers, have been the objects of praise from Robert Duncan and Denise Levertov, both of whom have found in them new concepts of the nature of poetry that they have found useful in their own work. Taken as a whole, H. D.'s poems are an impressive achievement which also promise to have a lasting influence on American poetry.

The only poet to appear in both Amy Lowell's *Some Imagist Poets* (1915) and the southern Fugitives' *I'll Take My Stand* (1930) is John Gould Fletcher (1886–1950). This fact says a lot about the two sides of a poet who began as an Imagist but after a twenty-four-year exile returned to his native Arkansas to write poems on regional and religious themes.

As a young man Fletcher was the kind of poetic prodigy who could impress Pound with his productivity and his innovations. Like many Harvard men of his generation, he had read Arthur Symons and the French Symbolist poets; unlike most of them, he published five books of poetry in 1913 at his own expense. He later contributed the remaining copies of all but one of these to the British Government as pulp during the wartime paper shortage, but by that time he had already become known to readers of *Poetry* as an Imagist poet. Fletcher could write Imagist poems with the best of them, and even though Pound did not include any of his poems in *Des Imagistes* (1914), he had given him encouragement and recommended him to Harriet Monroe. When Fletcher broke with Pound and refused to associate himself with the Vorticist movement, he was taken under the wing of Amy Lowell and became one of those to whom Pound derisively referred as "Amygists." This association with Lowell probably did Fletcher more harm than good, since he was for too long typed as an Imagist, even after he had moved into a new phase.

His Imagist style may be seen in the first half of *Irradiations: Sand and Spray* (1915); while in the second half are *vers libre* poems about the sea that reflect his first attentive reading of Whitman. The Whitman influence is still apparent in the poems most closely associated with Fletcher's name: the "symphonies," which he published in *Goblins and Pagodas* (1916). These, he once said, were attempts to create "analogies between my own moods and those of nature," and although at first glance this seems to border on the pathetic fallacy, the symphonies are actually—and literally—tone poems. Fletcher was searching for a new poetry that would, like Symbolist poetry, fuse the effects of poetry, painting, and music under what he said was "the triple influence" of Stéphane Mallarmé, Paul Gauguin, and Claude Debussy. The result was a series of poems in the post-Impressionist manner: the "Blue Symphony," "Green Symphony," "White Symphony," etc.; however, they now seem faded and decadent rather than fresh and vital. Since the effect of each poem is supposed to be cumulative, short quoted passages do not adequately illustrate their quality. They are made up in part of Imagist fragments, however, such as this from one of the better ones, "Green Symphony":

> The glittering leaves of the rhododendron
> Are shaken like blue-green blades of grass,
> Flickering, cracking, falling:
> Splintering in a million fragments.

By 1921, with the publication of *Breakers and Granite*, Fletcher had begun to abandon his early style, and his return to tradition became steadily more apparent, particularly in the semi-epic *Branches of Adam* (1926). During a visit to the United States in 1927 he met John Crowe Ransom, Allen Tate, and Donald Davidson, who were then preparing their manifesto of Southern agrarianism, *I'll Take My Stand*. When they asked him to contribute, he gave them not a poem but a weighty and highly conservative treatise on education. This essay was one indication of his discovery that he could no longer remain an expatriate; he had overstayed his exile in Europe and needed to return to the scene of his southern boyhood in order to find fresh sources for his art. He had already used his memories of the South as early as 1916 in "The Ghosts of an Old House"; now he turned again to sharp and direct treatments of them in place of the vague and abstract word-music of his "symphonies."

Fletcher is a master craftsman, a highly skilled practitioner of verse, and when he applies his craft to such subjects as the Ozarks he gets some excellent results:

These are the lonely Ozarks. Fold on fold
The crumbling limestone, mossy, drips. It carries
The hidden stream between the twisted roots
Of oak and hickory down. Through the steep hollow
Where nothing but shadow is and the dense weight
Of jungle-branches blocks the sky—the haunt
Of the rattlesnake and the spider—it crawls down,
That stream milk-grey with limestone, brown with leaves
Blown by innumerable autumn blasts to pierce
To a wilderness in which no living man
Has ever dared to walk.

("The Ozarks," 1940)

A lot of his later things are quite flat, however; the ideas are rather commonplace and are too prosaically stated when not fortified by his own brand of symbolism. His elegies, highly regarded by some, seem like a prettified version of something written by Whitman in collaboration with Archibald MacLeish. What Harriet Monroe said of him is still quite generally true: "One rarely feels in Mr. Fletcher's art the true lyric rapture, the emotion that seizes the singer and carries him away. But one does feel something only a little less impassioned—the absorption of the contemplative spirit in its object, the self uplifted and transcended into ecstasy."

If ecstasy is too strong a word to apply to Fletcher, one can still agree with Monroe's sense of the contemplative spirit in his best poems. This is particularly apparent in "Journey Day" (1941), a poem dedicated to his second wife, in which he has achieved a near-perfect blend of his earlier Symbolist manner with deep feelings for his native region:

> At the edge of the stream beyond which is no passing,
> The delicate lights flash, moving athwart pine-shadows:
> Boles going down to stream-banks where gleam white
>   button-willows,
> Against the clear green water-surface shimmering
>   athwart the trees.
>
> At the edge of the margin of the sharp rock and the water
> The jewel-weed flares upward; orange bracts that catch
>   at sunlight.
> Upon them, black with spots of gold, a butterfly poises
>   slowly,
> Shutting his fans upon the dust-filled sunset light.

A belief in the moral integrity of the work of art was widespread in the twenties, partially as an outgrowth of the poetry and criticism of Pound and Eliot. When this attitude fell into disrepute in the thirties under the impetus of Marxist criticism, those who were still searching for purity of line through the maximum of exposure were condemned for frivolity. Wallace Stevens came in for this kind of attack, which he attempted to answer in such poems as "Stanley Burnshaw and the Statue." Archibald MacLeish attacked such poets from another direction in 1940 when he labeled them the "irresponsibles" for not standing up to be counted for democracy.

In MacLeish's sense, John Peale Bishop (1892–1944) is one of the irresponsibles for refusing to heed the social muse and writing poetry in the thirties that perpetuated the commitment to art made in the twenties. In the eyes of critics like Horace Gregory this was a reprehensible position, but it is apparent that such criticism is an unfair judgment against the work of a poet who by the time of his death was coming into his own as a writer of fine lyrics, passionately and sensitively dedicated to both art and life. No one of Bishop's poems more strongly emphasizes the need to apply the poet-craftsman's delicate and subtle talents to the rough vigor of life than "Speaking of Poetry," published in *Now With His Love* (1933). There the metaphor for the blending of poetry and life is the wedding of Desdemona to Othello. Desdemona is the craftsman, the artist, who "once continued to imitate in the needlework / her father's shield, and plucked it out / three times, to begin again, each time with diminished colors." The Moor, on the other hand, is barbarous and uncouth. What is needed for this wedding of art and life is more than the violent act of coming together; there must be a sense of ritual, a ceremony

> Traditional, with all its symbols
> ancient as the metaphors in dreams;
> strange, with never before heard music; continuous
> until the torches deaden at the bedroom door.

This desire for the union of flesh and spirit, of form and content, or whatever combination seems appropriate, underlies much of Bishop's work; we find in his poems his sense of the vitality of life as both a necessary ingredient of art and a counterpart to death. His wartime poem "And When the Net Was Unwound Venus Was Found Ravelled with Mars" (1933), for example, is a celebration of "perfect lust" enacted in the context of a war in which "More of the young / must die." And the bawdy acrostic of "A Recollection" (1936) comically and brilliantly emphasizes the sensual basis of artistic purity:

All loveliness demands our courtesies.
Since she was dead I praised her as I could
Silently, among the Barberini bees.

Like Conrad Aiken, Bishop refused to become involved
in literary coteries, preferring to go his own way. Still, he was
unusually susceptible to the influence of other poets, and
only MacLeish went through more changes of style than he
did. His two masters were Eliot and Yeats, but there are imitations of Browning, cummings, Pound, and even MacLeish
in his work. As Allen Tate has remarked, however, "If a poem
in Yeats's manner appears in Bishop's book, and is as good as
Yeats's, it is as good there as it is anywhere else." Eliot echoes
are everywhere, as in "October Tragedy" (1933), a poem about
a French peasant finding a murdered girl whose drawers are
"maculate with blood": an image of the corruptness of the
flesh reminiscent of Eliot's "Apeneck Sweeney" with the "ze-
bra stripes along his jaw / Swelling to maculate giraffe." One
of Bishop's best poems is "The Return," a poem about war
in a Roman setting that in spite of its specific references still
remains magically indefinite and symbolic. It is not "about"
anything—any more than Pound's poem of the same title is
about anything—yet the vivid pictorial sense of Bishop's poem
works to create a strong but generalized statement about the
destruction of a civilization:

We did not know the end was coming: nor why
It came; only that long before the end
Were many wanted to die. Then vultures starved
And sailed more slowly in the sky.

A friend and literary associate of F. Scott Fitzgerald and
Edmund Wilson at Princeton, a student of Christian Gauss,
and probably the model for Tom D'Invilliers in *This Side of
Paradise* (1920), John Peale Bishop in his criticism, his fiction,
and his poetry stood for intellectual discipline and a commit-

ment to technical experimentation and mastery that his later poems fully illustrate. One of his most ambitious poems is the elegy he wrote on the death of Fitzgerald. "The Hours" (1941) is as much a critical estimate of Fitzgerald's strengths and shortcomings as it is a tribute to his friend, but he did not allow his grief to overwhelm his art, just as he would not allow Othello to tup Desdemona with unrestrained lust. These two stanzas from the final section are evidence of Bishop's ability to objectify grief in the formal sounds and rhythms of his verse:

> And I have seen the sea-light set the tide
> In salt succession toward the sullen shore
> And while the waves lost on the losing sand
> Seen shores receding and the sands succumb.

> The waste retreats; glimmering shores retrieve
> Unproportioned plunges; the dunes restore
> Drowned confines to the disputed kingdoms—
> Desolate mastery, since the dark has come.

Bishop is a minor poet—a talent meticulous in restraint but more complex than one first assumes. As Stanley Edgar Hyman observed, he is "one of a half-dozen lyric poets in America in our century . . . who without a 'great' or large-scale work, have produced a body of poems that seems assured of survival."

The interest in Donne and the poetry of other Metaphysical poets, which was stimulated by the essays and poetry of Eliot and by the criticism and poetry of John Crowe Ransom, is reflected in several women poets in the twenties. Lizette Reese and Louise Imogen Guiney had already evoked the spirit of the Cavalier poets and had written poems in a Metaphysical vein; in the work of three poets associated more directly with the twenties we see an even closer attention to craftsmanship, to precision in language, and to the construction of poems full of carefully developed conceits. Three of

these poets who share a number of characteristics are Elinor
Wylie, Louise Bogan, and Léonie Adams.

The poetry of Elinor Wylie (1885–1928) never completely disassociated itself from its Shelleyan beginnings, but
as her work matured, it took on a firmness and depth that
went beyond her often brilliant surfaces. The poems in her
early collection, *Nets to Catch the Wind* (1921), already reveal her fondness for beautiful words and fanciful images.
Many of them are written in the short two- and three-syllable
lines that she continued to use in her later work. "The Fairy
Goldsmith" (1921) is a typically Shelleyan poem, with language and imagery reminiscent of "Queen Mab"—or of Joseph
Rodman Drake's "The Culprit Fay":

> Here, if you please
> Are little gilt bees
> In amber drops
> Which look like honey,
> Translucent and sunny,
> From clover-tops.

This love for "Pretty Words" is half-ironically, half-seriously
described by the poet herself in the sextet of a late sonnet
(1932) with that title:

> I love bright words, words up and singing early;
> Words that are luminous in the dark, and sing;
> Warm lazy words, white cattle under trees;
> I love words opalescent, cool, and pearly,
> Like midsummer moths, and honied words like bees,
> Gilded and sticky, with a little sting.

But when she was not being self-indulgent, she could create
the almost perfect lyric, with the right combination of image,
language, and sound, such as we see in that widely anthologized piece, "Velvet Shoes" (1921), or "South" (1923), with its
rich assemblage of Keatsian images of physical sensation:

Spotted by sun, and visible
Above me in a wave-green vault,
With that thick sticky linden-smell
Saturate, as the sea with salt.

In *Trivial Breath* (1928) Wylie's sure sense of structure and her developing taste and restraint are evident in such lyrics as "Lament for Glasgerion" and "Address to My Soul." In the latter poem, certainly one of her best, she learned from Donne and Herbert how to use a cluster of images in a complex conceit. Her developing intelligence and wit led to "Little Elegy," "Hymn to Earth," and the nineteen-sonnet sequence called "One Person," all published posthumously in *Angels and Earthly Creatures* (1929). In Sonnet XVI she again demonstrates her ability to develop a conceit with artistry and wit. "Hymn to Earth" is a sustained work of seven eleven-line stanzas in an irregular form, in which her debts to Donne are apparent. It also is concerned with death, as much of her poetry came to be. One of her last poems, "Little Elegy," shows the subtle balance of tone she was able to achieve:

Withouten you
No rose can grow;
No leaf be green
If never seen
Your sweetest face;
No bird have grace
Or power to sing;
Or anything
Be kind, or fair,
And you nowhere.

Louise Bogan (b. 1897) is also clearly a member of her generation; like Edna St. Vincent Millay she works toward a new freedom of attitudes toward physical passion, and like Léonie Adams and Elinor Wylie she is highly conscious of craft. Her most obvious literary antecedents, in technique if

not necessarily in subject matter, are Emily Dickinson and
the seventeenth-century Metaphysicals. Her tightly constructed,
carefully tuned lyrics treat sexual passion, death, and the passage of time with a combination of intellectual brilliance and
sensuality. "Rhyme," for example, displays a subtle interplay
of the language of religion and sexual love that becomes a
modern version of Herbert, with the emphasis on the flesh
rather than the spirit:

> What laid, I said,
> My being waste?
> 'Twas your sweet flesh
> With its sweet taste,—
>
> Which, like a rose,
> Fed with a breath,
> And at its full
> Belied all death.
>
> It's at springs we drink;
> It's bread we eat,
> And no fine body,
> Head to feet,
>
> Should force all bread
> And drink together,
> Nor be both sun
> And hidden weather.
>
> Ah no, it should not;
> Let it be.
> But once heart's feast
> You were to me.

Other lyrics, too, are stripped bare of rhetoric, and they radiate
with a pulsating emphasis on the endurance of the flesh. In
"The Alchemist" Bogan writes of burning her life, "that I
might find / A passion wholly of the mind." When the fire
burned low, she found "unmysterious flesh— / Not the mind's

avid substance—still / Passionate beyond the will." The titles of her collections suggest some of the quality of her work: *The Sleeping Fury* (1937), *Dark Summer* (1929), and *Body of This Death* (1923). The themes of renunciation and lost love are the obverse of her poems of sexual yearning—all done with the same subtlety and restraint. The end of her "Ad Castitatem," an invocation to chastity, reveals her ambivalent feelings toward a life of renunciation:

> In this ravaged country,
> In this season not yours,
> You having no season,
> I call upon you without echo.
> Hear me, infertile,
> Beautiful futility.

Like the poems of Elinor Wylie and Léonie Adams, these poems make uncompromising demands upon the reader for his attention, his sympathy, and a cultivated sensibility. For one willing or able to meet these demands, Louise Bogan's poetry will have its rewards; and the forty-five years of her work printed in *The Blue Estuaries* (1968) support Theodore Roethke's claim that "her poems can be read and reread: they keep yielding new meanings, as all good poetry should."

Although the early lyrics of Léonie Adams (b. 1899), published in *Those Not Elect* in 1925, bear some resemblance to the lucid and somewhat transparent poetry of Millay and Wylie, the reader quickly senses that he is in the presence of an original voice, much more in tune with the twentieth century. Lacking the wit and surface grace of Elinor Wylie, and rejecting the romantic posing of Edna St. Vincent Millay, Adams charges her lines with a mystic intensity and fervor that express her response to the metaphysical puzzles of existence. Fred B. Millett has called her a sort of Vaughan to the Donne of Wylie, a comment that suggests both the spirituality and the toughmindedness of her poetry. "Pity of the

Heavens," an early poem, opens with lines strongly reminiscent of Vaughan's "I saw Eternity the other night":

> Light all day from heaven was streaming,
> But the last hour gathered earth with light,
> Steeping the darkened air with a blue colour;

Léonie Adams has published two later collections: *High Falcon* (1929) and *Poems: A Selection* (1954). The latter opens with a provocative quotation from Blake: "The child's toys and the old man's reasons / Are the fruits of the two seasons." Her poems are subtle and delicate explorations of the relationship between man and eternity, between his sense of desolation and his sense of beauty in a universe of baffling change. Moments of change, from season to season, and especially from day to night, evoke her finest responses in poems with such titles as "Light at Equinox," "Winter Solstice," "Midsummer," "Twilit Revelation," "Sundown," and "Twilight of the Wood." These simple titles belie the concentration of feeling and intellectual force that we can see in such lines as these from the end of one of her best lyrics, "Evening Sky" (1929):

> O desolation rent by intolerable blue
> Of the living heaven's core,
> Nor death itself at last the heavenly whim.
> For how can an eye sustain
> To watch heaven slain and quickening, or do
> To stretch in its little orbit and contain
> Sky balancing chaos in an inconstant rim?

The reader is struck also by the difference in the quality of language in these poems from those of Millay and Wylie. There is a strong sense of the sound-values of words, combined with a liking for precise but unusual language and a predilection for wrenched syntax and ellipses that mark her as a poet of the modern temper:

Husk, seed, pale straw, pale ear the year reposes,
And a thinned frieze of earth rims round
The whey-gleamed wet-ash-dimming sky,
And whole trodden floor of light,
Where that slant limb winds with its shadowing closes.

("Light at Equinox," 1954)

We are aware in Léonie Adams's work of the influence of several poets fashionable in the twenties and thirties: Hopkins and Dickinson as well as Donne and Vaughan. And we are aware, too, that we are in the presence of a subtle, discriminating mind and ear.

CHAPTER TEN

New Thresholds, New Anatomies

e. e. cummings, Marianne Moore, Conrad Aiken, Archibald MacLeish, Robinson Jeffers, John Crowe Ransom, Robert Penn Warren, Allen Tate, Hart Crane, Wallace Stevens, William Carlos Williams

The literature of the 1920s in America is dominated in the minds of many by Hemingway, Fitzgerald, and other writers of fiction, yet at no time in the history of American poetry were more poets of distinction writing. Frost, Robinson, Pound, and Eliot had already established themselves; in addition, a large number of newer poets, most of them born between 1880 and 1900, were continuing the transformation of language that began with Whitman and continued with Pound, Eliot, Joyce, and Stein. These poets were affected by the underlying psychology of the modernist movement: a conscious avant-gardism, a desire to shock and even infuriate one's audience, and a sense of the artist's alienation from society. These attitudes led to some extreme and often ridiculous experiments, such as those of the Surrealists and Dadaists in Europe, but they stimulated new ways of looking at things and of saying things that became the basis of modern poetry. Pound's exhortations to his friends and followers to "make it new" emphasized the need for language "free from emotional slither." As he wrote to Harriet Monroe in 1915, the requirements for modern poetry were "objectivity, and again objectivity, and expression: no hindside-beforeness, no straddled adjectives (as 'addled mosses dank'), no Tennysonianness of speech; nothing—nothing that you couldn't, in some circumstance, in the stress of some emotion, actually say. Every literaryism, every book word, fritters away a scrap of the reader's patience, a scrap of his sense of your sincerity."

This new aestheticism was in part a reaction to World War I and its failure to provide political answers to human problems; nevertheless, it was not an attempt to escape from reality but rather to see it in nonpolitical perspectives. As Frederick Hoffman has observed, the revolution in form was also a moral revolution; these writers were "profoundly concerned with the moral value of literary form."

This concern with form was a starting point for many, but not all, of the poets in this period. Wallace Stevens, William Carlos Williams, e. e. cummings, and Hart Crane found their way largely through formal experiments; the same is true of Marianne Moore and Conrad Aiken, different as their styles are from each other and from other poets. The sociopolitical starting point of the Fugitive poets—John Crowe Ransom, Robert Penn Warren, and Allen Tate—was different from the others, but they, too, were affected by changing standards of criticism and taste, which they in turn helped to change still further. Archibald MacLeish began as a deeply committed member of the avant-garde, later becoming a poet of social comment in response to the changing mood of the thirties. Standing apart and alone, Robinson Jeffers was one of the most widely read poets of the twenties, perhaps because of the explosive combinations of Nietzsche, nihilism, sex, and violence that permeated his long, tragic narratives.

Through all these poets, Jeffers included, runs a streak of rebelliousness and adventurousness that makes them seem to be, in spite of the individual and often profound differences between them, a homogeneous group. All of them, in their commitment to innovation, succeeded to an extraordinary degree in redefining the literature of their time.

Although it has lost virtually all of its original shock value as experimental poetry, the poetry of e. e. cummings (1894–1962) still represents for many the iconoclastic, irreverent, and defiant avant-gardism of the "literary left." His typographical eccentricities and syntactical distortions typify the spirit of experiment and daring that are associated with the twenties. Along with other experimentalists, including James Joyce, Gertrude Stein, and the French Surrealists Guillaume Apollinaire and Tristan Tzara, cummings was learning his craft as a poet at a time when syntax was being rejected, the upper-case alphabet ignored, and a playful attitude toward the sacred cows of poetry and art was the order of the day. "Little" magazines, such as *transition, Secession,* and *Broom,* proclaimed by their titles and their typography their independence, their sense of historical destiny, and their forward-looking spirit. Although cummings later thought Gertrude Stein subordinated the meaning of words to the beauty of words themselves, he shared with her at least one attitude toward language that is central to his work: words are symbols that can embody concepts independently of their syntactical function. This is the principle underlying such lines as "through sames of am through haves of give," in his poem "my father moved through dooms of love" (1940). And, like Joyce, whose "Work in Progress" was being published in *transition* during the twenties, cummings liked to play with words and with his readers' expectations in order to come up with the unexpected.

Cummings cannot be lumped with the Imagists, whom he knew only incidentally, or with other members of the avant-garde. Always an individual, he went his own way, affirming his humanity on the one hand and his individuality on the other. For cummings, these were the same—like Emerson, he believed that to be human was to be individual, and he had a lifelong contempt for the dehumanizing and conformist behavior of the great mass of humanity whom he dubbed "mostpeople." "Mostpeople," cummings wrote, "have less in common with ourselves than the squarerootofminusone. You and I are human beings;mostpeople are snobs."

The son of a Harvard professor who later became a Unitarian minister, cummings was graduated from Harvard in 1915, when he delivered the commencement address, entitled "The New Art." Like many other Harvard men of his generation he went to Europe in 1917 to serve in a Red Cross ambulance corps in France. Some inept bureaucratic fumbling led to his arrest by French authorities, who held him prisoner in a concentration camp for about three months. His experiences with officialdom and petty functionaries during his internment had a profound and lasting influence on his attitude toward all authority. The immediate result of that experience was *The Enormous Room* (1922), a book which characterized his captors as cruel and inhuman and his fellow prisoners as embodiments of those human virtues that stem from the love of the individual and the worship of beauty. His lifelong antagonism to the dehumanizing effects of modern society became the basis for many satirical attacks, such as "pity this busy monster, manunkind" (1944), which ends, "listen:there's a hell / of a good universe next door;let's go."

Cummings published a total of thirteen volumes of verse, beginning with *Tulips and Chimneys* (1923), one of his few conventional titles, and ending with the posthumous *73 poems* (1963). Generally, the titles simply describe the number of poems in them: *XLI Poems* (1925), *50 poems* (1940), and *95 Poems* (1958). In all of them are attempts at classification and order. *&* (1925) is divided into three main sections: "A" "N" and "D"; *Tulips and Chimneys* into "Tulips" and "Chimneys," which at this point seem to represent the rough division between the Romantic and realistic aspects of his art. *Is 5* (1926) derives its title from cummings' anti-empiricist conception of truth as an unmeasurable mystery, in which two plus two does not necessarily equal four.

The combination in cummings' work of sharply satirical poems and simple lyrics about love and beauty is not paradoxical, but stems from his central vision of life as a "supremely welcome mystery," not to be violated by stupidity, greed, hypocrisy, or cant. His fundamental pose is that of the youthful lover—anti-intellectual, but not unintelligent, reacting against pomposity and lack of feeling. Cummings started out writing rather simple and flat love lyrics, but as he developed, he felt the need to break away from conventional forms and to explore new subjects. Many of his early poems, printed in *&*, are about the world of the demimonde: its prostitutes,

burlesque queens, and bar-girls. The mood of the twenties
with its "liberated" attitudes toward sexual love is obvious in
these poems, yet cummings' poetry did more than merely reflect this atmosphere; it was actually instrumental in defining it.

Cummings began writing satirical poems around 1926,
the year he published *is* 5. The objects of his satire cover a
broad spectrum: "mostpeople," Santa-Claus-haters, virginal
tourists, Louis Untermeyer, flag-wavers, and Marxists; in general, he hated all evidence of man's inhumanity to man, all
false rhetoric, all restraints of freedom and spontaneity, particularly of sex. His "Cambridge ladies [who] live in furnished
souls," his "substantial dollarbringing virgins" on European
tours, and his "certain Young Woman unacquainted with the
libido / and pursuing a course of instruction at radcliffe college" are all variants of the same sexually inhibited and therefore "notalive undead" women who repress the pleasures of
the flesh.

But sex alone is not the measure of one's "aliveness";
one's responsiveness to beauty and sensitivity to language are
also means to redemption. In one of his few titled poems,
"POEM, OR BEAUTY HURTS MR. VINAL," cummings
writes:

> . . . i would
> suggest that certain ideas gestures
> rhymes, like Gillette Razor Blades
> having been used and reused
> to the mystical moment of dullness emphatically are
> Not To Be Resharpened.

And many of his poems similarly emphasize his desire to avoid
clichés of thought and language: "slightly before the middle
of Congressman Pudd," "next to of course god america i,"
and "as freedom is a breakfastfood." Another aspect of his humanism may be found in such antiwar poems as "the season
'tis, my lovely lambs," "I sing of Olaf glad and free," "it's
jolly," and "my sweet old etcetera." His irreverent attitudes
toward public figures and toward the sanctity of the dead are
reflected in his references to Robinson Jefferson, Theodore

Odysseus Graren't, William Cullen Longfellow, Amy Sandburg, and Algernon Carl Swinburned.

Cummings' technique is the most immediately striking
thing about his poetry, yet it tends to obscure the fact that he
wrote a number of different kinds of poems using a variety
of verse forms, including sonnets and quatrains. His early
love poems and satires are supplemented by comic poems, impressions of scenes, and sketches: an ugly man nobody loves, a
girl sleeping, a Negro playing the guitar, and the poet's own
father. Norman Friedman has observed that, in general, cummings used metrical stanzas for his more "serious" poems, re-
serving his tricks for satire, comedy, and description: "Parody,
pun, slang, and typographical distortion are called into being
by the urgencies of the satirical mode . . . Violence in the
meaning; violence in the style." The experiments are nearly
always interesting, but extreme examples become merely frus-
trating or boring, such as this poem, which William Carlos
Williams found unintelligible and indefensible as poetry:

> (im)c-a-t(mo)
> b,i;l:e
>
> FallleA
> ps!fl
> OattumblI
>
> sh?dr
> IftwhirlF
> (Ul) (lY)
> &&&

But Williams did admire other aspects of cummings' art,
and we can see how cummings influenced the way he arranged words on the page in such poems as "Rain" and in
many sections of *Paterson*. Like Williams, cummings was interested in reproducing the vernacular, but he depended more
heavily than Williams on phonetic spelling, in such poems
as "oil tel duh woil doi sez," "ygUDuh," and "buncha hard-
boil guys from duh A. C. fulla."

Cummings' best poems are his love lyrics, such as the

lyric of courtly love, "All in green went my love riding" (1923), and the very tender love poem, "somewhere i have never travelled, gladly beyond" (1931). The anthologists have done well by him; his best poems are the ones most frequently anthologized, including the eloquent tribute to his father, "my father moved through dooms of love" (1940). The poems of his last years became increasingly grim and disillusioned, however, as though in the face of more and more evidence of man's inhumanity he could no longer sustain his defiant youthfulness and spirit. The cynicism of some of the *73 poems* is the cynicism of a disillusioned idealist; but even in "now does our world descend" (1963) he affirms once again, without being entirely convincing, the transcendence of the soul in the face of a situation where no and yes have become the same, which makes it "time you unbecame":

> but from this endless end
> of briefer each our bliss—
> where seeing eyes go blind
> (where lips forget to kiss)
> where everything's nothing
> —arise,my soul;and sing

One poet who was always on the side of the modernists and the experimenters was Marianne Moore (1887–1972). The respect shown for her by the leading avant-garde poets of the time is shown in Ezra Pound's letters, in the autobiography of William Carlos Williams, and in the tribute T. S. Eliot pays to her in his introduction to the English edition of her poems, where he asserts that she is "one of those few who have done the language some service in my lifetime."

Moore's reputation as a poet dates from 1915, when five of her poems were published in *Poetry*. She was quickly recognized by Pound, Alfred Kreymborg, H. D., and others as a major new talent, and her close association with H. D. led in 1921 to the publication in London of *Poems*. Moore herself (like Anne Bradstreet before her) had no knowledge of this generous effort on her behalf, but unlike the "Tenth Muse," she was, in her words, "intensely grateful." Her poems were not published in book form in this country, in *Observations*, until 1924. This book won the prestigious Dial Award for that year, and this recognition in turn led to wider critical acceptance and fame. Her work on *The Dial* and her eventual editorship of that publication, from 1926 to 1929, established her as one of the leading American literary figures of the 1920s.

The talent of Marianne Moore is a unique one. The reader's first encounter with her poetry is likely to be a baffling experience and may even result in the verdict, frequently stated, that it is not poetry at all. One may indeed be put off by the opening stanza of such a poem as "He 'Digesteth Harde Yron' " (1941):

> Although the aepyornis
> or roc that lived in Madagascar, and
> the moa are extinct,
> the camel-sparrow, linked
> with them in size—the large sparrow
> Xenophon saw walking by a stream—was and is
> a symbol of justice.

The combination of unusual, pedantic diction and esoteric bird-lore with the offhand, casual tone of the speaker's voice plays havoc with our expectations. Are we being lectured at or are we being asked to savor word-sounds offered to us with Sitwellian extravagance? Rhyme is there, and so is rhythm, though not of a conventional sort. The "Notes" to the poem, diffidently offered at the end of the *Collected Poems* (1951), increase our understanding somewhat while perhaps diminishing our conception of it as a poem. They tell us that the title is from Lyly's *Euphues;* that the reference to Xenophon was discovered in *Animals for Show and Pleasure in Ancient Rome* by George Jennison; and that various allusions to ostriches are from a book called *Ostrich Egg-shell Cups from Mesopotamia* by Berthold Laufer. These facts are offered to us not only for themselves, but also as illustrations for conclusions to be drawn from them. The conclusions themselves often are not so memorable as the grace and style with which they are put, yet the fact that they are so well put is enough.

This admirer of Henry James and friend of Ezra Pound followed Pound's dictum that poetry should be at least as well written as prose. And although technique was by no means the exclusive province of Marianne Moore, certainly no modern poet devoted more attention to it than she did. Her poems are constructions, carefully wrought upon the page according to some preconceived formal pattern, and designed as much for the eye as for the ear. Her stanzas, she said, take shape as she goes along, yet she built many of them according to syllabic principles—a rigorous stanzaic form in which each line contains a predetermined number of syllables. She owes much here to the Japanese haiku, with its form of seventeen syllables. One is reminded, too, of the *cinquains* of Adelaide Crapsey (1878–1914), who was also fascinated with the possibilities of syllabic verse. Moore's rhymes are famous for their ingenuity and subtlety. T. S. Eliot called her the master of the light rhyme, and she herself wrote that after 1929 she "wrote no verse that did not (in my opinion) rhyme." The rhymes are not always immediately apparent; she will rhyme *of* with *dove, the* with *Scarlatti*. These features of her technique, along with the device of including the title of her poem as part of its first line, are illustrated well in "The Fish" (1921):

THE FISH

wade
through black jade.
    Of the crow-blue mussel-shells, one keeps
    adjusting the ash-heaps;
        opening and shutting itself like

an
injured fan.
    The barnacles which encrust the side
    of the wave, cannot hide
        there for the submerged shafts of the

Her lifelong concern with precision of language and thought, with polish, and with grace is evident in every line. She was a poet of the intellect, without being an intellectual. Although ideas were important to her, they did not lie at the root of her poetry, and they finally are not so important as the play of intelligence. We come away from her poems with no clearly established sense of her vision, but with the impression of having attended an eighteenth-century salon. Because ultimately what we realize about Moore is that she is a conversationalist; her prosaic, stylized poems retrieve the lost art of conversation through versification—they dance a courtly minuet through a set of intricate steps and measures for which she has set the rhythm and called the tune.

Yet to assume that her poems are dry or lacking in feeling and passion is to fail to recognize the extent to which Marianne Moore took life to herself. The best definition of her poetry is not that often-quoted and somewhat cryptic phrase in her first version of "Poetry": "imaginary gardens with real toads in them," but rather is contained in a remark made apropos of Hebrew poetry: "Ecstasy affords / the occasion and expediency determines the form." She ranges far and near for her subjects, but once settling upon a subject she concentrates on close observation and the accumulation of relevant and accurate detail. Her poems about animals are famous: "The Jerboa," "The Pangolin," "The Buffalo," "The Frigate Pelican." What she admired in animals was their ingenuity, their dexterity, and their lack of self-consciousness in doing what they do. These are the same qualities she admired in baseball players; therefore, she looked at the little desert rat called the jerboa, whose "leaps should be set / to the flageolet," in the same way she looked at the centerfielder: "versed / in an extension reach far into the box seats—he lengthens up, leans and gloves the ball." The range of her subjects goes far beyond the zoo and the ballpark, however; the S's alone would include swans, strawberries, steeplejacks, Scarlatti, salamanders, snails, skunks, steamrollers, and Saint Nicholas.

Marianne Moore's poems are made up not only of images and objects from life but also of verbal fragments from her reading and conversation. The sources of her quotations vary widely: telephone company leaflets, the *National Geographic,* a lecture by Padraic Colum, the *Book of Change,* a progress report of the Sloan-Kettering Institute for Cancer Research, and *The New York Times,* to name a few. One could apply her own animal imagery and say that Moore is a literary jack-daw, picking up and storing bright and shiny bits of phrases, and then weaving them into original structures. These phrases, embedded in her poems between pairs of inverted commas and documented in her notes at the end of her volumes, are not intended to work as allusions, as they do in Eliot's poems. They carry no associations outside the specific context of their origin and so mean pretty much what they say. The method works sometimes, as in "To a Snail" (1924), in which the quoted phrase, "compression is the first grace of style," becomes a way to elaborate the particular qualities of the snail that interest her. Or in the title of her poem, " 'Nothing Will Cure the Sick Lion but to Eat an Ape' " (1924)—laconically attributed to "Carlyle"—which allows her to explore an attitude in the manner of the fabulist. But overdone, as it tends to be in her later work, this technique becomes a reflex, resulting in mere pastiche.

Moore once remarked that a poem must be a closed system, and hers resist quotation: they have to be read entire, since each is an attempt to develop an idea through a series of subtle variations. A poem like "The Pangolin" (1936), for example, which seems to be about an animal but turns out to be about man, or the first part of "The Jerboa" (1935) called "Too Much"—one of the great poetic studies of excess—or "No Swan So Fine" (1935), a dense accumulation of images and phrases, cannot be illustrated by short passages. On the other hand, it is possible to find some memorable lines, such as her image of the mind as "the glaze on a / katydid-wing / subdivided by sun / till the nettings are legion," her description of America (in a poem called "England," 1921) as a "languageless country in which letters are written / not in Spanish, not in Greek, not in Latin, not in shorthand, / but in plain American which cats and dogs can read!" or the beautiful ending of "Nevertheless" (1935):

> What is there
>
> like fortitude! What sap
>> went through that little thread
>> to make the cherry red!

One is tempted to go on, using quotation as a method of criticism—the method Moore herself favored. In spite of their difficulty, in spite of their resistance to easy classification or description, the reader feels that the poems of Marianne Moore are the poems of a fully integrated individual whose tone of voice, like Emily Dickinson's, is heard in every line. Even when she faltered, as she did in her collection, *Tell Me, Tell Me* (1966), she did so with dignity. She was a connoisseur's poet, for whom one must work to acquire a taste, yet her poems are the product not of a barren aestheticism, but of a deep and passionate commitment to poetry.

The best description of this position are these words of William James that she chose in her Foreword to *A Marianne Moore Reader* (1961) to apply to herself: "man's chief difference from the brutes lies in the exuberant excess of his subjective propensities. Prune his extravagance, sober him, and you undo him."

How can a poet who has published over twenty-five volumes of verse (not to mention five novels, a play, an autobiography, and several collections of short stories) be virtually unread today? Yet such is the case with Conrad Aiken (b. 1889), who would seem by sheer weight of output to demand some serious critical attention. He does indeed have his apologists and exegetes, yet much of his complicated symbolism still awaits a competent critic. A tireless and dedicated critic, one might add, since the fulsomeness and voluminousness of his poems require a patient and steady attention that their facile verbal sensuousness continually threatens to distract.

The firm strands of intellectual rigor and emotional honesty that run through these poems are often obscured by the technique itself. Like Shelley, whose vaporous and often inflated verse suffers from some of the same weaknesses, Aiken thinks and feels "poetically." The entire consciousness is enveloped in an experience that defies the separation of form and content—and Aiken's purpose is to place himself and his reader on this higher plane. He succeeds in many poems and in brilliant isolated passages, but often he does not know when to stop or when to edit lines that are merely facile or vacuous. As Horace Gregory and Marya Zaturenska observed many years ago, "his was among the most luxuriant of fine lyrical talents ever to be squandered in America." But having noted this, we must still insist that in the course of such squandering Aiken has produced some memorable poems.

The central fact of Aiken's career—a fact documented in painful detail by Aiken himself—was the death of both his parents by his father's act of murder and suicide when the boy was eleven. This event has been the stimulus for Aiken's continuing return to his consciousness, to his youth, to the room and time when he simultaneously found and lost an identity in an instant of horror. But the complexity and subtlety of his reactions to that event go far beyond anything we can conceive of as a psychic scar. Aiken pushes his poems to the limits of metaphysical speculation and linguistic experimentation in order to respond to the ancient dictum to know thyself. In his autobiographical "essay" *Ushant* (1952) Aiken wrote what can be taken to be the guiding impulse of all his work in many genres:

> *Gnothi seauton*—that was still the theme, the open sesame. Freud had merely picked up the magic words where Socrates, the prototype of highest man, had let them fall, and now at last the road was being opened for the only religion that was any longer tenable or viable, a poetic comprehension of man's position in the universe, and of his potentialities as a poietic shaper of his own destiny, through self-knowledge and love. The final phase of evolution of man's mind itself to ever more inclusive consciousness: in that, and that alone, would he find the solvent of all things.

In his poems Aiken adopts a succession of personae in order to explore what he considers the central fact of the self: one's own consciousness as it exists in its heights and its depths. "The problem of personal identity," he wrote, "the struggle of the individual for an awareness of what it is that constitutes his consciousness; an attempt to place himself, to relate himself to the world of which he feels himself to be at once an observer and an integral part"—this is the direction not only of the long, loosely autobiographical series of "Symphonies" called *The Divine Pilgrim,* but of all his poetry and his fiction as well.

These six poems of *The Divine Pilgrim,* "The Charnel Rose: A Symphony," "The Jig of Forslin," "The House of Dust," "Senlin: A Biography," "The Pilgrimage of Festus," and "Changing Mind" were (with the exception of the last) written between 1915 and 1920 and occupy 262 pages of closely printed verse in the 1953 *Collected Poems.*

In the second of these, Forslin is a clown-figure, like Stevens' Crispin, who responds in a jiglike fashion to the variety of human experience. He cannot act, but can only react, to the stimuli from within and without that play upon his consciousness. Aiken's technique reinforces the dreamlike quality of Forslin's existence by deliberately trying to recreate the dilatory and repetitive activity of the mind—to evoke this through a verbal music (with a tiresome repetition of the word *music*) that progresses through modulations of rhythm and tone and seeks to appeal less to the intellect than to the feelings. We recall Poe's definition of poetry, and perhaps are inspired to apply it with some modification to Aiken's poetry as the rhythmical creation of consciousness. Yet the rhythm of individual lines is not so compelling or obvious as Poe's. The rhythmic unit of the "Symphonies" is what Reuel Denney has called the subsection, a group of two, three, or four lines built around a single cluster of sense impressions and words. Aiken then rang variations on these smaller units, building up stanzas and "movements" on them. The word *music* itself becomes almost omnipresent, as though he hoped by its constant reiteration to create the thing itself. His resemblances to Poe have been mentioned; one also recalls Sidney Lanier and his attempts to write musical poetry. But, like Lanier, Aiken was capable of sharp observation, and his early association with the Imagists led him to write lines as direct and concrete as anything H. D. or Pound ever wrote.

The autobiographical explorations in "The Jig of Forslin" are present in other parts of *The Divine Pilgrim*, most notably in "Senlin: A Biography," whose hero, like Aiken's other hero-personae, is a projection of Man who stands questioning himself and the reflection of himself and his consciousness in his universe. Senlin is a more everyday, and more comic, figure than Forslin, but still elusive and intangible. In the last "movement," called "His Cloudy Destiny," Senlin walks away and disappears, leaving "Only the soulless brilliance of the blue skies":

> Yet we would say, this was no man at all,
> But a dream we dreamed, and vividly recall;
> And we are mad to walk in wind and rain
> Hoping to find, somewhere, that dream again.

From his early poem "Discordants" (1914), beginning "Music I heard with you was more than music," to his late poem "Count the Summer," collected in *The Morning Song of Lord Zero* (1963), Aiken has demonstrated his mastery of craft. Once he had absorbed the influence of Freud, which threatened for a time to engulf his work, Aiken followed the experimental "Symphonies" with many different kinds of poems. "Tetélestai" (1917), for instance, is a great statement on the subject of death. The title poem of *And In the Hanging Gardens* (1933) illustrates the decadent, Yellow-Book quality of much of his work; it is an overripe "Eve of St. Agnes":

> And in the hanging gardens there is rain
> From midnight until one, striking the leaves
> And bells of flowers, and stroking boles of planes,
> And drawing slow arpeggios over pools,
> And stretching strings of sound from eaves to ferns.

The princess reads. The knave of diamonds sleeps.
The king is drunk, and flings a golden goblet
Down from the turret window (curtained with rain)
Into the lilacs.

Other good short poems are "Sea Holly" (1925), in which
he uses metamorphosis as a device to establish the symbiotic
relationship of man and his world; "The Room" (1919), a
painful psychological study of horror; and "Goya" (1923?),
in which he evokes the painter's world with vivid imagery.
One of his most successful attempts to create a dream landscape is "Psychomachia" (1922?), where Aiken becomes Poe
redivivus in his use of word-music and symbolic setting. In
Time in the Rock: Preludes to Definition (1936) Aiken faced
more squarely the problem of the relation of language and
reality. These poems, in their intention, subject matter, and
tone, come close to the meditative poems of Wallace Stevens
in their effort to define man's new religion as a celebration of
his consciousness and a discovery of the self. And like Stevens'
poems, Aiken's are part of a process, a process that is itself
definition but never arrives at a stasis or a conclusion. These
poems again demonstrate Aiken's intellectual subtlety and
sophistication, and they still await the kind of dedicated
exegesis that has been devoted to Stevens' poetry in recent
years.

Much more accessible are the *Brownstone Eclogues* (1942),
closely observed vignettes that take up some of the themes
of city life explored earlier in *The House of Dust* (1920). No
one has more sympathetically captured the heartbreakingly
lonely quality of city life than Aiken in "Doctor's Row," or in
"South End":

The benches are broken, the grassplots brown and bare,
the laurels dejected, in this neglected square.
Dogs couple undisturbed. The roots of trees
heave up the bricks in the sidewalk as they please.

Nobody collects the papers from the grass,
nor dead matches, nor the broken glass.

The elms are old and shabby; the houses, around,
stare lazily through paintless shutters at forgotten ground.

Out of the dusty fountain, with the dust,
the leaves fly up like birds on a sudden gust.
The leaves fly up like birds, and the papers flap,
or round the legs of benches wrap and unwrap.

Here, for the benefit of some secret sense,
warm-autumn-afternoon finds permanence.
No one will hurry, or wait too long, or die:
all is serenity, under a serene sky.

Dignity shines in old brick and old dirt,
in elms and houses now hurt beyond all hurt.
A broken square, where little lives or moves;
these are the city's earliest and tenderest loves.

Aiken is a man of many shapes who has both absorbed and enriched the tradition of which he is a part. He has never been fashionable, nor wished to be involved in literary coteries or movements. From the beginning of his career he was aware that he would have to make his own way, standing somewhere in the middle of the road, taking to himself the rhythms of St. John Perse, the images of Eliot, the irony of Laforgue, the Imagism of Pound, the word-music of Poe and Lanier, but throughout his career striving to *"stand clear,"* as he wrote, in order to preserve "that sort of impersonal anonymity, and that deep and pure provincialism, in which the terms approach universals, and in which alone [he] will find, perhaps, the freedom for the greatest work."

Reading the poetry of Archibald MacLeish (b. 1892) reminds one of Allen Tate's remark that a poem should fall pleasantly on the ear and remind us of the hour of our death. His skillful handling of rhyme and meter, the clarity of his language, and the lucidity of his thought give us the feeling we are reading a modern poet, but with few of the obscurities or complexities of Pound or Eliot. Our pleasure in MacLeish's

craftsmanship is matched by our sense of a deep moral earnestness and sincerity in a poet whose awareness of death and its
function in giving meaning to life is a recurring theme. He
sees the world as a circus tent, for instance, in "The End of
the World" (1926), where the last lines of the poem describe
what is revealed when the top blows off: "There in the sudden blackness the black pall / of nothing—nothing at all."
The dramatic abruptness of these lines gives the poem a shock
value and effectiveness far more impressive than the modish
nihilism they express; it is a good illustration of MacLeish's
ability to push technique to the limits of credibility. Mac-
Leish makes us aware of the ironies of death in other poems,
such as "Immortal Helix" (1926), with its closing line about
the body of a hundred-year-old man: "Dead bones roll on,"
and the quatrain called "Mother Goose's Garland" (1926):

> Around, around the sun we go:
> The moon goes round the earth,
> We do not die of death:
> We die of vertigo.

From his early participation in the expatriate movement
of the twenties through his various positions as an editor of
Fortune Magazine, Librarian of Congress, wartime agency
director, and Assistant Secretary of State, MacLeish has combined an active public career with a commitment to poetry,
and in many cases each has benefited from the other. Still,
most readers would agree with Richard Eberhart that Mac-
Leish's poetry is best when it is nonpolitical, and, one might
add, when he works in the lyric-elegiac mode.

After graduation from Hotchkiss and Yale, MacLeish became an artillery officer in France, returning to Harvard Law
School to earn a degree and then teach constitutional and
international law. After a three-year career as a lawyer in
Boston he became an expatriate poet, identifying himself
with the avant-garde in Paris, adapting his style to the new
techniques of Pound and Eliot. He echoed other poets, too,
and worked in a variety of styles before arriving at the clear

and controlled "modern" voice that was his by the time he published *Poems, 1924–1933*. During those ten years, Mac-Leish moved from the conventional college verse of *Tower of Ivory* (1917) through a period of widely diversified experimentation to a point where he became an accomplished craftsman. During those years also he shifted from his art-for-art's-sake position to a strong stand for social consciousness. Mac-Leish's early manner was introspective and despairing, consciously in the mode of Eliot and Pound, with possible debts also to the "Symphonies" of Conrad Aiken. He even created his own version of Mauberley, Prufrock, and Forslin in *The Hamlet of A. MacLeish* (1928), a long dramatic monologue in which MacLeish's highly personal sense of frustration and despair is couched in a combination of Eliotian stammering and Elizabethan rant. With its themes of inward confusion and outward chaos, it is both a poem of its time and a personal statement.

The poems in the 1926 collection *Streets in the Moon* borrow from many poets and are written in many styles. The title of "L'an Trentiesme de Mon Eage" is an allusion to an allusion: Pound's reference in *Mauberley* to Villon's *Grand Testament*. "March," "Way-Station," and "No Lamp Has Ever Shown Us Where to Look" are in the Imagist manner, with similarities to Amy Lowell and e. e. cummings. In "Le Secret Humain" MacLeish pays his debts to Eliot and Laforgue in these lines:

> We know beyond the doors we press and open,
> Beyond the smell of breakfast in the hall,
> Beyond the soggy towel and the soap—
> Wait! We shall know all.

What would have been parody five years later was at that point an assimilation of the new cult of sensibility into his own developing style.

Having learned his craft abroad, MacLeish showed a new maturity and a new commitment to his native land in *New Found Land* (1930), published two years after he returned to live on his farm in Conway, Massachusetts. The fourteen poems in this volume are spoken by an American who has found his voice and come home to sing. They include three of his best lyrics: "You, Andrew Marvell," " 'Not Marble Nor the Gilded Monuments,' " and "Immortal Autumn," all of them about the passage of time and, if not primarily about death, still reminding us of its inevitability. In " 'Not Marble . . .' " and "Immortal Autumn" MacLeish uses the long, supple line with its marked rhythms that he was to use with such success in his later, longer poems. "You, Andrew Marvell" uses an iambic tetrameter *abab* quatrain with almost no punctuation in order to heighten the effect of the continuous westward motion of darkness that is the poem's central theme and metaphor.

MacLeish had come home to Massachusetts by way of Mexico, following the route of Cortés on foot and muleback, and the result of this Mexican experience was *Conquistador* (1932), an epic based on the account of the conquest of Mexico by Bernal Diaz del Castillo. The poem's most striking technical feature is MacLeish's adaptation of *terza rima* to English, which he does by rhyming the last stressed syllable of the line, giving him a latitude and flexibility in rhyme that has always been denied to the writer of *terza rima* in English.

In *Frescoes for Mr. Rockefeller's City* (1933), MacLeish again used this rhyming device, this time in various types of stanzas: couplets, quatrains, and *terza rima*. But *Frescoes* is interesting for reasons other than its technique. It is evidence of MacLeish's new and growing concern with social issues and with the relationship of the poet to politics. With a strong sense of the poet's duty to both define and uphold the ideals of the republic, MacLeish had published an "Invocation to the Social Muse" ten days before Franklin Roosevelt was elected President in 1932. In it he replied to the rigid Marxist position that writers must propagate and publicize a social ideology and become actively involved in writing about issues. "How to conceive in the name of a column of marchers?" he asks, and concludes the poem with another bantering question:

> I remind you, Barinya, the life of the poet is hard—
> A hardy life with a boot as quick as a fiver:

> Is it just to demand of us also to bear arms?

In *Frescoes for Mr. Rockefeller's City* he continued his needling of the Communists, and also poked fun at the capitalists, by writing about the ludicrous situation the Rockefellers had found themselves in when they commissioned Diego Rivera, the Mexican Communist painter, to paint a mural in the main lobby of the RCA Building in Rockefeller Center. The murals were destroyed because Rivera refused to remove the head of Lenin from one of them, and MacLeish satirically treated the excesses of both sides of the controversy, particularly in "Oil Painting of the Artist as Artist" and in "Background With Revolutionaries," which mocks the doctrinaire Communists' ignorance of America:

> Also Comrade Devine who writes of America.
> Most instructively having in 'Seventy-four
> Crossed to the Hoboken side on the Barclay Street Ferry.

The reaction from both camps was violent, but MacLeish had by this time become committed to the goal of reexamining America's values in a series of pronouncements throughout the decade of the 1930s culminating in *America Was Promises* (1939), a long polemic in verse against the dangers of giving in to special-interest groups. The earlier writer of manifestoes on aesthetics in the manner of the 1920s, particularly his famous "Ars Poetica" (1926), with its closing line: "A poem must not mean but be," had become transformed into an ardent spokesman for political engagement and a reexamination of democratic values. In terms of his art, the transformation was not an altogether happy one. Although he retained a high degree of faithfulness to the literary values of the twenties, MacLeish's work of the thirties lost its vibrancy and its commitment to the life of the heart. The poems in *Public Speech* (1936), for example, are neither good poems nor good speeches. After MacLeish left public life to teach at Harvard in the fifties, he returned to a more comtemplative mode in *Songs for Eve* (1954), which explores in positive fashion man's possibilities as a human being. And in *Collected Poems* (1962) are many poems addressed to questions of aesthetics, and exploring the thesis that the art of poetry makes the whole man. It is clear from these poems as well as from his dramatic writing, such as his competent but much overpraised *J. B.* (1958), that the public side of MacLeish's career has led him to see man as both a private and a social being: in Frost's terms, he is a poet of outer as well as inner weather.

The picture that most readily comes to mind when one thinks of Robinson Jeffers (1887–1962) is of a lonely misanthrope gazing out upon the Pacific Ocean from atop his hand-hewn tower in Carmel, California. Consorting with hawks and eagles, splitting granite boulders, and admiring the lichens, the mosses, and the redwoods more than man or any of his works, Jeffers appears to be a worshiper of violence and hater of humanity and civilization who turns his back to America and the land to contemplate the ocean, a "staring unsleeping / Eye of the earth," and shares its indifference to the fate of man. Such a static and somewhat stereotyped picture of Jeffers seems an inevitable response to his poetry today, a poetry that has lost some of its ability to shock its readers and now seems to be only an outdated manifestation of post-Spenglerian despair.

The shocking quality of Jeffers' verse derived from his choice of violent and unusual themes: incest, rape, and murder in long verse narratives full of allegory and symbolism underscoring his love of nature and his hatred of society. But once the sensational aspects of poems such as *Tamar* (1924) and *Roan Stallion* (1925) are digested, we can see more clearly what Jeffers as a poet was doing. Trained in the science of medicine, although he never intended to practice, and deeply affected by his reading of Nietzsche, Jeffers looks at humanity as the extreme result of the development of consciousness, a consciousness harmful to the inanimate and eternal universe of silent galaxies and space dust. He shares Nietzsche's arrogant contempt for humanity—the "communal people"—as well as his conviction of the impossibility of discovering the true nature of God. But Jeffers, as Radcliffe Squires has pointed out, also differs from Nietzsche in his desire for strict morality and religion and in his acceptance of the idea of God as the mystical One. But the fundamental difference between them lies in Jeffers' "Inhumanism": a turning away from the contemplation of self to the contemplation of God; Nietzsche, on the other hand, held that in order for man to surpass himself he must turn away from the contemplation of God to an exclusive contemplation of himself.

Jeffers' repeated use of the incest theme illustrates the importance he attaches to this idea of Inhumanism: for him incest is a metaphor for the harmfulness of turning inward upon oneself rather than outward to nature and to God. *Tamar,* for example, is built around the incestuous strain that runs through the Cauldwell family, beginning with David and his sister Helen. In the next generation, David's daughter Tamar becomes pregnant by her brother Lee. The spirit of Helen, now dead, returns through her sister Stella, acting as a psychic medium, and wreaks revenge by pushing Tamar into another incestuous crime, this time with her father. This melodramatic series of events ends tragically with all the principal characters trapped in a house set afire by an idiot aunt. Ending in violent death and desolation, the poem is a warning to humanity against introversion and a celebration of violence as a good because it cleanses the world of human consciousness. This poem appeared in 1924, in the same volume with another long poem, "The Tower Beyond Tragedy," using the incest theme in a reworking of the Orestes-Electra legend; and such shorter poems as "Shine, Perishing Repub-

lic," with Jeffers' warning to his sons to "be in nothing so
moderate as in love of man."

Jeffers' preference for hawks, "the great unsocial birds," is
seen in "Hurt Hawks," published in *Cawdor, and Other
Poems* (1928), and there are many other passages in his poems
in which he describes himself standing "here on the foam-
wet granite sea-fang" where "it is easy to praise / Life and
water and the shining stones." But as he comes closer to humanity his disgust with the very idea of consciousness becomes
overwhelming, as in "Margrave" (1932):

> But man is conscious,
> He brings the world to focus in a feeling brain,
> In a net of nerves catches the splendor of things,
> Breaks the somnambulism of nature . . . His distinction per-
>   haps,
> Hardly his advantage. To slaver for contemptible pleasures
> And scream with pain, are hardly an advantage.
> Consciousness? The learned astronomer
> Analyzing the light of most remote star-swirls
> Has found them—or a trick of distance deludes his prism—
> All at incredible speeds fleeing outward from ours.
> I thought, no doubt they are fleeing the contagion
> Of consciousness that infects this corner of space.

The power of Jeffers' poetry is unmistakable. In its long,
sweeping lines, its sharp images of sea-swept cliffs, lonely redwoods, and other features of the California landscape it is
arresting and compelling. His supple and forceful free-verse
line, alternating between five and ten stresses, is a powerful
instrument in his longer narratives, such as *The Women at
Point Sur* (1927), "Cawdor" (1928), and "Thurso's Landing"
(1932). Shorter poems, such as "Apology for Bad Dreams"
(1925), "The Bloody Sire" (1941), and "Ocean" (1928), are
typical of his continuing concern with a world in which the
basic condition of life is "to eat each other."

Jeffers, finally, is not unaware of the paradox inherent in
an enemy of consciousness expressing himself in poetry:

I have humanized the ancient sea-sculptured cliff
And the ocean's wreckage of rock
Into a house and a tower,
Hastening the sure decay of granite with my hammer,
Its hard dust will make soft flesh;
And have widened in my idleness
The disastrous personality of life with poems,
That are pleasant enough in the breeding but go bitterly at
    last
To envy oblivion and the early deaths of nobler
Verse, and much nobler flesh.

("Margrave")

It is in such lucid perceptions of the tragedy of consciousness
that Jeffers' poetry is most compelling today.

The poetry of John Crowe Ransom (b. 1888), Robert
Penn Warren (b. 1905), and Allen Tate (b. 1899) is associated
in the minds of many with the Fugitives, a group consisting
of over a dozen writers who lived in Nashville, Tennessee,
between 1922 and 1926. Their acknowledged leader was Ransom; others included Donald Davidson (b. 1893) and Cleanth
Brooks (b. 1906). When they first gathered in the home of ·
James Frank, a Nashville citizen and man of the world, Ransom was a thirty-six-year-old English professor who had been
on the Vanderbilt University faculty for eight years and had
published one volume of verse, *Poems About God,* three years
before, which went almost entirely unnoticed. The magazine
they called *The Fugitive* came about as the outgrowth of discussions about poetry and poetic theory, which had been
largely stimulated by Ransom. *The Fugitive*'s first issue in
1922 was directed, as were they all, against southern smugness
and insensitivity to aesthetic values, from which, apparently,
they felt they were fleeing. They all thought of themselves as
outcasts, a view expressed in a poem by Ransom called "Ego"
and printed under the pseudonym of Roger Prim:

I have run further, matching your heart and speed
And tracked the Wary Fugitive with you.

It is not exactly clear who was pursuing them, however, since the South, as they well knew, was more than indifferent to their efforts. But *The Fugitive* rather rapidly gained national prominence, and Ransom's style began to show a maturity that went far beyond the blackberry-pie and baked-yam quality of his *Poems About God*.

The body of Ransom's work by which he wishes to be remembered is largely a product of his *Fugitive* years. In 1924, two years before the magazine folded, he published a volume of distinguished poetry, *Chills and Fever,* which rather suddenly reveals a fully matured poet in complete control of his craft. The qualities for which Ransom is best known—his gentle irony, his carefully poised wit, his subtle modulations of tone, his human sympathy, and his awareness of the finality of death and the inevitability of decay are all present in this remarkable volume. It was followed three years later by *Two Gentlemen in Bonds.* After these two volumes Ransom became increasingly concerned with criticism, and he published no more verse until his *Selected Poems* (1945). This includes selections from the second and third volumes, with nothing from his *Poems About God,* and adds five or six more poems. In 1952, 1963, and 1969 Ransom brought out revised editions of *Selected Poems* in which he made changes in some and added a few new ones. Of this continuing process of selection Randall Jarrell remarked: "few poets have ever picked their own best poems so surely, or disliked their weak or impossibly mannered poems so effectively: the whole *Selected Poems* is a little triumph of omission and revision, a piece of criticism that makes a great deal of the criticism one might otherwise write entirely unnecessary." When we talk about Ransom as a poet, then, we are talking almost entirely about a rather small collection of poems, most of them written in a period of about five years. These are the basis for Ransom's claim as an important American poet.

Ransom's forms are strongly traditional. He uses conventional stanzaic patterns: iambic pentameter quatrains, five-line stanzas with two-line and three-line rhymes, ballad stanzas, sonnets, and rhymed couplets. In many poems he is consciously

Spenserian, evoking a world of chivalry and romance through the use of such archaisms as *lissome, sward, wight, thole, leman,* and the like. One of his most characteristic poses is achieved through his ironic, consciously literary diction, by means of which he seems to be handling his subjects with detachment and Jamesian fastidiousness. *Beautifully, untidy, unseemly, hatefully,* are some of these words, but we cannot appreciate their full effect until we come across them in context.

The landscape of Ransom's world is mostly southern and rural, but more often it is not clearly identifiable as belonging to any one region. Among those settings that we can identify are a Virginia county, a southern town, a moldy garden, a piazza—presumably southern—and southern mansions, cornfields, and farms. In many other poems, however, the landscape is incidental or undefined, even in some where there is some unidentifiable sense of its southern setting. Ransom uses his settings, it would seem, to give what he would call "texture" to his poems—that is, to give them a feeling of concreteness— but he can hardly be thought of as a poet who is celebrating the South.

This is made clear by a look at his characters and themes. One is struck by the extent to which his poetic landscape is peopled by the dead, the dying, the forsaken, and the unlucky in love. Death becomes the great overbearing fact of life; one's response to life is measured by the presence of the "old gentleman in a dustcoat." Love, too, is viewed in terms of life and death, and those who renounce their lovers or deny physical passion are in effect dead. In "Parting, Without a Sequel" (1926), a girl writes a letter of rejection, "with characters venomous and hatefully carved," which she gives to a postman described as "the blue-capped functioner of doom." As she watches the "serpent's track" of his bicycle, she is consumed with physical pain, suggestive of death "hot as fever / And cold as any icicle."

Ransom is too sophisticated and cultured a gentleman to appear to be emotionally involved with his subject, however. His own poetry is not a poetry that, as he says of romantic poetry, proceeds out of failure. It is not the kind of poetry whose author has received too many "blows, privations, humiliations, and silences" from the natural world and who therefore "invents a private world where such injustices cannot be, and enjoys it as men enjoy their dream." Instead, Ransom feels that we should be interested in poetry that is the act not of a child but the act of an adult mind, "and I will add, the act of a fallen mind, since ours too are fallen."

Writing of Freud, whom he describes as a tragic ironist, Ransom says, "To be a tragic ironist is to be aware sharply and grimly, but not too painfully, of the constant involvement of life with death"; and in another context, his contribution to the collection of Southern Agrarian essays called *I'll Take My Stand* (1930), is another statement that applies to his poetry: "I believe there is possible no deep sense of beauty, no heroism of conduct, and no sublimity of religion, which is not informed by the humble sense of man's precarious position in the universe."

Such statements help us understand the reason for all those deceased maiden ladies and child corpses. Man's mortality is an essential fact of life, and our awareness of this—though not too painful, as Ransom reminds us—constitutes a knowledge of the world. In "Bells for John Whiteside's Daughter" (1924) he captures for us the irony of the contrast between an active young girl who chased geese with a stick and her stillness in death: "There was such speed in her little body, / And such lightness in her footfall, / It is no wonder her brown study / Astonishes us all."

Life versus death is only one of many oppositions by means of which Ransom views the world. In his vision, there are positive human values that need to be asserted in opposition to those negative ones that would thwart or destroy them. Ransom believes in a life of feelings, a life full of a sense of the world's reality. Associated with this is a belief in the necessity for the individual to feel his own worth, to have roots in a cultural heritage and a strong identification with place. This is a kind of humanism, and Ransom is an aesthetic humanist committed to a life in which the intelligence and the imagination play upon a tangible world. "I will cry with my loud lips and publish / Beauty which all our powers shall never establish, / It is so frail," he writes.

Ransom's brand of humanism is opposed to, but does not deny, science. "What we cannot know constitutionally as scientists," he has said, "is the world which is made of whole and indefeasible objects, and this is the world which poetry recovers for us." Ransom images the scientific man as a "Persistent Explorer," who gazes at the water but sees and hears nothing beyond its literal quality as water: "water, only water . . . the insipid chemical H_2O." When the sound threatens to draw out from "the deep thickets of his mind" some imaginary creatures, he feels compelled to beat them down. Plagued by a sense of his own dual nature and the conflict within him of the contrary tendencies toward opposite ways of looking at the world, his plight becomes perhaps the plight of modern man.

A similar dilemma is confronted by another of Ransom's characters whose label is equally descriptive: "Man Without Sense of Direction" (1945). He is unable to respond to the beauty of his world: the songs of birds offend his ear. He is fervorless, cold, without physical passion, unresponsive to his bride. He is noble in mind and physically strong, but, the poet says, "cannot fathom or perform his nature." His response is frustration, bewilderment, and despair—typical twentieth-century attitudes: he writhes, flails his arms, and mutters. "He is punished," Ransom says, "not knowing his sins / And for his innocence walks in hell."

Perhaps more difficult to understand is the way Ransom relates the South and its traditions to these other values. For him the South represents a dying way of life, an anachronism in an industrial, progressive age, which, in spite of his own inability to identify wholly and uncritically with it, still holds a charm. "Declension looks from our land, it is old," the speaker of "Antique Harvesters" (1925) says. But he urges the young men to resist the temptations of a new way of life and instead remain to the end upholding the ideals of their fathers. In this poem most specifically about the South, it is clear that Ransom is not an uncritical apologist for it. Like Faulkner, he uses the dying away of the Old South as a fable to protest against the dying out of a whole collection of values that are loosely identified with but not restricted to it. In John Crowe Ransom we can see a classical balance and restraint: he is a poet of feeling who refuses to be disillusioned or cynical, and who affirms the values of the mind and the imagination without excluding the senses.

The work of Robert Penn Warren (b. 1905) in verse and prose has a remarkable uniformity and coherence. He has been preoccupied with a number of basic themes for at least forty years, through six volumes of verse, a book-length poem, eight novels, and a volume of short stories. As an associate of Allen Tate and John Crowe Ransom he was early tagged with the Fugitive label, but although the southerner's dreams of agrarian simplicity and feudal order are present in his books, Warren has applied his southern experience to much wider themes. What has developed in Warren's work is an all-encompassing and complex vision of evil, coupled with a sense of the human penchant for violence, which he has explored more and more lingeringly and with greater and greater attention to detail.

Warren's early poems did in fact follow pretty much the formal and tonal patterns of Tate's and Ransom's poetry—the controlling metaphor or conceit, the irony and ambiguity, the mixture of love and theology that they used to adapt the tradition of Donne and Marvell to a southern setting. "Love's Parable," collected in *Thirty-Six Poems* (1935), is, in its handling of syntax and diction, Warren's tribute to Donne, while "Bearded Oaks" shows his familiarity with Marvell. But in that volume also are poems that combine his sense of place, his sense of history, and his sense of self—poems like "Revelation," in which a boy discovers the evil in himself and through it discovers love. These poems teem with Confederate veterans, coon dogs, peacocks: all the traditional features of the southern landscape, from poor white to army colonel, as Warren struggles with both time and place in an effort to define himself. They are composed of a mixture of Faulknerian horror and local-color humor, but contain a Puritan preoccupation with man's sinfulness that makes Warren seem almost a New Englander. *Thirty-Six Poems* is full of poems about man's share in the world's evil, many of them marked by images of rotting and decay.

Eleven Poems on the Same Theme (1942) continues Warren's search for self-knowledge and shows a more subtle and complex handling of incident and theme as well as a more inclusive vision of evil. In "Original Sin: A Short Story" he describes the frightening and ubiquitous, but slightly ludicrous, aspect of sin, which "acts like the old hound that used to snuffle your door and moan." In lines playfully echoing Eliot, he writes of our discovery that sin returns even when we think we have escaped it:

> But there it stood, after all the timetables, all the maps,
> In the crepuscular clutter of *always, always,* or *perhaps.*

Another poem exploring the relation of the self to time is "Variation: Ode to Fear," a mock ode in which a variety of ridiculous situations such as sitting in a dentist's chair, overdrawing one's bank account, and reading of the diseases of famous people are related to an all-engrossing fear of death, relentlessly emphasized in the refrain *"Timor mortis conturbat me."* He was to treat this obsession again with some flippancy in a later poem, "Nocturne: Traveling Salesman in Hotel Bedroom," which begins:

> The toothbrush lies in its case,
>   Like you in your coffin when
> The mourners come to stare
>   And the bristles grow on your chin.

In *Selected Poems, 1932–1943* (1944), the exploration of evil, violence, time, and history continues, and in an especially fine poem, "The Ballad of Billie Potts," Warren called upon a range of voices and styles that he had cultivated in order to raise a murder story to the level of Greek drama. The story concerns the murder of a prodigal son by parents who habitually made a living by ambushing, killing, and robbing unsuspecting guests at their inn. The father, by causing the death of his son, has violated the principle of trust upon which man can flourish in his community. As this poem suggests, man does not live in isolation but in relation to his physical and temporal setting. In a speech at Columbia University, Warren said that man is

> in the world with continual and intimate interpenetration, an inevitable osmosis of being, which in the end does not deny, but affirms, his identity. It affirms it, for out of a progressive understanding of this interpenetration, this texture of relations, man creates new perspectives, discovers new values—that is, a new self—and so the identity is a continually emerging, an unfolding, a self-affirming and, we hope, a self-corrective creation.

The idea that violence is an essential part of this self-corrective creation is a familiar one to the reader of any of Warren's novels, since for him self-fulfillment and self-discovery come not from a retreat to innocence, but paradoxically by acceptance of the guilt and sin that are a part of human nature. It was his desire to explore these ideas at length and in leisurely detail that led Warren into the novel, and when he returned to poetry, it was to write a book-length poem, *Brother to Dragons: A Tale in Verse and Voices* (1953). This is another violent story, first shown to him by Katherine Anne Porter, about the brutal ax-slaying of a Negro slave by two of Thomas Jefferson's nephews. Warren lifts the events out of the normal time order of history by putting them into a dramatic dialogue between Jefferson and a character called R. P. W. The facts in the case are tangled and confused enough, the distance in time far enough, and the murder bloody enough to satisfy Warren's desire to use the story to explore once again his preoccupation with the past and self-definition. As he says at one point: "All life lifts and longs toward its own name, / And toward fulfillment in the singleness of definition."

In *Promises: Poems 1954–1956* (1957) Warren displayed a new sureness, a new simplicity and directness of style, as well as new techniques that seem not experimental but the confident work of a mature and experienced writer. Five of the poems are addressed to his daughter Rosanna; the rest, "Promises," are nineteen poems, some of them multisectional, to his son Gabriel. History again appears—and the South—but not always subsumed under personal history. "Founding Fathers, Nineteenth-Century Style, Southeast U.S.A." combines sympathy with debunking of his ancestral past, and ends:

So let us bend ear to them in this hour of lateness,
And what they are trying to say, try to understand,
And try to forgive them their defects, even their greatness,
For we are their children in the light of humanness, and under
                the shadow of God's closing hand.

Although *You, Emperors, and Others: Poems 1957–1960* (1960) does not compare in quality to the preceding volume, Warren continues his practice of writing long poems composed of shorter ones linked together. In this way he is able to use a variety of tones and images to develop a complex set of ideas or feelings. One of the best of these, "Prognosis: A Short Story, the End of Which You Will Know Soon Enough," is about a woman facing death from cancer. In another sequence, "Mortmain," the first poem has another of the unwieldy titles Warren frequently uses: "After Night Flight Son Reaches Bedside of Already Unconscious Father, Whose Right Hand Lifts in a Spasmodic Gesture, as Though Trying to Make Contact: 1955." In the last stanza, the poet makes real his anguish at his father's death, as he becomes aware of the loss of his most important link with the past:

But no. Like an eyelid the hand sank, strove
Downward, and in that darkening roar,
All things—all joy and the hope that strove,
The failed exam, the admired endeavor,
Prizes and prinkings, and the truth that strove,
And back of the Capitol, boyhood's first whore—
Were snatched from me, and I could not move,
Naked in that black blast of his love.

The sureness of tone in Warren's voice continues undiminished in the new poems published as part of *Selected Poems: New and Old, 1923–1966.* A six-part sequence called "Tale of Time," about his responses to the death of his mother, brings in the familiar Warren themes of memory and horror in language that sounds sometimes like Eliot and sometimes like Lowell but is still characteristically his own. Both the new and the old poems remind us once again of Warren's secure position as an important American man of letters.

In one of those curious reversals of cultural history one of the two younger poets who dominated the Fugitive group in the 1920s and was acclaimed one of America's outstanding poets in the 1930s now seems less significant as a poet than his friend Robert Penn Warren. Allen Tate (b. 1899), essayist, critic, novelist, teacher, poet, has an equal claim with Warren as one of America's great men of letters, but as a poet his performance continues to be disappointing, and he will probably be remembered as a critic. The poems are disappointing because of the early evidence of his talent and the continuing but spotty evidence of his intensity of feeling and his mastery of craft. Unlike Warren, however, Tate has not developed and broadened.

He has not imitated himself, either, but has changed, searching for a basis of commitment and set of ideas upon which he could focus his fierce intellectual energy and passionate devotion to poetry. He has at last come to rest on the rock of the Roman Catholic Church, finding in its orthodoxy a certainty not present in the agrarians' shifting and elusive ideal of the Old South. But rest does not imply complacency, since his tortured sense of the brutal modern world in which he is living remains as excruciatingly alive as ever. Tate shares with John Crowe Ransom the assumption that we live in a fallen world—a world of spiritual chaos and social disorder cut off from history and therefore violent and disoriented. Tate pursued the agrarian dream of giving history a life-sustaining mythic quality with the same demonic obsessiveness with which Crane sought the mythos of the Brooklyn Bridge. For ten years he wrestled with the problem as he wrote and rewrote his "Ode to the Confederate Dead" (1930). The theme of the ode, he later said, was "the cut-off-ness of the modern 'intellectual man' " from his acquisitive modern society. But the poet's attempts to experience the past by studying the gravestones in a Confederate cemetery end in frustration; "the wind whirrs without recollection," and he, too, is turned to stone. Like Eliot's Gerontion, he finds that mere knowledge frustrates true experience, and his own dissociation of sensibility leads him into a hopeless solipsism signified by the image of the narcissistic jaguar who "leaps / For his own image in a jungle pool, his victim."

Looking over the five decades of his writing, we can see the long and continuing influence of Dante on Tate's work: from "Seasons of the Soul" through his most recent autobiographical long poem. For although he has made it apparent that the source of a unifying myth is to be found in one's personal history, the pattern and the imagery of his quest come from the *Divina Commedia*. In "Seasons of the Soul," his finest poem, Tate seeks the meaning of life through a series of confrontations with his own obsessions. The poem makes many references to Dante, some of which merely clutter it, but we can see that his intention is to use the allusions to call attention to the connection he feels exists between his personal agony and the apparent disintegration of western civilization.

But it was Baudelaire from whom Tate learned to use the violent and often bizarre imagery that appears in his poems of the twenties. The obscurity and concentration of these poems, as well as their extremely personal symbolism, remind us of Hart Crane, as in this well-known passage from "The Subway," written in 1924:

> I am become geometries, and glut
> Expansions like a blind astronomer
> Dazed, while the worldless heavens bulge and reel
> In the cold revery of an idiot.

Tate seems to lack a natural melodic ear; he is, to use a phrase from one of his poems, "harshly articulate." This lack of melody is sometimes deliberate, however, as in this polysyllabic and Latinate passage from "Ode to the Confederate Dead":

> Our heads with a commemorial woe
> In the ribboned coats of grim felicity,
> What shall we say of the bones, unclean,
> Whose verdurous anonymity will grow?

But he is most eloquent when his sense of history, his ear for rhetoric, and his moral outrage combine in that fine poem about Aeneas and his founding of Rome, "The Mediterranean." Aware of the contrast between the fulfillment of Aeneas' hopes in Rome and the failure in modern America to establish a society based on law, stability, and order, Tate concludes:

> Now, from the Gates of Hercules we flood
>
> Westward, westward till the barbarous brine
> Whelms us to the tired land where tasseling corn,
> Fat beans, grapes sweeter than muscadine
> Rot on the vine: in that land were we born.

Out of a total of about two hundred and fifty poems Tate has chosen only ninety-nine to include in *The Swimmers and Other Selected Poems* (1971) as a representative selection. Of these, one would list "Seasons of the Soul," "The Mediterranean," "The Ancestors," and "Shadow and Shade" as his best, while others such as "Mr. Pope," "The Subway," and "Ode to the Confederate Dead" contain, like much of his poetry, striking passages mixed with major and minor flaws. This collection includes three sections of a long, unfinished, and untitled autobiographical sequence: "The Maimed Man," "The Swimmers," and "The Buried Lake." This sequence, written in *terza rima,* is also modeled on Dante and seems to represent Tate's efforts to find the source of myth in personal history. Highly personal allusions are given symbolic significance in a hellish and nightmarish agony of the soul, using a Dantean "symbolic imagination" to describe what is perhaps a progress toward salvation. If we cannot judge the poem as a whole, we can still admire its parts, particularly "The Swimmers," a vivid recollection of the poet's own experience of evil and an awakening to redemption through love, a poem strikingly similar in subject and theme to Robert Penn Warren's "Revelation."

To an extraordinary degree Hart Crane (1899–1932) was formed by the disordered home life of his childhood, which left him an emotional cripple. His father was a successful and hard-driving candy manufacturer in Cleveland, Ohio; his mother a neurotic, possessive woman who after several separations and reconciliations with her husband eventually had a complete mental breakdown. The effect of this unstable relationship on Crane was a lasting one, and his lack of self-confidence, his drinking, and his homosexuality are some of the evidences of this early turmoil in which he took sides with his mother against the tyrannical harshness of his father. Some of the quality of this boyhood is reflected in these lines from *The Bridge* (1930):

> Is it the whip stripped from the lilac tree
> One day in spring my father took to me,
> Or is it the Sabbatical, unconscious smile
> My mother almost brought me once from church
> And once only, as I recall—?

Crane first went to New York in 1916, and, after a period in which he wrote advertising copy and a period in which he tried unsuccessfully to work in his father's candy factory, he returned to New York, where he lived a marginal existence, half the time drunk in sailors' bars, the other half associating with various literary friends, such as Waldo Frank, Gorham Munson, Malcolm Cowley, and Allen Tate. He became friendly also with Otto Kahn, a banker, who supported him through much of the writing of *The Bridge*, and later in Paris he met Harry and Caresse Crosby, who encouraged him to finish it. These meager and depressing external facts do little to reflect the intense inner life that Crane was living—his wide and impassioned reading in Plato, Nietzsche, Blake, and Rimbaud for example, or his enthusiastic discovery of the American poets he considered to be of the first rank: Whitman, Poe, Melville, and Emily Dickinson.

His early poems show a great variety of influences: Swinburne, Yeats, the English Romantics, and the French Symbolists. He soon began writing poems in the manner of T. S. Eliot and Laforgue, such as "Chaplinesque" (1926), in which the clown figure of Charlie Chaplin as comic hero-poet was suggested at least in part by Laforgue's Pierrot. The ironic self-deprecation in this poem reflects Crane's own sense of the poet's pathetic position in the modern world. After seeing Chaplin's film *The Kid* (1921), Crane was struck by the comic melancholy of his characterization and wrote the poem to express his sense that the poet is "in the same boat."

But the "new thresholds, new anatomies" that become the basis of Crane's romantic quest for a poetry of the Absolute had their origin in a peculiarly twentieth-century mystical experience. Although there is a ludicrous aspect to Crane's having found his greatest moment of spiritual exaltation in a dose of laughing gas, it is still appropriately related to his search for a means by which to achieve a mystic fusion of the new technology and the romantic vision that is the task of *The Bridge*. In the dentist's chair he felt his mind "spiraled to a kind of seventh heaven of consciousness" and heard a voice saying, "you have the higher consciousness." "I felt the two worlds," he wrote to Gorham Munson in a description of this experience; "O Gorham, I have known moments in eternity." Crane's attempts to reproduce this experience radically changed the nature of his poetry. Rimbaud's poetry of drunkenness and ecstasy became his model, and he sought a variety of stimuli for his own writing. Drinking in bars, or alone in his room with a phonograph blaring at full volume, Crane's pursuit of the "higher consciousness" led him to occasional lyric flights, but also led him into a downward-spiraling path of drunkenness, remorse, and self-loathing that made each effort to achieve his ideal more difficult than the one before. Nevertheless, it was during this period that he wrote his greatest poems, one of which has as its subject the very squalor he was seeking to transcend. "The Wine Menagerie" (1926) is both an affirmation of his need for the stimulation of alcohol and a recognition of the sordid surroundings in which he found it. The poem opens with a series of sharply observed vignettes in a barroom—bottles ranged on a shelf, the "imitation onyx wainscoting," couples quarreling, an urchin buying a canister of beer—but as the wine begins to take effect the poet experiences a tremendous sense of release:

> New thresholds, new anatomies! Wine talons
> Build freedom up about me and distill
> This competence—to travel in a tear
> Sparkling alone, within another's will.

His own puritan conscience has been subdued and his "blood dreams a receptive smile / Wherein new purities are snared."

A poem that more fully exemplifies the method of this visionary poetry—a term rightly insisted upon by R. W. B. Lewis—is "For the Marriage of Faustus and Helen." In it he made his first concerted attempt to reach out beyond the despair and death of Eliot and his followers in order to affirm his own joy in life and to unite himself with the world of ideal beauty. "For the Marriage of Faustus and Helen" is an effort to create a kind of positive *Waste Land* in which past and present are fused and classical attitudes toward beauty are reconstructed in modern terms. To do this Crane took the classically pure Helen out of Poe's "Nicéan barks of yore" and placed her in a streetcar, thereby, he later wrote, "building a bridge between so-called classic experience and many divergent realities of our seething, confused cosmos of today." From there the poet explores the fallen world in which both he and she find themselves, and discovers that in spite of its limitations it is not all bad. The poem moves indirectly through some of the most difficult and compressed lines ever written. Language and images are piled upon one another in a dizzying crescendo that reaches its climax in the third section of the poem, where Crane achieves the Dionysian intoxication and ecstasy of Rimbaud and a mystical, Blakean vision of the Absolute.

An even more impressive performance is the lyrical sequence called "Voyages," which Crane placed at the end of his first collection, *White Buildings* (1926). In this series of love poems, frankly written about a homosexual affair with a sailor, Crane reaches through and beyond physical love toward a transcendent vision of the poetic ideal. Nowhere else in his poetry are the elements of sea imagery, sexual union, the Platonic striving for the ideal, and the poet as inspired prophet and lover so harmoniously united. The "Voyages" sequence is preceded in *White Buildings* by the lyric "At Melville's Tomb," a tribute to that writer's close identification with the sea, and, we sense, Crane's further identification with Melville —as well as Whitman—in his frank acceptance of the ambiguities of sexual love. Underlying "Voyages" is the story of his relationship with this sailor-lover: discovery, love, sexual fulfillment, loss, and reconciliation with the sense of loss through an identification of love and poetic harmony. The opening poem establishes the dominant image of the sea and strikes the note of foreboding for the role the sea is to play in the poet's earthly life: "The bottom of the sea is cruel." The sea undergoes a series of metamorphoses throughout the six sections of the poem: in Section II it is "this great wink of eternity"; in Section III, a powerful analogue of physical love; and then, in various ways, a destroyer, a rival for his love; and finally a source of redemption in its role in leading the poet to discover the "Belle Isle" of his poetic vision in Section VI. We see here clear parallels with the "Cathay" of *The*

Bridge and the complex symbolic structures of the "Atlantis" of the same poem, in which purified love and Platonic harmony are merged in the one transcendent symbol of the "Bridge of Fire." But "Voyages" is not an exercise in preparation for *The Bridge;* it confronts more directly and without that poem's added complexities of history, modern technology, and epic aspiration, the central issue of Crane's mature work: the transcendence of space and time and the union of love and poetic vision in the one redeeming Word. Like his other poetry, it presents serious difficulties to the reader and critic; its density of texture, its defiance of logic for its own "logic of metaphor," and its straining for the kind of ultimate poetry that strikes directly at the imagination, leave many passages undecipherable and unparaphrasable. Yet few will deny that this is a great poem, and some will agree with Yvor Winters' categorical statement that it is "one of the most powerful and one of the most nearly perfect poems of the last two hundred years."

There is certainly some interplay of attitudes and ideas between "Voyages" and Crane's most ambitious work, *The Bridge* (1930), his not entirely successful effort to transform modern America into a self-defining and self-sustaining myth. He selected the basic image of the Brooklyn Bridge partly because it represented an achievement of modern technology, partly because it supplied a present-day image of spanning and crossing similar to Whitman's Brooklyn Ferry. As a symbol it tries to do many things, and although the poem tries continually to use it as the basis for still another soaring flight, it remains curiously static and inert. The bridge is one of the two major symbols; the other is Pocahontas, conceived of as a mythical earth-mother representing America's lost mythic past, which the narrator attempts to rediscover and to link with the present and the future.

In "Proem" Crane first establishes the central role of the bridge; it composes in its span a perfect arc, a fleeting embodiment of the Absolute, the Logos, or God's Word. Addressing it as the "terrific threshold of the prophet's pledge"—a clear clue to his visionary conception of its role—he demands:

O sleepless as the river under thee,
Vaulting the sea, the prairies' dreaming sod,
Unto us lowliest sometime sweep, descend
And of the curveship lend a myth to God.

This opening section of the poem is balanced at the end by "Atlantis." The two together work as a kind of frame, the "Proem" setting forth the problems, "Atlantis" approaching the point of religious ecstasy and joy toward which the entire sequence is directed. In between these two poems are seven sections of varying lengths. The first is "Ave Maria," a poem in which the poet's wavering religious doubts are expressed through the story of Columbus' ambiguous success: he was the discoverer and therefore destroyer of "Cathay," but he was also the instrument for possible future redemption by those who would achieve social and religious harmony. Part II, "Powhatan's Daughter," consists of five poems in which we are led back into the mythic past and discover the "body" of Pocahontas and the secret of religious mystery in her ritual dance. In these sections, particularly in the magnificent "The River," Crane worked to establish the sense of myth that he felt informed the lives of his ancestors. And in "The River" he spans both time and space to end with the image of the Mississippi River, symbol of time, merging with the timeless as it flows into the sea.

Two other outstanding sections are "Cape Hatteras," in many ways the central poem of the sequence, as well as his greatest tribute to Whitman, and "The Tunnel," an underworld vision of the modern city as a Dantesque hell that is every bit as nightmarish as the "unreal city" of Baudelaire and Eliot. Crane comes dangerously close in the latter to affirming the very Eliotian view of the modern world that the poem was intended to reject, and this can be explained only by our sense of the powerful impact of the ugliness of an urban civilization upon a sensibility that could not deny it even in the act of trying to transcend it. But this section must also be read as a dark night of the soul, a purgatorial episode before the final beatific vision of "Atlantis"—and the clue is provided for us by the epigraph from Blake's "Morning":

> To find the Western path
> Right thro' the Gates of Wrath.

The best poetry is in "Atlantis," where Crane's mystical striving for the "multitudinous Verb"—the Logos contained in the symbol of the bridge itself—reaches its apotheosis. This concluding poem contains some of the most intense and stimulating passages in modern poetry and goes far to redeem *The Bridge* as a whole. Our sense of formlessness, of an impassioned effort to bring together the many strands of the poem, of, finally, the failure of the poem to achieve an impossible goal, still does not blind us to the greatness of many of its incomparably brilliant passages.

Crane's fatal leap from the taffrail of the steamship *Orizaba* in the spring of 1932 ended the tortured career of a poet whose visionary poetry strove to reconcile or transcend the contradictions of a life he found simultaneously beautiful and hideous. Crane may be said to embody two aspects of the American romantic tradition. From Poe he inherited his desire for pure poetry, his vision of the poet as living in a fallen world, his systematic *"dérèglement de tous les sens"* through the use of various stimulants, and, finally, his sense of hostility to and alienation from contemporary society, which led Baudelaire to characterize Poe as *"le poète maudit."* But at the same time he had a Whitmanesque vision of spiritual fulfillment through a mystical belief in man's ability to transform himself into a transcendent being. This was a conflict so basic in both Crane himself and in the society of which he was a part that suicide may have seemed the only possible solution.

The publication in 1923 of a small book of poems called *Harmonium* represents the first phase of a poet who was to undergo a number of transformations, largely unnoticed by most of his readers until after his death. Today, many still know Wallace Stevens (1879–1955) only as the poet of *Harmonium*, even though from the late 1930s until his death he exhibited an inventiveness and intellectual fertility that belied his established reputation as an exotic offshoot of the Imagist movement. His later poetry, published in *Parts of a World* (1942), *Transport to Summer* (1947), and *The Auroras of Autumn* (1950), explores with tireless energy the artistic and philosophical implications of his inexhaustible subject: poetry. In 1954, on his seventy-fifth birthday, he published what he wanted preserved in *The Collected Poems,* and three years later Samuel French Morse edited the *Opus Posthumous,* containing further riches, including the invaluable and fascinating collection of aphorisms he called "Adagia."

Harmonium is full of gaudy poems with such playful titles as "Thirteen Ways of Looking at a Blackbird," "The Emperor of Ice-Cream," "Le Monocle de Mon Oncle," and "The Man Whose Pharynx Was Bad." The tone of these poems is a kind of intellectualized elegance, with elements of self-mockery and buffoonery in which the poet seems to be guarding against taking himself too seriously. Stevens' critics accused him of preciousness and dandyism in his use of bizarre images, out-of-the-way allusions, and freakish diction, such as *rattapallax, nincompated, diaphanes, emprize, pendentives,* and the like. These qualities are indeed there. But the roles Stevens plays— the comedian, the vaudevillian, the literary dandy or aesthete —are all central to his conception of the poet as celebrant— a master of ceremonies to the world of reality whose language and deportment often have the sonorities and flair of the circus ringmaster. Stevens' world—especially the *Harmonium* world—is in an important sense a circus, in which wonders never cease, and the everyday is transformed by art into the miraculous.

Although there is an apparent contradiction between Stevens' life as an insurance executive and his life as a poet, the recent publication of his letters has given us a glimpse into the mind of a man so sensitive to shading and nuance that only the most comfortable and routine life could provide

him with the leisure to pursue them. Stevens made up his
mind early to become a writer. When he left Harvard he
struggled in the slums of New York to lead a Bohemian life
at about the same time that Edwin Arlington Robinson was
eking out his life as a poet in squalid West Side flats. But
whereas Robinson remained bitterly faithful to his determination to be nothing but a poet, Stevens took a law degree at
New York University and in 1908 left his "window in the
slums" for an insurance office in Hartford. For the rest of his
life his material security was to exert a subtle influence on his
sense of spiritual as well as physical well-being. As a cultivated
epicure and connoisseur, he indulged himself in collections of
miniature porcelains, French prints, and books and sent to
Ceylon for rare blends of tea. He lived, in other words, the
roles of dandy and aesthete that he found essential in the
process of developing some of the most serious and profoundly
meditative poetry ever written.

Stevens' poetry first attracted public notice in 1915 when
Harriet Monroe published "Sunday Morning" (in a truncated
version) in *Poetry*. This poem, a landmark in the history of
twentieth-century poetry and quite possibly Stevens' greatest
poem, is a blank-verse meditation centered around the question of belief. It is, as he later described it, a pagan poem, full
of sensuous images and a control over sound and rhythm that
give the words themselves a life and richness of their own.
The poem is a dialectic between the poet and a woman who
feels twinges of conscience for staying home from church and
enjoying the physical beauty of "late coffee and oranges in a
sunny chair, / And the green freedom of a cockatoo / Upon a
rug." In eight flawless stanzas Stevens develops the argument
of a stoic hedonist who asserts the need to enjoy the pleasures
of this world, as well as suffer the pains, since there is no life
after death. "Divinity must live within herself," he argues, and
in reply to her plea for an "imperishable bliss," offers the
answer that "death is the mother of beauty": we live in a state
of change and chaos in which our awareness of the transitory
quality of beauty is its very essence. The poet's exuberant cele-

bration of an earthly religion is followed by the brilliant and moving last stanza, added later by Stevens, which tempers this exuberance with a delicate and ambiguous evocation of death:

> Deer walk upon our mountains, and the quail
> Whistle about us their spontaneous cries;
> Sweet berries ripen in the wilderness;
> And, in the isolation of the sky,
> At evening, casual flocks of pigeons make
> Ambiguous undulations as they sink,
> Downward to darkness, on extended wings.

"Sunday Morning" contains the germ of practically everything Stevens later wrote. As a "connoisseur of chaos," he devoted himself over and over to the proposition that "the essence of poetry is change and the essence of change is that it gives pleasure." "Beauty is momentary in the mind," he writes in "Peter Quince at the Clavier" (1915), another early poem. He adds: "The body dies; the body's beauty lives. / So evenings die, in their green going." In his abiding concern with the fact of death, coupled with his celebration of earthly beauty, his poetry has echoed and reechoed many of the ideas and phrases of "Sunday Morning."

The central poem of his next volume, *Ideas of Order* (1936), takes us in a new direction, as Stevens focuses his attention on the artist rather than on his art—the poet as maker, seen in the art of creation. The protagonist in "The Idea of Order at Key West" is a woman singing by the sea. The sounds of the sea furnish the substance of her song, yet "it was she and not the sea we heard. / For she was the maker of the song she sang." The interaction of the singer's imagination and reality is the process that creates the song, or poem:

> She was the single artificer of the world
> In which she sang. And when she sang, the sea,
> Whatever self it had, became the self
> That was her song, for she was the maker.

In "Like Decorations in a Nigger Cemetery" (1935) closer in manner to the *Harmonium* poems, Stevens defined poetry this way:

> Poetry is a finikin thing of air
> That lives uncertainly and not for long
> Yet radiantly beyond much lustier blurs.

But however uncertain its existence, the poem came more than ever to be Stevens' central concern. In *The Man With the Blue Guitar* (1937), he asserted flatly that "Poetry is the subject of the poem." In an age that had rejected religious belief, Stevens felt that poetry had to satisfy man's need for spiritual sustenance:

> Poetry
>
> Exceeding music must take the place
> Of empty heaven and its hymns.
> ("The Man With the Blue Guitar")

This is the position he had taken earlier in "A High-toned Old Christian Woman" (1922), where he said, "Poetry is the supreme fiction," preferable to a "haunted heaven" with palms "like windy citherns hankering for hymns." By this time in his career Stevens was embarked on a quest for the discovery of what must be rejected and what must be affirmed. It was clear to him, as he noted in his journals, that "after one has abandoned a belief in God, poetry is that essence which takes its place as life's redemption."

Stevens' aesthetic begins with the proposition that reality is a combination of the physical world and the imagination; the action of man's imagination upon his surroundings constitutes his sense of the world and, finally, the world itself. The poet is continuously engaged in the process of imposing order on his world by putting his perceptions into words. He has a "rage for order" but is aware that inherent in his universe of change is a central paradox: "A great disorder is an order," he says in "A Connoisseur of Chaos" (1938). As a firm believer that the world we live in is the only world, he insists on the need to respond to it:

> Let's see the very thing and nothing else.
> Let's see it with the hottest fire of sight.
>   ("Credences of Summer")

But the world alone is not enough without the saving presence of man's imagination:

> There would still remain the never-resting mind,
> So that one would want to escape, come back
> To what had been so long composed.
> The imperfect is our paradise.
>   ("The Poems of Our Climate")

In such an imperfect and changing world the order that the poet establishes through the poem is only a momentary, unstable order, with disintegration implied in it. The poet, who is himself changing, can see an object one moment in one way and a moment later see it in another way—an idea explored in one of his famous early poems, "Thirteen Ways of Looking at a Blackbird." The poem becomes, therefore, not a revelation of truth, but one truth among many revealed through the interaction of the seeing eye of the imagination and the images it perceives:

> We live in a constellation
> Of patches and of pitches,
> Not in a single world.

For Stevens, these acts of perception and creation became analogous to the religious experience, as he searched for ways to celebrate the world and the poet's perception of it which would release him from "the malady of the quotidian." As it was for both Poe and his spiritual descendants, the Symbolists, the poem for Stevens was an unparaphrasable reality that exists wholly within its language and elevates both poet and reader to a state of transcendence in which their sense of the renewing powers of poetry become identical with the poem itself. But in another sense, he is not working toward transcendence. In his "Notes Toward a Supreme Fiction" (1942), he sets down the criteria for the formation of the "ultimate poem," the "supreme fiction" that enables man to accept himself and his world on their own terms. The supreme fiction, as Roy Harvey Pearce has noted, "was to be a poem which all men could come to behold, stripped of its antecedents and consequences, that which made them human." The pursuit of this poem, which of course was never actually attainable, was the preoccupation of Stevens' later years. In such late poems as "Credences of Summer" (1946), "An Ordinary Evening in New Haven" (1949), "Notes Toward a Supreme Fiction" (1942), and the group of poems contained in "The Rock" (1950), Stevens evolves into a meditative poet, writing "The poem of the mind in the act of finding / What will suffice" ("Of Modern Poetry," 1940). In these poems, meditation is both subject and technique: meditation with the purpose of adducing innumerable particular poems as "notes" toward finding "the essential poem at the centre of things." He writes of this poem in "A Primitive Like an Orb" (1948):

> We do not prove the existence of the poem.
> It is something seen and known in lesser poems.
> It is the huge, high harmony that sounds
> A little and a little, suddenly,
> By means of a separate sense. It is and it
> Is not and, therefore, is. In the instant of speech,
> The breadth of an accelerando moves,
> Captives the being, widens—and was there.

The poet who thus unites himself and the world celebrates himself as an indispensable part of the process; he is the "capable man," the "impossible possible philosopher's

man . . . in [whose] poems we find peace" ("Asides on the
Oboe," 1940). Like Whitman, he celebrates the world by depending upon the evocative power of language; Stevens'
world, his "fluent mundo," is a world only fully realized when
it is imaginatively heightened by words. In his only reference
to Whitman (in "Like Decorations in a Nigger Cemetery,"
1935), Stevens describes him "walking along a ruddy shore":

> singing and chanting the things that are part of him,
> The worlds that were and will be, death and day.
> Nothing is final, he chants.

Although Stevens nowhere adopts the cosmic view of Whitman, he is still, as Joseph Riddel has said, centrally concerned
with the poet as mythmaker and creative center of vision,
transforming the ordinary world by his touch. For Stevens,
as the title of one of his late poems states, "Reality is an Activity of the Most August Imagination" (1954), an activity
that leads one to a fresh conception of his world. "Many sensitive readers of poetry," he wrote, "without being mystics or
romantics or metaphysicians, feel that there probably is available in reality something accessible through a theory of poetry
which would make a profound difference in our sense of the
world."

Not only the theory but the poetry itself works this way,
if the reader allows himself to become immersed in it. One
can object to his philosophical preoccupations, to his mannered style, to the flatness of his later poetry, which often
approaches the language of technical philosophers, yet one
can never doubt the seriousness and sense of spiritual commitment to his art that ultimately approaches the "vital center" of Eliot's *Four Quartets,* as in this passage from "Credences of Summer":

> Trace the gold sun about the whitened sky
> Without evasion by a single metaphor.
> Look at it in its essential barrenness
> And say this, this is the centre that I seek.

Stevens has an individuality and richness of invention unmatched by any poet in English since Yeats, and a technical virtuosity in language and form that rivals Eliot and Pound. As he moved away from the tricks and flukes of his early manner, he became more and more aware of the need to make himself understood—to speak, like Wordsworth, as a man speaking to men. In this endeavor, Stevens is joined by both Robert Frost and William Carlos Williams—an endeavor to purify the dialect of the tribe that has made American poetry of the twentieth century truly vital and readily distinguishable from English poetry.

William Carlos Williams (1883–1963) during his career remained much more closely associated than Stevens with the principal figures of the modern movement. From his early years as a medical student at the University of Pennsylvania, where he formed lifelong friendships with Ezra Pound and H. D., to his last years as a sort of guru to the young hopefuls of a new, postmodernist generation, such as Robert Creeley and Allen Ginsberg, Williams stood spiritually in the center of much that was and is new in American poetry. On the one hand abiding by Pound's exhortations to "make it new," but on the other hand refusing to adopt his elitist aesthetics, Williams stubbornly went his own way, much of his life, against the prevailing taste for obscurity, complexity, and ambiguity established by Eliot and Pound, to fashion a tough, original, and elastic language of his own.

Language lies at the heart of his poetry—an obvious statement, but, like many of the obvious critical pronouncements Williams himself makes, it assumes a kind of innocent conviction and special relevance to his own work. Williams was a seeker and a searcher—for the words and the qualities of words that form the substance of his poems. Words themselves become objects, with which larger objects, the poems, are formed. Like the "environments" of Louise Nevelson, created from scraps of wood, or the constructions of painters using *objets trouvés,* Williams' poems began with recognizing the properties of the individual words and built up from there. He could incorporate a sign into a poem:

```
*  *  *
*  S  *
*  O  *
*  D  *
*  A  *
*  *  *
```

or bring in prose passages from letters, history books, and newspaper articles, as he did in *Paterson*.

He was convinced (as was Pound) that Americans speak "a distinct, separate language in a present [new era] and that it is NOT English." This position led him to look and listen for rhythms and expressions that were typically American, even to the point of jotting down his patients' remarks on the backs of prescription blanks. Many of these found their way into his poems, and some of them he even tried to make stand on their own as poems. Like Whitman, Williams was fascinated by the possibilities of slang and the idiom of everyday speech, but unlike Whitman, he never made them seem affected when he used them in his poems; instead, they seem to capture some essential human quality by imitating something in the human being himself: "Doc, I bin lookin' for you / I owe you two bucks." Just as important as his conception of language, and related to it, is his sense of place, of the local, his need for roots. As the second-generation son of immigrant parents (his father was English and his mother was from Puerto Rico), Williams reacted typically in rejecting his foreign antecedents and putting down roots in his native soil. His search for roots took several directions. *In the American Grain* (1925) is a study of American history in which he tried "to find out for myself what the land of my more or less accidental birth might signify." His search is most fully satisfied, of course, in his long epic of the city of Paterson, which becomes "an image large enough to embody the whole knowable world about me." In that poem his "local pride" as he called it, enabled him "To make a start, / out of particulars / and make them general," a process typical not only *of Paterson* but of all his poetry, in which he sought to perceive the essence of the objects in his world by first discovering their existence.

Williams was born and died in Rutherford, New Jersey. After eight years of education in Rutherford public schools, two in schools abroad, and three at Horace Mann High School in New York, he entered the medical school of the University of Pennsylvania, where he met Ezra Pound, Hilda Doolittle, and the painter Charles Demuth. Between 1906 and 1909 he interned at hospitals in the Hell's Kitchen district of New York City, and at the same time was writing Keatsian lyrics about the search for beauty. In 1909 he published *Poems* at his own expense with an epigraph from "Ode on a Grecian Urn." These misty yearnings for some unobtainable ideal are entirely derivative in form and language and give virtually no indication of what he was to become. But after visiting Pound in London in 1909–1910 Williams found a new model and turned out poems defying both an outworn poetic tradition and the society that fostered it. This new freedom and looseness, as well as a growing self-confidence, were Williams' greatest debts to Pound. However, he came to sympathize less and less with Pound's ideas of the poet-outcast, as he realized that the source of his own poetic strength lay in the misery, ugliness, violence of life, and even in the stupidity of the lower classes and waste products of humanity whom Pound contemptuously rejected.

Williams' associations with other poets continued to grow as he met Marianne Moore through Alfred Kreymborg and began contributing to Kreymborg's *Others* and Harriet Monroe's *Poetry*. Later he met the American expatriate writer and publisher Robert McAlmon (1895–1956), with whom he edited the first issue of the magazine *Contact*. In 1923 McAlmon's Contact Publishing Company published Williams' *Spring and All*, a mixture of poems and experimental writing in the manner of Gertrude Stein, James Joyce, and the Dadaists. Williams continued to write prolifically—novels, short stories, plays, and essays, as well as poems—but pub-lished much of his writing at his own expense or with small independent publishers, since few commercial publishers were interested. The poetry volumes included *Collected Poems 1921–1931* (1934), with a preface by Wallace Stevens; *The Complete Collected Poems of William Carlos Williams 1906–1938* (1938); the five books of *Paterson,* published separately from 1946 to 1958; and *Pictures from Breughel and Other Poems* (1962); all published by his friend James Laughlin of New Directions.

By the time Williams published the poems in *Al Que Quiere!* in 1917 he had begun to find his own way. He was working under the twin influences of the Imagists and of Whitman; from Whitman he derived mainly the impulse to-ward freedom and release of the self—a conception of the role of the poet as seeking renewal through the tapping of the power of the word as it resides in the speech of the people. As James Breslin has written, Williams, having grown up after the closing of the frontier, saw that his poetic task was to affirm the self-reliant, sympathetic consciousness of Whit-man in a broken, industrialized world. But unlike Eliot, who responded negatively to the harsh realities of this world, Wil-liams saw his task as breaking through restrictions and gen-erating new growth: "Saxifrage is my flower that splits / the rock" ("A Sort of a Song," 1944). But in spite of his spiritual affinities with Whitman, Williams rejected his free verse and orotund voice for the sharp images and precise diction of the Imagists. More than any of the poets closely associated with the Imagist movement—Pound, H. D., Richard Aldington, or John Peale Bishop—Williams adhered to Imagist principles. His intention was to show things—and to *show* them meant to describe them, or more basically, to name them. Naming things, in fact, became an end in itself—as though by an ac-curate concentration on the physical object he could some-how make it a part of himself. His relation to the physical world was of the utmost importance, not because he was in-terested in objects for their own sake but because they re-lated back to him. His subject was himself—his personal feelings—and, by extension, every man; but the way to himself was through an objectified response to his surroundings, rather than the subjective responses of Wordsworth or Keats. Here is the scene, he seems to be saying in so many of his poems; it is not important what was or what will be, but what is. This is the kind of response that his famous poem, "The Red Wheelbarrow," from *Spring and All* (1923) demands:

> so much depends
> upon
>
> a red wheel
> barrow
>
> glazed with rain
> water
>
> beside the white
> chickens

It was poems like this that led Kenneth Burke to call him "the master of the glimpse," and when they work, they work well. Although not all of his early poems are this type of Imagist *aperçu,* many, such as "This is Just to Say" (1934), "Proletarian Portrait" (1935), and "Pastoral" (1917), use this technique.

But in other poems much more is at work than mere perception of objects. In "The Young Housewife" (1916), for example, there is a nervousness and tension between the perceived and the perceiver as the speaker's sexual desire flows just beneath the surface of carefully selected diction and imagery. And in "The Bull" (1922), "Young Sycamore" (1927), and "Fine Work With Pitch and Copper" (1935) he develops his aesthetic principles by the use of symbolism and oblique statements.

Many of his poems are about flowers and trees: Queen Anne's lace, asphodel, sycamores, saxifrage, locust, lily, mullen, daffodil; some of these are simple nature poems, while in others the flowers are used as symbols of sexual desire, artistic vitality, or love. Whatever Williams looks at he looks at directly—and often the directness of his gaze and his refusal to temper it with conventional pieties is the source of the poem's interest. In "Danse Russe" (1916) he looks at himself dancing naked in front of a mirror and asks, "Who shall say I am not the happy genius of my household?" Robert Lowell admires "The Catholic Bells" (1955) for similar reasons: Williams hears the bells "in the yellow-brick tower / of their new church . . . ring in / the new baby of Mr. and Mrs. Krantz." The statements are factual, incongruous, and "real," in the sense of seeing things as they are. His poems finally defy easy categories, however. His range is one of the widest of twentieth-century poets—from Imagist fragments to more complex and more fully developed poems, such as "St. Francis Einstein of the Daffodils" (1936), "Burning the Christmas Greens" (1944), "The Pink Church" (1946), "The Desert Music" (1951, a small masterpiece), "Asphodel That Greeny Flower" (1955), which Auden has called one of the greatest love poems in the language, and *Paterson*.

Although *Paterson* is typical of Williams in many ways, it is still a departure in form and conception from his earlier work. He became aware of the shortcomings of both Imagism and Objectivism, which limited him to describing or rendering the concrete "thing," and saw that he needed a new, more flexible structural principle; this, as Linda Wagner sees it, was *design*. As an epic poem, *Paterson*, like other modern epics such as Crane's *The Bridge* and Pound's *Cantos*, departs from traditional ideas of what the epic is and what it is supposed to achieve. Williams wanted his epic to contain what he saw as the principal features of modern life: man and the city. These he embodied in a single, composite figure, Noah Faitoute Paterson, the poet-city-man-hero of his originally projected four-part poem. In addition to rejecting a traditional epic hero, such as Columbus, as his protagonist, Williams also rejected a narrative, or logical, structure, preferring instead to build his poem as a kind of montage or collage composed of scraps of local history, old letters, and narrative fragments concerning a variety of real fictional characters, together with lyrical and Imagist passages. All of these are combined, using a technique that owes something to Dos Passos' *U.S.A.* (1938) and something to modern painting. Looking back on his work, Williams could see a kinship between the structure of his poem and that of the "action painting" of Jackson Pollock. But in its complexity and its use of abundant detail he saw also that it worked toward the inclusiveness one finds in medieval tapestries and in the paintings of Pieter Breughel.

Each of the first four parts of *Paterson* was published separately between 1946 and 1951; in 1958 Williams published Book Five, which in a sense is a continuation but more accurately, perhaps, is an attempt to rethink and consolidate the themes in the earlier books. Of Book Five Williams wrote to his publisher: "I have been forced to recognize that there can be no end to such a story I have envisioned with the terms which I had laid down for myself. I had to take the world of Paterson into a new dimension if I wanted to give it imaginative validity . . . the composition began to assume a form which you see in the present poem, keeping, I fondly hope, a unity directly continuous with the Paterson of *Pat. 1 to 4.*"

The best description of the poem is Williams' own:

> *Paterson* is a long poem in four parts—that a man in himself is a city, beginning, seeking, achieving, and concluding his life in ways which the various aspects of a city may embody—if imaginatively conceived—any city, all the details of which may be made to voice his most intimate convictions. Part One introduces the elemental character of the place. The Second Part comprises the modern replicas. Three will seek a language to make them vocal, and Four, the river below the falls, will be reminiscent of episodes—all that any one man may achieve in a lifetime.

The method is, as he announces in the "Preface":

> To make a start,
> out of particulars
> and make them general, rolling
> up the sum, by defective means—

There is a good deal of stammering and hesitancy throughout the poem, as the poet tries to discover the language that will energize man and allow him to fulfill his creative potential. Williams derives the symbols for this process from the topography of Paterson itself. Paterson, the city, is the male principle, the reason, and the intellect, while Garrett Mountain, which lies next to the city, is the female principle, embodying feelings and creativity. But both are asleep and deaf to the language of the Great Falls of the Passaic River, which carry the Word the poet-Paterson seeks to discover:

> (What common language to unravel?
> . . combed into straight lines
> from that rafter of a rock's
> lip.)

The Falls' secret lies largely in the frequently repeated exhortation: "Say it, no ideas but in things," which is to say that the objects of the physical world imitated in poetry will themselves give us a new knowledge of reality. If there is an echo of Stevens here, it is even more strong in this stanza from Book Three:

> The province of the poem is the world.
> When the sun rises, it rises in the poem
> and when it sets darkness comes down
> and the poem is dark

The torrent of the Passaic River and the plunging of the Falls contain the secret of life that the shape-shifting poet-protagonist attempts to unlock. Borrowing his conception of man-as-city partly from James Joyce, and indulging in a "wasteland" vision of contemporary society that often resembles Eliot's, Williams constructed *Paterson* on the theme of divorce: divorce from the soil, divorce from cultural and historical roots, divorce from love and creativity. The inhabitants of Paterson, the modern city, are automatons, "Who because they / neither know their sources nor the sills of their / disappointment walk outside their bodies aimlessly for the most part, / locked and forgot in their desires—unroused." And believing that "knowledge, undispersed, is its own undoing," Williams uses the technique of dispersal—a moving outward and forward from the objects and people and events he records —to restore vitality and meaning to them. Knowledge locked up in books or men's minds, or restricted to university professors, "spitted on fixed concepts like roasting hogs," is useless knowledge. To the question in Eliot's "Gerontion," "After such knowledge, what forgiveness?" Williams would answer, write poetry:

> Let the words
> fall any way at all—that they may
> hit love aslant.

Paterson is Williams' masterpiece—the testimony to his efforts to seek and to find life's redemption through language. Running through the poem and interconnected by a complex set of unifying images are the themes of the sacredness of life, the regenerative powers of sex and love, the need for beauty, and the dignity of man. It is a poem that is impressive in the desperation and daring of its attempt to redefine the epic in modern terms.

One senses, and is confirmed in his feeling by closer analysis, that Williams has achieved far greater control over his materials than is at first apparent. They have been orchestrated, to use Randall Jarrell's term, in a way that gives all five books a thematic and even a structural unity that at individual points threatens to break down under the sheer weight and diversity of the material. As uneven as the poem is, the reader is made aware that Williams will not compromise with his principles—his commitment to love, to art, to the full realization of the energies of the self, and to his search for the vital principle linking language and life. Nor does he look for an escape into transcendence—the "Cathay" of Crane, the "still point" of Eliot, or the "supreme fiction" of Stevens—instead, he finds his answer in "the thing itself."

In spite of its many digressions and distractions, the poem has an internal consistency of attitude throughout and is a testimony to Williams' own lifelong search for form and for meaning within form. Considered in this way, it is fascinating as a poem-in-process (like the *Cantos*) in which the poet simultaneously expresses his view of the world and works out the formal problems connected with his desire to express it. In his efforts to find "how to begin to find a shape," he finds he must comb out the language himself, and in so doing affirm, often eloquently, that "we know nothing, pure and simple, beyond our own complexities."

CHAPTER ELEVEN

The Middle Generation

Robert Lowell, Theodore Roethke, Elizabeth Bishop,
Stanley Kunitz, Randall Jarrell, Karl Shapiro, John
Berryman, Howard Nemerov, Richard Wilbur, Rich-
ard Eberhart, J. V. Cunningham

The rapidly changing quality of life in America during the forties and fifties had a profound effect on the poets reaching maturity during those years. They were witnesses to the accelerated growth of an urban and technological society, while still remembering the relative innocence of their youth in the years before World War II. The Depression, Marxism, the labor movement, and the shift from an agricultural to an industrial economy all played a part in shaping their ideas and attitudes. It is no wonder, then, that when W. H. Auden showed how the poet could use the play of irony and irreverent wit to dissect the economic and social ills of modern civilization his influence on the idiom of this generation of American poets threatened to become all-pervasive.

These poets, whose first encounter with *The Waste Land* was likely to have been in college courses, were also being exposed to some of the early enthusiasms of the New Criticism. They became, through the criticism of T. S. Eliot and John Crowe Ransom, admirers of Donne and the Metaphysicals; they looked for the tensions of irony and ambiguity as well as for the difficulty and erudition that were then widely regarded as essentials of the good poem. Recalling the literary atmosphere of those years, Richard Wilbur writes: "We were led by our teachers and by the critics whom we read to feel that the most adequate and convincing poetry is that which accommodates mixed feelings, clashing ideas, and incongruous images." Some of his contemporaries have held to these views, others have tried, more or less successfully, to move away from them, and one, Karl Shapiro, has openly declared war against them. All seem to have been able to assimilate the lessons their elders had learned in their years of artistic rebellion, to use the new forms and techniques with less self-consciousness and pugnacity.

These are the poets of the middle generation: overshadowed often by their elders, who in their last years were writing some of their greatest poetry. When Theodore Roethke was in his late forties, William Carlos Williams was publishing *Journey to Love,* Wallace Stevens his *Collected Poems,* and Ezra Pound his Rock Drill *Cantos.* No wonder, then, that Roethke, along with Lowell, Shapiro, and Berryman, all around forty, was considered one of the younger poets. That is the label they seemed fated to carry with them forever, even when a new generation of adventurous poets began publishing "contemporary poetry" in the sixties.

Since the publication of *Lord Weary's Castle* (1946), Robert Lowell (b. 1917) has been recognized as the strongest and most original voice among the many who have made the post–World War II period an exciting one in American poetry. Lowell's early work is written in a mood of anger and frustration, giving vent to a deep-lying resentment against his own New England Puritan background. His feelings of being stifled by the virtues of hard work, clean living, and gentility that remained as legacies of the Puritans were coupled with his awareness of the violence and harshness that gave rise to and sustained those traditions. His conversion to Catholicism was a rebellion against this heritage, but he created as many problems as he solved, since he felt more strongly than ever the tension that exists between his spiritual impulses and the secular life.

Lowell's early poems are full of violence and somber fury, with grotesque images and a syntax to match. For Lowell, the modern world is not a wasteland awaiting the rains of spiritual renewal, but Saint Bernard's nightmarish Land of Unlikeness, where the unhappy inhabitants have lost their likeness to God but are still aware of the falsity of the material world. Lowell himself, choosing the poems he wanted to reprint in *Lord Weary's Castle*, felt there had been "too much twisting and disgust" in *Land of Unlikeness* (1944), his first book; and that is the reaction of the reader today to such poems as "Christ for Sale" or "Satan's Confession," the very titles of which suggest the overt use of religious imagery and symbolism and the strained efforts at irony that characterize many of them. In both of these early collections Lowell was trying to combine his horror of war, social criticism, the irony of history, and the torments of a wavering religious faith in highly compressed, allusive poems using severely restricting forms.

The most impressive of these poems is "The Quaker Graveyard in Nantucket," an elegy in the great tradition. The deaths by water of Edward King and John Keats are echoed in Lowell's celebration of the drowning of his cousin Warren Winslow. The poem bears more than a superficial resemblance to Milton's "Lycidas" in its effort to come to grips with the puzzling question of a young man's death. The opening five sections are typical of Lowell in their harsh descriptions of man's rapacity, violence, and greed, personified in the figures of the Nantucket whalemen who, in the "mad scramble of their lives" for wealth, make a cruel mockery of the biblical passage that appears as the epigraph: "Let man have dominion over the fishes of the sea . . ." Lowell's references to *Moby-Dick* underscore his agreement with Melville that the Quaker shipowners were a grasping lot. The connection between these nineteenth-century whalers and the violence of the present is implied throughout the poem, which is resolved in the superb sixth section by a rejection of his own heritage and a discovery of the means for redemption in a statue of Our Lady of Walsingham, whose serene mysticism goes beyond the world. In this transcendence of earthly terror Lowell sees the source of hope.

The violent imagery and language of this poem are matched in "Colloquy in Black Rock," an extremely difficult and compressed dialogue between self and soul. The poem's difficulty comes from the odd juxtaposition of references to the martyrdom of Saint Stephen and the Feast of Corpus Christi interspersed with images of destruction, rubble, and mud. The connection between all of these is made in the last stanza with the image of Christ walking on the black water. In a dazzling Hopkins-like line, Lowell evokes Christ as the spiritual redeemer of man's broken and battered flesh:

> the mud
> Flies from his hunching wings and beak—my heart,
> The blue kingfisher dives on you in fire.

The number of religious allusions in these lines alone indicates Lowell's heavy reliance in this period on an overt Christian symbolism for dramatizing his concerns with the destructive effects of alienation from God.

In *The Mills of the Kavanaughs* (1951) Lowell began to abandon his Catholic symbolism, although several of the poems, such as "Mother Marie Therese" and "Thanksgiving's Over," make some use of it. The title poem is a monologue by the young widow of a naval officer who has committed suicide. The poem itself would be even more difficult than it is were it not for a long prefatory note containing some biographical details essential to an understanding of the poem. We see here Lowell's growing sense of the need for some way of maintaining the compression of his verse and at the same time avoiding a baffling obscurity. He may have found a solution to his problem in William Carlos Williams' *Paterson,* where the prose passages are used as a background for the lyrical ones. Lowell was to use this device more effectively and with more attention to its structural and thematic possibilities in *Life Studies.*

Life Studies (1959), most readers agree, marks a new and significant departure in Lowell's career. With this book he seems to have found his voice—a strong, powerful, free voice, still strident, but less shrill, less at the mercy of form. What he has discovered principally is himself, and himself in relation to his own past. That past was there in such earlier poems as "Mary Winslow" and "In Memory of Arthur Winslow," but his sense of it was still clotted by the conflict between the demands and aspirations of his Puritan New England heritage and the equally rigorous demands of his new-found Catholic faith. The pathetic irrelevance of Mary Winslow's death, for example, was bitterly expressed in the opening lines:

> Her Irish maids could never spoon out mush
> Or orange-juice enough

Now, in "Grandparents," he combines a flippancy of tone and a looseness of language in a way that suggests both sympathy and detachment from the world and the values his grandparents stand for:

> They're altogether otherworldly now,
> those adults champing for their ritual Friday spin
> to pharmacist and five-and-ten in Brockton.
> Back in my throw-away and shaggy span
> of adolescence, Grandpa still waves his stick
> like a policeman;

In these lines are the widely praised Lowell concreteness and particularity of image, qualities he admires in the poetry of Elizabeth Bishop; his playfulness in the first line is a sign of a new self-confidence, and in the fourth line he even glances sidewise at Dylan Thomas.

These poems are studies of his own life—his boyhood, his parents, his grandparents, their lives and deaths, their houses, cars—and his marriage, his friendships, his experiences in jail as a conscientious objector and in a mental institution. But his personal memories are also viewed against a larger backdrop: a world where secularism, violence, political paralysis, and uncontrolled sexuality have reached alarming stages. The book opens with four poems: "Beyond the Alps," written in 1950, the year Pius XII defined the dogma of Mary's bodily assumption; "The Banker's Daughter," about Marie de' Medici after the assassination of her husband, Henri IV; "Inauguration Day: January 1953"; and "A Mad Negro Soldier Confined at Munich." By what route, Lowell seems to ask, did he arrive at the end of the decade of the fifties, full of malaise, casting doubtful and anguished looks at his marriage and his life? To retrace these painful steps he first characterizes the sensibility of his own times by contrasting the present with the past and then casually and prosaically renders the immobility and spiritual paralysis of the Eisenhower years through images of ice, snow, and death.

Part Two, the prose autobiography, "91 Revere Street," lies at the heart of the volume. These ironically detached reminiscences provide the factual data and establish the tone for the "life studies" in Part Four. By making us see the pathetic qualities of his father, who tried to maintain stature and dignity in a naval career for which he was unsuited, Lowell is able to be compressed and allusive in the poems that follow. The power of his observation in the poem "Commander Lowell," that "Having a naval officer / for my Father was nothing to shout / about," comes from his having shared —confessed is a better word—the often painful details of his childhood. This confessional quality, most fully discussed by M. L. Rosenthal, grew partly out of Lowell's association with W. D. Snodgrass, whose *Heart's Needle,* a frank and honest exploration of his failing marriage and divorce, also appeared in 1959. What raises Lowell's confessional poetry above the level of self-indulgence or self-therapy is his own acute awareness of the link between the public and the private sensibility. Even in his most personal and painful revelations he manages to suggest the universality of his anguish, a quality he recognized and admired in the poems of Sylvia Plath. The most powerful and at the same time most personal poem in *Life Studies* is the concluding one, "Skunk Hour." Here, in the depths of despair, living on an island where an heiress longs to retain the symbols of her decayed grandeur and where he has his own doubts about his capacity for love or any human relationship, the poet cries out from the imprisonment of his own mind. The phrase is Satan's from Milton's *Paradise Lost:* "I myself am hell." The flatness of the words themselves, completely appropriate to the tone and setting of the poem, ring with the eloquence of Milton and raise the poem to a level of universality with chilling abruptness. The poem and the book end with a tentative grasp on a concrete reality that takes the form of a mother skunk and her young foraging for food.

Lowell's poetry since *Life Studies* has been written with his usual technical mastery. *Imitations* (1961) are ostensibly translations from Baudelaire, Rimbaud, Rilke, Montale, and others, but they are as free if not freer than Pound's translations and may be read as original poems. In *For the Union Dead* (1964) Lowell writes with new assurance and a kind of flippancy and playfulness that suggest his partial liberation from the night sweats of *Life Studies.* The title poem is an eloquent meditation on the purposelessness and drift of modern society. His use of the statue of Colonel Robert Shaw on the Boston Common as a central image recalls William Vaughn Moody's "Ode in Time of Hesitation" (1900) and suggests that this is an updating of that poem. Several of his poems, such as "Hawthorne" and "Jonathan Edwards in Western Massachusetts," return to the American past for images of relevance to our own time. This search for usable truth has continued in three plays published in 1964: *The Old Glory, Benito Cereno,* and *My Kinsman, Major Molineux.*

Near the Ocean (1967) seems to be a lull, a regathering of forces, and a return to some of the obscurity of his earlier years, but the poems, none of which is individually memorable, show him nevertheless to be a poet more sure of himself than ever.

From 1967 onward, Lowell has become more and more

political-minded and has identified himself as a public figure with various causes related to the peace movement. He marched with Norman Mailer at the Pentagon in October 1967, campaigned for Eugene McCarthy in the 1968 Presidential primaries, and took part in the events in Chicago surrounding the Democratic National Convention in August 1968. Lowell's sense of outrage, disgust, or frustration at the political and social events of the years 1967–1970 found expression in a series of fourteen-line unrhymed blank-verse sections, which he first collected in *Notebook 1967–1968* (1969). But he continued to write more of these sections and to revise those he had written, reissuing them in a third, revised and expanded edition, titled simply *Notebook,* in 1970. The book as a whole, the poet tells us in an "Afterthought," is to be read as one long poem, intuitively arranged. The form, the arrangement, and the manner of publication inevitably remind one of Berryman's *Dream Songs,* but here there is no Henry-persona to act as intermediary between the poet and his reader. Lowell gives himself: his mind and emotions stripped bare. The poem is his personal history, but he avoids self-pity and self-indulgence by using his own experience, as do all great poets, as the raw materials for art. Although it appears to have been assembled piecemeal, the poem is a long, sustained meditation on the chaos of the spirit that prevailed publicly and personally for Lowell in the turbulent years of the late sixties. Paradoxically, they have an easiness and suppleness of tone in spite of their intensely private and allusive, even hermetic, quality. *Notebook* is a major work, in which the voices of the past and of Lowell's contemporaries speak through him, but the prevailing voice is his own, speaking out of his agonies in an eloquent rage for order.

In his search for identity in *Life Studies,* Lowell was participating in what has become an almost universal literary enterprise in this century. No poet, however, has taken his search farther or deeper than Theodore Roethke (1908–1963). His poems reach back and reclaim his own lost infancy and childhood, taking him on a voyage of exploration into Jungian depths of consciousness where he finds a world animate with the primordial life-urges of nonthinking plant and animal life. This wet, green world, full of bugs and grubs, is the realm of the irrational and the animistic, which becomes for Roethke a point of departure for a return to feeling and spiritual wholeness.

The poems throb with mice capering in straw, toads brooding in wells, roses breathing in the dark; all Roethke's images conspire to plunge the reader into this pungent and fecund world in order to loose him from his moorings and take him along on a journey of self-identification. "A man goes far to find out what he is," Roethke once said, and his words about the function of poetry are a gloss on that remark: "We must permit poetry to extend consciousness as far, as deeply, as particularly as it can." Roethke did not reveal his purpose early and relentlessly pursue it, however. His career was a process of finding his way and shifting his style as he moved toward a genre of meditative poetry that complements in its mystical serenity the meditative poems of Eliot and Stevens. His early poems, collected in *Open House* (1941), are spare and precise, written with controlled passion and emotion, as though the act of disciplining his feelings kept him from flying apart. The title poem hints at Roethke's continuing preoccupation and prescribes his means for dealing with it:

> I'm naked to the bone,
> With nakedness my shield.
> Myself is what I wear:
> I keep the spirit spare.

These early poems, although they are obviously the work of a richly talented poet, lack an inner cohesiveness, a sense of clear purpose and direction. But the poems at the end of the volume suggest he was finding a way, and these, together with the amazing poem about his father, "The Premonition," lead us directly into the startling greenhouse world of *The Lost Son and Other Poems* (1948).

It was his boyhood as the son of a nurseryman in Saginaw, Michigan, that gave Roethke the memories and the images that he used with increasing imaginativeness. His rediscovery of boyhood is a discovery of Paradise, a return to the smells of roses, orchids, and begonias, the feel of vines and roots. These poems about a small boy playing and working in his father's greenhouse have such titles as "Cuttings," "Root Cellar," "Transplanting," and "Flower Dump." Diction and image merge in "Root Cellar" to produce the rich, earthy quality that characterizes Roethke's world:

> Roots ripe as old bait,
> Pulpy stems, rank, silo-rich,
> Leaf-mold, manure, lime, piled against slippery planks.

The greenhouse becomes in these poems, as he himself has said, a symbol "for the whole of life, a womb, a heaven-on-earth." The feelings associated with it are simple and innocent: a pleasure in watching things grow, a curiosity about the shapes and smells of living—and dying—plants, the satisfactions of working and touching life with one's hands. But in his "The Lost Son" sequence at the end of the volume Roethke becomes much more interested in making the greenhouse symbolism vitally operative. Two poems preceding that sequence prepare us for the shift. One is "The Minimal," in which he explicitly describes his subject matter:

> I study the lives on a leaf: the little
> Sleepers, numb nudgers in cold dimensions,
> Beetles in caves, newts, stone-deaf fishes,
> Lice tethered to long limp subterranean weeds,
> Squirmers in bogs,
> And bacterial creepers

The other is "My Papa's Waltz," where his father, strong and volatile, both frightening and benign, appears as a god of power and order.

"The Lost Son" sequence opens with the boy's anxious thoughts of death, then moves into a mysterious, subterranean world of worms, snails, and roots, through which he moves in a kind of Alice-in-Wonderland fantasy in which he is reduced to their size. This move downward and inward is a prelude to a movement back out again toward light and order: he loses himself in order to find himself. He returns to the womb: "I feel the slime of a wet nest"; then in a kind of prenatal state of unreason he searches for "the old rage, the lash of primordial milk!" In the fourth poem, images of light begin to dominate as the darkness recedes and he hears the paternal voice of authority: "Ordnung! Ordnung! / Papa is coming!" The pattern of this poem, with its movement from confusion to order, from dark to light, becomes a familiar one in Roethke's poetry as he moves through the slime and loam of his embryonic memories in what he describes as "an effort to be born, and later, to become something more." The titles of his poems are suggestive: "The Long Alley," "A Field of Light," "The Shape of the Fire." The second of these, all of which are part of a sequence, ends with the lines: "And I walked, I walked through the light air; / I moved with the morning."

The rest of Roethke's major works are steps in the process of restoring the fragmented and unintegrated self to a state of mystical wholeness and communion with the life principle of nature. Substance takes precedence over form as his lines are by turns short and almost primitive, then long, loose, and rhythmically powerful. The sequence, a series of loosely related poems, which he first used in *The Lost Son,* became a useful device for tracing the progress of his meditations. The sequence at the end of that volume, in fact, was continued in a series of poems in his next volume, *Praise to the End!* (1951), and concluded with still another poem, "O Thou Opening, O" in *The Waking* (1953).

In another sequence from *Praise to the End!* Roethke makes heavy demands on the reader by asking him to become a child again and see the world through the eyes of a growing child. The perceptions and the language of the poems are infantile, but the sensations have an immediacy that removes completely all literary trappings for the sake of the sensations themselves. As the child grows, the rhythms and language of the nursery are replaced by others, as in that exuberant poem of awakened sexuality, "Give Way, Ye Gates."

But he moves away from these explorations into celebrations of pure being that assert the primacy of feeling. "We think by feeling," he says in one poem, and, in another: "Being, not doing, is my first joy." Love also becomes a kind of ordering, however, and his marriage to Beatrice O'Connell in 1953 brought forth a new burst of energy stemming from his discovery of love as another way out of the self. The nature imagery of the earlier poems that he shaped to suggest the womb now works in reverse to impart to the woman herself the virtues he discovered in the world of weeds and seeds. He dances and sings, finds music, rhythm, and otherness in crying out in triumph at the end of the title poem of *Words for the Wind* (1958):

> And I dance round and round,
> A fond and foolish man,
> And see and suffer myself
> In another being, at last.

From the time of *Words for the Wind* onward Roethke's thoughts turned increasingly toward death, and his poems establish a complex interaction between love, death, dancing, and sensuality that is difficult to describe but that seems a natural development of his feelings. Like Dylan Thomas, who exhorts his dying father to "rage, rage against the dying of the light," Roethke rages against death and yet looks at it as a fulfillment of life. In his moving tribute to Yeats, "The Dying Man" (1958), he develops the relationship between life, order, and dancing that he did so well in "Four for Sir John Davies" (1953) and reaches a state of mystical oneness with nature where he is able to say, "I shall undo all dying by my death."

This attitude provides the basis for the meditative sequences of the posthumous volume *The Far Field* (1964), such as the *North American Sequence,* with the remarkable "Meditation at Oyster River" and "Journey to the Interior"; the *Mixed Sequence* and *Sequence, Sometimes Metaphysical.* The second of these begins with the poem called "The Abyss," somewhat typical in its variations of form and tone. In Kunitz' *Twentieth-Century Authors* Roethke said these longer poems "try in their rhythms to catch the very movement of the mind itself, to trace the spiritual history of a protagonist (not 'I' personally), of all haunted and harried men." In "The Abyss" he invokes Whitman, the "maker of catalogues," as his sense of the world invades him. But terrified by his hunger for objects, he sees himself as a caterpillar crawling down a string toward death—toward a still point where consciousness and unconsciousness meet. The world of objects recedes as he approaches this stillness and re-creates his sense of it in this meditative passage:

> I rock between dark and dark,
> My soul nearly my own,
> My dead selves singing.
> And I embrace this calm—
> Such quiet under the small leaves!—
> Near the stem, whiter at root,
> A luminous stillness.

It is clear from this and many other passages in these meditative poems that Roethke's attitude toward death is ambivalent. He fears it, he shrinks from its horror, yet he is moving toward an embrace of the very thing he fears. The concreteness of his imagery becomes often obsessive and repetitious as he seems to be trying to define himself through the particularity and oneness with nature that characterized "The Lost Son." But he has gone beyond the womb, beyond sensuality, to a mystical still point of being and consciousness, which echoes, indeed seems almost to parody, Eliot's voice in *Four Quartets.* But his affinity is perhaps even more with Stevens (to whom he once paid tribute in that exuberant line, "Brother, he's our father!"), whose meditative later poems were poems "of the mind in the act of finding / What will suffice" ("Of Modern Poetry," 1940). What suffices for Roethke is a recognition of the oneness of God and the mind—a mind that climbs out of its fear of death to a mystical transcendence that accepts and resolves the paradox of spirit and created matter. It is this mystical serenity that finally triumphs over the rage, the questioning, and the dark soul-fear of the later poems, as in this moving passage in the closing section of "The Far Field":

> A man faced with his own immensity
> Wakes all the waves, all their loose wandering fire.
> The murmur of the absolute, the why
> Of being born fails on his naked ears.
> His spirit moves like monumental wind
> That gentles on a sunny blue plateau.
> He is the end of things, the final man.

From the publication of her first collection of poems, *North and South* (1946), Elizabeth Bishop (b. 1911) has been recognized as a meticulous observer of her surroundings with an ability to absorb and relate them to her own experience. Like the early Imagists, Bishop blends language and image to re-create a fleeting *aperçu*, but she draws out and sustains this kind of experience through a loving attention to the things themselves. Like Wallace Stevens and Richard Wilbur, she is called to the things of this world, and she seems to possess an instinctive awareness of the thingness—the *quidditas*—of things that makes her poems much more than mere descriptive pieces. Take this passage from one of her best poems, "Brazil, January 1, 1502" (1965):

> A blue-white sky, a single web,
> backing for feathery detail:
> brief arcs, a pale-green broken wheel,
> a few palms, swarthy, squat, but delicate;
> and perching there in profile, beaks agape,
> the big symbolic birds keep quiet,
> each showing only half his puffed and padded,
> pure-colored or spotted breast.

This is a poem about the similarities in appearance between the Brazil the original explorers saw and the Brazil of today. Unobtrusively yet quite deliberately she places in the middle of this passage of description the "big symbolic birds"—a phrase that allows her to project her own responses to the landscape into this and the stanzas following it. We feel here, as we do in other poems, such as "Quai d'Orleans" (1946) or "Florida" (1946), that a sense of place is for her a kind of existential sense, providing her with the means for seeing the conditions of life as they are in the here and now.

Saying even this much is perhaps to suggest that her poems are erected on some philosophical footing, even though they are not. Each is an individual response to an experience or a situation. She writes about her travels to Cape Cod, Florida, Paris, Nova Scotia, and Brazil, where she has made her home for many years. Some of her lighter poems are triumphs of wit and intelligence, such as "Sleeping on the Ceiling," "The Colder the Air," and "Chemin de Fer," all from 1946. She writes very movingly about her visits to Ezra Pound in the Washington mental hospital in "Visits to St. Elizabeths." Her most successful poems are those that perfectly blend imagery, diction, and music in dazzling brilliance, such as her beautifully controlled and modulated "A Miracle for Breakfast" (1946) and the poem that is undoubtedly her best, "The Fish" (1946). As she describes a fish she has caught, she sees its ugliness, its "frightening gills, / fresh and crisp with blood," its eyes returning her stare. It has five hooks in its mouth and four broken lines that he had snapped, "a five-haired beard of wisdom trailing from his aching jaw." As she looks at this often victorious fish against the ugly backdrop of her rented, rusted, and oil-soaked boat she experiences what must be called an epiphany:

> until everything
> was rainbow, rainbow, rainbow!
> And I let the fish go.

The fish in its ugly splendor becomes a symbol of hope and renewal that emphasizes once again Bishop's modest but enduring faith in the redemptive possibilities of combining observation and wonder.

In her lighter moments she indulges in wit and fantasy, as in "The Man-Moth" (1946), inspired by a newspaper misprint for "mammoth." The Man-Moth is a creature that comes out at night and thinks the moon is "a small hole at the top of the sky" that he can climb through by scaling a skyscraper. But what starts out as whimsy closes with a serious statement:

> (Man, standing below him, has no such illusions.)
> But what the Man-Moth fears most he must do, although
> he fails, of course, and falls back scared but quite unhurt.

Her debts to Marianne Moore are evident in this poem—in the tone of intelligent and detached speculation and in the techniques of the fabulist. In "Roosters" (1946) Moore's influence is apparent in similar ways. Elizabeth Bishop makes her devotion most explicit in a lighthearted tribute, "Invitation to Miss Marianne Moore" (1955), a loose reworking of a Pablo Neruda poem that becomes a typical Bishop poem as well:

> Come with the pointed toe of each black shoe
> trailing a sapphire highlight,
> with a capeful of butterfly wings and bon-mots,
> with heaven knows how many angels all riding
> on the broad black brim of your hat,
> please come flying.

The very warm sympathy for her fellow human beings evident here is one of Bishop's most engaging qualities. It makes it possible for her simultaneously to laugh at and feel genuine affection for all kinds of people, as she does in the case of a poor Cuban-American in "Jerónimo's House," a black maid in "Cootchie," and a Brazilian gardener, "the world's worst gardener since Cain," in her comic portrait of "Manuelzinho" (1965), to whom she says: "You helpless, foolish man / I love you all I can, / I think." The last of these was published in

Questions of Travel (1965), and *The Complete Poems* were published in 1969.

"I suffer the twentieth century," Stanley Kunitz writes in his fine poem, "Night Letter." The strain of quiet terror that runs through the poetry of Stanley Kunitz (b. 1905) is its most distinctive as well as its most unnerving quality. His poems record a series of encounters with experience in a voice of intelligent candor. Coming to maturity in Eliot's generation, Kunitz seems to have absorbed much of the sensibility of his elders and responded with some of the same shock to their sense of the world's violence and cruelty. But his own toughminded response is much less doctrinaire, less eager to furnish answers or to offer the consolations of religion and philosophy. "I face the hard and inescapable phenomenon that we are living and dying at once," he writes. "My commitment is to report the dialogues." "Hermetic Poem" both describes and illustrates these qualities in his work:

> The secret my heart keeps
> Flows into cracked cups.
>
> No saucer can contain
> This overplus of mine:
>
> It glisters to the floor,
> Lashing like lizard fire
>
> And ramps upon the walls
> Crazy with ruby ills.
>
> Who enters by my door
> Is drowned, burned, stung, and starred.

In his first volume, *Intellectual Things* (1930), Kunitz was under the influence of Donne and Herbert; these poems are hard, dry, metaphysical examinations of the mind and the self, such as "Geometry of Moods" and "Lovers Relentlessly." Although they are impeccably crafted works of art, one does not read them primarily for the sake of their style.

Kunitz considers himself, in fact, to be working in counter style to Eliot, and he puts a heavy reliance on the need in poetry for Blake's "minute particulars"—those hard, tangible facts that tie poetry down to experience itself.

Kunitz' output has been small but of consistently high quality. A second volume, *Passport to the War,* appeared in 1944, and in *Selected Poems 1928–1958* he carefully winnowed out his best and rearranged them thematically under such headings as "The Serpent's Word," "The Terrible Threshold," and "Prince of Counterfeits." The second of these groups contains his most startling and terrifying poems. "Open the Gates" is a nightmare vision in which the speaker knocks on the door of his youth with the "great bone of my death"; when it opens, "I stand on the terrible threshold, and I see / The end and the beginning in each other's arms." "Father and Son," his best poem, is a dream-pursuit of a father-figure through a landscape of personal boyhood reminiscences. The quest is an archetypal one: for enlightenment, reassurance, love. But at the water's edge, to which the pursuit has led, the speaker, like Robin in Hawthorne's "My Kinsman, Major Molineux," undergoes a trauma of separation and disillusion:

> Among the turtles and the lilies he turned to me
> The white ignorant hollow of his face.

In the "Prince of Counterfeits" group are some of his most striking lines. One poem ends: "The thing that eats the heart is mostly heart." In another, "The Fitting of the Mask," the self utters this cry of despair as he is presented by a mask-maker with his most suitable mask:

> "O Prince of Counterfeits,
> This is the Self I hunted and knifed in dreams!"

Kunitz' most recent volume, *The Testing-Tree* (1971), once again displays his versatility and range. His translations of the Russian poets, Osip Mandelstam, Anna Akhmatova, and Yevgeny Yevtushenko, are both his and theirs as poems —as good translations must be. "Journal for My Daughter" is a richly sentimental tribute to his daughter's girlhood, and in "Three Floors" and "King of the River" he sounds like his good friend Theodore Roethke.

We can see in many of his poems what Jean Hagstrum has called Kunitz' "imagistic surrealism," a terse, understated, but extremely effective vision of the terror of life welling up from the subconscious. Blake is often present in his imagination, as well as the terrifying ecstasy of Hopkins. But most apparent of all is Kunitz himself, searching persistently for a self-integration that will admit the worlds of the living and the dead; for the "spiral verb that weaves / Through the crystal of our lives, / Of myth and water made / And incoherent blood."

The distinctive quality of the poetry of Randall Jarrell (1914–1965) is its unusual, disconcerting combination of compassion and uncompromising intellectual honesty. But complementing his wit and pathos was his deep learning. Jarrell knew more English poetry than most professors of English, yet he despised academic poetry or anything with the smell of the classroom, and he turned his knowledge—in painting, music, and German, as well as English literature—to use in poems that give new freshness to the idea of a life of the mind.

Jarrell was a poet of childhood, a poet of war, and a poet of women. All three of these subjects gave him the opportunity to write about victims of suffering or of loss, of change or of defeat; a thread of compassion runs through all his work, from the child in "A Story" (1955)—a "new boy lost" in the impersonality of his school—to the child in "The Lost World" (1955) who wonders whether it is really possible for the mad science-fiction scientist to blow up the world. In all his poems Jarrell remains a personal poet, a lyrical voice expressing his own pain and anguish in a world promising to destroy itself through war or technology.

Jarrell had already made a name for himself through his criticism and through his first book of poems, *Blood for a Stranger* (1942), when he fulfilled his early promise in the poems coming out of his Air Force experiences in World War II. *Little Friend, Little Friend* (1945) contains some of the best poetry to come out of the war—poems about individual human beings finding themselves in situations of extreme violence who respond not as heroes but as men full of revulsion at the degradation and impersonality of war. "Second Air Force" and the famous five-line poem, "The Death of the Ball Turret Gunner," make us see soldiers as we might see children caught up in the horrors of war.

Jarrell published some more poems about war in *Losses* (1948), including his own favorite, "Eighth Air Force." But he went on to new subjects, many of them arising from his love of fairy tales, German ones in particular. In this volume and in *The Seven-League Crutches* (1951) are "Hansel and Gretel," "The Märchen," "The Black Swan," and many others that in one way or another use the fairy tale as a means for escaping from life or facing death through metamorphosis. The magical world of the fairy tale allows one to avoid unpleasantness by changing into something else, or by becoming invisible. In "The Märchen," his poem about Grimm's tales, the poet addresses Hansel:

Had you not learned—have we not learned, from tales
Neither of beasts nor kingdoms nor their Lord,
But of our own hearts, the realm of death—
Neither to rule nor die? to change, to change!

The fairy tale is itself a product of the subconscious and thus closely linked to dreams. A great number of Jarrell's poems are about dreams and in them the dream / reality conflict takes many forms. In "The Black Swan" (1955), for example, a child tries to understand her sister's death by dreaming that she has been turned into a swan. In "Losses" (1955) an airman dreams he is dead on the night he dies, and in "The

Dream of Waking" (1945) a wounded soldier dreams he is a child waking before he really awakes to the grim reality of the present. In these and other poems dreams are associated with death as they work to remove the actual pain of loss through the magic of transformation. As Sister Bernetta Quinn has said of these poems, the conversion of one thing into another "is an attempt to go back to that principle of change, natural to the child and common in dreams, in order to live more adequately our mortal measure of years."

His desire for the innocence of childhood led Jarrell to the Wordsworthian reverie of a late poem, "The Lost World" (1965) in which he recalls his strange, half-real, half-make-believe boyhood years in Hollywood. The poem opens with a description of a motion-picture lot where he sees

> a dinosaur
> And pterodactyl, with their immense pale
> Papier-mâché smiles, look over the fence
> Of *The Lost World.*

In this childhood world, reality and fantasy are hopelessly mixed; he visits the foundry where his father works and there watches a man hammering metal suddenly become "a dwarf hammering out the Ring / In the world under the world." This fantasy-reality confusion persists to the poem's end, where he tells his father about the mad scientist's plan to blow up the world:

> "He couldn't really, could he, Pop?" My comforter's
> Eyes light up, and he laughs. "No, that's just play,
> Just make-believe," he says. The sky is gray,
> We sit there, at the end of our good day.

The effect of this poem depends on our reading it with a sense of the speaker's own aesthetic distance from the events he narrates. Jarrell here demonstrates he is a master of the dramatic monologue, but the monologist is both in and out of character; he is the boy grown to manhood recalling his past as well as the poet seeing himself with the irony of his own intelligence.

In *The Woman at the Washington Zoo* (1960) there are few really good poems, with the exception of the translation from Rilke and possibly the title poem. Many of Jarrell's readers have noticed his sympathy with women and his fondness for speaking through and about female characters. He draws attention to this tendency himself when he remarks about "The Woman at the Washington Zoo" that she is "a distant relation of women I have written about before, in 'The End of the Rainbow' and 'Cinderella' and *'Seele im Raum.'* " This woman is a government worker who feels colorless and drab, as "The saris go by me from the embassies." Her longing for change is the longing of the grown-up child for her lost innocence, as out of her repressed sexual desire she cries to the animals:

> You know what I was,
> You see what I am: change me, change me!

The woman in a more recent dramatic monologue, "Next Day" (1965), shops in a supermarket for Cheer and Joy and All and sees her life as a nightmare of change: "As I look at my life, / I am afraid / Only that it will change, as I am changing."

This poem, from *The Lost World* (1965), proves Jarrell to be a master of the dramatic monologue, but still with a lyric quality that shows his affinity with Wordsworth and with Rilke. The Wordsworthian quality is apparent in two ways: in his almost reverential awe of the innocence and wonder of childhood, and in his use of the language of real men. His poems have always had a conversational tone; in this last, best volume he achieves a deliberate flatness of language that is the result of an unseen craftsmanship belying its simple surface. Only a poet with great skill and daring could arrange these seven nonstop lines about a guard in an Italian art museum in a way to make the climax seem inevitable:

When at last he takes a magnifying glass
From the shiny pocket of his uniform
And shows you that in the painting of a woman
Who holds in her arms the death of the world
The something on the man's arm is the woman's
Tear, you and the man and the woman and the guard
Are dumbly one. You say *Bellissima!*

("In Galleries")

Jarrell returns once again to the lost world of his childhood in "Thinking of the Lost World" (1965), a poem in which
all of his thoughts about the essential value of childishness
are celebrated in a spiritual return to a state recoverable only
in the imagination. His longing for childhood is not so much
a regret for having aged as it is an affirmation of the vital
presence of his lost youth. For Jarrell, the secret of life lay
in its "dailiness"; and the facts of change and death were to
be faced unflinchingly with both wit and composure. His
women, his solitaries, his children, his men all confront their
world as the speaker does in "The Orient Express" (1955):

"Behind everything
An unforced joy, an unwilling
Sadness (a willing sadness, a forced joy)
Moves changelessly"

As in the case of Randall Jarrell, the important early influences on Karl Shapiro (b. 1913) were W. H. Auden and
World War II. The satire, the social consciousness, the urban and technological orientation, the supple colloquial
idiom of Auden all found their admirers on this side of the
Atlantic. To his poems about barbershops, drugstores, the university, and other aspects of the American scene Shapiro
brings much of Auden's particularity, wit, and closeness of
observation. The title of his first collection is *Person, Place
and Thing* (1942)—an indication of his sense of the role of
external reality in his world. This volume, published while
he was on army duty in Australia and the South Pacific, was

followed by the Pulitzer-Prize-winning *V-Letter and Other Poems* (1944). The war poems in this second collection are the poems of an individual caught up in a war where he does not matter. In "V-Letter" (those letters written on forms to be microfilmed and sent back to the States), a young soldier writes a love letter back home to his fiancée full of homesickness, sexual longing, and the heroism born of love: "our love is whole whether I live or fail." In "Elegy for a Dead Soldier," the best of Shapiro's war poems, he pays tribute to a young, unformed, in many ways unthinking boy who, although he did not know very clearly what he was fighting for, was nevertheless willing to die for his country. The complex mixture of attitudes toward the war and toward the boy sensitively brings into play the wide range of feelings that citizens of a democracy have about fighting wars to defend their beliefs. Somewhere in the background one hears Wilfred Owen and A. E. Housman, but Shapiro replaces their detached irony and suppressed anger with subjective innocence and simplicity.

Shapiro as a young poet in *Person, Place and Thing* attracted wide attention with his poems about the American scene as he remembered it from afar. In "Drug Store" he mixes satire with a pity for wasted lives in his masterful evocation of the atmosphere of a small-town institution. In "Haircut" he recalls the gaudy setting of the barbershops where getting a haircut seemed to be an irrevocable loss of a part of himself. In "Buick," one of his best-known poems, Shapiro deals with the same kind of sexual attraction to machinery that cummings did in "she being Brand / –new." But while cummings used the automobile ride as a metaphor for the sex act, Shapiro created a piece of social commentary by making explicit the American male's attitude toward his car as a mistress. In "Auto Wreck" Shapiro uses a grimmer aspect of our machine culture in order to look not at sex but at death. The poem moves abruptly from an evocation of the scene of an accident and the arrival of the ambulance, "Its quick soft silver bell beating, beating," to a sudden glimpse of horror, in which a cop "douches ponds of blood / Into the street and gutter." Opening with lots of carefully described details, the poem ends with a philosophical speculation on the precariousness of life and the unpredictability of death:

> Already old, the question Who shall die?
> Becomes unspoken Who is innocent?

As we look through these poems we begin to observe two preoccupations, one having to do with the sense of loss, the other with identity, and in some the two are related. In "The Leg" (1944) he writes about a wartime amputation that causes the patient to feel a profound sense of separation from a part of himself—a sense momentarily put in sharp perspective by a shift to the point of view of the leg itself, "wondering where [the soldier] is." In "A Cut Flower" (1942) he also adopts the point of view of an inanimate object as he describes the fading and dying of a cut flower as it might itself experience them:

> Yesterday I was well, and then the gleam,
> The thing sharper than frost cut me in half.

This strong desire to retain the whole of one's identity through a kind of physical integrity occurs also in "Haircut" (1942), in which the shorn boy bleats like a lamb and the act seems related to the rite of circumcision: "Does the barber want blood in a dish?" And in that group of autobiographical lyrics called "Recapitulations" published in *Trial of a Poet* (1947), he begins the account of his Jewish boyhood by referring to his circumcision.

That title and those of his next two collections, *Poems of a Jew* (1958) and *The Bourgeois Poet* (1964), show even more plainly his concern with identity. The first of these is a collection of some new and some old poems in which he defiantly and somewhat petulantly seems to be asserting the one aspect of himself of which he can be absolutely certain. Many of the poems are better than the title would suggest, however, and mitigate somewhat this blatant cry for attention.

By 1950 Shapiro had pretty well severed his connections

from the Eliot-Pound literary establishment, and in his polem-
imical essays in *Beyond Criticism* (1953) he threw out all his
past allegiances with the modernist movement. For inspiration he went back to Whitman and perhaps Carl Sandburg
as models of anti-intellectual, anti-"Culture Poetry," creating
for himself a persona full of rebelliousness, deliberate vulgarity, and a freedom from rhyme or rhythm in a collection of
prose poems called *The Bourgeois Poet*. There are ninety-six
of these, divided into three sections: the first discursive, the
second autobiographical, the third epigrammatic. In form and
technique they owe something to Baudelaire, Max Jacob, St.
John Perse, and René Char, as well as to Whitman and Williams. In their talkiness and often in their tone of invective they
resemble the *Cantos* of the Pound whom Shapiro at other times
has specifically repudiated. Like Berryman's *Dream Songs*
(1964), these poems are efforts to find a new language, but in
Shapiro's case the persona of the bourgeois poet is itself such
a depressing oxymoron that it is not sustained by, nor does
it sustain, that language. His hostility to convention seems to
become a *raison d'être* rather than a means to arrive at some
particular end; nevertheless, there are some good poems and
some good passages, full of satire, sexuality, and outspoken-
ness on a wide range of topics. Here is a passage from Number
23, "From the Top Floor of the Tulsa Hotel I Gaze at the
Night Beauty of the Cracking-Plant":

> From the top floor of the Tulsa hotel I gaze at the night
> beauty of the cracking-plant. Candlelit city of small gas
> flames by the thousands, what a lovely anachronism
> dancing below like an adolescent's dream of the 1880s,
> the holy gas redeemed from Baudelaire's mustachioed
> curses. Elsewhere are the white lights of the age, but
> here, like a millionaire who frowns on electricity, the
> opulence of flame. Descending on Rome from the air at
> night, a similar beauty: the weak Italian bulbs like
> faulty rheostats yellowly outline the baroque curves of
> the Tiber, the semicircles of the monstrous Vatican,
> endless broken parabolas.

These are interesting, often successful experiments that suggest that Shapiro is still a poet of vitality and promise.

No one reading the early verse of John Berryman (1914–1972) could have predicted the act of self-liberation that from the time of *Homage to Mistress Bradstreet* (1956) gave him a voice, or, rather, a congeries of voices, with which to speak about himself and about his world. In the forties Berryman was the clever and rather brittle young man of the quarterlies: writing his poems of irony and paradox, bowing to Tate here, Auden there, molding his considerable talents in the language of his masters. By the time of his death, he had moved far beyond this role to become one of the most powerful and original poets of our time.

Berryman always gave the impression of a heightened consciousness, of a man of painful intellectual awareness with an undercurrent of sensuality and a desire for freedom. Reading the early poems we sense his desire to know other people and other people's minds—to enter somehow into the sensibility of others in order to escape the overwhelming demands of the self. In a series of "Nervous Songs," published in *The Dispossessed* (1948), Berryman divides himself by looking at a series of characters both objectively and subjectively in such poems as "Young Woman's Song," "The Song of the Young Hawaiian," and "The Song of the Bridegroom." The young woman, looking at her body in the bath, muses:

> What I am looking for (*I am*) may be
> Happening in the gaps of what I know.
> The full moon does go with you as you go.
> Where am I going? I am not afraid.
> Only I would be lifted lost in the flood.

The young Hawaiian lusts after girls, the bridegroom both trembles at and yearns for the consummation of his marriage. In many of these poems there is, in addition to the projection of the poet into the mind and feelings of another person, an element of sexual curiosity that recurs in Berryman's later work.

In the poems printed in *The Dispossessed* one finds Metaphysical conceits, compressions of syntax, allusion, and other devices fashionable during the forties. But Berryman in his twenties was not a mere imitator. The title poem is a nightmarish Dantesque vision of disaster in a contemporary world that lacks feeling and a sense of social responsibility. The images of irrationality and of emotional coldness—an icy dove, a songless child, the "spidery business of love"—are arranged in frightening patterns in order to suggest the absence of individuality and responsibility in the atomic age. At the poem's close, however, Berryman ironically reduces this vision of cosmic disaster to the level of cheap melodrama:

> no soul of us all was near was near,—
> an evil sky (where the umbrella bloomed)
> twirled its mustaches, hissed, the ingenue fumed,
>
> poor virgin, and no hero rides. The race
> is done.

This is the horror of war as seen by Shapiro and Jarrell by a writer who did not fight it. In it, too, is the barely contained terror of Stanley Kunitz. Another poem in that volume, "Boston Common: A Meditation upon the Hero," uses the statue of the Civil War hero Robert Gould Shaw as the basis for meditation. In his reflections on the vicissitudes of heroism and its rewards in relation to the present, Berryman leads us backward to Moody's "Ode in Time of Hesitation" (1900) and, curiously, forward to Robert Lowell's "For the Union Dead" (1964).

But still straining to be let out was a voice that was neither Auden's nor Kunitz' nor Tate's, but his own. In his ambitious long poem, *Homage to Mistress Bradstreet* (1956), Berryman at last was able to become a ventriloquist by projecting his own attitudes and language backward into seventeenth-century America and breathing new life into the

"Tenth Muse." That he was able to take such an unpromising subject and make a major poem out of it is a result as much of his desire to find a voice as it is to recover the past. The poem consists of fifty-seven eight-line stanzas, each similarly constructed of lines of varying length and a flexible rhyme scheme. For Berryman, Anne Bradstreet was not so much the quaint Puritan poetess as she was an uprooted English girl of sixteen, transported with Simon, her new husband, to a strange and hostile wilderness where she was to bear nine children and write poetry. She became for him a seventeenth-century version of the alienated poet who was spiritually and sexually at odds with her environment. Berryman reached out to her and identified with her:

> Outside the New World winters in grand dark
> white air lashing high thro' the virgin stands
> foxes down foxholes sigh,
> surely the English heart quails, stunned.
> I doubt if Simon than this blast, that sea,
> spares from his rigour for your poetry
> more. We are on each other's hands
> who care. Both of our worlds unhanded us

The language of the poem is a language of artifice, to use Kunitz' phrase, heavily influenced by Hopkins and, in some places, by Pound's translations of Anglo-Saxon verse:

> Strange ships across us, after a fortnight's winds
> unfavouring, frightened us;
> bone-sad cold, sleet, scurvy

Berryman's attempts to merge with Anne Bradstreet's identity actually become sexual, and he even tries to make love to her across the years. His own sexual curiosity, which is evident in the earlier poems, reappears here in some of the weaker sections where he describes the physical sensations of giving birth to a child. The poem is a major achievement, both in its sensitive evocation of a rare plant growing in alien soil and in the liberation of its creator from the restraints of linguistic convention.

Like Karl Shapiro, Berryman seems to have felt the necessity to shape for himself a language and form that implicitly deny his own earlier work and the work of his contemporaries. But while Shapiro made a clean break with his past, Berryman grew; he allowed Hopkins, Auden, and Pound to shape him but found a new maturity, flexibility, and confidence that are widely evident in his exciting major work, the *Dream Songs*.

The first group of these, appearing in *77 Dream Songs* (1964), were described in a note as sections of a poem in progress. The songs, all written in three six-line stanzas, are spoken—or sung—by a character named Henry, "a white American in early middle age sometimes in blackface," who is as much an outsider as Anne Bradstreet and has a much greater colloquial range. Here is a fascinating and delightful use of a persona through whom Berryman is able to project an astonishing variety of moods, tones, and attitudes. Henry speaks in blackface dialect, mingling ungrammatical constructions with ironic asides and sophisticated throwaway lines; the jauntiness of tone serves sometimes for comic effect, sometimes to mask the sadness underneath. In his use of this traditional American minstrel-show clown, Berryman has found the native equivalent of the classic tragic harlequin. The opening poem sets the tone for much of what follows:

> What he has now to say is a long
> wonder the world can bear & be.

A typical stanza is this one:

> God bless Henry. He lived like a rat,
> with a thatch of hair on his head
> in the beginning.
> Henry was not a coward. Much.
> He never deserted anything; instead
> he stuck, when things like pity were thinning.

The subjects range from sexual desire to autobiography —some having to do with his father's suicide, an obsession that he gradually works through and out—and contemporary literature. He makes gossipy references to Eliot (Old Possum), and to Hemingway and Faulkner ("the shooter, and the bourbon man"). There is an elegiac group on Frost and "A Strut for Roethke." The general tone, in spite of the poems about death and alienation, is lighthearted. With the publication of the rest of the series in *His Toy, His Dream, His Rest* (1968) we can see the astonishing range and energy that went into eleven years of work. In this volume are 308 new songs (beginning with Number 78), which make up Books IV, V, VI, and VII of the completed poem. The poem, he says, in an effort to clarify his position, is "essentially about an imaginary character (not the poet, not me) named Henry . . . who has suffered an irreversible loss and talks about himself sometimes in the first person sometimes in the third, sometimes even in the second; he has a friend, never named, who addresses him as Mr. Bones and variants thereof."

With the publication of *His Toy, His Dream, His Rest* Berryman seemed to be riding high on a crest of energy and achievement. His *Short Poems* and *Berryman's Sonnets* were published the year before, and in 1970 an entertaining collection of pieces appeared, which seem to have been written by the left hand, so casual and effortless are they. *Love and Fame* is about those two things, chronicling Berryman's rise to fame by means of his memories of past love affairs. The poems are sprinkled with famous names and places, and follow his career through boarding school, Columbia, Cambridge, and beyond, peopled with nymphets, sweethearts, faculty wives, mistresses, and lost opportunities. What make the poems more than a celebration of lust are the evocations of the prewar literary world, through Berryman's early contacts with the great, his reading, and his literary enthusiasms. Berryman speaks here in his own voice, and it is a voice warm with reminiscences of other times and other girls.

In 1972, shortly after his death, the posthumous volume *Delusions, Etc.* was published. These are difficult, introverted, meditative poems, many of which echo his earlier style. In retrospect they seem to forecast his suicide, with their preoccupation with death and madness. But they do not diminish the achievement of a man who had at the time of his death become a major poet.

Another poet formed by the forties is Howard Nemerov (b. 1920), whose dry wit and irony rather carefully echo Auden and whose attitudes toward literature and art are those of the liberal academic starting out when *Partisan Review* was becoming a bona fide literary magazine and the New Criticism held excesses of the imagination in check. This is not to say that Nemerov is an imitator or that he writes according to some formula. His nature poetry, such as "A Spell Before Winter" (1962), has a tone strongly reminiscent of Robert Frost, as do many of his "talk poems," which follow the relaxed rhythms of everyday speech. Nemerov's stance is informality and offhandedness, itself an essential quality of the modern poem. There are no full-dress performances; even his Harvard Phi Beta Kappa poem, carefully built though it is, seems less a public address than a private fantasy. Reading through the poems in *The Image and the Law* (1947), *The Salt Garden* (1955), *The Next Room of the Dream* (1962), and *The Blue Swallows* (1967), one has the impression of a powerful intelligence at work and at play.

Nemerov gives us the wry thought, the startling image, and more than one glimpse into the abyss. In "The Town Dump" (1958) he sees the dump as a "city / Which seconds ours," where "Being most Becomingly ends up / Becoming some more." The objects hurled on the trash heap—lobster claws, oyster, crab, and mussel shells—have been returned to nature in an unnatural way. But although these objects lie there in heaps, "savage as money hurled / Away at the gate of hell," he finds it too easy to make of this a paradigm of our own civilization, since in the middle of this ugliness are not only hidden treasures, such as pearl necklaces and Hepplewhite chairs, but also the strange beauty of the scavenging birds, "their wings / Shining with light, their flight enviably

free, / Their music marvelous, though sad, and strange."
These grotesquely beautiful aspects of nature perversely keep
the spectator from indulging in sentimental hand-wringing
and viewing-with-alarm at the excesses of modern civilization.

In "The Goose Fish" (1955), nature is again grotesque,
enigmatically and even obscenely so. Two lovers on a beach,
"emparadised" by their solitary moment of sexual passion, find
their latent feelings of guilt aroused by the presence of a dead
goose fish, whose "wide and moony grin" intrudes upon their
private Eden. What "that rigid optimist" meant to them is
not revealed, but its image is as disturbing and chilling to
the reader as it is to the lovers. Nemerov leads us even more
abruptly to the edge of the abyss in "Lobsters" (1967), which
starts out innocently enough with a shopping trip to the "Super
Duper," where he watches the "beauty of strangeness" of the
creatures in the tanks: "Philosophers and at the same time
victims / Herded together in the marketplace." As he looks
at them he puts himself in their place and ends with a line
that narrowly—but perhaps not altogether willingly—avoids a
facile cynicism:

> a mind sinks down
> To the blind abyss in a swirl of sand, goes cold
> And archaic in a carapace of horn,
> Thinking: There's something underneath the world. . . .
>
> The flame beneath the pot that boils the water.

Nemerov assembles his poems with a considerable amount
of skill and careful attention to structure and diction. "The
Rope's End" (1967), written in iambic trimeter quatrains,
winds its way down the center of the page, making as it goes
a witty analogy between the unraveling of the rope and "crazy
man's" tendency to "leave / Nothing continuous / Since
Adam's fall / Unraveled all." The echo of McGuffey's readers
in these lines is typical of Nemerov's fondness for using familiar phrases and even clichés in unusual or fresh ways. He
once remarked that there are very few original, striking, or

profound thoughts, that the poet just puts his platitudes in the right places. Such phrases as "the peace that passeth understanding," "separate but equal," "pictures any child can understand," and "sweat it out" are used in this way. In "Grace to Be Said at the Supermarket" (1967) the echo of a well-known ungrammatical cigarette commercial is effective:

> That we may look unflinchingly on death
> As the greatest good, like a philosopher should.

Many of Nemerov's reflective poems, such as "The Pond" (1955) and "Lives of Gulls and Children" (1955), make use of natural objects, and he is particularly fond of using trees, as in "Trees" (1955), "Learning by Doing" (1967), "An Old Colonial Imperialist" (1967), and "Burning the Leaves" (1962). But Nemerov is by no means limited to philosophical and nature poems; actually he seems more at home with subjects relating to literature or to the life of the artist. Such poems as "The Map-Maker on His Art," "To Lu Chi" (1958), the sonnet sequence "Runes" (1960), and "The Painter Dreaming in the Scholar's House" explore the relationship between art and life or art and ideas. And various aspects of the literary scene become targets of his satire. One of the best of many parodies of Eliot's *The Waste Land* is Nemerov's "On the Threshold of His Greatness, the Poet Comes Down with a Sore Throat" (1962), complete with footnotes, including one identifying the Waldorf-Astoria as "An hotel in New York City." In "A Chromium-Plated Hat: Inlaid With Scenes from Siegfried" (1947) he mocks the pallid style of *The New York Times Book Review*. He calls into question his own role as poet in "On the Platform" (1967), his poem about reading his poems at public readings, and in "A Full Professor" (1967), in which the subject of the poem, who started his career with "some love of letters," is now "a dangerous committeeman" who "publishes and perishes at once." This poem, and one addressed "To the Governor & Legislature of Massachusetts" (1967) about the loyalty oath required of teachers in that state, shade over into general social commentary. A group of poems in *The Blue Swallows,* including these two, are collected under the heading "The Great Society." The titles "Grace to be Said Before Committee Meetings," "The Great Society, Mark X," "A Negro Cemetery Next to a White One," and "Santa Claus," give one an idea of the range of their subjects. His reactions to them are incisive, though somewhat predictable, as in "Boom!" a satirical poem about the apparent religious revival in the fifties, in which the chief delight is in the language and wordplay.

In a note to Robert D. Harvey in 1962, Nemerov wrote, "Poetry is an art of combination, or discovering the secret valences which the most widely differing things have for one another. In the darkness of this search, patience and good humor are useful qualities. Also: The serious and the funny are one." The cool, rather distant, but still somehow committed poems he writes reflect this attitude toward life and art.

The poetry of Richard Wilbur (b. 1921), also, is the poetry of an intelligent and gifted man. More often than not, when one thinks of the poetry of the fifties one thinks of Wilbur as a typical poet of those years. Witty, versatile, good-humored, intelligent, and technically dazzling, Wilbur's poems cover a wide variety of subjects, from aesthetics to potatoes, celebrating with a warm and sensuous delight the things of this world. Wilbur has changed or developed very little in his eight collections of verse from *The Beautiful Changes* (1947) to *Digging for China* (1970). What we admire in all his poems are his apparently effortless shapings of everyday reality into lyrical expressions of beauty and candor.

In "Cicadas" (1947)—later changed to "Cigales"—he begins a description of the cry of the insects and moves to reflections both moral and aesthetic on the meaning of their "thin uncomprehended song." As a creature living and singing somewhat apart from the world, "heedless of ants," the cicada is a source of wonder—even more so, when we learn in the last stanza that "cicadas cannot hear." The aesthetic implications of this observation are unstated and complex.

One of Wilbur's most carefully and successfully inte-

grated poems is "Lightness" (1947). The technique alone is
worth careful study, since he breaks up his rhymed pairs by
rhyming them in lines alternating between four and five
beats. A long sentence describing the slow, delicate fall of a
bird's nest from the top of an elm tree combines rhythm,
diction, and sound effects in a dazzling display of virtuosity.
The lightness of the nest and the airiness of its fall are emphasized by the repetition of short *i* sounds, both in the line
endings and internally. But the nest is used also in a simile
comparing it to the attitude of his Aunt Virginia, slowly
dying and rejecting the offered sympathy of her friends. Those
looking at her sitting in her garden, "in her gay shroud,"
are led to think of "legerity" and "of the strange intactness
of the gladly dying." Wilbur has a talent for such effectively
worded phrases. In "The Death of a Toad" (1948) he describes the toad amputated by a power mower: "with a hobbling hop has got / To the garden verge." In "First Snow in
Alsace" (1947) he talks about the snowfall that "Fills the
eyes / Of soldiers dead a little while." And in "Bell Speech"
(1947) the rhythm underscores the language in his address to
the bell in London's St. Paul's Cathedral:

> Great Paul, great pail of sound, still dip and draw
> Dark speech from the deep and quiet steeple well.

These poems are celebrations, each a self-contained experience for the poet as well as the reader, who feels himself
in the presence not of a philosopher or a thinker, but of a
maker and sayer who discovers his humanity in the gift of
language. He likes the challenge of rhyme and meter: the
terza rima of "First Snow in Alsace," the varying line lengths
coupled with a rhyme scheme in such poems as "Castles and
Distances" (1948), "The Beautiful Changes" (1947), and "A
Black November Turkey" (1956). He likes the wordplay of
the title of "A Simile for Her Smile" (1948) and in the stanza
of "Lamarck Elaborated" (1956), in which he talks about the
physical objects in the world that "Attired in sense the tact-
less finger-bone / And set the taste-buds and inspired the

nose." We can admire the language of such vivid nature description as "Years-End" (1948) or the beginning of "Winter Spring" (1947) even while we deplore the false Shakespearean line in that poem: "Now all this proud royaume / Is Veniced." Still another example of his versatility is "Junk" (1956), written in an Anglo-Saxon form imitated from Waldere:

> An axe angles
> > from my neighbor's ashcan;
> It is hell's handiwork,
> > the wood not hickory,
> The flow of the grain
> > not faithfully followed.

Wilbur has also demonstrated his ability as a translator in his brilliant translations from Molière: *The Misanthrope* (1955) and *Tartuffe* (1963), and in lyrics by Guillén, Nerval, and Quasimodo. He can be witty, as he is in "Pangloss's Song," written for the libretto of Lillian Hellman's and Leonard Bernstein's musical version of *Candide* (1957). But some of his best poems go beyond the everyday or the clever. One such poem is "Altitudes" (1956), a meditation on the more than geographical distance separating the dome of St. Peter's basilica in Rome from the cupola of Emily Dickinson's house in Amherst, Massachusetts. Another is "Marginalia" (1956), a distillation of his reading in Poe, which uses Poe's own dream imagery to describe the unquiet workings of the imagination. As Frederic E. Faverty has observed of him in an essay called "Well-Open Eyes," Richard Wilbur is essentially a poet of affirmation. He looks at the world about him, often with the eyes of a Dutch genre painter, and makes us aware, in a phrase he borrows from Thomas Traherne and turns to his own use, that "A World without Objects is a Sensible Emptiness."

Like Wallace Stevens and Richard Wilbur, Richard Eberhart (b. 1904) is concerned with celebrating the things of this world: "my flesh is / Poetry's environment" ("The Place," 1964). The direct rendition of experience, simultaneously perceived and recorded, is the effect he seeks, in a poetry that, like Wordsworth's, frequently reaches peaks of intensity that belie the apparently bland and commonplace milieu in which they occur. Eberhart is a pleasant poet, a nice guy, who reacts with healthy good humor to the incongruities of the world and with solemnity to intimations of its end. He notices such incongruity in the sight of a ragpicker on the Princeton campus, but observes that he still shares the human condition in the midst of "towers, books, professors, ideas." "Santa Claus in Oaxaca" (1967) begins, "Nothing seemed so incongruous." But this opening is deceptively simple, as many of his openings are, and it works into a poem with many colorful details of an unusual south-of-the-border Christmas celebration.

Eberhart's career began in 1930 with a book-length autobiographical poem, *A Bravery of Earth*, which contains some good lyrical passages, such as the section, "This fevers me, this sun on green," but much of it is weak and confused. In *Reading the Spirit* (1937) his lyrical gifts are much more evident, but in the same volume he was working the metaphysical vein in such poems as "When Golden Flies Upon My Carcass Come." His poems are full of a sensitivity to death, as in "The Cancer Cells," both as a sobering reminder of the transiency of life and as a stimulus to the imagination. One of the best of these is "The Groundhog," in which he recounts a series of visits to the animal's corpse, each time in a more advanced state of decay. After three summers, when only the whitening bones are left, he is led to reflect on the transiency of empires, of Alexander, of Montaigne, and "Of Saint Theresa in her wild lament." And in "On a Squirrel Crossing the Road in Autumn, in New England," after noting the squirrel's inability to reason, he compares the animal's state with that of man, who in turn knows nothing of God. The analogy is suddenly thrown into shocking and illuminating reverse by the last line: ". . . Just missed him!"

Like Emily Dickinson, Eberhart treasures the odd phrase, the whimsical image that captures the fleeting perception. In one poem, "Vision" (1964), he attempts a similar pithy stanza as well as borrowing the diction from "A Route of Evanescence," one of Dickinson's best-known poems:

> Two hummingbirds as evanescent as
> Themselves
> Startled me at my study window

At other times he echoes the elegance of Stevens, as in "The Place" (1964), his poem about the locale of poetry:

> Alas! One thought of a gold
> Hullabaloo, a place of glass

but some of these attempts to define the poet's role, such as "The Supreme Authority of the Imagination" (1960), promise more than they deliver.

On the whole, we can be grateful for the poetry of Richard Eberhart, a man working steadily and patiently to record those moments of inward vision and emotion that come spontaneously and unsought in a voice of humility capable of rising to a high pitch of religious feeling:

> O Christ of Easter, impossible Man, Lord, and God
> I, cold geographer, map Your clear estate
> As one sentient, yet a prisoner, clashing Thy
> Cymbal in the gliding sound of my dying

"Style is the perfection of a point of view," he writes in *The Quarry* (1964), and the style of his own poems confirms his view that style should "amplify and refine man's poise, / Be an instrument as lucid as the best of his knowing." In 1972 he published a new collection, *Fields of Grace*.

One poet who has persistently gone his own way against all prevailing tendencies is J. V. Cunningham (b. 1911). As a scholar and teacher whose interests are in Latin and the English Renaissance, Cunningham has practiced the art of poetry with a firm sense of its origins in the mind. Discounting for his own purposes poetry based on visual experience and poetry based on fictional experience, Cunningham takes poetry to be "a way of speaking, a special way of speaking." Writing about his work in Howard Nemerov's *Poets on Poetry* (1966), Cunningham says, "a good poem is the definitive statement in meter of something worth saying." Definiteness leads to brevity, he adds, and the poet who holds this view becomes an epigrammatist.

Cunningham is an epigrammatist, certainly the most accomplished one writing in English today, yet this description of his work is hardly adequate. He writes in the mode of the seventeenth-century epigrammatists, particularly Ben Jonson, to whom he is closest in spirit and style. But the effect of his brief poems is cumulative, and the reader has great difficulty reading them in isolation. In *The Helmsman* (1942), *The Judge is Fury* (1947), and *Doctor Drink* (1950) one loses the interplay of irony and ambiguity between the poems if he reads them separately and takes them at face value. For this reason these groups of poems may best be considered as sequences, a term Cunningham himself uses when describing the need to provide some context for the short poem. For the idea of the sequence he finds an ancient precedent in Propertius' *Cynthia,* as well as in Sidney's *Astrophel and Stella* and Tennyson's *In Memoriam* and *Maud.* He goes furthest in this direction in *To What Strangers? What Welcome?* (1964), which actually follows a simple story line: a traveler drives west, falls in love, and comes back home to the East.

From the earlier collections, republished in one volume in 1960 as *The Exclusions of a Rhyme: Poems and Epigrams,* it is possible to pick out many excellent individual poems. "Choice" is one of his best; other good ones are "To the Reader," "Agnosco Veteris Vestigia Flammae," "Passion," and "Epigram 8" from *The Judge is Fury.* When reading Cunningham's verse one is constantly aware of a relentless irony and wit holding in check a fierce passion. The one contemporary whose work resembles his in tone is Stanley Kunitz, even though he uses none of Kunitz' surrealism or imagery of horror. Cunningham is not writing in the Romantic tradition; he is a classicist subjecting the vagaries of feeling to the rigorous scrutiny and subtle play of the mind. His ironies and ambiguities are couched not in the conceits of John Donne and George Herbert but in the plain style of Fulke Greville and Ben Jonson—a language of statement fully charged with the realities of hate, love, and anger.

CHAPTER TWELVE

Some Contemporaries

Isabella Gardner, Theodore Weiss, Louis Simpson, Jean Garrigue, W. D. Snodgrass, Anne Sexton, Kenneth Koch, John Hollander, Alan Dugan, Gregory Corso, Sylvia Plath, W. S. Merwin, James Wright, James Dickey, Anthony Hecht, John Ashbery, Allen Ginsberg, Gary Snyder, Charles Olson, Robert Creeley, Robert Duncan, Denise Levertov, Imamu Amiri Baraka

The number of good poets writing today is almost overwhelming, with new writers and new volumes appearing weekly. In addition, the last decade has institutionalized a new phenomenon, the anthology of new poets, directed at the growing market of consumers of culture as well as colleges and universities offering courses in contemporary poetry. One of the most significant and influential of these was Donald M. Allen's *The New American Poetry 1945–1960* (1960), which he put together as a kind of manifesto, asserting the existence of a number of poets who were mainly outside the academy. The three groups of relatively unknown poets he chose to represent included the San Francisco Beats, those associated with Charles Olson and Black Mountain College, and the New York group, including John Ashbery, Kenneth Koch, and the late Frank O'Hara. Another valuable collection is Donald Hall's, Robert Pack's, and Louis Simpson's *New Poets of England and America* (1957), with a second selection by Hall and Pack in 1962. These include many of the younger traditional poets of the fifties and sixties. The battle between these two groups ("the Palefaces and the Redskins") has since been waged on other fronts, particularly in such journals as *Evergreen Review,*

Yūgen, Trobar, Black Mountain Review, and *Big Table,* which opened their hospitable pages to many poets at first rejected by *Poetry, Partisan Review, Kenyon Review,* and other established journals.

One of the most interesting things about the poetry of the sixties is the movement away from the modernism of the twenties, thirties, and forties into a postmodernist, or contemporary, phase. The dominant influences on this generation are not Eliot, Yeats, and Donne, but the later Pound and Williams, as well as Blake, Hopkins, and Whitman. Most observers of the contemporary scene agree that there are two, or possibly three, groups into which it is possible to fit the poets writing today, corresponding roughly to the Allen and Hall anthologies. These are known variously as the Academics and the Beats, the Palefaces and the Redskins, the Establishment and the Underground, or the Conservatives and the Liberals. Such obviously crude labels can only suggest rather than define the kinds of distinctions that the poets themselves and their readers tend to make. But they do call attention to the fact that in poetry, as in the other arts, there is an official culture, an unofficial one, and an interaction between them: one looking toward the past, the other passionately denying it; one emphasizing form and ideas, the other, freedom of form and feelings.

Before looking at greater length at some of the new poets, we might look briefly at a sampling of well-established poets who command our attention. The work of Isabella Gardner, Theodore Weiss, Louis Simpson, and Jean Garrigue shows us that there is no shortage of highly accomplished craftsmen with considerable lyric gifts. Gardner's three books, *Birthdays from the Ocean* (1955), *The Looking Glass* (1961), and *West of Childhood* (1965), all shimmer with a surface brilliance of language and rhythm while revealing a strong lyric intensity. Like Denise Levertov, she is a believer in what Martin Buber has called the simple magic of life, and she celebrates its wonder in impassioned but skillfully controlled rhetoric.

Theodore Weiss (b. 1916) has been with us long enough to have established a firm reputation as a literalist of the imagination whose subtle intellect and rigorous formal discipline have given a classical grace and simplicity to the "real toads" of his everyday experiences.

Louis Simpson (b. 1923) is even more closely attached to his experience, which becomes specifically American in his poetry of this time and this place. Examining the plight of modern man through the particulars of the American scene, Simpson early developed a natural and conversational style that has become increasingly loose and open, with imagery more and more "subjective" as he has responded to the influence of Robert Kelly (b. 1935) and Robert Bly (b. 1926). As James Dickey has said of him, Simpson's tone of desperate sadness is close to Jarrell's, and he is "self-consciously more American than most of our other writers."

Jean Garrigue (1914–1972), too, forged the raw materials of her American experience into poetry that is private rather than public. Like Muriel Rukeyser (b. 1913), Garrigue drew her subjects from the social problems of the thirties and forties, but made them into personal statements. Both *The Ego and the Centaur* (1947) and *The Monument Rose* (1953) put lyricism and technical brilliance to the service of moving poems demonstrating her commitment to individual feelings in a hostile environment.

Several other poets defy categories, although two of them seem to have become permanently labeled as "confessional poets." W. D. Snodgrass (b. 1926) left nothing unsaid in his painful and moving chronicle of the disintegration of his marriage and the emotional trials of his divorce, which he told in *Heart's Needle* (1959). The complete honesty with which he examined these feelings stimulated Robert Lowell and others to make similar explorations. Snodgrass has continued in the self-revelatory mode in *After Experience* (1968), which also contains some excellent translations of Rilke. Anne Sexton (b. 1928) has followed Snodgrass; her particular hell has been her mental illness and her struggle to retain a grip on life both in and out of institutions. *To Bedlam and Part Way Back* (1960), *All My Pretty Ones* (1962), and *Live or Die* (1966) all subject the reader to uniquely horrifying revelations of these very personal experiences, seen with no compromise or attempts at self-deception. Her flirtations with death in the last volume recall her friend Sylvia Plath, to whom one of the poems is addressed. *Love Poems* (1969) are very frank, self-revelatory poems, passionate and sexually explicit.

Some of the poets in their forties who are interesting are Kenneth Koch (b. 1925), John Hollander (b. 1929), Alan Dugan (b. 1923), and Gregory Corso (1930). As different as these writers are from each other in many ways, they are related in their playfulness, their lack of reverence, and their high spirits: Koch's attacks on the literary establishment and his parodies of Williams and Frost; Hollander's elaborate conceits and bawdy-intellectual love poems; Dugan's loving, witty attention to the trivia and incongruities of everyday life; and Corso's outrageous attacks on our sense of propriety.

All these poets taken together begin to suggest the variety, inventiveness, and energy of American poetry today, and this impression is reinforced by thirteen poets whom I have chosen as examples of the continuing tradition of heterogeneity in American poetry: Sylvia Plath, W. S. Merwin, James Wright, James Dickey, Anthony Hecht, John Ashbery, Allen Ginsberg, Gary Snyder, Charles Olson, Robert Creeley, Robert Duncan, Denise Levertov, and Imamu Amiri Baraka.

The poems of Sylvia Plath (1932–1963) are even more painfully personal than those of Anne Sexton or Robert Lowell, going beyond the poetry of confession to become, in *Ariel* (1965), the poetry of hysteria. An intense, shy, and brilliant woman, Sylvia Plath suffered a breakdown when she was nineteen and was plagued thereafter with periods of extreme mental depression, particularly after the birth of her second child in 1962. Her first volume of poems was *The Colossus* (1960), but she came to consider most of these as preparation for her later work. One possible exception is "The Stones," a poem recording her experiences in a mental hospital. After reading Theodore Roethke and some African folktales, she was led into a primitivism of imagery and style in this poem that tended to free her work of some of its academic qualities.

She developed rapidly after *The Colossus,* as we can see in the poems recently collected in *Crossing the Water* (1971). Here she has become a mature poet, playful and serious by turns, but with a new sureness of tone. The Roethke influence continues to play a part in these poems, for example in the language and imagery of "Wuthering Heights" and "Heavy Women."

However, they contain little to prepare us for the terrifying—even sickening—poems she wrote with such feverish energy during the last year of her life. A selection of these, published posthumously in *Ariel,* secured her reputation as a disturbing poet of genius. *Winter Trees* (1972), which her husband, Ted Hughes, says in the preface, "are all out of the batch from which *Ariel* poems were more or less arbitrarily chosen," reinforces that impression. It is difficult to describe the quality of these poems, full of grotesque images of disease and death. "Fever 103°" combines images of radiation sickness with the bloated sensations of fever dreams in a way that links personal hysteria to public madness. Her references to Dachau, Hiroshima, and Belsen in the very personal context of madness illustrate her own stated belief that personal experience should be generally relevant. But this is no random outpouring of horror. It is a poetry of controlled hysteria—nightmare in retrospect dredged up à la Rimbaud and Poe and manipulated with the certainty and purposiveness of the artist.

In "Ariel," Sylvia Plath embodies the force that drives her on furiously and compulsively to a violent, apparently inevitable goal:

> And I
> Am the arrow,
>
> The dew that flies
> Suicidal, at one with the drive
> Into the red
>
> Eye, the cauldron of morning.

Not all of the poems are so directly about sickness and death. Some are about her children, such as "Morning Song" (1965), describing the birth of her son:

> Love set you going like a fat gold watch.
> The midwife slapped your footsoles, and your bald cry
> Took its place among the elements.

Several poems in one sequence are about her beekeeping and honey-making. But even in these domestic poems one senses a rising tension leading toward a headlong flight into the abyss. It is a dangerous and exhilarating flirtation with madness and death witnessed in poems that she was writing near the end of her life at the rate of two and three a day. As Robert Lowell wrote of them, they are not celebrations of a debauched existence; "they tell that life, even when disciplined, is simply not worth it."

In one of her most personally revealing poems, "Lady Lazarus" (1963), the speaker sees her return to life from a suicide attempt as a dramatic performance before a gaping crowd, and comments:

> Dying
>
> Is an art, like everything else.
> I do it exceptionally well.

Sylvia Plath put an end to both her life and her art on February 11, 1963.

One of the most interesting things about the poetry of W. S. Merwin (b. 1927) is the transformation taking place as he moves away from the technical brilliance and virtuosity of a prolific early career to a new, almost hesitant groping for forms with which to come to closer grips with his material. In his early volumes, published in startlingly rapid succession, *A Mask for Janus* (1952), *The Dancing Bears* (1954), and *Green with Beasts* (1956), Merwin was dazzling in his command of meter and language, but more than one critic felt a lack of involvement with his material. There was actually a strange pull between the highly polished stanzas of his poems and their mythical and archetypal subjects that were far removed from the contemporary world. In *A Mask for Janus* are poems about Sisyphus, Medusa, and Ulysses, and others set in the ancient and medieval worlds. These continue Eliot's search for unifying myths and archetypes, but in the course of this search Merwin also shows an interest in the art of poetry that reminds us of Stevens. His self-consciousness as artist is a recurrent theme appearing in various forms throughout his work. "Canso," in *The Dancing Bears,* for instance, blends these two strains of Merwin's sensibility as he makes the Orpheus myth the subject of a poem in which the speaker grapples with the loss of love and the attendant conditions of death. In one section is a Stevens-like meditation on the search for a poetry of renewal: "There must be found, then, the imagination / Before the names of things, the dicta for / The only poem, and among all dictions / That ceremony whereby you may be named / Perpetual out of the anonymity of death." Many such romantic self-portraits of the artist have a Stevensian cast, as in "East of the Sun and West of the Moon" (1954), a delightful long narrative poem. In one passage the young heroine remarks that "All metaphor is magic" and demands that the story itself "be an improvisation continually." Merwin's belief in the redemptive qualities of the creative act and the power of language to bring order out of chaos finds many such statements, even some in which he ironically turns upon himself. In "Fly," published in *The Lice* (1967), he describes his efforts to get a dying pigeon to fly by throwing it into the air and telling it to fly. When he finds it dead in the dovecote he looks at it and thinks that it "could not / Conceive that I was a creature to run from / I who have always believed too much in words."

But this believer in words had moved, by the early sixties, more closely and deeply into his own experience. In *The Drunk in the Furnace* (1960) we see evidence of the influence of the interest in autobiography and personal revelation that led W. D. Snodgrass to write *Heart's Needle* and Lowell to write *Life Studies*. Merwin wrote his own poems of personal reminiscence: about his grandparents; "Uncle Hess," a handyman in a summer resort; and the title poem about an old drunkard who "established / His bad castle" in an abandoned furnace.

In *The Moving Target* (1963) Merwin moved even further away from his earlier work by adopting freer, more open forms. He seems to be following the example of William Carlos Williams and Charles Olson in the use of increasingly free rhythms and longer, looser lines. The transformation is more nearly complete in *The Lice* (1967) and *The Carrier of Ladders* (1970), in which the eccentric arrangements of lines and words on the page give an emphasis to language and to individual words that occasionally approximates the concentration of verbal effects in the verse of Robert Creeley. "I Live Up Here" is a good example of this development in technique. It is narrated by a speaker who is reluctant to become engaged with life, who goes downstairs "only / For the accidents and then / Never a moment too soon." The poem ends in a typically open and inconclusive fashion, perhaps another indication of Creeley's influence:

> For I see
> What my votes the mice are accomplishing
> And I know I'm free
>
> This is how I live
> Up here and simply
>
> Others do otherwise
> Maybe

The subjects in *The Lice* are varied; there are poems about art, about the self, about death, and about war. His Vietnam poem, "The Asians Dying," is not propaganda but the same kind of matter-of-fact treatment of horror we have seen in such earlier poems as "Shipwreck," which links him to Stanley Kunitz and John Berryman:

Rain falls into the open eyes of the dead
Again again with its pointless sounds
When the moon finds them they are
    the color of everything,

Other good poems in *The Lice* are "For a Coming Extinction," "Whenever I Go There," "The Last One," and
the poem below, "The Dry Stone Mason," which demonstrates that Merwin's technical mastery has not been abandoned but merely transformed:

The mason is dead the gentle drunk
Master of dry walls
What he made of his years crosses the slopes
    without wavering
Upright but nameless
Ignorant in the new winter
Rubbed by running sheep
But the age of mortar has come to him

Bottles are waiting like fallen shrines
Under different trees in the rain
And stones drip where his hands left them
Leaning slightly inwards
His thirst is past

As he had no wife
The neighbors found where he kept his suit
A man with no family they sat with him
When he was carried through them they stood
    by their own dead
And they have buried him among the graves of
    the stones

Another poet of considerable interest for the direction
he is taking is James Wright (b. 1927), who has been compared at various times to such widely different poets as Edwin
Arlington Robinson and Theodore Roethke. Wright has

made some important shifts in technique in the course of his career. In *The Green Wall* (1957) and *Saint Judas* (1959) he was largely a derivative poet writing of his Ohio youth and his teaching years in Minnesota. Even in these, however, he took the point of view of the alienated individual, commenting on the society that had made him with both nostalgia and bitterness. The title of his second volume defines this conception of himself, as does an epigraph from Thoreau asserting his independence of vision. These early poems are quiet and conversational in tone and conventional in form, dealing with the physical details of reality in a matter-of-fact way. But they contain indications of Wright's ability to sympathize strongly with other people and project his own consciousness into the minds and feelings of others. In "At the Executed Murderer's Grave" (1959) he shows an awareness of the invisible bonds existing between people that reminds us of James Dickey's techniques in such poems as "The Fiend" (1965) or "A Screened Porch in the Country" (1962).

Wright's third volume, *The Branch Will Not Break* (1963), is a departure in style and approach. He abandons metrics entirely and shifts to free forms and images that carry with them a set of suggestive associations. He is influenced in his use of the "deep image" by his fellow-Minnesotan Robert Bly (b. 1926), who is also writing a poetry of "inwardness" that opens up a level of subconscious feelings and half-formed thoughts. The term *deep image* is more closely associated with two New York poets, Jerome Rothenberg (b. 1931) and Robert Kelly (b. 1935), who have described deep-image poetry as a pattern of associations that emphasizes the subjective as opposed to the objective Image of Pound, Williams, and Zukofsky. "Poetry," writes Kelly, "like dream reality, is the juncture of the experienced with the never-experienced. Like waking reality, it is the fulfillment of the imagined and the unimagined."

"A Dream of Burial" is a good example of Wright's use of the deep image, a simple but frightening surrealistic fantasy built upon a succession of images. "Twilights," the best poem in the volume, is a horrifying vision of the simultaneous destruction of his boyhood memories and the localities to which they are attached. In three progressively shorter stanzas Wright moves from images of life in the country and the past ("Locusts are climbing down into the dark green crevices / Of my childhood") to an ominous image that embodies all the threats of modern technology. The last stanza is the single line, "A red shadow of steel mills." Another good poem using similar techniques and structure is "Fear Is What Quickens Me." Wright also uses surrealism for comic effect. In the first poem of "Two Hangovers," the waking speaker describes the rising sun as a drunk mumbling Hungarian, and he hears a sparrow singing of the Hanna Coal Company. The second poem is a single image of a jay jumping up and down on a branch and abandoning himself to delight, "for he knows as well as I do / That the branch will not break." The last line gives the volume its title.

Wright makes his poems out of the scenes of his own Midwest: the blast furnaces, football stadiums, shopping centers, and bars in towns like Moundsville, West Virginia, and Mansfield, Bridgeport, Marion, Martins Ferry, and Tiltonville, Ohio; the names themselves suggest the flatness of a nowhere that is everywhere, inhabited by characters like the "ruptured night watchman of Wheeling Steel." This interest in local scenes, full of the poignancy of loneliness and despair, continues to be the basis of the poetry in *Shall We Gather at the River* (1968), which has poems with titles such as "Gambling in Stateline, Nevada" and "Outside Fargo, North Dakota." The surrealism of Dickey and Merwin are still an essential part of his technique; we find it in the very effective short poem, "Living by the Red River." Wright, as David Ignatow has said of him, has "made an organic graft of the surrealist technique upon the body of hard reality, one enhancing and reinforcing the other so that we have a mode as evocative as a dream and as effective as a newspaper account." Wright lives in the heart of his abundant land, looking out at it through the personal vision of his despair:

Dead riches, dead hands, the moon
Darkens,
And I am lost in the beautiful white ruins
Of America

("Having Lost My Sons, I Confront the
Wreckage of the Moon: Christmas, 1960")

The expansive-affirmative mood of James Dickey's poems
(b. 1923) continually raises the reader to a high level of ex-
pectation that is not always fulfilled by performance. Loose
in structure, many of them built upon an underlying anapestic rhythm, the poems rock with the upbeat, hard-driving
force of a man determined to fill his poems with life. The
early ones are filled with his own life, which Dickey has described as a continuous story with different episodes, "leading
from childhood in the north of Georgia through high school
with its athletics and wild motorcycle riding, through a beginning attempt at education in an agricultural college,
through World War II and the Korean War as a flyer in a
nightfighter squadron, through another beginning at college,
this time completed." These are memories of a southern boyhood, but they have little of Allen Tate's tortured sense of
history or Robert Penn Warren's profound sense of tragedy.

Dickey recalls such episodes as going hunting for Civil
War relics with his brother, making love in an automobile
junkyard, playing in a treehouse at night, and in all these
activities he reaches toward the heart of experience, arriving
at a mystical sense of insight or fulfillment. In "Hunting
Civil War Relics at Nimblewill Creek" (1962) he and his
brother, using a mine detector in their search, suddenly
become aware of each other in a moment of mutual perception that reaches beyond and through time. In "Cherrylog
Road" (1964) the situation is basically more humorous—a boy
and girl make love in the back seat of a junked car—but the
emotions of the boy after the experience are genuine, as he
races away on his motorcycle, "Wringing the handlebar for
speed, / Wild to be wreckage forever."

Beginning with his second volume, *Drowning with*

Others (1962), Dickey has become more and more interested in dreams, hallucinations, and fantasy, blurring distinctions between what is actually happening and what is happening in the mind of a character in a poem. As in the work of several of his contemporaries, including Robert Bly, James Wright, W. S. Merwin, and Louis Simpson, Dickey has moved away from rationalistic verse toward a poetry that releases the unconscious and irrational, often depending upon surrealism to produce his effects. In "A Screened Porch in the Country" his images are blurred by the night and by the subjective vision of the characters in the poem, giving them a dreamlike quality. A different kind of interaction between fantasy and reality occurs in "The Lifeguard," in which a boy who has failed to rescue a child from drowning creates a fantasy in which he walks out upon the water and undoes what has happened by raising the victim back to life.

The poems in *Buckdancer's Choice* (1965) and *The Eye-Beaters, Blood, Victory, Madness, Buckhead and Mercy* (1970) are quite different from those that appeared in *Helmets* a year earlier. Dickey was becoming interested in what he called the "open" poem, a poem without a formal neatness but full of imperfections, the idea being to draw the reader into the poem. His long poem, "The Firebombing," which describes the feelings of a bomber pilot twenty years after flying missions over Japan, is an example of his new interest in looseness of form, as well as his interest in surrealist techniques. The poem moves back and forth between the cockpit of the airplane and the suburban house of the veteran, as he subjectively links the Sunday afternoon quiet of the present with the similar atmosphere surrounding the Japanese victims waiting to be killed by his bombs. The purpose here is to create a fusion of the inner and outer states where everything partakes of the protagonist's mental state and creates a single impression.

Dickey's interest in the inner life of his subjects dates back to his early poems, including the remarkable poem "The Sheep Child" (1967), narrated by the dead offspring of a farm boy and a sheep, a poem exploring the anomalies of sexual passion. "In the Marble Quarry" (1964) has as its speaker a block of marble that is being made into part of a monument. Two poems in *Buckdancer's Choice,* "The Fiend" and "Slave Quarters," employ the new openness of form, together with an experimental spacing of words in the lines, to explore still further the possibilities in the unique point of view. "The Fiend" is an ironic title, referring to a peeping-tom speaker who describes himself and his pathetic lusts in the third person. "Slave Quarters" is a less successful poem done from the point of view of a slave. Dickey's *tour de force* in this genre is "Falling" (1967), which is prefaced by this note from a news item in *The New York Times:* "A 29-year-old stewardess fell . . . to her death tonight when she was swept through an emergency door that suddenly sprang open . . . The body . . . was found . . . three hours after the accident." The poem contains the thoughts of the stewardess as she falls to her death: memories, fears, irrelevant jokes, sexual longings, and fantasy. When she strips off her clothes, they "come down all over Kansas into bushes   on the dewy sixth green / Of a golf course." The poem's eerie mixture of horror, humor, and lyricism illustrates Dickey's particular strengths—an offbeat way of looking at the world around him, again by subjectively distorting reality. In all these poems there is a deliberate formlessness that frequently becomes a handicap, in spite of his professed interest in the "un-well-made poem." Big, general, sweeping forms are not always enough. Although they work well in "Falling," it is also helpful to know when and where to stop.

The patrician elegance of Anthony Hecht's (b. 1922) finely wrought poems seems to come from a painstaking attention to surface and texture. The reader finds himself admiring the way he says things as much as what he says. One of his most beautiful early poems, "The Gardens of the Villa D'Este," is an ornate and lush love poem that uses the riotously sensuous decorations of a sixteenth-century Italian garden as an extended metaphor for his own sexual longings. The design of the stanza itself, short lines at the beginning and the end with longer lines in the middle, gives the poem a pleasing and somewhat formal appearance on the page. Another poem, also about gardens and using a similar stanza, is "La Condition Botanique," a conceit on the idea of Eden being preserved in the Brooklyn Botanical Gardens. These two poems appeared in his first book, *A Summoning of Stones* (1954).

Hecht has continued to work slowly and carefully, publishing his second volume, *The Hard Hours,* in 1967. He follows no school and writes in no special idiom, but his poems shimmer with the formal polish of a writer who wants to say things well. He is capable of producing a civilized kind of *frisson* in a slight tale of illicit love, "The End of the Weekend," in which the lover, hearing a noise in the attic of their cabin, goes up to find an owl beating its wings in wrath, "among the shattered skeletons of mice." He creates a deeper horror in "Behold the Lilies of the Field," a free-verse, first-person narrative told by an eyewitness to the flaying alive of the Roman Emperor Valerian.

He also has a flair for the comic and ironic; in "The Dover Bitch: A Criticism of Life" (1959) the speaker talks about his own experiences with the girl whom Arnold supposedly addressed in "Dover Beach": "To have been brought / All the way down from London, and then be addressed / As a sort of mournful cosmic last resort / Is really tough on a girl, and she was pretty."

His best poems have a weight, an intensity, and a directness that admit neither inattention nor compromise on the part of the reader. Such poems as "Upon the Death of George Santayana," "The Origin of Centaurs," and "The Vow" illustrate in different ways Hecht's talent for writing intellectual poetry that still obeys the promptings of the heart. He illustrates this himself at the end of "A Letter," written by a man to the mistress he cannot forget:

> But I would have you know that all is not well
> With a man dead set to ignore
> The endless repetitions of his own murmurous blood.

John Ashbery (b. 1927) is one of our most relentlessly experimental poets. Much of his published work in *The Tennis Court Oath* (1962) and *Rivers and Mountains* (1965) seems to be sketches and notes toward poems rather than finished products. A glance at many of his poems in the first volume will reveal his heavy debts to the French surrealists; the hostile reader may see him as an anachronism, a throwback to Tristan Tzara and André Breton:

> The charcoal mines were doing well
> At 9½ per cent. A downy hill
> Announced critical boredom for the bottler
> Of labor tonic. It seemed there was no more
> Steering-wheel oil or something—you had better
> Call them about it—I don't know,
> I predisposed the pests toward blue rock.

Ashbery is the kind of poet who invites extreme reactions. His adventuresomeness, his willingness to try anything, lead readers to think he is frivolous or worse. He is capable of writing quite lucid and more nearly conventional poetry, as he demonstrates in such early poems as "Some Trees" (1956) and "The Instruction Manual" (1956); however, these are not typical of most of his work. His background in painting and music has led him to take an interest in the structure, or architecture, of verse. His arrangement of passages of surrealistic verse follows a random, free pattern that has been compared to the action paintings of Jackson Pollock. One can also see resemblances to the music of John Cage, and to the open forms of Charles Olson and Robert Duncan. In "Europe" (1960) Ashbery constructs a collage of 111 short sections of disconnected images and phrases that add up to an impression of his subject that could be achieved in no other way.

"The Skaters," an ambitious long poem in *Rivers and Mountains,* reveals most impressively the possibilities of his exploratory techniques. In one section of that poem he rejects the methods of the past, "the old, imprecise feelings, the / Common knowledge, the importance of duly suffering . . .

The world of Schubert's lieder." His own poem, he writes, is in the form of falling snow:

> That is, the individual flakes are not essential to the
>   importance of the whole's becoming so much of a truism
> That their importance is again called in question to be
>   denied further out, and again and again like this.
> Hence, neither the importance of the individual flakes,
> Nor the importance of the whole impression of the storm,
>   if it has any, is what it is,
> But the rhythm of the series of repeated jumps, from
>   abstract into positive and back to a slightly less
>   diluted abstract.
>
> Mild effects are the result.

The method is, of course, no assurance that good poems will result. Still, Ashbery is an interesting poet who has adopted an artificial voice and an aggressively playful attitude toward poetry as a way to avoid the easy lie.

The most widely known and widely publicized phenomenon of contemporary American poetry is the San Francisco Beat scene, which began as a colony of Bohemia, in some ways a West Coast branch of Greenwich Village, developed a jazz-Zen-drug culture of its own, produced several important poets, and brought many features of the underground into the mainstream of American life. When Allen Ginsberg and Lawrence Ferlinghetti (b. 1919) arrived in San Francisco in the mid-fifties, Kenneth Rexroth (b. 1905) was reading poetry to jazz in Bay-area coffeehouses, Robert Duncan was organizing poetry readings over radio station KPFA, and the Poetry Center at San Francisco State College was sponsoring readings by major American and British poets. There was, in addition, a large anti-establishment subculture consisting of dropouts from Berkeley, emigrants from the Village, artists and writers, and various disaffected hangers-on, all of whom were characterized in the national press as beatniks. The term *beat*, coined by Jack Kerouac (1922–1969), carries with it the connotations of both "beat down" and "beatitude." The Beat stance is difficult to characterize briefly, but it consists of various combinations of drug- or jazz-induced hallucination, childlike wonder at trivia, worship of sex and the orgasm, Zen Buddhism, Hinduism, and other Eastern religions, and freedom from every kind of tyranny. Although the beatniks, with their hair, their sandals, their squalor, and their indifference to middle-class values, were the subjects of sensational publicity, several serious poets emerged from this scene to give the poetry of the sixties new vitality and new directions.

The most important of these is Allen Ginsberg (b. 1926). His first public reading in 1956 of *Howl* at an artists' cooperative called the Six Gallery marks the beginning both of the Beat movement and of Ginsberg's career as a poet. Rexroth introduced him to the audience, which included Gary Snyder, Philip Whalen, Philip Lamantia, Jack Kerouac, Neal Cassady, and others, and he drunkenly read the entire poem. He quotes Rexroth as saying that *Howl* would make him famous "from bridge to bridge," which it did. The real credit for making the poem famous, however, must go to U.S. Customs officials and the San Francisco Police Department, who seized *Howl and Other Poems* (1956), published by Ferlinghetti's City Lights Books, on the grounds of obscenity. During the trial it sold thousands of copies.

Howl is a long, sustained cry of outrage against the injustice and inhumanity of an America that destroys the "holy" impulses and tendencies of its young men and forces them into excesses of drug-taking, sex, and alcoholism. The speaker of the poem is the alienated artist who tells how "the best minds of my generation" were destroyed. He lists in a Whitmanian catalogue a long series of bizarre, shocking, disgusting, and truly horrifying examples of human depravity and degradation. The technique is Whitman's, but the vision is Rimbaud's; a descent into a hell of furnished rooms, Turkish baths, subways, bus stations, and insane asylums reeking with sex and junk. There are echoes of Blake in Part II, where Ginsberg locates the source of this nightmarish existence in Moloch:

> Moloch the incomprehensible prison! Moloch the crossbone
> soulless jailhouse and Congress of sorrows! Moloch whose
> buildings are judgement! Moloch the vast stone of war!
> Moloch the stunned governments!

We can see here the strong paranoia that underlies much of
Ginsberg's work and becomes more and more explicit in later
poems. This paragraph from the San Francisco *Chronicle,*
written in 1959, carries the burden of themes he later developed at length:

> At the same time there is a crack in the mass
> consciousness of America—sudden emergence of in-
> sight into a vast national subconscious netherworld
> filled with nerve gases, universal death bombs, ma-
> levolent bureaucracies, secret police systems, drugs
> that open the door to God, ships leaving Earth, un-
> known chemical terrors, evil dreams at hand.

His long 1961 poem, "Television Was a Baby Crawling Toward That Deathchamber," is built on paranoia, as are parts
of "Wichita Vortex Sutra" (1966).

Part III of *Howl* is addressed to Carl Solomon, to whom
the poem is also dedicated, in the state asylum in Rockland.
We are to assume that Solomon's madness is symptomatic
of our social condition. In "Footnote to *Howl*" (1955), which
should be read as a separate poem, Ginsberg turns from negation to affirmation: everything is holy, in spite of all the defeat and despair:

> Everything is holy! Everybody's holy! everywhere is holy!
>   everyday is in eternity! Everyman's an angel!

This is the "beatific" vision of the Beat writers—their innocent
and mystical belief in decency and goodness that inspires some
to write powerful, freewheeling poems and others to descend
into bathos and banality. Ginsberg often but not always saves
himself from these pitfalls both by his technique and by his

sense of humor. Building on Williams' theories of rhythm (which he once told Williams he did not understand), Ginsberg developed a style in which each long line is a single breath unit. In his use of breathing as a rhythmical unit there is probably some connection with the Projective Verse theories of Olson and Duncan, but the influence of Whitman is also obvious. "Ideally each line of *Howl* is a single breath unit," Ginsberg has said. "My breath is long—that's the Measure, one physical-mental inspiration of thought contained in the elastic of a breath." Poetry written on these principles is obviously meant to be read aloud, and the fact that each line is unusually long for a single breath forces the performer, in Ginsberg's words, "to mouth more madly." This is oral poetry, and the printed page can only suggest the wide range of devices Ginsberg uses in his public readings: the shouting, the whispering, the carefully timed *sotto voce* asides, the comic Jewish inflections, the gestures of hands, arms, and waggling beard, the pauses and crescendos, the chanting, are all devices that relate his poetry to music and dance and help establish a new oral tradition. Ginsberg can use an electronic sound system as a weapon, bellowing into it to create a din unsurpassed by the most violent rock group, causing a physical reaction from his listeners that also goes far beyond what the printed page can create. As more than one critic has observed, the printed poems bear the same relationship to the actual poems as an orchestra score does to its performance.

Like Whitman, Ginsberg saves his poetry from becoming purely bombastic rant because he has a sense of humor. Some of it is satire, some self-deprecatory about his Jewishness or his homosexuality, some simply playful. In *Howl* he describes his rebel friends "investigating the F.B.I. in beards and shorts with big pacifist eyes sexy in their dark skin passing out incomprehensible leaflets"; in "A Supermarket in California" he fancies he sees Walt Whitman "poking among the meats in the refrigerator and eyeing the grocery boys"; in "America" (1955), one of his best satires, he asks when he can "go into the supermarket and buy what I need with my good looks"; he says, "I'm obsessed by Time Magazine. / I read it every week . . . / It's always telling me about responsibility. Businessmen are serious. Movie producers are serious. Everybody's serious but me."; and he confesses: "My ambition is to be President despite the fact that I'm a Catholic."

These comic asides are aspects of style, it must be remembered, and they do not mitigate the nightmarish vision of the collection as a whole. In his second volume, *Kaddish and Other Poems 1958–1960* (1961), Ginsberg gives us more specific reasons for his own state of despair. The title poem, "Kaddish for Naomi Ginsberg 1894–1956," takes the traditional form of the Hebrew lament for the dead; it is divided into six parts called "Proem," "Narrative," "Hymmnn," "Lament," "Litany," and "Fugue." It is an almost unbearably painful and often disgusting series of recollections about his Russian immigrant mother, her extreme paranoia, her confinement in a mental institution, her cancer, and her death. Her Socialist and Communist activities as a young woman are the background for her fears in 1938 of assassins sent by Hitler to kill her, and her madness and fantasies haunt Ginsberg's memory as reactions of a weak and vulnerable individual against the undercurrents of violence and repression that he himself senses in modern America. The poem is an attempt to come to terms with himself by wallowing in the madness, horror, and filth of his past.

Reality Sandwiches (1963) is an undistinguished collection for the most part, but *Planet News* (1968) reflects apparently contradictory tendencies: a new militancy and radicalism with increased opposition to the Vietnam war and the "military-industrial-complex," and a growing mysticism and drug-induced transcendence. These attitudes, of course, were widely shared by the college generation of the sixties, and his travels to hundreds of college campuses, his involvement in the Pentagon marches and the Chicago Democratic Convention have made him more politically aware and more radical in his opposition to society. His radicalism takes the form of universal love and brotherhood buttressed by Hinduism, Shintoism, Buddhism, and marijuana and LSD. The long poem "Television Was a Baby Crawling Toward That Deathchamber" (1961) is a paranoic rant against J. Edgar Hoover and "United Fruits" and a program for a "Breakthru to all other Consciousness." The other long poem, "Wichita Vortex Sutra" (1966), is, in his words, "mind-collage & keystone section of progressively longer poem on 'These States'—here Self sitting in its own meat throne invokes Harekrishna as preserver of human planet & challenges all other Powers usurping State Consciousness to recognize same Identity, thus 'I here declare the End of the War.' " The collection is also interesting for its return to other forms beside the long line. "The Change: Kyoto-Tokyo Express" is written in free-verse stanzas made up of short lines. "After Yeats" doesn't sound much like Yeats but looks like an Imagist poem. "Wales Visitation" is a serene, almost Wordsworthian, poem written while he was high on LSD and revised several days later. One can only speculate on the amount of revision he did, but the imagery and language are rich and strangely evocative. It is one of his best poems and reminds us again that in spite of the tastelessness, bombast, and rant that mar some of his work, Ginsberg is a very talented and accomplished poet.

Gary Snyder's (b. 1930) association with the Beats has been incidental but important. His subject matter covers a much wider range than the San Francisco scene and the preoccupations growing out of it, even though he has specifically acknowledged a kind of tripartite vow of allegiance to a set of principles he shares with them. Snyder's freewheeling life as lumberjack, forester, and merchant seaman, scholar of Japanese and classical Chinese, and student of Zen under a Japanese master has given his work a unique substance and texture. He has taken what he calls the religious tendencies of the Beat movement and incorporated them into his own work. In a 1959 essay in *Liberation* he names the three aspects of religiosity as contemplation (with and without the aid of drugs), morality (the love and respect for life coming from such varied sources as Quakerism, Walt Whitman, Shinshu Buddhism, and Sufism), and wisdom (coming from discipline in the traditions of some religion).

This religious, contemplative approach to life gives Snyder's poetry a serenity and sweetness, whether it is about logging in the High Sierras or cooking a stew in the Arizona desert. Snyder reduces living to its essentials: hard physical work alternating with spiritual rapture. The rhythms of his poems, as he noted in Donald Allen's *The New American Poetry*, follow the kind of work he is doing. In his first collection, *Riprap* (1959), he worked for hard, spare poems, with short words and short lines. His definition of riprap, a word used by trail crews in the Sierra Nevada, is "a cobble of stone laid on steep slick rock / to make a trail for horses in the mountains." The hard surface texture of his free-verse poems attempts to imitate this quality:

> Lay down these words
> Before your mind like rocks.
> > placed solid, by hands
> In choice of place, set
> Before the body of the mind
> > in space and time:
> Solidity of bark, leaf, or wall
> > riprap of things

In this collection are poems about his logging days, a trip to Japan, and a job on a tanker in the Mediterranean. "Milton by Firelight" and "Kyoto: March" are among the best.

Snyder's encounters with Oriental culture gave him the language and subject matter he needed to make statements about the necessity to search for the essentials of life. In *Cold Mountain* (1965) he tells the story of a legendary Chinese hermit, Hanshan, whose residence, Cold Mountain, gives him his name. This solitary existence is also a state of mind, which inspired a following of wild-haired hermits, who, Snyder says in his introductory note, "became Immortals and you sometimes run in to them today in the skidrows, orchards, hobo jungles, and logging camps of America."

This romantic love for the little guy is part of a modern Thoreauvian stance against the encroachments of a materialistic society. Two other collections develop similar themes: *Myths and Texts* (1960) and *The Back Country* (1967). The first of these, made up of three long sections, "Logging," "Hunting," and "Burning," mixes Oriental religion, social criticism, sharp imagistic impressions and drug hallucinations in a complex but integrated poem, influenced in its technique by Olson's Projective Verse. *The Back Country* shows a growing self-confidence and maturity and makes it clear that Snyder is one of the most promising of the Beat poets.

In 1950 Charles Olson (1910–1971) wrote "Projective Verse," a theoretical essay that became a seminal one for himself and his followers. It was written about the time William Carlos Williams was discovering the possibilities of the triadic foot and working toward the open forms of the later books of *Paterson* and of *Desert Music*. Olson defined Projective Verse as verse that moves out of a closed system into open forms. Quoting Robert Creeley, he maintained that "form is never more than an extension of content." Olson also talked about "field composition," defining a poem as a "high-energy construct" that transfers energy or life force from the poet to the reader. Field composition, as Olson saw it, involves a steady stream of dense perceptions: "one perception must immediately and directly lead to a further perception." On the basis of this position, Olson's Projective Verse shares some characteristics with the Objectivist verse of Louis Zukofsky, George Oppen, and Williams, and is illustrated also by Williams' statement in *Paterson:* "No ideas but in things." This process of free association and dense juxtaposition of perceptions is also related to the technique of Pound's *Cantos*.

Olson's theories are not always clear; nevertheless, they and his poems have been an important influence on a number of poets who knew him and each other at Black Mountain College in the 1950s. The shape of their poetry is governed by the idea that various elements of the poem, the image, the sound, the sense, all interact as in a kinetic field. The syllable and the line are especially important, growing as they do out of the poet's own involvement with his material. The syllable

expresses the relationship between sound and sense and therefore gives the verse its particular quality, while the line is governed by the poet's actual breathing, his own life-rhythm, as
it were, injected into the line as he composes it. The result is
poetry that looks "open" on the page: lines of varying length,
words divided at the ends of lines, short stanzas alternating
with longer ones, etc. There are obvious similarities in appearance between Olson's Projective Verse and the poems of cummings and Williams, particularly in *Paterson.* The poets most
closely associated with Projective Verse have each gone their
own way and represent a school only in the sense of their
early connections with Black Mountain College. Although
there are noticeable similarities in their work, the poems of
Charles Olson, Robert Creeley, Robert Duncan, and Denise
Levertov are quite different from each other. Other poets
who have been influenced by this movement include the late
Paul Blackburn, Edward Dorn, Imamu Amiri Baraka, and, indirectly, the San Francisco poets Allen Ginsberg, Gregory
Corso, Gary Snyder, and Michael McClure.

Although Charles Olson published many of his poems
separately as broadsides or in small collections during the fifties, they are most conveniently found in two books published
in 1960, *The Distances* and *The Maximus Poems.* The first of
these collects such poems as "Letter for Melville," written in
1951 as a protest against a gathering of scholars at Williams
College to celebrate the centennial of *Moby-Dick,* and "There
Was a Youth Whose Name Was Thomas Granger," a grim
comic narrative about a young man who was tried and executed for sodomy in the Plymouth Plantation. A more impressive poem is "The Kingfishers," a difficult, ruminative
poem about the decay of meaningful forms of life in the face
of an advancing civilization. The kingfisher is developed as a
complex archetypal symbol from which Olson feels free to
digress in propagandistic or didactic passages. The theme is
change and decay, particularly the decay of society brought
about by materialism, cheapness, and sham, all embodied in
his term "pejorocracy," which had for him the same force as
usura had for Pound in *Cantos.*

"Pejorocracy" becomes a central item in *The Maximus Poems*, a loosely arranged set of poems, "songs," and "letters" written in and about Gloucester, Massachusetts, and spoken through a persona, Maximus, who functions in a way similar to that of Dr. Paterson in Williams' *Paterson*. Olson characterizes his speaker at the end of "Letter 3" of "Maximus, to Gloucester":

Isolated person in Gloucester, Massachusetts, I, Maximus,
address you

you islands
of men and girls

Local history and local personages are woven into what we must assume are high-energy constructs. Inhabitants past and present, shipping magnates, town characters, fishermen, etc., appear and disappear and are set side by side with bills of lading, ships' logs, and records of town meetings. These are held together by a dreaming or speaking Maximus, who writes letters, sings songs, and places himself in ironic or comic juxtaposition to the prevailing tendencies of his age. Although it has much less coherence than *Paterson*, the similarities of *The Maximus Poems* to that poem are apparent, in its attitudes as well as its techniques. In a two-line utterance at the end of "Maximus, at Tyre and Boston" Olson wrote: "we are only / as we find out we are," a statement that echoes Williams' statement: "we know nothing, pure and simple, beyond our own complexities." *The Maximus Poems* are uneven, but many passages demonstrate Olson's considerable talents as a poet. Critical recognition is beginning to catch up with his achievement, with the recent publication of *Maximus Poems, Four, Five, and Six* (1969) and *Archaeologist of Morning* (1971).

One of the poets most closely associated with Olson is Robert Creeley (b. 1926). Creeley went to Black Mountain

College in 1954 to teach writing and edit the *Black Mountain Review*. In 1955 his fourth book of poems was published
by Jonathan Williams' Jargon Books. In 1962 he collected the
contents of seven earlier volumes in *For Love: Poems 1950–
1960*. Creeley's poems are bare, stripped, laconic in the extreme. They are indirect and ironic, depending not so much
on the words themselves as on their connotations and on the
rhythms derived from their arrangement on the page. The
theory upon which these poems are composed is interesting.
In his preface to *For Love* Creeley writes, "the discovery of
an external equivalent of the speaking self is felt to be the object of poetry." Elsewhere, in his essay on Projective Verse,
Olson credited Creeley with one of his basic tenets: that
"form is never more than an extension of content." These
theories are interesting, if not particularly new—one thinks
of Eliot's objective correlative and Emerson's meter-making
argument—and they help to explain what his poetry is. The
poems, composed of three- or four-line stanzas, two or three
words to a line, seem efforts at communication in a media-
saturated world by a man groping for words and trying desperately and even self-consciously to avoid cliché. His minimal
forms call attention to themselves as antiverbal messages, using words sometimes almost resentfully, as if they could not
hope to contain the inwardness of feeling he is trying to convey. To hear Creeley speak his poems in person is to be
aware of his intense honesty with language; one feels that his
words are semiprecious stones, and that certain ones must be
separately treasured and placed with care among others that
seem to matter less. He is like Olson in his concern with the
function of the word within the line and within the poem,
working for a rhythm that derives from American, the "speech
of the place," as it does in the later poems of Williams.

Creeley's major subject is love, which he treats both seriously and with a wry and sometimes coy humor: courtship,
married love, infidelity contemplated and actual. Many of
them are about the small, daily ups and downs of living with
and loving another person, such as the husband who never

has a towel where he can find it, or the wife who thinks of a bed mainly as a place to sleep. A more serious poem, "Distance" (1967), explores the difficulty of two people getting to know each other in the context of physical intimacy. This "domestic" side of Creeley is perhaps best summed up in these lines from "The Way" (1959):

> Oh well, I will say here,
> knowing each man,
> let you find a good wife too,
> and love her as hard as you can.

Other good poems are "Kore" (1959), "The Language" (1967), and "The Riddle" (1955).

The most powerful and original of the Projectivist poets is Robert Duncan (b. 1919), a poet of cosmic consciousness who creates intricate, highly complex, and interacting constructions out of words. Duncan is a very intelligent, widely read, anti-intellectual poet working to unite the body and the soul through a rich and randomly organized poetry of living, breathing, and feeling. "Poetry is the very life of the soul: the body's discovery that it can dream. And perish into its own imagination," he writes in a statement for Donald Allen's *The New American Poetry*. This is just one of many orphic statements he makes, both as prefaces to his poems and in the poems themselves, about the nature of his art. Duncan's object is to return to wholeness and fullness of feeling by recognizing the variety of life and the interdependence of public and private experience. "Everywhere dissenting, contradictory voices speak up," he writes. "I don't seek a synthesis, but a melee . . . The problem is that we dread all inconsequential experience; our taboo is at root against unintelligible passions."

The results of such attitudes toward his craft are poems widely varying in form, length, subject matter, and quality. Reading through *Roots and Branches* (1964) or his latest volume *Caesar's Gate* (1972), one has the impression of a powerful personality with a sense of mission, whose combined playfulness and high seriousness strike a familiar note. We recognize the tone of Pound in the *Cantos* and Olson in *The Maximus Poems*—both of whom view poetry as a moral and spiritual force working toward man's redemption. We are reminded also by this attitude toward poetry of Wallace Stevens' observation in his "Adagia" that "poetry is a means of redemption," and Duncan is certainly close to Stevens in many of his poems about poetry. Duncan gives a substantial list of influences on his work; they include Pound, Stein, Woolf, Joyce, Stevens, Lawrence, Edith Sitwell, Mallarmé, Yeats, Swift, St. John Perse, and particularly H. D. It is possible to detect all these influences; he describes himself as an "artist of abundancies," and his method is that of the maker of jigsaw puzzles or the creator of collages, taking things apart and putting them back together in new shapes and in different order. This technique of seeing things always in relation to other things is related to Olson's field-composition theories, as well as to Pound's *Pisan Cantos* (1948) and to Williams' *Paterson*. Like those three writers, Duncan has experimented with the open-ended poem, the poem larger than the volume in which it is contained. In *The Opening of the Field* (1960) he began a long work called "The Structure of Rime," which continues through his next two volumes. In *Bending the Bow* he writes of a new open-ended poem, *Passages:* "I number the first to come *one,* but they belong to a series that extends in an area larger than my work in them. I enter the poem as I entered my own life, moving between an initiation and a terminus I cannot name." *Passages* is a long quest-poem about the poet's search for "It," the mystical spirit of poetic creation immanent in the physical world, by means of which the poet explores the cosmic unity of life and re-creates himself through the act of creation. Here is a section from "Passages 1," "Tribal Memories," which illustrates the poet's sense of the vital connection between life and poetry as he searches his memory for clues for his quest:

Mnemosyne, they named her, the
        Mother with the whispering
  feather'd wings. Memory,
the great speckled bird who broods over the
      nest of souls, and her egg,
    the dream in which all things are living,
I return to, leaving my self.

I am beside myself with this
    thought of the One in the World-Egg,
enclosed,   in a shell of murmurings,
        rimed round,
           sound-chamberd child.
  It's that first!   The forth-going to be
           bursts into green as the spring
    winds blow watery from the south
and the sun returns north.   He hides

   fire among words in his mouth

and comes racing out of the zone of dark and storm

      towards us.

No quotation can give an adequate idea of Duncan's virtu-osity: his capacity for allusion, for puns, for passages of intense mystical beatitude next to passages of horrifying despond-ency. Formal demands in themselves are meaningless to him, yet he demonstrates his mastery of form in such *tours de force* as "Shelley's *Arethusa* set to new measures" and "After a Passage in Baudelaire" (1961–1963). Of all the poets associated with the Black Mountain group Duncan is the most inter-esting and the most promising. Although it is impossible to sympathize with everything he writes and not at times be put off by his pretentiousness, one cannot fail to be impressed with a genuine and original poetic talent.

    Denise Levertov (b. 1923) is a poet who has evolved her own style but was influenced at a crucial point in her career by the poetry of William Carlos Williams and Wallace Stevens and by Robert Duncan and Robert Creeley, whom she considers the chief poets among her contemporaries. Levertov was born and raised in England, and her first book of poems, *The Double Image* (1946), is a competent collection of typically British poems of the period, full of war-weariness, damp emotions, and vague echoes of the Georgians written in traditional English meters. She was, in her own words, a British Romantic with an almost Victorian background. When she met and married the American writer Mitchell Goodman and moved to New York, she underwent nothing less than a total revolution in her conception of the function of language, of rhythm, and of life. Her reading of Williams directed her attention to the possibilities of finding poetry in everyday experience, in transforming the insignificant into art, and making the personal reaction or insight an experience to be valued for its own sake. Her interest in the rhythms of American speech was also spurred by Williams' experiments in the "variable foot" as well as by Olson's essay on Projective Verse, and her second volume, *Here and Now* (1957), reflects, even in the title, these new attitudes. This volume was followed by four others, *Overland to the Islands* (1958), *With Eyes at the Back of Our Heads* (1959), *The Jacob's Ladder* (1961), and *O Taste and See* (1964).

In all of these Levertov concentrates on discovering the marvelous in the ordinary, obeying in her own way Williams' exhortation to find "no ideas but in things":

> Marvelous Truth, confront us
> at every turn,
> in every guise, iron ball,
> egg, dark horse, shadow,
> cloud
> of breath on the air,
>
> dwell
> in our crowded hearts
> our steaming bathrooms, kitchens full of
> things to be done, the
> ordinary streets.

Thrust close your smile
that we know you, terrible joy.

This "poetry of the immediate," as Ralph J. Mills has
described it, is not confined to strictly literal renditions of
life. Levertov finds in her experiences a source of transcendence, but even though these experiences move her to a higher
plane, they retain their original uniqueness and concreteness.
In "The Instant" (1958), for example, she describes a mush-
room-gathering expedition with her mother, during which
the mist suddenly lifts to reveal Mount Snowdon, fifty miles
away. The walk up the hill, the feel of the mushrooms, the
dampness of the grass are all described as a preface to her
mother's sudden outcry when she sees the mountain. The
poem ends simply, and factually, but with a heightened sense
of reality transformed:

> Snowdon, home
> of eagles, resting-place of
> Merlin, core of Wales.
>
> Light
> graces the mountainhead
> for a lifetime's look, before the mist
> draws in again.

In her latest volume, *The Sorrow Dance* (1967), is a series of
restrained and meticulously crafted love poems called "Bride
of Abel," of which "Face to Face" and "Hymn to Eros" are
particularly good. She has become more and more preoccupied with change and death, and in her longest poem yet, the
"Olga Poems" (1965), she has written a series of meditations
in memory of her older sister.

An important source of Levertov's recognition of joy in
the physical world are the ideas of Hasidism with which she
first became acquainted in her childhood through her father,
a Russian Jew who became an Anglican priest. Later, reading
Martin Buber, she recognized in his writings her own sense

of wonder at creation; once she remarked that "that's what poems are all about." In her poems she cures the malady of the quotidian by reveling in it, by searching in it for what she calls "the authentic," and making it the substance of her life as well as her art.

We should not leave Levertov's poetry with the impression that she is a member of a school of poets. She is a highly original, personal poet who has wrestled with the angel, Art, and evolved a style and themes of her own. Her increasing social consciousness and humanitarianism may be seen in her long poem, "During the Eichmann Trial" (1961), and more particularly in her impassioned poems about the Vietnam war, as well as her own deep involvement in antiwar causes. The last section of *The Sorrow Dance,* "Life at War," contains nine poems that contradict to a certain extent a statement she made ten years ago: "I do not believe that a violent imitation of the horrors of our times is the concern of poetry. . . . Insofar as poetry has a social function it is to awaken sleepers by other means than shock." These are public poems, meant to be read at antiwar rallies and meant to shock. In "Didactic Poem" and "Second Didactic Poem" she speaks about the denial of life-giving wonder in war and bloodshed in language that remains consistent with her other poems but departs from them in their direct involvement. Like Muriel Rukeyser and W. S. Merwin, Levertov has usually not allowed her sense of outrage to distort or debase her art.

In 1959 LeRoi Jones, who now calls himself Imamu Amiri Baraka (b. 1934), wrote in Donald Allen's *The New American Poetry* that the greatest influences on his work were Federico García Lorca, William Carlos Williams, Ezra Pound, and Charles Olson. His desire was to be free, to say what he wanted to say in the way he wanted to say it—an attitude he shared with the Black Mountain poets. His poems bear out these statements: they are playful, elliptical, irreverent, and stylistically adventurous. He worked in the hip vein, full of references to his friends, sentimental recollections of the radio programs of his boyhood, and Imagistic pastiche, coming through as a bright young man who knew his way around the intellectual and hip worlds and was capable of writing competent poetry. This is the kind of poetry he published in his first volume, *Preface to a Twenty Volume Suicide Note* (1960). In this, and in *The Dead Lecturer* (1964), Baraka shows an ear for rhythm, for the cadences of what he calls "Melican speech," and a talent for surrealism and free association that make his poems become projections of an inner eye; such poems as "The Measure of Memory (The Navigator)" and *"The invention of comics"* resemble poems of Duncan and Olson.

There is also, however, a noticeable strain of black consciousness in these poems, in which Baraka seems to be trying to deal with that subject in artistic rather than political or propagandistic ways. "BLACK DADA NIHILISMUS" is an example. Indirect and allusive at the beginning, the poem rises to a scream of accusation and outrage.

This tendency toward militancy has continued through the sixties as the events of those years and Baraka's own racial consciousness have moved in similar directions. He has found that the real outlet for giving artistic expression to his militancy is the theatre, as can be seen in his plays *The Toilet* (1964), *Slave Ship* (1964), and *Dutchman* (1964). He has continued to write and publish poetry, however; gravitating toward mysticism in his latest collection, *Black Magic Poetry 1961–1967* (1969).

Since the mid-sixties, there has been a resurgence of energy in black poetry, largely because of the new militant mood of blacks. Gwendolyn Brooks, still one of the best black poets, has been able to turn her talents more and more to black subjects and is consciously continuing the tradition of Langston Hughes. Much black poetry is published in black magazines, such as *Kenyatta* and *Black Expressions,* and by independent publishers, such as Detroit's Broadside Press. The best of the Broadside poets is a protégé of Brooks, Don L. Lee (b. 1942), whose five books, from *Think Black!* (1967) to *Directionscore:*

Selected and New Poems (1971), demonstrate his ability to express strong feelings of outrage in language shaped by sensitivity and wit.

Black poetry, according to Lee, is poetry that reflects the black experience; it is therefore black first and poetry second. The function of such poetry is purposefully social, yet its best practitioners are writing a vital poetry that promises much for the future. Some of these writers are young; others have been around a while and are now emerging as spokesmen for the black experience. Among the best are Conrad Kent Rivers (b. 1933), Dudley Randall (b. 1914), Raymond Patterson (b. 1929), James Emanuel (b. 1921), Sonia Sanchez (b. 1943), Nikki Giovanni (b. 1943), and Keorapetse Kgositsile (b. 1938), an immigrant from South Africa.

These are some of the signs of vigor in American poetry today. Everywhere we look we can see that poetry is being written, read, and heard by more and more people. For a while in the fifties it looked as though poetry was about to follow the novel to a premature grave, but poetry readings, the paperback book industry, and the growing number of college-educated young people have helped give poets a new and larger audience. Folk and rock musicians, too, have added their own impetus to a new language awareness, and some respectable lyrics are appearing on the backs of record jackets. In a sense, we have returned to an oral tradition, even though we must now think of it as part of McLuhan's electronic global village. The line between "serious" and "popular" poetry therefore seems less distinct than it once did, and one of these days we may find ourselves with a new poet who has turned the folk-rock idiom into really good poetry. Until that time, however, we can go on reading the contemporaries mentioned in the last few chapters, who continue to flourish at a rate too fast for me to keep up with them.

When reading American poets, one is struck by their desire to exploit the possibilities of language to the fullest: to make it over in their own image, as though they were the first to discover it. Since the time of Poe and Emerson and Whitman, our poets have been giving "a purer sense to the words of the tribe," as Stéphane Mallarmé said of Poe in his sonnet to him. This, I would say, is the great accomplishment of our poets: they have found "the speech of the place" and, rooting themselves in that soil, have produced the "autochthonous song" Walt Whitman called for. There can be no better conclusion to this book than the words with which Whitman closed his own reminiscences in "A Backward Glance O'er Travel'd Roads": "First, what Herder taught to the young Goethe, that really great poetry is always (like the Homeric or Biblical canticles) the result of a national spirit, and not the privilege of a polish'd and select few; Second, that the strongest and sweetest songs yet remain to be sung."

Bibliographies

The following bibliographies are designed to serve two purposes: to list works consulted and to list specific references to which I have referred in the text. For the convenience of the reader, I have compiled a bibliography for each chapter and, in addition, a general bibliography. The reader should be able to locate every reference in the text by consulting the appropriate *chapter* bibliography. I have frequently listed the same source in several chapters, when I have had occasion to refer to it in connection with different poets. For bibliographies of works by each poet, the reader should consult standard reference works such as Spiller *et al.*, *Literary History of the United States* and Rosalie Murphy ed., *Contemporary Poets of the English Language* (Chicago and London: St. James Press, 1970).

CHAPTER ONE

BERRYMAN, JOHN. *Homage to Mistress Bradstreet*. New York: Farrar, Straus & Giroux, 1956.

BLAU, HERBERT. "Heaven's Sugar Cake: Theology and Imagery in the Poetry of Edward Taylor." *New England Quarterly*, 26 (1953), 337–360.

BOYS, RICHARD C. "The English Poetical Miscellany in Colonial America." *Studies in Philology*, 42 (1945), 114–130.

BRADFORD, WILLIAM. "A Word to Boston." *Massachusetts Historical Society Collections*, 3rd Series, 7 (1838), 27–28.

CROWDER, RICHARD. "Meat Out of the Eater." *Boston Public Library Quarterly*, 11 (1959), 179–192.

———. *No Featherbed to Heaven: A Biography of Michael Wigglesworth*. East Lansing, Mich.: Michigan State University Press, 1962.

FEIDELSON, CHARLES, JR. *Symbolism and American Literature*. Chicago: University of Chicago Press, 1953.

GRABO, NORMAN S. *Edward Taylor*. New York: Twayne, 1961.

———. "How Bad is the *Bay Psalm Book?*" *Papers of Michigan Academy of Science, Arts & Letters*, 46 (1961), 605–615.

HALBERT, CECELIA L. "Tree of Life Imagery in the Poetry of Edward Taylor." *American Literature,* 38 (1966), 22–34.

HARASZTI, ZOLTÁN. *The Enigma of the Bay Psalm Book.* Chicago: University of Chicago Press, 1956.

HOPKINS, F. E., ed. *The Poems of Mrs. Anne Bradstreet (1612–1672) Together With Her Prose Remains.* New York: The Duodecimos, 1897.

JANTZ, HAROLD S. *The First Century of New England Verse.* Worcester, Mass.: American Antiquarian Society, 1944.

LITTLEFIELD, GEORGE EMERY. *The Early Massachusetts Press.* Boston: The Club of Odd Volumes, 1907.

MATHER, COTTON. *Magnalia Christi Americana; or, The Ecclesiastical History of New England.* Edited by REV. THOMAS ROBBINS, D.D. [1702]. New York: Russell & Russell, 1967.

MATTHIESSEN, F. O. "Michael Wigglesworth: A Puritan Artist." *New England Quarterly,* 1 (1928), 491–504.

MILLER, PERRY, and JOHNSON, THOMAS H. *The Puritans.* New York: American Book Co., 1938.

MORISON, SAMUEL E. *The Intellectual Life of Colonial New England.* New York: New York University Press, 1956.,

MURDOCK, KENNETH B., ed. *Handkerchiefs from Paul: Being Pious and Consolatory Verses of Puritan Massachusetts.* Cambridge: Harvard University Press, 1927.

MURDOCK, KENNETH B. *Literature and Theology in Colonial New England.* Cambridge: Harvard University Press, 1949.

MURPHY, FRANCIS. "Edward Taylor's Attitude Toward Publication: A Question Concerning Authority." *American Literature,* 34 (1962), 393–394.

MURPHY, HENRY CRUSE. *Anthology of New Netherland.* New York: n.p., 1865.

PEARCE, ROY HARVEY. *The Continuity of American Poetry.* Princeton: Princeton University Press, 1961.

PIERCY, JOSEPHINE K. *Anne Bradstreet.* New York: Twayne, 1965.

RAESLY, ELLIS L. *Portrait of New Netherland.* New York: Columbia University Press, 1945.

Samuel Sewall's Diary. Edited by MARK VAN DOREN. New York: Macy-Masius, 1927.

SHEPERD, EMMY. "Edward Taylor's Injunction Against Publication." *American Literature,* 33 (1962), 512–513.

STANFORD, DONALD E. "Edward Taylor's 'Spiritual Relation.'" *American Literature,* 35 (1964), 467–475.

TAYLOR, EDWARD. *Poems of Edward Taylor.* Edited by DONALD STANFORD. Foreword by LOUIS L. MARTZ. New Haven: Yale University Press, 1960.

TYLER, MOSES COIT. *A History of American Literature, 1607–1765.* New York: G. P. Putnam's Sons, 1878.

WARD, NATHANIEL. *The Simple Cobler of Aggawam* [1647]. New York: Scholars' Facsimiles and Reprints, 1937.

WARREN, AUSTIN. "Edward Taylor's Poetry: Colonial Baroque." *Kenyon Review,* 3 (1941), 355–371.

WEGELIN, OSCAR. *Early American Poetry: A Compilation of the Titles of Verse and Broadsides.* 2d ed. New York: Peter Smith, 1930.

WILLIAMS, ROGER. *The Complete Writings.* 7 vols. New York: Russell & Russell, 1963.

WILLIAMS, STANLEY T. *The Beginnings of American Poetry (1620–1885).* Uppsala, Sweden: Almqvist & Wiksells Boktryckeri Ab, 1951.

WRIGHT, LOUIS B. *The Cultural Life of The American Colonies, 1607–1763.* New York: Harper, 1957.

CHAPTER TWO

ADKINS, NELSON F. *Philip Freneau and the Cosmic Enigma.* New York: New York University Press, 1949.

BECKER, CARL L. *The Heavenly City of the Eighteenth-Century Philosophers.* New Haven: Yale University Press, 1932.

BOWDEN, EDWIN T., ed. *The Satiric Poems of John Trumbull: The Progress of Dulness and M'Fingal.* Austin, Tex.: University of Texas Press, 1962.

COWIE, ALEXANDER. *John Trumbull: Connecticut Wit.* Chapel Hill, N.C.: University of North Carolina Press, 1936.

CUNINGHAM, CHARLES E. *Timothy Dwight, 1752–1817: A Biography.* New York: The Macmillan Co., 1942.

FRENEAU, PHILIP. *Poems.* Edited by HARRY HAYDEN CLARK. New York: Harcourt Brace, 1929.

HOWARD, LEON. *The Connecticut Wits.* Chicago: University of Chicago Press, 1943.

LEARY, LEWIS, ed. *The Last Poems of Philip Freneau.* New Brunswick, N.J.: Rutgers University Press, 1946.

LEARY, LEWIS. *That Rascal Freneau: A Study in Literary Failure.* New Brunswick, N.J.: Rutgers University Press, 1949.

LEE, ROBERT EDSON. "Timothy Dwight and the Boston *Palladium.*" *New England Quarterly,* 35 (1962), 229–239.

MORE, PAUL ELMER. "Philip Freneau." *Shelburne Essays, Fifth Series.* Boston: Houghton Mifflin & Co., 1908.

PARRINGTON, VERNON L. *Main Currents of American Thought.* New York: Harcourt Brace, 1927.

PATTEE, FRED L. *Poems of Philip Freneau, Poet of the American Revolution.* 3 vols. Princeton: The University Library, 1902–1907.

TINKER, CHAUNCEY B. "Joel Barlow's *Vision of Columbus.*" *Essays in Retrospect.* New Haven: Yale University Press, 1948, pp. 37–42.

TYLER, M. C. *The Literary History of the American Revolution, 1763–1783.* 2 vols. New York: G. P. Putnam's Sons, 1897.

WOODRESS, JAMES. *A Yankee's Odyssey: The Life of Joel Barlow.* Philadelphia: J. B. Lippincott, 1958.

CHAPTER THREE

ADERMAN, RALPH M. "James Kirke Paulding's Contributions to Literary Magazines." *Studies in Bibliography,* 17 (1964), 141–151.

ADKINS, NELSON F. *Fitz-Greene Halleck: An Early Knickerbocker Wit and Poet.* New Haven: Yale University Press, 1930.

ALLEN, GAY WILSON. *American Prosody.* New York: American Book Co., 1935.

ALLSTON, WASHINGTON. *Lectures on Art, and Poems.* Edited by RICHARD HENRY DANA, JR. New York: Baker & Scribner, 1850.

BEWLEY, MARIUS. "James Fenimore Cooper; William Cullen Bryant." *Major Writers of America.* Edited by PERRY MILLER. New York: Harcourt, Brace and World, 1962, I, pp. 279–293.

BRADLEY, WILLIAM A. *William Cullen Bryant.* New York: The Macmillan Co., 1905.

BRONX SOCIETY OF ARTS AND SCIENCES. *Papers and Proceedings of the Drake Memorial Celebration May 29, 1915. Together with a Bibliography of the Writings of Dr. Joseph Rodman Drake by Victor Hugo Paltsits.* New York, 1919.

BRYANT, WILLIAM CULLEN, II. "The Genesis of Thanatopsis." *New England Quarterly,* 21 (1948), 163–184.

BRYANT, WILLIAM CULLEN. "Poets and Poetry of the English Language." *A Library of Poetry and Song.* New York: J. B. Ford, 1871.

CAMPBELL, KILLIS. *The Mind of Poe and Other Studies.* Cambridge: Harvard University Press, 1933.

CLARK, HARRY H., ed. *Transitions in American Literary History.* Durham, N.C.: Duke University Press, 1953.

DRAKE, JOSEPH RODMAN. *The Culprit Fay and Other Poems.* New York: George Dearborn, 1835.

ELIOT, T. S. *From Poe to Valéry.* New York: Harcourt Brace, 1948.

FLAGG, JARED BRADLEY. *The Life and Letters of Washington Allston.* New York: Scribner's, 1892.

HALLECK, FITZ-GREENE. *The Poetical Writings.* Edited by J. G. WILSON. New York: Appleton, 1869.

HEROLD, AMOS L. *James Kirke Paulding: Versatile American.* New York: Columbia University Press, 1926.

HUXLEY, ALDOUS. *Vulgarity in Literature.* London: Chatto and Windus, 1930.

LEONARD, WILLIAM ELLERY. *Byron and Byronism in America.* New York: Columbia University Press, 1907.

LOWELL, JAMES RUSSELL. Review of Halleck's *Alnwick Castle, with Other Poems. Broadway Journal* (May 3, 1845).

McDOWELL, TREMAINE, ed. *William Cullen Bryant: Representative Selections.* New York: American Book Co., 1935.

McLEAN, ALBERT F., JR. "Bryant's 'Thanatopsis': A Sermon in Stone." *American Literature,* 31 (1960), 474–479.

———. *William Cullen Bryant.* New York: Twayne, 1964.

PARRINGTON, VERNON L. *Main Currents of American Thought.* New York: Harcourt Brace, 1927.

PAULDING, WILLIAM I. *The Literary Life of James K. Paulding.* New York: Scribner's, 1867.

POE, EDGAR A. *Complete Poems.* Edited by RICHARD WILBUR. New York: Dell, 1959.

———. Review of *The Culprit Fay and Alnwick Castle. Southern Literary Messenger* (April, 1836).

QUINN, PATRICK F. *The French Face of Edgar Poe.* Carbondale, Ill.: Southern Illinois Press, 1957.

ROBBINS, J. ALBERT. "Some Unrecorded Poems of James Kirke Paulding: An Annotated Check-List." *Studies in Bibliography,* 3 (1950), 229–240.

TATE, ALLEN. *The Forlorn Demon.* Chicago: Henry Regnery, 1933.

WHITE, ROBERT L. "Washington Allston: Banditti in Arcadia." *American Quarterly,* 13 (1961), 387–401.

WHITMAN, WALT. "Edgar Poe's Significance." *The Critic* (June 3, 1882).

CHAPTER FOUR

ADKINS, NELSON F. "Emerson and the Bardic Tradition." *PMLA,* 63 (1948), 662–677.

BARTLETT, WILLIAM I. *Jones Very: Emerson's "Brave Saint."* Durham, N.C.: Duke University Press, 1942.

BEACH, JOSEPH WARREN. *The Concept of Nature in Nineteenth-Century English Poetry.* New York: The Macmillan Co., 1936.

CAMERON, KENNETH W., ed. *Poems of Jones Very: James Freeman Clarke's Enlarged Collection of 1886. Reedited with a Thematic and Topical Index.* Hartford, Conn.: Transcendental Books, 1965.

CARPENTER, FREDERIC I. *Emerson Handbook.* New York: Hendricks House, 1953.

CARPENTER, HAZEN C. "Emerson and Christopher Pearse Cranch." *New England Quarterly,* 37 (1964), 18–42.

FOERSTER, NORMAN. "Emerson." *Nature in American Literature: Studies in the Modern View of Nature.* New York: The Macmillan Co., 1923, pp. 37–68.

FORD, ARTHUR L., JR. "A Critical Study of the Poetry of Henry Thoreau." Ph.D. dissertation (Bowling Green, 1964).

FOSTER, CHARLES HOWELL. *Emerson's Theory of Poetry.* Iowa City, Iowa: Midland House, 1939.

GROSS, SEYMOUR L. "Emerson and Poetry." *South Atlantic Quarterly,* 54 (1955), 82–94.

HOPKINS, VIVIAN C. *Spires of Form: A Study of Emerson's Aesthetic Theory.* Cambridge: Harvard University Press, 1951.

LEVENSON, J. C. "Christopher Pearse Cranch: The Case History of a Minor Artist in America." *American Literature,* 21 (1950), 415–426.

LOWELL, JAMES RUSSELL. "Thoreau." *North American Review,* 101 (1865), 597–608.

MCEUEN, K. A. "Emerson's Rhymes." *American Literature,* 20 (1948), 31–42.

MATTHIESSEN, F. O. *American Renaissance: Art and Expression in the Age of Emerson and Whitman.* New York: Oxford University Press, 1941.

METZGER, CHARLES R. *Thoreau and Whitman: A Study of Their Esthetics.* Seattle, Wash.: University of Washington Press, 1961.

PAUL, SHERMAN. *The Shores of America: Thoreau's Inward Exploration.* Urbana, Ill.: University of Illinois Press, 1958.

ROBERTS, J. R. "Emerson's Debt to the Seventeenth Century." *American Literature,* 21 (1949), 298–310.

RUSK, R. L. *The Life of Ralph Waldo Emerson.* New York: Charles Scribner's Sons, 1949.

SCOTT, LEONORA CRANCH, ed. *The Life and Letters of Christopher Pearse Cranch.* Boston: Houghton Mifflin & Co., 1917.

THOREAU, HENRY D. *Collected Poems.* Edited by CARL BODE. Enl. ed. Baltimore: Johns Hopkins Press, 1964.

VAN DOREN, MARK. *Thoreau: A Critical Study.* New York: Houghton Mifflin & Co., 1916.

WELLS, H. W. "An Evaluation of Thoreau's Poetry." *American Literature,* 16 (1944), 99–109.

WHICHER, STEPHEN E. *Freedom and Fate: An Inner Life of Ralph Waldo Emerson.* Philadelphia: University of Pennsylvania Press, 1953.

WHITAKER, THOMAS. "The Riddle of Emerson's Sphinx." *American Literature,* 27 (1955), 179–195.

WINTERS, YVOR. *In Defense of Reason.* New York: The Swallow Press and William Morrow & Co., 1947.

CHAPTER FIVE

ANDERSON, CHARLES R. *Emily Dickinson's Poetry: Stairway of Surprise.* New York: Holt, Rinehart, & Winston, 1960.

ARVIN, NEWTON. *Herman Melville.* New York: William Sloane Associates, 1950.

——. "Melville's Shorter Poems." *Partisan Review,* 16 (1949), 1034–1046.

ASSELINEAU, ROGER. *The Evolution of Walt Whitman.* Cambridge: Harvard University Press, 1960–1962.

BARRETT, LAURENCE. "The Differences in Melville's Poetry." *PMLA,* 70 (1955), 606–623.

BEZANSON, WALTER. "Melville's 'Clarel': The Complex Passion." *ELH,* 21 (1954), 146–159.

——. "Melville's Reading of Arnold's Poetry." *PMLA,* 69 (1954), 365–391.

CHASE, RICHARD. *Herman Melville: A Critical Study.* New York: The Macmillan Co., 1949.

——. *Walt Whitman Reconsidered.* New York: William Sloane Associates, 1955.

COHEN, HENNIG, ed. *Selected Poems of Herman Melville.* New York: Doubleday & Co., Anchor Books, 1964.

COLERIDGE, SAMUEL TAYLOR. *Coleridge's Shakespearian Criticism.* Edited by T. M. RAYSOR. 2 vols. Cambridge: Harvard University Press, 1930.

DICKINSON, EMILY. *The Letters of Emily Dickinson.* Edited by THOMAS H. JOHNSON. 2 vols. Cambridge: Harvard University Press, 1958.

FOGLE, RICHARD HARTER. "Melville's *Clarel:* Doubt and Belief." *Tulane Studies in English,* 10 (1960), 101–116.

——. "Melville's Poetry." *Tulane Studies in English,* 12 (1963), 81–86.

——. "The Themes of Melville's Later Poetry." *Tulane Studies in English,* 11 (1961), 65–86.

GOLDEN, SAMUEL A. *Frederick Goddard Tuckerman.* New York: Twayne, 1966.

GRIFFITH, CLARK. *The Long Shadow: Emily Dickinson's Tragic Poetry.* Princeton: Princeton University Press, 1964.

HOWARD, LEON. *Herman Melville: A Biography.* Berkeley, Calif.: University of California Press, 1951.

JAMES, WILLIAM. *The Varieties of Religious Experience.* New York: Longmans Green, 1902.

JOHNSON, THOMAS H. *Emily Dickinson: An Interpretive Biography.* Cambridge, Mass.: The Belknap Press, 1955.

LANIER, SIDNEY. *Centennial Edition of the Works.* Edited by CHARLES R. ANDERSON. 10 vols. Baltimore: Johns Hopkins Press, 1945.

MACLEISH, ARCHIBALD, BOGAN, LOUISE, and WILBUR, RICHARD. *Emily Dickinson: Three Views.* Amherst, Mass.: Amherst College Press, 1960.

MARCUS, MORDECAI. "Frederick Goddard Tuckerman's 'The Cricket': An Introductory Note." *Massachusetts Review,* 2 (1960), 33–38.

MATTHIESSEN, F. O. *American Renaissance: Art and Expression in the Age of Emerson and Whitman.* New York: Oxford University Press, 1941.

———. *The Responsibilities of the Critic: Essays and Reviews.* New York: Oxford University Press, 1952.

MELVILLE, HERMAN. *Clarel: A Poem and Pilgrimage in the Holy Land.* Edited by WALTER BEZANSON. New York: Hendricks House, 1960.

———. *Selected Poems.* Edited and Introduction by ROBERT PENN WARREN. New York: Random House, 1970.

MILLER, JAMES E., JR. *A Critical Guide to Leaves of Grass.* Chicago: University of Chicago Press, 1957.

———. *A Reader's Guide to Herman Melville.* New York: Farrar, Straus & Giroux, 1962.

———. SLOTE, BERNICE, and SHAPIRO, KARL. *Start with the Sun.* Lincoln, Nebr.: University of Nebraska Press, 1960.

MIMS, EDWIN. *Sidney Lanier.* Boston: Houghton Mifflin & Co., 1905.

MOMADAY, N. SCOTT, ed. *The Complete Poems of Frederick Goddard Tuckerman.* With a Critical Foreword by YVOR WINTERS. New York: Oxford University Press, 1965.

———. "The Heretical Cricket." *Southern Review,* 3 (1967), 43–50.

MONTAGUE, GENE B. "Melville's *Battle-Pieces.*" *University of Texas Studies in English,* 35 (1956), 106–115.

PEARCE, ROY HARVEY. *The Continuity of American Poetry.* Princeton: Princeton University Press, 1961.

PERRY, BLISS. *Walt Whitman: His Life and Work.* Boston: Houghton Mifflin & Co., 1906.

STARKE, AUBREY HARRISON. *Sidney Lanier: A Biographical and Critical Study.* Chapel Hill, N.C.: University of North Carolina Press, 1933.

UNDERHILL, EVELYN. *Mysticism: A Study in the Nature and Development of Man's Spiritual Consciousness.* New York: Dutton Paperbacks, 1961.

WARREN, ROBERT PENN. "Melville the Poet." *Kenyon Review,* 8 (1946), 208–223.

WILLIAMS, STANLEY T. "Sidney Lanier," in JOHN MACY, ed., *American Writers on American Literature.* New York: Horace Liveright, 1931, pp. 327–341.

WILSON, EDMUND. *Patriotic Gore.* New York: Oxford University Press, 1962.

CHAPTER SIX

ARMS, GEORGE. *The Fields Were Green: A New View of Bryant, Whittier, Holmes, Lowell, and Longfellow.* Stanford, Calif.: Stanford University Press, 1953.

ARVIN, NEWTON. *Longfellow: His Life and Work*. Boston: Little, Brown, 1963.

BEATTY, RICHMOND CROOM. *James Russell Lowell*. Nashville, Tenn.: Vanderbilt University Press, 1942.

BEWLEY, MARIUS. "The Poetry of Longfellow." *Hudson Review*, 16 (1963), 297–304.

BRODERICK, JOHN C. "Lowell's 'Sunthin' in the Pastoral Line.'" *American Literature*, 31 (1959), 163–172.

CARPENTER, G. R. *Whittier*. Boston: Houghton Mifflin & Co., 1903.

CLARK, HARRY HAYDEN, and FOERSTER, NORMAN. *James Russell Lowell: Representative Selections*. New York: American Book Co., 1947.

DUBERMAN, MARTIN. *James Russell Lowell*. New York: Houghton Mifflin, 1966.

———. "Twenty-seven Poems by James Russell Lowell." *American Literature*, 35 (1963), 322–351.

HAYAKAWA, S. I., and JONES, HOWARD MUMFORD, eds. *Oliver Wendell Holmes: Representative Selections*. New York: American Book Co., 1939.

HOWARD, LEON. *Victorian Knight-Errant: A Study of the Early Literary Career of James Russell Lowell*. Berkeley, Calif.: University of California Press, 1952.

JONES, HOWARD MUMFORD. "Longfellow." *American Writers on American Literature*. Edited by JOHN MACY. New York: Horace Liveright, 1931.

KERN, ALEXANDER C. "Dr. Oliver Wendell Holmes Today." *University of Kansas City Review*, 14 (1948), 191–199.

LEARY, LEWIS. *John Greenleaf Whittier*. New York: Twayne, 1961.

LEWISOHN, LUDWIG. *Expression in America*. New York: Harper & Brothers, 1932.

LONGFELLOW, SAMUEL, ed. *The Life of Henry Wadsworth Longfellow*. 2 vols. Boston: Ticknor and Co., 1886.

MILLER, PERRY. "John Greenleaf Whittier: The Conscience in Poetry." *Harvard Review*, 2 (1964), 8–24.

MORE, PAUL ELMER. "Whittier as Poet." *Shelburne Essays, Third Series*. New York: Houghton Mifflin & Co., 1906.

NEMEROV, HOWARD. "On Longfellow." *Poetry and Fiction: Essays*. New Brunswick, N.J.: Rutgers University Press, 1963, pp. 143–158.

PARKS, EDD WINFIELD. *Henry Timrod*. New York: Twayne, 1964.

PEARSON, NORMAN HOLMES. "Both Longfellows." *University of Kansas City Review*, 16 (1950), 245–253.

PICKARD, JOHN B. *John Greenleaf Whittier: An Introduction and Interpretation*. New York: Barnes & Noble, 1961.

PICKARD, SAMUEL T. *Life and Letters of John Greenleaf Whittier*. 2 vols. Boston: Houghton Mifflin & Co., 1894.

SMALL, MIRIAM R. *Oliver Wendell Holmes*. New York: Twayne, 1962.

THOMPSON, H. T. *Henry Timrod: Laureate of the Confederacy*. Columbia, S.C.: University of South Carolina Press, 1928.

TIMROD, HENRY. *The Collected Poems: A Variorum Edition*. Edited by EDD WINFIELD PARKS and AILEEN WELLS PARKS. Athens, Ga.: University of Georgia Press, 1965.

VOSS, ARTHUR. "Backgrounds of Lowell's Satire in 'The Biglow Papers.'" *New England Quarterly*, 23 (1950), 47–64.

WAGENKNECHT, EDWARD. *John Greenleaf Whittier: A Portrait in Paradox*. New York: Oxford University Press, 1967.

———. *Longfellow: A Full-Length Portrait*. New York: Longmans, Green and Co., 1955.

WILLIAMS, CECIL B. *Henry Wadsworth Longfellow*. New York: Twayne, 1964.

CHAPTER SEVEN

BEATTY, RICHMOND CROOM. *Bayard Taylor: Laureate of the Gilded Age*. Norman, Okla.: University of Oklahoma Press, 1936.

BEER, THOMAS. *Stephen Crane: A Study in American Letters*. Garden City, N.Y.: Garden City Publishing Co., 1927.

BERRYMAN, JOHN. *Stephen Crane*. New York: William Sloan Associates, 1950.

BOKER, GEORGE HENRY. *Sonnets: A Sequence on Profane Love*. Edited by EDWARD SCULLEY BRADLEY. Philadelphia: University of Pennsylvania Press, 1929.

BRADLEY, EDWARD SCULLEY. *George Henry Boker*. Philadelphia: University of Pennsylvania Press, 1927.

BRAWLEY, BENJAMIN. *Paul Laurence Dunbar: Poet of His People*. Chapel Hill, N.C.: University of North Carolina Press, 1936.

BROWN, ALICE. *Louise Imogen Guiney*. New York: The Macmillan Co., 1921.

DICKEY, JAMES. "Introduction" to *Selected Poems of E. A. Robinson*. Edited by MORTON DAUWEN ZABEL. New York: The Macmillan Co., 1965.

EMERSON, RALPH WALDO. *Letters to Emma Lazarus in the Columbia University Library*. Edited by RALPH L. RUSK. New York: Columbia University Press, 1939.

GARLAND, HAMLIN. "Stephen Crane as I Knew Him." *Yale Review*, 3 (1914), 494–506.

HALPERN, MARTIN. *William Vaughn Moody*. New York: Twayne, 1964.

HENRY, D. D. *William Vaughn Moody: A Study*. Boston: Bruce Humphries, 1934.

HOFFMAN, DANIEL G. *The Poetry of Stephen Crane*. New York: Columbia University Press, 1957.

JACOB, H. E. *The World of Emma Lazarus.* New York: Schocken Books, 1949.

JONES, HOWARD MUMFORD. *The Bright Medusa.* Urbana, Ill.: University of Illinois Press, 1952.

KINDILIEN, CARLIN T. *American Poetry in the Eighteen Nineties.* Providence, R.I.: Brown University Press, 1956.

LAZARUS, EMMA. *The Poems of Emma Lazarus.* Boston and New York: Houghton Mifflin & Co., 1889.

LOVETT, ROBERT M. "Introduction." *Selected Poems of William Vaughn Moody.* Boston: Houghton Mifflin & Co., 1931, pp. ix–xcii.

LOWELL, AMY. "Introduction." *The Work of Stephen Crane.* Edited by WILSON FOLLETT. Vol. 6. New York: Knopf, 1925.

MATTHIESSEN, F. O. *The Responsibilities of the Critic: Essays and Reviews.* New York: Oxford University Press, 1952.

NELSON, HARLAN S. "Stephen Crane's Achievement as a Poet." *Texas Studies in Language and Literature,* 4 (1958), 564–582.

PEARCE, ROY HARVEY. *The Continuity of American Poetry.* Princeton: Princeton University Press, 1961.

PECK, RICHARD E. "Stephen Crane and Baudelaire: A Direct Link." *American Literature,* 37 (1965), 202–204.

RIGGS, THOMAS, JR. "Prometheus 1900." *American Literature,* 22 (1951), 399–423.

TENISON, E. M. *Louise Imogen Guiney: Her Life and Works 1861–1920.* London: Macmillan, 1923.

WENDELL, BARRETT. *A Literary History of America.* New York: Scribner's, 1900.

ZIFF, LARZER. *The American 1890's.* New York: Viking, 1966.

CHAPTER EIGHT

ADAMS, RICHARD P. "The Failure of Edwin Arlington Robinson." *Tulane Studies in English,* 11 (1961), 97–151.

ATKINS, ELIZABETH. *Edna St. Vincent Millay and Her Times.* Chicago: University of Chicago Press, 1936.

BARNARD, ELLSWORTH. *Edwin Arlington Robinson: A Critical Study.* New York: The Macmillan Co., 1952.

BAYM, NINA. "An Approach to Robert Frost's Nature Poetry." *American Quarterly,* 17 (1965), 713–723.

BROWER, REUBEN A. *The Poetry of Robert Frost: Constellations of Intention.* New York: Oxford University Press, 1963.

CESTRE, CHARLES. *An Introduction to Edwin Arlington Robinson.* New York: The Macmillan Co., 1930.

COOK, REGINALD L. *The Dimensions of Robert Frost.* New York: Holt, Rinehart & Winston, 1958.

Cox, James M., ed. *Robert Frost: A Collection of Critical Essays.* Englewood Cliffs, N.J.: Prentice-Hall, 1961.

Cox, Sidney. *A Swinger of Birches: A Portrait of Robert Frost.* New York: New York University Press, 1957.

Crowder, Richard. *Carl Sandburg.* New York: Twayne, 1964.

Deutsch, Babette. *Poetry in Our Time.* New York: Holt, Rinehart & Winston, 1952.

Dickey, James. "Introduction" to *Selected Poems of E. A. Robinson.* Edited by Morton Dauwen Zabel. New York: The Macmillan Co., 1965.

Emanuel, James. *Langston Hughes.* New York: Twayne, 1967.

Fussell, Edwin. *Edwin Arlington Robinson: The Literary Background of a Traditional Poet.* Berkeley, Calif.: University of California Press, 1954.

Gerber, Philip L. *Robert Frost.* New York: Twayne, 1966.

Hagedorn, Hermann. *Edwin Arlington Robinson: A Biography.* New York: The Macmillan Co., 1938.

Jarrell, Randall. *Poetry and the Age.* New York: Knopf, 1953.

Kaplan, Estelle. *Philosophy in the Poetry of Edwin Arlington Robinson.* New York: Columbia University Press, 1940.

Lynen, John F. *The Pastoral Art of Robert Frost.* New Haven: Yale University Press, 1960.

Neff, Emery. *Edwin Arlington Robinson.* New York: William Sloane Associates, 1948.

Robinson, Edwin Arlington. *Untriangulated Stars: Letters of Edwin Arlington Robinson to Harry de Forest Smith, 1890–1905.* Edited by Denham Sutcliffe. Cambridge: Harvard University Press, 1947.

Smith, Chard Powers. *Where the Light Falls: A Portrait of Edwin Arlington Robinson.* New York: The Macmillan Co., 1965.

Squires, Radcliffe. *The Major Themes of Robert Frost.* Ann Arbor, Mich.: University of Michigan Press, 1963.

Thompson, Lawrance, ed. *Selected Letters of Robert Frost.* New York: Holt, Rinehart & Winston, 1964.

Trilling, Lionel. "A Speech on Robert Frost: A Cultural Episode." *Partisan Review,* 26 (1959), 445–452.

Williams, William Carlos. *The Autobiography of William Carlos Williams.* New York: Random House, 1951.

Winters, Yvor. *Edwin Arlington Robinson.* Norfolk, Conn.: New Directions, 1946.

———. *Maule's Curse.* Norfolk, Conn.: New Directions, 1938.

CHAPTER NINE

Coffman, Stanley K., Jr. *Imagism, a Chapter for the History of Modern Poetry.* Norman, Okla.: University of Oklahoma Press, 1951.

DAVIDSON, DONALD. "In Memory of John Gould Fletcher." *Poetry,* 77 (1950), 154–161.

DEUTSCH, BABETTE. "A Host Address." *Poetry,* 52 (1938), 347–351.

DREW, ELIZABETH. *T. S. Eliot: The Design of His Poetry.* New York: Charles Scribner's Sons, 1949.

ELIOT, T. S. *Selected Essays.* New ed. New York: Harcourt Brace, 1950.

ESPEY, JOHN J. *Ezra Pound's "Mauberley": A Study in Composition.* Berkeley, Calif.: University of California Press, 1955.

FULKERSON, BAUCOM. "John Gould Fletcher." *Sewanee Review,* 46 (1938), 275–287.

GARDNER, HELEN. *The Art of T. S. Eliot.* New York: Dutton Paperbacks, 1950.

GREGORY, HORACE, and ZATURENSKA, MARYA. *A History of American Poetry, 1900–1940.* New York: Harcourt Brace, 1946.

HYMAN, STANLEY EDGAR. "Notes on the Organic Unity of John Peale Bishop." *Accent,* 9 (1949), 102–113.

KENNER, HUGH. *The Invisible Poet: T. S. Eliot.* New York: Ivan Obolensky, 1959.

———. *The Poetry of Ezra Pound.* Norfolk, Conn.: New Directions, 1951.

MACLEISH, ARCHIBALD. *The Irresponsibles: A Declaration.* New York: Duell, Sloan and Pearce, 1940.

MATTHIESSEN, F. O. *The Achievement of T. S. Eliot: An Essay on the Nature of Poetry.* 3rd ed. New York: Oxford University Press, 1958.

MILLETT, FRED B. *Contemporary American Authors.* New York: Harcourt Brace, 1940.

MONROE, HARRIET. *A Poet's Life.* New York: The Macmillan Co., 1938.

NORMAN, CHARLES. *Ezra Pound.* New York: The Macmillan Co., 1960.

POUND, EZRA. *The Letters of Ezra Pound 1907–1941.* Edited by D. D. PAIGE. New York: Harcourt Brace, 1950.

QUINN, VINCENT. *Hilda Doolittle (H. D.).* New York: Twayne, 1967.

ROETHKE, THEODORE. "The Poetry of Louise Bogan." *Critical Quarterly* 3 (1961), 142–150.

ROSENTHAL, M. L. *A Primer of Ezra Pound.* New York: The Macmillan Co., 1960.

STEPHENS, EDNA B. *John Gould Fletcher.* New York: Twayne, 1967.

SULLIVAN, J. P. *Ezra Pound and Sextus Propertius: A Study in Creative Translation.* Austin, Tex.: University of Texas Press, 1964.

SUTTON, WALTER, ed. *Ezra Pound: A Collection of Critical Essays.* Englewood Cliffs, N.J.: Prentice-Hall, 1963.

SWANN, THOMAS BURNETT. *The Classical World of H. D.* Lincoln, Nebr.: University of Nebraska Press, 1962.

TATE, ALLEN. *Collected Essays.* Denver, Colo.: Alan Swallow, 1959.

THOMPSON, ERIC. *T. S. Eliot: The Metaphysical Perspective.* Carbondale, Ill.: Southern Illinois University Press, 1963.

UNGER, LEONARD, ed. *T. S. Eliot: A Selected Critique.* New York: Holt, Rinehart & Winston, 1948.

WHITE, ROBERT L. *John Peale Bishop.* New York: Twayne, 1966.

YEATS, WILLIAM BUTLER. "To Ezra Pound." *A Vision.* New York: The Macmillan Co., 1938.

CHAPTER TEN

AIKEN, CONRAD. *Ushant.* New York and Boston: Duell, Sloan and Little, Brown, 1952.

ALDRICH, JENNIFER. "The Deciphered Heart: Conrad Aiken's Poetry and Prose Fiction." *Sewanee Review,* 75 (1967), 485–520.

BAUM, S. V., ed. *EΣTI: eec: E.E. Cummings and the Critics.* East Lansing, Mich.: Michigan State University Press, 1962.

BEACH, J. W. "Hart Crane and *Moby-Dick*." *Western Review,* 20 (1956), 183–196.

BLACKMUR, R. P. "The Method of Marianne Moore." *Form and Value in Modern Poetry.* New York: Doubleday & Co., Anchor Books, 1957, pp. 225–252.

BLOOM, HAROLD. "The Central Man: Emerson, Whitman, Wallace Stevens." *Massachusetts Review,* 7 (1966), 23–42.

BOHNER, CHARLES H. *Robert Penn Warren.* New York: Twayne, 1964.

BORROFF, MARIE, ed. *Wallace Stevens: A Collection of Critical Essays.* Englewood Cliffs, N.J.: Prentice-Hall, 1963.

BRADBURY, JOHN M. *The Fugitives: A Critical Account.* Chapel Hill, N.C.: University of North Carolina Press, 1958.

BRESLIN, JAMES G. *William Carlos Williams: An American Artist.* New York: Oxford University Press, 1970.

BROWN, ASHLEY, and HALLER, R. A., eds. *The Achievement of Wallace Stevens.* Philadelphia: Lippincott, 1962.

BURKE, KENNETH. "Heaven's First Law." *The Dial,* 72 (1922), 197–200.

CASPER, LEONARD. *Robert Penn Warren: This Dark and Bloody Ground.* Seattle, Wash.: University of Washington Press, 1960.

CECIL, C. D. "An Audience for Wallace Stevens." *Essays in Criticism,* 15 (1965), 193–206.

COWAN, LOUISE. *The Fugitive Group: A Literary History.* Baton Rouge, La.: Louisiana State University Press, 1959.

CRANE, HART. *The Complete Poems and Selected Letters and Prose.* Edited and Introduction by BROM WEBER. New York: Doubleday & Co., 1966.

DENNEY, REUEL. *Conrad Aiken.* Minneapolis, Minn.: University of Minnesota Press, 1964.

DUPEYRON-MARCHESSON, HÉLÈNE. *William Carlos Williams et le renouveau du Lyrisme.* Paris: Presses Universitaires de France, 1967.

ENGEL, BERNARD F. *Marianne Moore.* New York: Twayne, 1964.

FALK, SIGNI. *Archibald MacLeish.* New York: Twayne, 1965.

FRIEDMAN, NORMAN, *E.E. Cummings: The Art of His Poetry.* Baltimore: The Johns Hopkins Press, 1960.

FUCHS, DANIEL. *The Comic Spirit of Wallace Stevens.* Durham, N.C.: Duke University Press, 1963.

———. "Wallace Stevens and Santayana." MARSTON LA FRANCE, ed. *Patterns of Commitment in American Literature.* Toronto: University of Toronto Press, 1967, pp. 135–164.

HEMPHILL, GEORGE T. *Allen Tate.* Minneapolis, Minn.: University of Minnesota Press, 1964.

HOFFMAN, FREDERICK J. *Conrad Aiken.* New York: Twayne, 1962.

———. *The Twenties: American Writing in the Postwar Decade.* New York: Viking, 1955.

HORTON, PHILIP. *Hart Crane: The Life of an American Poet.* New York: W. W. Norton, 1937.

HUGHES, GLENN. *Imagism and the Imagists.* Stanford, Calif.: Stanford University Press, 1931.

JARRELL, RANDALL. *Poetry and the Age.* New York: Knopf, 1953.

KENNER, HUGH. "The Experience of the Eye: Marianne Moore's Tradition." *Southern Review,* 1 (1965), 754–769.

KERMODE, FRANK. *Wallace Stevens.* Edinburgh: Oliver & Boyd, 1961.

LEWIS, R. W. B. *The Poetry of Hart Crane: A Critical Study.* Princeton: Princeton University Press, 1967.

LONGLEY, JOHN LEWIS, JR. *Robert Penn Warren: A Collection of Critical Essays.* New York: New York University Press, 1965.

MACLEISH, ARCHIBALD. *The Collected Poems.* New York: Houghton Mifflin, 1962.

MARKS, BARRY A. *E.E. Cummings.* New York: Twayne, 1964.

MARTIN, JAY. *Conrad Aiken: A Life of His Art.* Princeton: Princeton University Press, 1962.

MEINERS, ROGER KEITH. *The Last Alternatives.* Denver, Colo.: Alan Swallow, 1963.

MILLER, J. HILLIS, ed. *William Carlos Williams: A Collection of Critical Essays.* Englewood Cliffs, N.J.: Prentice-Hall, 1966.

NORMAN, CHARLES. *The Magic-Maker: E.E. Cummings.* New York: The Macmillan Co., 1958.

O'CONNOR, WILLIAM VAN. *The Shaping Spirit: A Study of Wallace Stevens.* Chicago: Henry Regnery, 1950.

OSTROM, ALAN. *The Poetic World of William Carlos Williams.* Carbondale, Ill.: Southern Illinois University Press, 1966.

PEARCE, ROY HARVEY. *The Continuity of American Poetry.* Princeton: Princeton University Press, 1961.

RANSOM, JOHN CROWE. *The New Criticism.* Norfolk, Conn.: New Directions, 1941.

———. *The World's Body.* New York: Charles Scribner's Sons, 1938.

RIDDEL, JOSEPH. "Hart Crane's Poetics of Failure." *ELH*, 38 (1966), 473–496.

———. *The Clairvoyant Eye: The Poetry and Poetics of Wallace Stevens*. Baton Rouge, La.: Louisiana University Press, 1965.

SQUIRES, RADCLIFFE. *The Loyalties of Robinson Jeffers*. Ann Arbor, Mich.: University of Michigan Press, 1956.

STERLING, GEORGE. *Robinson Jeffers the Man and the Artist*. New York: Boni & Liveright, 1926.

STEVENS, WALLACE. *The Necessary Angel: Essays on Reality and the Imagination*. New York: Knopf, 1951.

STEWART, JOHN L. *The Burden of Time: The Fugitives and Agrarians*. Princeton: Princeton University Press, 1965.

TATE, ALLEN. *Collected Essays*. Denver, Colo.: Alan Swallow, 1959.

WAGNER, LINDA. *The Poems of William Carlos Williams*. Middletown, Conn.: Wesleyan University Press, 1964.

WEBER, BROM. *Hart Crane: A Biographical and Critical Study*. New York: The Bodley Press, 1948.

WEST, PAUL. *Robert Penn Warren*. Minneapolis, Minn.: University of Minnesota Press, 1964.

WILLIAMS, WILLIAM CARLOS. "Marianne Moore." *The Dial*, 78 (1925), 393–401.

WINTERS, YVOR. *In Defense of Reason*. New York: The Swallow Press and William Morrow & Co., 1947.

CHAPTER ELEVEN

BURKE, KENNETH. "The Vegetal Radicalism of Theodore Roethke." *Sewanee Review*, 58 (1950), 68–108.

ENGEL, BERNARD. *The Achievement of Richard Eberhart*. Glenview, Ill.: Scott Foresman, 1968.

FAVERTY, F. E. "Well-Open Eyes; or, The Poetry of Richard Wilbur." In *Poets in Progress*, edited by EDWARD HUNGERFORD. Evanston, Ill.: Northwestern University Press, 1962.

FIEDLER, LESLIE A. "On the Road; or the Adventures of Karl Shapiro." *Poetry*, 96 (1960), 173.

FLINT, R. W. "Randall Jarrell." *Commentary*, 41 (February 1966), 79–81.

HAGSTRUM, JEAN H. "The Poetry of Stanley Kunitz: An Introductory Essay." In *Poets in Progress*, edited by EDWARD HUNGERFORD. Evanston, Ill.: Northwestern University Press, 1962.

HARVEY, ROBERT D. "A Prophet Armed: An Introduction to the Poetry of Howard Nemerov." In *Poets in Progress*, edited by EDWARD HUNGERFORD. Evanston, Ill.: Northwestern University Press, 1962.

KUNITZ, STANLEY. "News of the Root." *Poetry*, 73 (1949), 222–225.

————. *Twentieth Century Authors: A Biographical Dictionary of Modern Literature.* First Supplement. New York: Wilson, 1955.

LOWELL, ROBERT, TAYLOR, PETER, and WARREN, ROBERT PENN, eds. *Randall Jarrell—1914–1965.* New York: Farrar, Straus & Giroux, 1967.

LUPHER, DAVID. "Stanley Kunitz on Poetry: A Yale Lit Interview." *Yale Literary Magazine* (April 1968), 6–13.

MILLS, RALPH J., JR. *Contemporary American Poetry.* New York: Random House, 1965.

————, ed. *Selected Letters of Theodore Roethke.* Seattle, Wash.: University of Washington Press, 1968.

————. *Theodore Roethke.* Minneapolis, Minn.: University of Minnesota Press, 1963.

QUINN, SISTER M. BERNETTA. *The Metamorphic Tradition in Modern Poetry.* New Brunswick, N.J.: Rutgers University Press, 1955.

ROETHKE, THEODORE. "Some Remarks on Rhythm." *Poetry,* 97 (1960–61), 35–46.

ROSENTHAL, M. L. *The New Poets: American and British Poetry Since World War II.* New York: Oxford University Press, 1967.

RUBIN, LOUIS D., JR. "The Search for Lost Innocence: Karl Shapiro's *The Bourgeois Poet.*" *The Hollins Critic,* 1, No. 5 (December 1964), pp. 1–16.

SEAGER, ALLAN. *The Glass House: The Life of Theodore Roethke.* New York: McGraw-Hill, 1968.

SHAPIRO, KARL. *Randall Jarrell.* Washington, D.C.: Library of Congress, 1967.

SPENDER, STEPHEN. "Roethke: The Lost Son." *New Republic* (August 27, 1966), pp. 23–25.

STAPLES, HUGH B. *Robert Lowell: The First Twenty Years.* New York: Farrar, Straus and Cudahy, 1962.

STEIN, ARNOLD. *Theodore Roethke: Essays on the Poetry.* Seattle, Wash.: University of Washington Press, 1965.

STEVENSON, ANNE. *Elizabeth Bishop.* New York: Twayne, 1966.

THORSLEV, PETER L., JR. "The Poetry of Richard Eberhart." In *Poets in Progress,* edited by EDWARD HUNGERFORD. Evanston, Ill.: Northwestern University Press, 1962.

WILBUR, RICHARD. "On My Own Work." *Poets on Poetry.* Edited by HOWARD NEMEROV. New York: Basic Books, 1966.

WILLIAMS, WILLIAM CARLOS. "Shapiro is All Right." *Kenyon Review,* 8 (1946), 123.

CHAPTER TWELVE

BENSTON, ALICE N. "Myth in the Poetry of W. S. Merwin." In *Poets in Progress,* edited by EDWARD HUNGERFORD. Evanston, Ill.: Northwestern University Press, 1962.

DICKEY, JAMES. *Babel to Byzantium*. New York: Farrar, Straus & Giroux, 1968.

IGNATOW, DAVID. Review of James Wright's *Shall We Gather At the River*. *The New York Times Book Review* (March 9, 1969), p. 31.

JONES, ALUN R. "Necessity and Freedom: The Poetry of Robert Lowell, Sylvia Plath, and Anne Sexton." *Critical Quarterly*, 7 (1965), 11–30.

MILLS, RALPH J., JR. *Contemporary American Poetry*. New York: Random House, 1965.

———. "Denise Levertov: The Poetry of the Immediate. In *Poets in Progress*, edited by EDWARD HUNGERFORD. Evanston, Ill.: Northwestern University Press, 1962.

———. "The Poetry of James Dickey." *Tri-Quarterly*, 11 (1968), 231–242.

OSSMAN, DAVID. *The Sullen Art: Interviews With Modern American Poets*. New York: Corinth Books, 1963.

ROSENTHAL, M. L. *The New Poets: American and British Poetry Since World War II*. New York: Oxford University Press, 1967.

STEPANCHEV, STEPHEN. *American Poetry Since 1945: A Critical Survey*. New York: Harper, 1965.

GENERAL

ALLEN, GAY WILSON. *American Prosody*. New York: American Book Co., 1935.

AUDEN, W. H. *The Dyer's Hand and Other Essays*. New York: Random House, 1962.

BATE, WALTER JACKSON. *From Classic to Romantic*. Cambridge: Harvard University Press, 1946.

BLACKMUR, R. P. *The Double Agent*. New York: Arrow Editions, 1935.

BOGAN, LOUISE. *Achievement in American Poetry*. Chicago: Henry Regnery, 1951.

BRENNER, RICA. *Twelve American Poets Before 1900*. New York: Harcourt Brace, 1933.

BROWN, JOHN RUSSELL, EHRENPREIS, IRVIN, and HARRIS, BERNARD, eds. *American Poetry*. London: Edward Arnold, 1965.

CLARK, HARRY H., ed. *Transitions in American Literary History*. Durham, N.C.: Duke University Press, 1953.

DAVIE, DONALD. *Articulate Energy*. New York: Harcourt Brace, 1955.

DEMBO, L. S. *Conceptions of Reality in Modern American Poetry*. Berkeley, Calif.: University of California Press, 1966.

DEUTSCH, BABETTE. *Poetry in Our Time*. New York: Holt, Rinehart & Winston, 1952.

DONOGHUE, DENIS. *Connoisseurs of Chaos*. New York: The Macmillan Co., 1965.

DUNCAN, J. E. *The Revival of Metaphysical Poetry: The History of a Style, 1800 to the Present.* Minneapolis, Minn.: University of Minnesota Press, 1959.

FEIDELSON, CHARLES, JR. *Symbolism and American Literature.* Chicago: University of Chicago Press, 1953.

GREGORY, HORACE, and ZATURENSKA, MARYA. *A History of American Poetry, 1900–1940.* New York: Harcourt Brace, 1946.

GROSS, HARVEY. *Sound and Form in Modern Poetry: A Study in Prosody from Thomas Hardy to Robert Lowell.* Ann Arbor, Mich.: University of Michigan Press, 1964.

HART, JAMES D. *Oxford Companion to American Literature.* New York: Oxford University Press, 1965.

HUBBELL, JAY B. *The South in American Literature, 1607–1900.* Durham, N.C.: Duke University Press, 1954.

I'll Take My Stand: The South and the Agrarian Tradition: by Twelve Southerners. New York: Harper & Bros., 1930.

JARRELL, RANDALL. *Poetry and the Age.* New York: Knopf, 1953.

KETTELL, SAMUEL. *Specimens of American Poetry.* 3 vols. Boston: S. G. Goodrich & Co., 1829.

KREYMBORG, ALFRED. *A History of American Poetry: Our Singing Strength.* New York: Coward-McCann, 1929.

LAWRENCE, D. H. *Studies in Classic American Literature.* New York: Thomas Seltzer, 1923.

LEWIS, R. W. B. *The American Adam: Innocence Tragedy and Tradition in the Nineteenth Century.* Chicago: University of Chicago Press, 1955.

LOWELL, AMY. *Tendencies in Modern American Poetry.* New York: The Macmillan Co., 1917.

LUDWIG, RICHARD M., ed. *Aspects of American Poetry: Essays Presented to Howard Mumford Jones.* Columbus, Ohio: Ohio State University Press, 1962.

MATTHIESSEN, F. O. *The Responsibilities of the Critic: Essays and Reviews.* New York: Oxford University Press, 1952.

MILLER, J. HILLIS. *Poets of Reality.* Cambridge: Harvard University Press, 1965.

MONROE, HARRIET. *A Poet's Life.* New York: The Macmillan Co., 1938.

NEMEROV, HOWARD. *Poets on Poetry.* New York: Basic Books, 1966.

O'CONNOR, WILLIAM VAN. *Sense and Sensibility in Modern Poetry.* Chicago: University of Chicago Press, 1948.

ONDERDONK, JAMES L. *History of American Verse (1610–1897).* Chicago: A. C. McClurg & Co., 1901.

OSTROFF, ANTHONY. *The Contemporary Poet as Artist and Critic.* Boston: Little, Brown, 1964.

OTIS, WILLIAM BRADLEY. *American Verse, 1625–1807: A History.* New York: Moffat, Yard & Co., 1909.

PARRINGTON, VERNON L. *Main Currents of American Thought.* New York: Harcourt Brace, 1927.

PATTERSON, SAMUEL WHITE. *The Spirit of the American Revolution . . . A Study of American Patriotic Verse from 1760–1783* (Ph.D. thesis). Boston: R. G. Badger, 1915.

PEARCE, ROY HARVEY. *The Continuity of American Poetry.* Princeton: Princeton University Press, 1961.

QUINN, SISTER M. BERNETTA. *The Metamorphic Tradition in Modern Poetry.* New Brunswick, N.J.: Rutgers University Press, 1955.

ROSENTHAL, M. L. *The Modern Poets: A Critical Introduction.* New York: Oxford University Press, 1960.

SHAPIRO, KARL. "Is Poetry an American Art?" *College English,* 25 (1964), 395–405.

SPILLER, ROBERT E., *et al. Literary History of the United States.* 3 vols. New York: The Macmillan Co., 1948.

STEDMAN, EDMUND C., and HUTCHINSON, ELLEN M., eds. *A Library of American Literature from the Earliest Settlement to the Present Time.* 11 vols. New York: C. L. Webster & Co., 1888–1890.

———. *Poets of America.* Boston: Houghton Mifflin & Co., 1885.

STEPANCHEV, STEPHEN. *American Poetry Since 1945: A Critical Survey.* New York: Harper, 1965.

STERNER, LEWIS G. *The Sonnet in American Literature.* Philadelphia: University of Pennsylvania Press, 1930.

TATE, ALLEN. *Reactionary Essays on Poetry and Ideas.* New York: Charles Scribner's Sons, 1936.

WAGGONER, HYATT H. *The Heel of Elohim: Science and Values in Modern American Poetry.* Norman, Okla.: University of Oklahoma Press, 1950.

WELLS, HENRY W. *The American Way of Poetry.* New York: Columbia University Press, 1943.

WILSON, EDMUND. *Patriotic Gore.* New York: Oxford University Press, 1962.

WINTERS, YVOR. *In Defense of Reason.* New York: The Swallow Press and William Morrow & Company, 1947.

———. *Maule's Curse.* Norfolk, Conn.: New Directions, 1938.

Index

Italicized page numbers indicate major discussion of and quotation from the named poet.